The Natural History *of* Love

The
NATURAL
HISTORY
of
LOVE

by Morton M. Hunt

Decorations by Warren Chappell

New York: Alfred ·A· Knopf

1 9 5 9

L. C. catalog card number: 59-11050

© Morton M. Hunt, 1959

THIS IS A BORZOI BOOK,
PUBLISHED BY ALFRED A. KNOPF, INC.

FIRST EDITION

To Lois
with my love

A PREFATORY NOTE

❦   ❦

❦

WHEN I first read Boswell's *London Journal* some years ago, I was fascinated by the details of his love affair with a young actress named Louisa Lewis. The words, the manners, and the intimate details of his report on that peccadillo seemed to me infinitely more real and convincing than those of almost any novel or play. Though I might have been more deeply moved by a work of fiction, I *believed* what Boswell wrote; his reportorial account allowed me the unforgettable experience of living with him in his own time and almost in his own skin. I wondered if it were possible to learn about other men in other times from sources equally credible and equally intimate, and so got the idea of writing this book—an attempt to recreate, from historical materials, a series of realistic portraits of love in each of the major eras of Western history.

Love, to be sure, is a quicksilver word; though you see plainly where it is, you have only to put your finger on it to find that it is not there, but someplace else. What I do not mean by it in this book is, at least, clear enough: this is neither a *Perfumed Garden* nor a historian's Kinsey Report, but primarily the history of emotional relationships between the sexes. Sexual behavior plays a large part in it, to be sure, but what I have wanted most to show is how people have felt about each other. Making this invasion of their private lives has both gratified my curiosity about other people's business and helped me understand, to some degree, what has made modern love the thing it is. The reader need not share the latter motive; I would be delighted if he merely came here seeking enjoyment, and found it.

[vii]

SOURCES

ANYONE who undertakes to write on love naturally faces the hazard of being challenged by scholars and experts; what is worse, he is apt also to be challenged by everyone else, for what man does not consider himself qualified to argue about love? I have, therefore, from time to time indicated in a footnote the source of some hard-to-believe quotation or the justification for some controversial interpretation. For the rest, the more useful and important works drawn upon in each chapter are named in the section at the back of the book entitled "Notes on Sources."

THANKS

To THOSE learned and busy people who were good enough to read various chapters and give me their suggestions, I owe thanks for ferreting out at least some of my errors. I am grateful to Professor Richard Haywood of New York University for his comments on Chapters Two, Three, and Four; to Professor Helaine Newstead of Hunter College for hers on Chapter Five; to Professors Garrett Mattingly and Peter Gay of Columbia University, the former for his comments on Chapters Six and Seven, and the latter for his on Nine; to Professor Raymond G. Carey of the University of Denver for his on Chapter Eight; and to Dr. Abraham Stone, Director of the Margaret Sanger Research Bureau, for advising me on Chapter Ten.

I am indebted more than I should reveal to my friend Robert L. Heilbroner for putting aside his own writing and providing me with a meticulous and invaluable critique of the style and content of every chapter. Of the several people who assisted me in research, Dr. Katharine M. Rogers deserves my special thanks for her persistence and professional skill in verifying worrisome points and relocating mislaid or missing references. Miss Violet Serwin was more than an expert typist, being also a comber-out of repetitions, lacunae, and other snags.

Finally, it is considered good form to say that one's wife has borne, with infinite patience and understanding, the trials and dolors of the literary work; I cannot in all conscience say this, since my own wife has been fully as impatient as I to see the book finished. But she has done something far more important than show patience and understanding; she has consistently and immoderately admired my efforts chapter by chapter, and with this indispensable support to my ego, I was able to finish after all.

ACKNOWLEDGMENTS

GRATEFUL acknowledgment is hereby made to the following publishers and persons for permission to reprint the materials specified:

Blackie & Son, Ltd., and Mrs. M. Leon: selections from E. P. Moore's translation of Ovid's *Ars Amatoria;*

Cambridge University Press: lines from R. C. Trevelyan's translation of *Idylls of Theocritus;*

The Clarendon Press, Oxford: lines from Sophocles' "Fragment 678" as translated in R. W. Livingstone's *Greek Genius and Its Meaning to Us;*

Norma Millay Ellis: for Edna St. Vincent Millay's sonnet, "I Shall Forget You Presently, My Dear," © 1922, 1950 by Edna St. Vincent Millay;

Alfred A. Knopf, Inc.: the lines from Catullus' *Carmine* Nos. 8, 11, 68, and 85, as translated by Gilbert Highet in his *Poets in a Landscape;*

G. P. Putnam's Sons: lines from lyrics by Bernard de Ventadour, Jaucelm Faidit, and Sordello, as translated in Emil Lucka's *Eros;*

Routledge & Kegan Paul, Ltd.: lines from No. 72 of Catullus' *Carmine,* as translated by F. A. Wright in *Catullus: The Complete Poems;*

Charles Scribner's Sons: selections from Castiglione's *The Book of the Courtier,* translated by L. E. Opdycke;

Yale University Press: selections from the *Yale Edition of Horace Walpole's Correspondence.*

CONTENTS

❊   ❊

❊

Contents

Chapter I
INTRODUCTION

I

The Trouble with a Word

❀   ❀

❀

*V*oi, che sapete, che cosa è amor?" asked Cherubino in Mozart's
Marriage of Figaro. "Tell me, you who know, what is this
thing, love?" Cherubino was still a beardless adolescent and did not
know the answer, but he took it for granted there was one. So have
most other people, and many of them have tried to give it, but the
most noteworthy feature about all their answers is how thoroughly
they disagree. Sometimes, it seems, they cannot possibly be referring
to the same phenomenon, or even to related ones; after a while one
wonders whether there is something wrong with the question itself, or whether perhaps it employs a word of no fixed meaning and
can have no fixed answer.

Poets have written more about love than almost anyone else and
are somehow thought to be experts on it, but they continually con-
tradict each other in hopelessly irreconcilable terms. Some call it
"the sweetest thing on earth," while others assure us that it is "a
mighty pain" and "a sickness full of woes"; another calls it "a proud
and gentle thing" while yet another insists it is "an abject intercourse between slaves and tyrants." A poet will even disagree with
himself, with never a sign of discomfort. Shakespeare on one occasion answered Cherubino's question in the tones of an amiable and
slightly wicked satyr:

> *What is love? 'tis not hereafter;*
> *Present mirth hath present laughter;*
> *What's to come is still unsure;*
> *In delay there lies no plenty:*
> *Then come kiss me, sweet and twenty,*
> *Youth's a stuff will not endure.*

[3]

But another time he fervently and a trifle righteously took this
higher view:

> Love's not Time's fool, though rosy lips and cheeks
> Within his bending sickle's compass come;
> Love alters not with his brief hours and weeks,
> But bears it out even to the edge of doom.

Poets, of course, are a notoriously flighty lot, but sober philosophers have come no closer to agreeing with each other on the ultimate truth of love. Plato, for instance, held it to be an appreciation
of beauty, especially that of abstract ideas and mathematical concepts. Descartes, seeking to avoid this rather static view, injected
some desire and action into it; love, he said, is an emotion in which
the soul is incited to join itself willingly to objects which appear
agreeable to it. In our own time Ortega y Gasset analyzed such
philosophizing, and on the basis of modern psychology found it
wanting; in his little volume, *On Love*, he produced his own definition of love as "a centrifugal act of the soul in constant flux that
goes towards the object and envelops it in warm corroboration,
uniting us with it, and positively reaffirming its being." Even without an exegesis—which we clearly need to make anything of all
that—we can guess that he is talking about something else again. So
it is with the great minds; no wonder, then, that the average man
feels himself fully justified in having his own opinions on the subject.

But whatever the definition, is there not at least some agreement
as to the extent of love's power and influence? Not a bit. Dante, in
the closing line of his giant work, saw it as a macrocosmic force—
"love that moves the sun and the other stars." Marlowe's Faustus,
though not similarly cosmological in his outlook, nevertheless expected Helen to make him immortal with a single kiss, and Sir
Walter Scott epitomized the viewpoint of all the romantics who
have ever believed love to have an incomparable power over men's
lives:

> Love rules the court, the camp, the grove,
> And men below, and saints above;
> For love is heaven, and heaven is love.

Quite a few other men, however, have considered such talk to be
the purest nonsense. Francis Bacon tartly remarked that among the
great people of history "there is not one that hath been transported

to the mad degree of love." Samuel Johnson, a soul mate of his in a later century, believed that love "has no great influence upon the sum of life," and in modern times H. L. Mencken, as good a scoffer as any, called it merely "a state of perceptual anesthesia."

Semantic troubles with the word "love" are one of the main reasons for confusion and disagreement on the subject. Having remained undifferentiated, the single noun is freely used to refer to any one of several distinct entities. There is "making love" and "being in love," which are quite dissimilar ideas; there is love of God, of mankind, of art, and of pet cats; there is mother love, brotherly love, the love of money, and the love of one's comfortable old shoes. People who study animals have a particular weakness for applying the word to behavior which only externally resembles human love, and then drawing conclusions which they think should hold good for human beings. A Philadelphia psychoanalyst named Leon J. Saul wrote not long ago that birds, since they feed and care for their young with no thought of personal ambition or of being supported in old age, provide us with the perfect model of "true love." Unromantic biologists, however, know that much of this loving behavior consists of purely instinctive responses to "releasers," which are visual or other stimuli that cause the bird to respond automatically. Many songbirds will feed a painted, gaping, artificial mouth just as readily as a real one. Moreover, if a cuckoo, born in a songbird's nest, pushes the baby songbirds out, the loving parents will ignore the fallen ones and feed only the cuckoo; true love seems to be aroused only by the sight of baby-bird-within-nest.

Still, many naturalists have been unable to refrain from seeing human emotions throughout the animal world. In 1900 a German science-popularizer named Wilhelm Bölsche wrote rapturously of the "spiritual impetuosity" of the salmon who even goes hungry in order to find his beloved mate, while the Italian anthropologist, Paolo Mantegazza, a generation earlier offered in the name of natural history such lyrical rhapsodies as this in his book, *The Physiology of Love:*

> Fondly they caress each other with their wings. . . . The wing of one softly and slowly kisses the silk and velvet of his companion. . . . Two creatures, nude yet clothed, passionate and chaste, that love but once and one creature only, that kiss on earth and mate in the skies. . . . Why do we not also love in this way?

For good reason: we do not fly, and anyhow our clothes can come off, neither of which is true of the small brown butterflies he was discussing.

But butterflies were not the end; Professor Mantegazza claimed that flowers also had the power to caress each other, Bölsche held that even the bacillus has a love life, and a series of others reached the logical conclusion that the chemical bonds holding atoms together in molecules were the ultimate form of love. "Potassium and phosphorus entertain such a violent passion for oxygen," wrote a German physician and science writer named Büchner in 1885, "that even under water they burn, that is, unite themselves with the beloved object." Similar ideas are current today, though couched in less incandescent prose; even the learned anthropologist M. F. Ashley Montagu recently wrote that the tendency of matter to cohere is the most primitive form of love. The nuclear binding forces of the atom, he says, are a form of "cooperation," while the bonds holding atoms together in a molecule exemplify "interdependence"; these same characteristics are variously manifested by the amoeba, the plant, the animal, and man, and in the latter are called love.[1]

Perhaps we can simply ignore most of these excursions in meaning; neither Cherubino nor most of the other people who have been fascinated by love have had in mind anything but the love of human beings. Even so, the subject remains marvelously confounded by the variant uses of the word. One of the most famous books on love is the *Ars Amatoria* of Ovid, but he meant by it only a delicious game of seduction, with never a bit of nonsense about centrifugal acts of the soul. Almost at the same time, Platonists and Neoplatonists were using the same word to mean something spiritually ennobling and capable of leading the mind toward divinity. The early Christians fretted about the fact that in their time the name of love was applied with equal ease to pagan sexual orgies and to the Christian feeling for God; after several centuries they more or less succeeded in getting all sexual expression (even within marriage) referred to as "lust," while "love" referred only to religious and benevolent emotions. But the dichotomy would not hold; by the eleventh century men and women had re-appropriated the word for

[1] *The Meaning of Love*, pp. 12–16. But in his later and far more profound study of love, *The Direction of Human Development*, he omitted the atomic and molecular analogies.

feelings they had about each other, and since then it has been freely used to refer to everything from the lecheries of Restoration rakes to the domestic sentimentality of the Victorians. Afoot in this semantic jungle, we can have only sympathy for the anonymous compiler of *The Ladies Dictionary* of 1694, who hacked away briefly at the question and then hastily backed out:

> *Love*, what is it? Answ. 'Tis very much like light, a thing that everybody knows, and yet none can tell what to make of it. 'Tis not money, fortune, jointure, raving, stabbing, hanging, romancing, flouncing, swearing, ramping, desiring, fighting, dicing, though all those have been, are, and still will be mistaken and miscalled for it. . . . 'Tis extremely like a sigh, and could we find a painter who could draw one, you'd easily mistake it for the other.

And thus the question "What is this thing, love?" may be incapable of any good answer as long as it implies that there is a single entity. What, then, will this book be about? Not about the love of art, money, or pets; not about the love of God, mankind, or shoes; not about the loves of salmon, butterflies, or atoms. There is a simple criterion—not a definition, but merely a litmus-paper test—of love as it is meant in this book, and as it is thought of, I believe, by most people when they hear the word: it will be any and every form of relationship between human beings which makes sense when used in conjunction with the phrases "falling in love" or "being in love with."

So we must reword Cherubino's question for him a little, making it: "What are these things that have been called love?" In this somewhat inelegant form, the question might find an answer; and that, in fact, is precisely what this book will try to do.

2

Love in the Butterfly Net

❀   ❀

❀

I have called this a "natural history" of love. The term, to be sure, ordinarily refers to the scientific study of animals other than man; I have used it nevertheless because this is to be a data-gathering field expedition in which the author and his readers are the naturalists, the various eras of Western history are the jungles and plains we shall visit, mankind is the fauna that inhabit those regions, and his ways of loving are what we hope to observe and collect examples of.

Most of the learned people who write about love seem to equip themselves in advance with a special theory; with this as a kind of butterfly net, they then sally forth and attempt to capture cases to prove or exemplify their point. But with a single net one can bag only a very narrow range of creatures; if the mesh is the right size for butterflies, it will be too coarse to catch midges and singularly inappropriate for taking elephants. Moralists like Ortega y Gasset and psychoanalysts like Erich Fromm insist that love is not selfish, not a question of desire to possess, but involves a selfless, generous wish to give, to benefit, and to succor the beloved; with such a theory, however ethical it may sound, one cannot capture the love of Catullus for Lesbia, King Henry for Anne Boleyn, or indeed a great many others throughout history. Freudians explain love as arising from inhibited or delayed sexuality, but both pagan Romans and Catholic priests of the Dark Ages often fell deeply in love with their concubines after having uninhibitedly slept with them for months or years. The Marxist's critique of love, the marriage counselor's picture of love, the anthropologist's meaning of love,

are all useful and stimulating, but each manages by itself to encompass only some kinds of evidence and to miss the others.

We, on the other hand, will venture forth generously equipped
with nets both large and small, plus a complete array of lenses, field
glasses, stoppered bottles, traps, chains, and cages, so that we need
miss nothing. Most important of all, we will take with us a wide-
eyed readiness to observe the creatures just as they are, living and
making love in their own surroundings.

Even so, there are limits to what we will undertake. We will pass
up, for instance, the temptation to explore the curious jungles of
primitive love, for here the creatures are so unlike ourselves that we
may find it quite impossible to feel their emotions vicariously or
assess the meaning of love in any but the most detached fashion.
Even when the primitive man speaks as directly and as eloquently
as he can, his words hardly help us; most primitive languages are
so remote from modern Indo-European language in their structure
that the thought processes and undercurrents of meaning can
scarcely be translated, while the emotional significance of every
object and action is too alien to convey a mood to any but the professional anthropologist. This, for example, is how an intelligent
young Trobriand chieftain described a typical romantic rendezvous
to the anthropologist Bronislaw Malinowski:

> We make love: our fire, our lime gourd, our tobacco; food no,
> shame. We go, we go one tree tree big; we sit, we louse and eat;
> we tell to woman: "We copulate." It is finished, we go to village;
> in village we go to bachelors' house, we lie, we chatter. Supposing
> we are alone, we undo pubic leaf ours she undoes skirt we sleep.

Malinowski, recognizing the unintelligibility to outsiders of this
transcript, also made a free rendering, padded out with civilized
words and explanations, which went as follows:

> When we go out on a love-making expedition, we light our fire;
> we take our lime gourd (and chew betel-nut), we take our to-
> bacco (and smoke it). Food we do not take, we would be ashamed
> to do so. We walk, we arrive at a large tree, we sit down, we
> search each other's heads and consume the lice, we tell the woman
> that we want to copulate. After it is over we return to the vil-
> lage. In the village we go to the bachelors' house, lie down, and
> chatter. When we are alone he takes off the pubic leaf, she takes
> off her fiber skirt: we go to sleep.[2]

[2] B. Malinowski: *The Sexual Life of Savages in Northwestern Melanesia*, pp.
335–6.

It is certainly less formidable, grammatically speaking, but it is still emotionally impenetrable; the reader may be pardoned for saying, like the waspish Byron: "I wish he would explain his explanation."

And anthropologists do so, in the form of intensive, detailed descriptions of puberty rites, mate-selection, courtship, sexual practices, and married life among primitive peoples. But in the great mass of such writings there is almost nothing that seems to refer to love as Western man knows it. Primitive love has perhaps a hundred, perhaps more, different forms, but only a few resemble Western love at all; those few do so only superficially and usually only in certain aspects of sexual practice. For by and large, the clanship structure and social life of most primitive societies provide a wholesale intimacy and a broad distribution of affections; Western love, with its especially close and valued ties between two isolated individuals, is neither possible nor needed. Furthermore, most primitive peoples fail to see any great difference between individuals, and hence do not become involved in unique connections in the Western fashion; any number of trained observers have commented on the ease of their detachment from love objects, and their candid belief in the interchangeability of loves. Dr. Audrey Richards, an anthropologist who lived among the Bemba of Northern Rhodesia in the 1930's, once related to a group of them an English folk-tale about a young prince who climbed glass mountains, crossed chasms, and fought dragons, all to obtain the hand of a maiden he loved. The Bemba were plainly bewildered, but remained silent. Finally an old chief spoke up, voicing the feelings of all present in the simplest of questions: "Why not take another girl?" he asked.

Leaving such questions to be answered by the anthropologist, or anyone else who cares to try, we shall explore only the domain of civilized man, and in fact only Western civilized man, in the past 2,500 years. Even so, it will not be possible to do justice to all who lived in that period; of the love lives of the illiterate and the oppressed, for instance, very little record remains in most of history. We will therefore consider as love in each era that which the era itself meant by the word—the dominating ideas of the dominating classes.

About them, of course, there is plenty of information. But not all of it is reliable, and even the most acquisitive naturalist must have some rules as to what he will consider an acceptable specimen. It is generally supposed that great fiction and great drama bare the human soul and portray the secrets of the heart. But whose soul and whose heart? Those of the author or of his subject? Those of the era of the plot, or the era of the author's own life? The tale of Tristan and Iseult is often thought to convey transcendent truths concerning love, but if one tries to label them and identify them, they vanish or change form before his very eyes. Generations of high-school pupils have learned, through Tennyson, what the world of King Arthur was like in which Tristan and Iseult lived;[3] it greatly resembled a parcel of Victorian gentlemen in medieval costume. The college student, being more sophisticated, reads Sir Thomas Malory and learns that Arthur and his knights were actually rather like fifteenth-century English noblemen in medieval costume. The still more sophisticated graduate student reads Chrétien de Troyes and learns that in fact they were very much like the courtiers of twelfth-century France in medieval costume (and quite properly so). But the historical Arthur was only a minor chieftain rather than the king of a great civilization, and the events he is supposed to have played a part in took place in the sixth century, not the twelfth. He and his men, or their real counterparts, were uncouth Celtic warriors, while the real Tristan, or Drustan, was very likely an equally uncouth Pictish chieftain; neither Arthur, Tristan, nor Iseult could have been anything like the twelfth-century aristocrats in dress, morals, and culture, and their love patterns could not by any stretch of the imagination have been like those portrayed by Chrétien, much less Malory, and still less Tennyson.

Similarly, some of the most vivid characterizations of the seventeenth-century Puritans of New England are the figures created by Nathaniel Hawthorne, who lived two centuries after they did and saw them in retrospect as tormented, brooding, inhibited people. But the historian Henry Cabot Lodge (grandfather of the present Ambassador Lodge) remarked that he had looked on every page of New England history for Hawthorne's characters and never found them. When the diary of Judge Samuel Sewall, the Puritan equivalent of Samuel Pepys, was at last published in 1878, Lodge once again hoped he would discover the originals of Hawthorne's types, but could find not one in all its pages. The Puritan of fiction was, in large part, a fiction.

[3] Tristan (whom Tennyson calls Tristram) did not originally live in it at all, and his story had no connection with the Arthurian court. But by the Middle Ages he and Iseult had been enveloped by the growing Arthurian legend, and Tristan had been made into a knight of the Round Table.

So we will be chary of accepting the word of creative literature as primary evidence. It will surely be valuable, but more by way of corroboration and amplification than otherwise. Primarily we will look to biography, private correspondence, diaries, and the anecdotes and trivia recorded by chroniclers and amateur historians. The advice of fathers to their sons and daughters will be useful, and so will old books of domestic conduct, manuals of courtship technique and sexual methodology, the laws of adultery, divorce, and dowry, and the rules of etiquette. Even palace gossip may sometimes be illuminating; one senses a whole chapter of light-hearted cynicism in a little story about the father of Alexander the Great, repeated centuries later by Plutarch: "What said a woman to King Philip that pulled and hauled her to him by violence against her will? 'Let me go,' said she, 'for when the candles are out, all women are alike.' "

And now, having taken thought for the problems of gathering our specimens, and having outfitted ourselves with all the apparatus of an open mind, we are at last ready to embark on our expedition. The tide is full and it is time to cast off. With luck, we may bring back a museumful of treasures and a fat sheaf of field notes; then let who will visit our museum of love, see what we have collected, and make theories to suit himself.

Chapter II

DILEMMA IN GREECE

I

The Invention of Love

❀   ❀

❀

No wonder the Greeks had a word for nearly everything—
they invented nearly everything. Or, at any rate, a great
many of the things that have been important to Western civilization
ever since: the theory of atoms and the principles of punctuation,
democratic procedure and political dictatorship, metaphysics and
the forms of the drama, scientific terminology and a love of bathing,
and some of the oldest jokes in the world, as, for instance:

> *Talkative barber:* How shall I cut your hair, sire?
> *King Archelaus of Macedon:* In silence.

And that was not all; they also invented love, gave it two names—
eros (carnal love) and *agape* (spiritual love)—and elaborated upon
both its theory and its practice.

Love has never since divested itself of its Greek trappings. Cupid
(Eros) and his arrows are a Greek conceit; Sappho drew up a
formal symptomatology of lovesickness which has been faithfully
adhered to by lovers for twenty-five centuries; Platonic love, that
long-discussed and marvelously misapplied term, originated with
Plato's own attempts to build incorporeal metaphysics out of the
desires of the flesh; and a whole set of familiar love tales emerged
from Greek sources—Odysseus and Penelope, Daphnis and Chloe,
Cupid and Psyche, Dido and Aeneas, Hero and Leander, and many
others.[1] Greek literature of earlier times had been made up chiefly
of heroic histories, political diatribes, religious hymns, philosophic
inquiries, and the like, but beginning with the Golden Age (about

[1] And later many fictional love stories with Greek backgrounds came to be thought truly Greek; the legend of Troilus and Cressida, for instance, origi- nated in the Middle Ages in Western Europe, but is often taken for a genuine Trojan legend.

[15]

480 B.C. to 399 B.C.) it became progressively diluted with an ever greater admixture of love lyrics, amorous laments, and protracted romances ending either in bliss or misery. In some of these—even in the briefest epigrams—love sentiments occasionally achieved a quality quite unknown to the primitive peoples who preceded the flowering of Athenian culture:

> My soul was on my lips, as I kissed Agathon;
> It came there (poor soul!) longing to cross over to him.

Yet for all its familiar aspects, love in classic Greece was peculiarly, and even startlingly, different in character from later and contemporary Western conceptions of love. For it was considered not so much an ennobling and transforming goal of life, but an amusing pastime and distraction, or sometimes a god-sent affliction. And its heartfelt expressions were poured forth not by young men and women who desired each other as mates, but by married men serenading courtesans, and by homosexuals (or lesbians) wooing others of their kind. It is therefore a paradox of no mean order that modern love began with Greek love and owes so much to it, although the forms and ideals of Greek love are considered immoral and, to a large extent, illegal, in modern society.

2

Love Life of an Insolent Hero

❀   ❀

❀

The tastes and preferences of the Athenians of the time of Socrates were not as uniformly noble and elevated as they often seem in romantic perspective. They admired wisdom, it is true, but they admired physical beauty even more, even when it was accompanied by no wisdom whatever; they esteemed moderation and self-control, but they vastly admired *hybris* (insolent pride) and fiery passion; and though they praised virtue, they were entranced by cunning and trickery. In the realm of love it was much the same: they studied it, argued about it, exalted its pleasures, and lamented its pains—but in the main were able to feel it only for prostitutes and pederasts.

In an extreme form all this is well exemplified by the man who helped tarnish the luster of the Age of Pericles—his own foster son, Alcibiades, that man of extreme contrasts: pupil of Socrates and vulgar roisterer, superb warrior and idle wastrel, master politician and common lawbreaker, patriot and traitor, devotee of philosophy and oratory, and passionate lover of whores and boys.[2]

Born in 450 B.C. of a wealthy noble family, Alcibiades lost his father early, and was raised by his mother's kinsman Pericles, the great statesman and leader of Athens in her democratic zenith. In his teens, Alcibiades blossomed out as the tallest and handsomest youth in Athens, and soon was everywhere accompanied by a swarm of men who, in the fashion of the time, courted and flattered him as though he were a beautiful girl. He played the role of *demi-mondaine* expertly, taunting, flirting, and frustrating his lovers, and allowing homosexual favors when it pleased or profited him to. Youths aped his manners, his lisp, and his special style of shoes, and his latest pranks and dissipations were always the talk of the town.

Yet Alcibiades had a brilliant mind and a strain of moral sensibility. He studied with Socrates, and when the philosopher spoke to him of the virtuous life, tears would run from the lad's eyes. "If I did not shut my ears against him, and fly as from the voice of the siren," Alcibiades later said, "my fate would be like that of the others—he would transfix me, and I should grow old sitting at his feet. For he makes me confess that I ought not to live as I do. . . . And therefore I run away and fly from him." Fleeing from Socrates again and again, he reveled in dissolute pleasures and played discreditably at politics; yet he was brave and manly, and fought well at Potidaea at the age of twenty (though Socrates had to save his life on the battlefield), and six years later did still better at Delium (where he returned the favor).

[2] The principal classical sources of information about Alcibiades are Plutarch's "Life of Alcibiades," Xenophon's *Memorabilia*, and two dialogues of Plato; many other writers mention him, but anecdotally and often unreliably.

In the full flush of his youthful popularity, Alcibiades was atro-
ciously insolent, but he always went completely unpunished. When
Pericles said that he too, like Alcibiades, had talked too cleverly and
dogmatically of politics in his youth, his foster son sneered: "Would
that I had conversed with you, Pericles, when you were still acute in
such discussions!" Anytus, a wealthy lover of his, invited him to a
banquet; Alcibiades came only as far as the door, and wickedly
ordered his slaves to pick up and carry home half of the gold and
silver vessels spread before the other guests. The banqueters were
furious and protested to Anytus that Alcibiades had acted outrageously, but the lovesick man replied: "Not so, but moderately and
kindly; he might have taken all there were; he has left us half."

To meet the dare of fellow roisterers, Alcibiades once publicly
punched Hipponicus, one of the richest and most powerful citizens
of Athens, in the face, but the next morning he came to Hipponicus'
house, bared his body, and begged the older man to whip him.
Hipponicus was overcome. He not only forgave the youth, but
offered him his daughter, Hipparete, in marriage, with a dowry of
ten talents ($60,000)—which the glib Alcibiades promptly per-
suaded him to double when she should become a mother. To Alcibiades' way of thinking, this was just about his wife's only attraction. After marrying her, he paid no attention to her except to give
her household orders. With her dowry money, he filled his house
with costly furniture, had artists paint pictures on the walls, held
elegant banquets, and lived in luxury and splendor such as were rare
in Athens at that time. His wife's role in all this remained merely
that of his housekeeper—one who took orders, and was ignored
except when inefficient in serving him.

Alcibiades' attitude toward her was not the result of homosexuality. Like most upper-class Athenian men of his time, he was
equally attracted by both sexes. The women who intrigued him,
however, were those who sold their favors; these he liked thoroughly, from elegant courtesans to common brothel inmates, and
at all levels they were fond of him and much impressed by him. But
this did not in the least interfere with his continuing affection for
other men and for boys. In fact, so successful was he on all fronts
that he chose not an ancestral device for his shield, but a design of
Eros holding a thunderbolt, to indicate his own invincibility in love.

When Hipparete could stomach all this no longer, she returned
to her father's house and prepared to divorce Alcibiades, but the

day she appeared in court he and some of his friends burst in, snatched her up, and carried her off. No one protested or tried to free her, and she passively accepted the situation, remaining in his house quietly until her death a short time later. His reasons for carrying her off had nothing to do with hidden affection. Under Athenian law, when a wife divorced her husband, he had to return the dowry—and this Alcibiades had no intention of doing.

His political and military biography, entangled as it is with the complex Peloponnesian War, is too involved to bear telling here, but a few highlights of it will illuminate his personality. Through political and military exploits, he rose to be one of Athens' ten generals and successfully preached the need for a war against Syracuse in order to expand the Athenian economy. The Assembly endorsed his plan and in 415 B.C. built a great armada and dispatched an army in it, with Alcibiades as one of its two commanders. But a few days after its departure they sent a swift ship ordering him back to stand trial for the mischievous mutilation of the ears, noses, and phalli of the city's many statues of Hermes, as well as for certain religious impieties. The doughty general denied the charges, but jumped ship rather than stand trial. He then made his way to Sparta and appeared before its Assembly, arguing that Sparta should join Syracuse in the war against Athens. The Spartans listened and were impressed; unfortunately, before Alcibiades could fulfill the dream of conquering his own city at the head of an enemy army, he indulged in a love affair with the Spartan Queen, Timaea, and had to flee the wrath of King Agis. In this extremity he turned to the Persians, the traditional enemies of all Greeks, and found shelter among them.

The military fortunes of Athens declined seriously in the following years. After a series of overturns of the government, the democracy came back into power; the Athenian Assembly offered Alcibiades an amnesty after ten years' absence if he would return and take charge of their military forces. He heeded the call, promptly defeated two Spartan fleets, and entered Athens to the accompaniment of frenzied adulation, all his sins forgotten. But then came an unexpected naval defeat as a result of his temporarily leaving his post of command, whereupon the fickle Assembly turned upon him again. Once more he fled the city, and when the Athenian fleet, lacking his leadership, was completely destroyed by the Spartans, he had to flee still farther—as before, to the Persians. In Phrygia he put himself under the protection of General Pharnabazus, who lent him a house in which he lived, plotting and consoling himself with one, or some say two, courtesans. The Persian King, meanwhile, in order to curry favor with the conquering Spartans, secretly ordered Pharnabazus to kill his guest, and one day in 404 B.C. two assassins set fire to Alcibiades' house and riddled him with arrows and javelins as he ran forth naked, sword in hand—still brave, still beautiful, still full of *hybris*.

More fascinated than horrified by him, the Greeks made him a favorite subject of biographical and philosophic writing. At least half a dozen dialogues, including one doubtfully ascribed to Plato, bore his name in classic times, and he appeared briefly in scores of other works. Forgetful of his crimes but mindful of his charm, they set up a monument at his Phrygian grave; so great was his appeal even five centuries later that the Roman Emperor Hadrian had a marble statue of him put up at the monument and ordered an ox sacrificed there every year. This was the man the Athenians admired to distraction, and who wore into battle the likeness of Eros on his shield.

3

"Marriage Brings a Man Only Two Happy Days"

❁   ❁

❁

Not every Greek was an Alcibiades, but even those who were law-abiding, gentle, and kindly tended to look upon their wives as a necessary burden and expected to find love only outside the home. Their relationships with the women they married can be

hesitantly inferred from drama and comedy, but neither hesitancy
nor inference is necessary, for among the Greek writings that survived the Roman conquest and the Dark Ages there is one detailed,
authentic nonfictional portrayal of the life of the upper-class Athenian woman. It comes from the prolific historian Xenophon, who
found time among his more ambitious projects to dash off a brief
handbook on home and farm economics which he called *The
Economist.*[3] It gives advice on the management of a household, the
control of slaves and servants, and the proper techniques of farming; and when it deals with the handling and training of a wife, it
provides us with the best existing description of the well-to-do
woman's life in Athens at the end of the fifth century B.C. *The
Economist* is written in the form of a dialogue, most of it taking
place between Socrates (under whom Xenophon had studied) and
an excellent young man named Ischomachus. As with all dialogues,
it undoubtedly employs much literary artifice, but basically it is not
a work of fiction; it is a practical manual, offering a blueprint of the
well-run normal household.

In chapter seven Socrates first asks Ischomachus whether his wife
came to him well prepared for her role. "My dear Socrates,"
Ischomachus replies, "how could she have had sufficient knowledge
when I took her, since she came to my house when she was not
fifteen years old, and had spent the preceding part of her life under
the strictest restraint in order that she might see as little, hear as
little, and ask as few questions as possible?" Since his bride was only
an ignorant child, without glamour, sophistication, intellectuality,
or experience in the ways of attracting men, it is little wonder that
Ischomachus has almost nothing to say about loving her; love, in
fact, had nothing whatever to do with their marriage, as he himself
pointed out to the girl soon after their wedding.

"Tell me, my dear wife," he said one day, after the girl had become somewhat accustomed to him, "have you ever considered
with what view I married you, and with what object your parents
gave you to me? For I am sure it is as evident to you as to me that
there was no lack of other persons with whom we might have shared
our respective beds. But when I took thought for myself, and your
parents did for you, whom we might select as the best partner for a

[3] The title, in English, has a misleading sound; the Greek, *Oeconomicus,*
implied one who was expert not in
theoretical economics, but in the management of his farm and estate.

house and children, I preferred you, and your parents, it appears, preferred me." With this unromantic preamble, he began to explain the purpose of marriage, telling her that it rested first of all on co-operation in managing their common fortune and property.

"But in what respect could I co-operate with you?" asked the girl with due humility. "What power have I? Everything lies with you. My duty, my mother told me, was to conduct myself discreetly."

This being a modest and proper answer, Ischomachus generously said that she could indeed help him. The gods had made man and woman different so as to be of the greatest use to each other. By their union, man and woman produce offspring and keep the race alive, but even more important, they profit by a division of labor. There are two general kinds of work—outdoor and indoor—of which man is designed for the former, woman for the latter; man is fitted to travel, to work in the field, to fight, and to be active in public places, while woman is equipped to care for children, train and watch over the servants, store and guard the household goods, and perform other stay-at-home tasks. It is her success at these labors, Ischomachus tells his young wife, that will bring her joy in her marriage: "Be therefore diligent, virtuous, and modest, and give your necessary attendance on me, your children, and your house, and your name shall be honorably esteemed even after your death; for it is not the beauty of your face and shape, but your virtue and goodness, which will bring you honor and esteem which will last forever." Esteem, respect, honor—these are the greatest pleasures she can gain from marriage. If these might seem a threadbare reward to modern woman, they did not to Ischomachus' wife, for according to his own words, she was immediately inspired to begin trying her hand at household management.

In the next long session of instruction, he taught her the orderly arranging and storing of food and goods in the house. "How excellent a thing a regular arrangement of articles is, and how easy it is to find, in a house, a suitable place to put everything!" he rhapsodized after giving her full details. This too, he apparently felt, is an important element of woman's emotional life, for, as he says to Socrates in recounting the instruction he gave her that day: "It seems to be a provision of nature that as it is easier for a well-disposed woman to take care of her children than to neglect them, so it is more pleasing for a right-minded woman to attend to, rather than neglect, her property, which, being her own, affords her gratification." But despite such gratification, generously granted her, there seems to have sprung up in the foolish bosom of Ischomachus' young wife some fugitive desire to be thought ravishing and enchanting, for one day, as he explains to Socrates, he noticed that she had lightened her skin with white lead, touched her cheeks with vermilion, and put on high-heeled shoes. He dealt with her in a gentle, but firm, manner:

"My dear wife," he began, "were we not united that we might have personal intimacy with each other?"

"People say so, at least," she replied.

"I am not better pleased with the color of white lead and red dye than with your own," said Ischomachus, paying her what he conceived to be a loving compliment. He assured her on philosophic grounds that the human body is most beautiful in its natural state; than, rather inconsistently, he argued against a wife's use of cosmetics on the grounds that it could deceive a stranger, but not a husband, since the latter would see her in the morning or in her bath, and know the truth.

"And what in the name of the gods did she answer to those remarks?" asks Socrates.

"Her only answer," says Ischomachus, "was this, that she never afterwards practiced any such art, but took care to appear in a natural and becoming manner." Not being a hard man, however, Ischomachus very kindly offered her some advice on beauty care: she must not sit idle in her room, but preside over the loom, move constantly about the house to watch the servants, and trouble herself to do some of the kneading of dough and the shaking-out and folding of linens. "I assured her," he concludes, "that if she thus exercised herself she would take her food with a better appetite, would enjoy better health, and would assume a more truly excellent complexion. . . . And now, Socrates, be assured my wife regulates her conduct as I taught her."

Whether this impenetrably smug young man was a real person, whether his views are actually those of Socrates, or whether they are those of Xenophon himself, hardly matters; the cloistered, duty-bound, mentally circumscribed Athenian wife of these pages is no figment of satire or of romance, but a composite portrait of the normal, upper-class housewife of Athens, in about 400 B.C. And from other sources one can piece together many details to corroborate and complete the picture shown in *The Economist*. Athenian citizenship was a precious possession of women as well as men, but between the sexes yawned a gulf as great as that between citizen and slave. A boy began to go to school in his seventh year, filling his mind with grammar, poetry, music, arithmetic, legend, and the sports and studies of the gymnasium. By the age of eighteen or nineteen, when he adopted the *chlamys* or man's cloak and swore the oath of loyalty to the State, he had become a gentleman, a warrior, a property-manager, and an amateur philosopher. A girl, in contrast, remained confined to the house from birth to marriage, and learned nothing but a few domestic skills and possibly a little writing. When she reached her teens, her betrothal was arranged by her parents; her consent was not asked, and would have been valueless in any case, since she had hardly ever met or known any young men. Many a girl laid aside her dolls or dedicated them to Artemis only a day or two before her wedding.

The wedding thrust her into the limelight for one day. There was a ritual bath, a careful dressing-up in holiday clothes, and a ceremony at her own house followed by a banquet and libation. Toward evening the groom put her in a bridal chariot and led her home through the streets, while flutists and harp-players made music, and relatives and guests formed a merry procession. At his house the new husband carried her into the bridal chamber and closed the door; outside, the guests chanted *epithalamia* or wedding hymns, the gist of which was that he should attend to business and not fall asleep. By morning, when the bride unveiled herself to her new relatives, her moment of glory was over. Rarely would she again mingle with her husband's friends or go out into the streets, except accompanied by servants; never would she again be celebrated or sung to until she died.

When Pheidias designed the statue of Aphrodite at Elis, dedicated to marriage, he made her with one foot on the shell of a tortoise, wrote Plutarch, to signify that a virtuous woman stayed inside her house and kept quiet. Pericles, the man of his age, once said in a famous funeral speech that "the greatest glory of a woman is to be least talked about by man, whether they are praising you or criticizing you." The seclusion of Athenian women was not quite as complete as that in Oriental harem life: well-born girls marched in the procession in honor of Athena; wives apparently went occasionally to the theater and to a few public festivals; and to judge from vase paintings, women of the poorer classes had to go outside the house to get water from the public wells. But upper-class women sent slaves on all household errands, and could not even do their own shopping. At home, the female quarters (*gynaikonitis*) were physically separated from the men's hall and rooms (*andronitis*); when a husband brought company home to dinner, his wife and daughters were expected to remain unseen. Men sallied forth in the morning and spent their days in public places; when they finally came home at night, it was not to share with an ignorant woman the precious experiences of the day or the subtleties of current politics and warfare, but to go to sleep.

Custom established the distance between them, and the law maintained it. An Athenian female, even though a citizen, could neither make contracts nor incur debts for more than trifling sums. She could not bring actions at law, and at all times had to have a male guardian—either her father, some relative, her husband, or son. Although the law was completely permissive toward male philandering, it prescribed that a woman caught in adultery was not thereafter to attend public sacrifices; if she did, passers-by had the right to maltreat her in any way short of homicide. A husband could "dismiss" or "put away" his wife not only for adultery, but for any other reason, though he had to return the dowry with her. As for his property, though she spent her life caring for it, it went not to her but to his male heirs; for support, after his death, she had to return to her own people. In a famous court oration involving a prostitute who had tried to pass herself off as a married woman, Demosthenes clarified the whole subject of womanhood and marriage for the jury in one sentence: "Mistresses we keep for pleasure, concubines for daily attendance upon our persons, and wives to bear us legitimate children and be our housekeepers." [4]

Having set up such barriers against love within marriage, Greek men found the wedded state distasteful; it was expensive, bothersome, and a hindrance to one's personal freedom. Yet it was unavoidable: a man did need a housekeeper, and it was his duty to the State and to religion to have progeny. He tried to render marriage painless by thorough subjugation of his wife, but only with partial success, for he had to put up with her unless he was

---

[4] "Against Neaera." This oration is included among Demosthenes' writings in most collections, although its authenticity is uncertain. Scholars generally agree, however, that it dates from his time, is much in his vein, and gives a faithful portrait of the morals of that period.

willing to send her and her dowry back home. Like most overlords, he distrusted and disliked this vassal, and feared every evidence of power on her side.

Down through the centuries have come echoes of that fear, the most familiar of them being the gossipy tales of the terrible wife of that best of all men, Socrates. According to tradition, Xanthippe was a ferocious termagant, who even attacked Socrates physically; she not only drenched him with water during one argument, but once tore the cloak off his back in the market place. Yet these things were minor, compared to the waspishness of her tongue. "How is it," a friend once asked him, "that you do not educate Xanthippe, but are content to have her as your wife, although she is the most ill-trained of all women that are in existence?" "Since I wish to converse and associate with mankind," said the philosopher in his typical mocking way, "I chose this wife, well knowing that if I could learn to endure her, I should easily bear the society of all other people."

As early as the sixth century B.C., the great lawmaker Solon had seriously considered a law—and according to some sources, passed it—making marriage compulsory because it had already become so unpopular that the State was endangered. Similar measures were considered again and again as the problem grew worse, and in Periclean Athens the law actually specified that only married men could become orators or generals. Most men delayed marriage as long as possible, and entered upon it only when they dared no longer avoid it. It is against this background that one can judge the frequent splenetic attacks upon wives and marriage in the creative literature of the era. "He's married, I tell you!" says a character in one forgotten play. "What's that you say?" replies the other. "He's really married?—but I just left him, alive and well!" Euripides often portrayed women as adulterous and vicious; Aristophanes lampooned them as drunken, scheming, quarrelsome, and greedy; and after some centuries of this tradition, the Greek poet Palladas summed it up with one of the cruelest epigrams in literature:

> Marriage brings a man only two happy days:
> The day he takes his bride to bed, and the day he lays her
> in her grave.

The prevailing dislike of marriage was only part of a more general dislike of womankind. Greek anti-feminism began in the nursery, where naughty children were threatened with bogies—all of which were female—and as they grew up they heard such legends as that of Pandora, source of all human ills, and Helen, cause of the terrible Trojan War. Indeed, it was a cliché of Greek popular thought that there was a woman behind every war. Even philosophers subscribed to much of the general misogyny, though thinking themselves above it. Plato pleaded liberally for equal education and career opportunities for woman in Book Five of the *Republic:* "The gifts of nature," he wrote, "are alike diffused in both; all the pursuits of men are the pursuits of women also." Being a Greek gentlemen, however, he could not help adding: "—but in all of them a woman is inferior to a man." Even his famous proposal, in the *Republic,* for a system of communal marriage, superficially seeming to be a liberation of woman from her secluded destiny, is actually no great elevation of her role or status as a love partner; it makes of womankind a mere collective pool of depersonalized fertility, and can be interpreted as the fantasy of a man who has no interest in a close relationship with an individual female.

Sane, sensible Aristotle rejected his teacher's communal-marriage plan, but agreed with him that the male was by nature superior not only in mind and body, but even in the procreative process, on the grounds that semen bears the principle of soul, while female secretions contribute only the material of body. From this and similar considerations, Aristotle arrived at a philosophic principle on married love which nicely rationalized the status quo: because the wife is inferior to her husband, he wrote in the *Nichomachean Ethics,* she ought to love him more than he her; algebraically, this would compensate for their inequality and result in a well-balanced relationship. There is no particular evidence that Greek women agreed with this view.

But what did Greek women actually feel? Did they love their husbands, or hate them, or merely suffer them in boredom? Unfortunately, in the war of the sexes, as in other wars, history is written by the victors; there are no books on love by Greek housewives. We might make a synthesis of their feelings toward men by distilling and collecting samples from the tragedies of Sophocles and Euripides, the scandalous comedies of Aristophanes, and the like; but it would remain unverified and unproven, for all this literature was written by and chiefly for men. The product, in fact, would probably be not so much a reproduction of the attitudes of the real

Greek wife, but of a fiction of the Greek male mind—a phantom shrew, created by him to justify his own hostile and oppressive attitude toward real women.

But we have already seen the objective facts of Greek marriage; in them lies the only reliable answer, and a better guide than the bitter thrusts of creative literature. The Athenian wife had no real contact with any free men except her husband. He was all-important to her, regardless of the inner separateness of their lives. He was her master, the father of her children, the provider for her home. As human beings everywhere tend to feel loyalty and affection for the authorities over them—even when they grumble against and frequently hate those authorities—so Greek wives must have felt a kind of love for their husbands, though it could hardly have been anything that would satisfy the expectations and requirements of women in more recent centuries.

A good objective measurement of the Greek wife's love for her husband is its strength as compared to familial, clan-like ties. A wealth of details concerning Greek marriage, divorce, and property inheritance, some of which we have already seen, make it clear that her ties to her own family always remained far stronger than those to her husband. And this does corroborate a portrait in drama: that of Antigone, in the play by Sophocles, who explains her act of self-sacrifice for her brother by saying that a brother is irreplaceable, though a husband is not—a passage so distasteful to the romantic mind that Goethe once remarked: "I would give a great deal to have an apt philologist prove that it is interpolated and spurious." The Greeks were not similarly offended.

Even more impressive is an instance of the identical sentiment appearing not in drama, but in history; the character in the case is Persian, but her actions were reported with approval by a Greek, Herodotus, in his monumental *History*, as exemplifying noble conduct in a woman. King Darius of Persia, Herodotus related, had convicted one Intaphernes and his kin of conspiring at insurrection, and condemned them all to death. But taking pity on Intaphernes' weeping wife, he sent a messenger to her, who said: "Madam, King Darius gives you one of the prisoners to be reprieved: take which one you choose." Her course was clear. "If the king grants me the life of one only," she said without hesitation, "I choose, above all, my brother." As for Intaphernes, she would weep for him—and let him die.

4

The Descent from Primitivism

❀   ❀

❀

How did it come about that, in the very flowering of this superb civilization, woman was so lowly and unloved? In general, one expects woman's place in a civilized society to be rather better than that in a primitive society, where she is apt to be exploited, treated as property, and subjected to numerous strict taboos. Yet many classicists have claimed that in the Golden Age of Greece, which we have just been visiting, her position was far inferior, both socially and in the hearts of men, to what it had been six to eight centuries earlier in the savage society of the Homeric era. The *Iliad* and *Odyssey* tell of no such extreme seclusion as existed in the time of Pericles, and the women in these epics often exercise considerable influence over their men and over the course of history. Some are shown as archetypes of faithfulness and loyalty. Penelope, who waited twenty wretched years for the return of Odysseus and steadfastly held off a horde of importunate suitors, is the very embodiment of wifely fidelity. In Book Six of the *Iliad*, Andromache and her husband, Hector, are shown to be a devoted and loving couple, and the scene when Hector is about to set out for battle is often cited as evidence of the closeness that could exist in Homeric marriage. Says Andromache:

> When I lose you I might as well be dead. There will be no comfort left, when you have met your doom—nothing but grief. . . . You, Hector, are father and mother and brother to me, as well as my beloved husband. Have pity on me now; stay here on the tower; and do not make your boy an orphan and your wife a widow.

Hector replies that he would dishonor himself if he failed to fight the Greek enemy, but adds:

[29]

Deep in my heart I know the day is coming when holy Ilium
will be destroyed, with Priam and the people of Priam of the good
ashen spear. Yet I am not so much distressed by the thought of
what the Trojans will suffer, or Hecabe herself, or King Priam,
or all my gallant brothers whom the enemy will fling down in the
dust, as by the thought of you, dragged off in tears by some
Achaean man-at-arms to slavery.

Certain other ancient legends also show women in a favorable
light: the stories of Alcestis, Polyxene, Iphigenia, and others all
center about heroines who not only are admirable, but who act
with far more freedom and initiative than later Greek women.
Literary scholars long racked their brains to find explanations for
this perplexing state of affairs. Possibly the most ingenious of them
all was Samuel Butler, who, after translating both the *Iliad* and
Odyssey, decided that Homer had been a woman, and had portrayed society inaccurately, with a feministic bias.

Homer, however, was a very thorough and excellent reporter of
folkways, and if one considers in the light of anthropological science the data so liberally strewn through the *Iliad* and *Odyssey*, a
rather different conclusion appears.[5] The world that Homer de-
picted existed about 1300 to 1100 B.C.; if judged by its technology,
its social organization, its degree of literacy, and other basic criteria,
it was a primitive society about as developed as those of the more
advanced American Indians before they came in contact with
white men. Woman's place in Homeric society, despite such occasional hints of sentiment as those quoted above, was typically
that of the primitive female. She was denied any place at ceremonial
banquets, and even the youth Telemachus could tell his mother,
Penelope, to leave the banquet hall and return to her proper wom-
anly tasks. Marriages were arranged entirely by men, without the
participation or consent of the women. The woman was purchased
by her husband, and could be traded, lent, or given away like his
other property. She was accumulated in large numbers by the
wealthy, and enslaved, abused, or killed on the spot by conquering
enemies.

Sexually she had no rights, though her lord had many: Penelope
was faithful, but Odysseus was a potent lover who enlivened his
tedious travels with many affairs, and though Zeus, chief of the

[5] Just such anthropological analyses
have been made by sociologist A. G.
Keller some decades ago in his book
Homeric Society, by historian Moses
Finley very recently in *The World of
Odysseus*, and by others.

gods, boastfully recited to his wife a list of his extramarital triumphs, she dared offer no word of reproach. Above all, between man and woman there was hardly ever the depth, intensity, or quality of feeling that existed between father and son or between male friends. "The poems," wrote Professor Finley, "are rich in such images as this: 'as a father greets his dear son who has come from a distant land in the tenth year'; but there are no similes drawn from a husband's joy in his wife. . . . The meaningful social relationships and the strong personal attachments were sought and found among men."

Nevertheless, even if meaningful relationships and strong attachments were rare between husbands and wives, women in Homeric society were genuinely important to their men, as in all primitive societies. They were food-preparers, makers of clothing, breeders of offspring, nurses to the sick, caretakers of the household and farm during the warriors' absence, and much else. No wonder, then, that they may well have been more active, resourceful, and important than their descendants of six hundred years later; seclusion—and intellectual misogyny—would only come with the emergence of a society wealthy enough to take most of woman's vital functions away from her and leave her nearly useless.

As civilization gradually ripened, long centuries after the barbaric Homeric era of tribal warfare and agrarian economy, the Greek city-states developed both manufacturing and mercantile activities. Finally, after the Greeks threw back the great Persian attacks of the fifth century B.C., Athens emerged as a leading sea power and industrial center. Mines, factories, farms, and other enterprises were profitably operated by slave power. In Attica, the district around and including Athens, there lived some 25,000 citizens and 10,000 free noncitizens; since the average slave cost only two *minae* (about $100 to $200, depending on which decade of the fifth century B.C. one considers), these citizens and freemen lived and prospered by the labors of some 150,000 to 300,000 slaves. Using this great pool of manpower as we use machinery today, Athens passed rapidly from a semi-primitive household economy to an urban economy, and thence to an imperialistic one. Among the results were wealth, leisure, and a great flourishing of art and ideas; but another, and less happy, result was the severe whittling-away of the purposes of family life.

When the home lost its position as the only source of food, clothing, and other essentials, it ceased to be the center of a man's existence and became merely an expensive social obligation. A husband's ties to his wife and household were no longer those of personal survival and close co-operation, but of *noblesse oblige* and absentee overlordship. Women retained their primitive disadvantages, but lost much of their onetime importance; in fact, with leisure, wealth, and slave power at their command, they themselves became enslaved. Meanwhile, as small tribes evolved into the imperialistic city-state, the ancient clanship ties wasted away, leaving Greek men and women with a need to redirect their love feelings and reorganize their deteriorating web of affectional ties. A state is not as warm as a clan, and neither a tyrant nor a democracy fills the gap left by tribal elders.

Affectional ties therefore shifted toward individuals. Greek wives, more closely than ever bound to the home, could partly fill their emotional needs with their children. But Greek men cast about uncertainly, seeking the proper persons with whom to develop a new set of relationships to replace the old ones. Their wives, clearly, were not the answer, since they were totally ignorant of educated ideas, and knew nothing of the richness of Athenian mental and spiritual life. Yet the Greeks enjoyed sex and admired female beauty; their legends, their religion, and their art were full of idealized and highly desirable goddesses, nymphs, and women. Greek men were willing to experiment with a new and more intense relationship to women, if they could find any who offered both gratification to the body and entertainment to the mind.

5

The Noble Companion

❀   ❀

❀

The hiring of the female as a sexual outlet and a companion was one of the many innovations of city life. According to several ancient authors, the wise Solon himself first established brothels throughout Athens. "You did well for every man, O Solon," exulted one Greek poet. "You, seeing that the State was full of men, young and possessed of all the natural appetites, and wandering in their lusts where they had no business, bought women and in certain spots did place them, ready for all comers." It not only protected wives from philanderers, but was a sound business venture; tradition says that Solon was able to build the temple of Aphrodite Pandemos with the profits.

The supplying of sexual partners later passed into private hands, and became specialized. In the Golden Age and afterwards, there were three categories of hired women. The common prostitutes were called *pornae;* they lived in ordinary brothels, the nature of which was made unmistakable by a wooden or painted phallus near the door. Higher than the *pornae* in the social scale were the *auletrides* or flute-players; these girls were hired out by their teachers or by their masters (many of the girls being slaves) to play, dance, and amuse the men at private dinners. Often they would spend the night, or part of it, with one or more of the dinner guests. The upper-class Greek man had a condescending and mildly contemptuous attitude toward both of these types. He felt no moral loathing for them, but as a man of taste and education he recognized that short-order harlotry was trivial, unaesthetic, and often vulgar.

But at the top level, prostitution was something quite different. In the sixth century B.C., Sappho had first used the word *hetaerae*—

companions—to mean intimate female friends. Much later the word
degenerated to mean prostitutes in general, but during the fifth and
fourth centuries B.C. it was still the dignified label of the high-grade
courtesan. She was often a woman of good blood and Athenian
citizenship, but unlike the usual wellborn girl, she had been carefully trained to be sexually exciting, mentally stimulating, full of
charm and graces, and capable of infatuating intelligent men. The
hetaera lived independently, usually in a house of her own, and en-
tertained such lovers as she chose to admit to it; she might allow a
number of them to pay court to her, or she might for a while become the exclusive companion of one man. Her gown, her hair,
and her make-up were elegant and full of artifice; her table was
artistically set and well spread; her home was a place of beauty and
refuge where a man could pass the time agreeably; and she herself
was a captivating and complex woman. All this gave her a status
vastly higher than that of the housewife. Greek literature of this
period refers again and again to the hetaera as a real friend, a noble
companion, and a woman of golden character, immeasurably superior to the virtuous woman. As the poet Philetaerus remarked: "No
wonder there is a shrine to the Companion everywhere, but nowhere in all Greece is there one to the Wife."

Such was the hetaera; perhaps only a few were quite so ideal and
idealized, but they made up in impact what they lacked in numbers.
In the fifth century B.C., for example, no woman was more influential than Aspasia, a courtesan who learned and practiced her profession in Miletus until about 450 B.C., and then came to Athens.
She is said to have had golden hair, a silvery voice, and a small high-
arched foot, and undoubtedly her physical charms included much
more, of which, unfortunately, there is no record. Her ability to
captivate, however, rested upon the fact that her beauty was allied
to other and more compelling qualities. She was widely read, highly
skilled in speaking, and talented in philosophic discussions. According to some, she gave lectures in her own home on rhetoric and
philosophy, and won such respect for her knowledge and her fine
manners that it is even said some men brought their wives to hear
her speak. (In view of the prevailing feeling about wives, this may
be a doubtful detail.) In the *Menexenus* of Plato, Socrates says that
he studied rhetoric with Aspasia, and that she was responsible for
the training of some of the finest Athenian orators. Pericles himself
was named among them, and a large part of the *Menexenus* con-

sists of Socrates' recollection of a funeral oration which he says was written by Aspasia and delivered by Pericles.

It is a pity that there is no credible record of the first meetings of Pericles and Aspasia; one would like to know if he came to learn rhetoric and stayed to love, or came to dally and was captivated by her mind and soul. Whichever was the case, Pericles and his wife were soon divorced and he brought Aspasia into his own home as his exclusive mistress. From then on she was the uncrowned Queen of Athens. To conservatives, however, she was an irritant, a disgrace, and a danger; they accused her of being a procuress, a schemer, and a malevolent power in politics; it was even said by gossips that the long, dreadful Peloponnesian War was started at her request merely because two of her maidservants were stolen by pranksters from the city of Megara.

Pericles was completely devoted to her, and would have married her except that the law forbade citizens to marry noncitizens. Plutarch wrote that he "loved her with wonderful affection," citing as proof that "every day, both as he went out and as he came in from the market place, he saluted and kissed her." He did much more: he not only willed his fortune to their illegitimate son, but once publicly defended her against malicious charges of impiety, risking his honor and reputation to plead with a jury of fifteen hundred citizens, to whom he appealed even with his tears. The Athenians acquitted her by a handsome vote, and later on even granted citizenship to their son.

A good deal of biographical material was written about other hetaerae in Greek times, but the bulk of it was lost or destroyed in early Christian times. Most of what remains owes its existence, by improbable circumstance, to the abnormal passion of a gastronome of the third century A.D. for collecting quotations. His name was Athenaeus and he lived in Naucratis, in Egypt; almost nothing else is known about him. He wrote an interminable dialogue called *The Deipnosophists* (*The Banquet-table Philosophers*) which is a kind of philosophizing cookbook filled with menus, discussions of various foodstuffs, and advice on table matters. Because Athenaeus could omit nothing that came to hand, it also happens to include a great variety of extraneous discussions and quotations concerning, among other things, hedonism, wars, dirty jokes, literary style, love, women, and courtesans. Athenaeus was probably the least original writer of classic times, and his book is a deadly dull patchwork of quotations from over eight hundred authors. Still, *The Deipnoso-phists* happened to survive, and with it survived scraps and bits of information from scores of works that were otherwise completely lost.

We learn from his quotes, for instance, that like Aspasia, many hetaerae wielded great power over even the highest-placed men. Athenaeus furnishes lists of kings, dictators, and generals who were influenced in state affairs by their mistresses, or married their cour-tesans and made them queens, or passed their thrones on to their bastard sons. Intellectuals, too, sought the companionship of he-taerae. Sophocles, despite his gloomy opinion of love, conceived a sincere passion for a hetaera, Theoris, in his later years and had children by her. Both Plato and Aristotle are said by Greek anec-dotalists to have had favorite courtesans, and the gossip, if doubtful, is not impossible; various hetaerae did study with each of them, and in Athens, as elsewhere, one thing could lead to another. Epicurus, that decent and serious thinker whose name was later wrongly at-tached to philosophies of self-indulgence, lived with Leontion, a courtesan who became learned enough to write a notable attack on certain ideas of the philosopher Theophrastus. The courtesan Gna-thaena, though not so philosophic, was an Emily Post of her time and wrote a treatise on table etiquette, and presumably other he-taerae were similarly intellectual.

Socrates not only studied rhetoric with Aspasia, but when he dis-coursed on higher and nobler forms of love he asserted that he was merely repeating what he had learned from Diotima, a priestess or hetaera at Mantineia. This may be only a literary device, but it probably indicates that he did discuss the subject with her. One may not find this so astonishing, but one *is* rather startled to learn that Socrates could also offer a courtesan practical pointers on tech-nique.[6] Someone had told him of the indescribable beauty of Theo-dota, and he hastened to see her for himself. After praising her beauty, he asked how she could afford such luxurious surroundings, and she replied that her income came from lovers, whereupon Socrates promptly offered her some unsolicited business advice.

"You must not imagine that it is such a simple matter to catch that noble animal, a lover," he said, pointing out that lovers are like

[6] What follows rests on the authority of Xenophon (*Memorabilia*, III, xi), who had been a pupil of Socrates and was one of his admirers.

hares, which have to be chased by skilled dogs into the hunter's nets.

"What sort of contrivance should I use, then, in hunting for lovers?" she asked.

"You should get a man, of course, to take the place of the dog," answered the good philosopher; "someone able to track out and discover wealthy amateurs for you; able also to find ways of driving them into your nets." No matter what exegesis one seeks for this, the meaning is plain: Socrates was urging her to use procurers. Nor was this all. He continued at some length, telling her how to excite and gratify her lovers—and not only in terms of intellectual converse.

"You will charm them best," he said, "if you never surrender except when they are sharp-set. You have noticed that the daintiest fare, if served before a man wants it, is apt to seem insipid, while, if he is already sated, it even produces a feeling of nausea. Create a hunger before you bring on your banquet. . . . Seem not to wish to yield. Fly from them—and fly again, until they feel the keen pang of hunger. That is your moment. The gift is the same as when the man did not want it: but wondrous different now its value." Impressed by his technical *expertise*, Theodota asked Socrates to be the agent who would help her net more game; he lightly replied that he was too busy, but that she should call on him if she needed him.

How much of all this actually happened, one cannot be certain, but Xenophon, who included it in his recollections of Socrates, portrayed the philosopher throughout in a fashion that tallies with Plato's portrait of him; one can therefore assume it represents Socrates' attitude, if not a genuine occurrence. It does nothing to enhance our image of the philosopher, but it does show that a better-class hetaera could be on intimate and cordial terms with a man of his stature and serious purpose.

To capture the imagination of philosophers as well as of lesser men, the hetaera did not need to be learned, like Aspasia, Diotima, or Leontion, but she did have to be quick-witted and ready with barbed puns, clever references to popular plays, and allusions (preferably salacious) to famous men. The jokes and quips of courtesans became famous; Machon, a comic poet, even compiled an anthology of them, part of which was preserved by the tireless Athenaeus. Many are puns which do not survive translation, and others are too obscene even for scholars (who translate them as far as Latin, but no further). Even those which labor under neither disadvantage suffer from the effects of time and the sea-crossing. Gnathaena, for instance, was serving to Diphilus, a writer of comedies, wine that had been secretly chilled with snow. When he complimented her on its coldness, she casually answered: "Yes, we always take care to pour into it the prologues of your plays." In her time, and to those who knew Diphilus' lack of emotional intensity, it may have seemed a capital jest.

Whether one can appreciate Machon's examples or not, it is evident that the Greeks considered badinage and sharp wit one of the charms of the hetaerae. They held court, sparred verbally with their suitors, played hard to get, teased, tormented, and frustrated their admirers, and all in all provided them with an experience compounded of intellectual, emotional, and sexual excitement that was vastly more desirable than sex alone; at least, so one would suppose from the market value of the respective commodities. The going price for lying with a common *porna* was two drachmas (about two dollars). Phryne, however, charged at least a mina (roughly one hundred dollars), and sometimes much more. Gnathaena asked one elderly moneybags for a thousand drachmas for one night with her granddaughter, Gnathaenion, and Lais had the effrontery to quote the repulsively ugly Demosthenes a fee of ten thousand drachmas.

That same Phryne, incidentally, reigned supreme as the love queen of Athens about a century after Aspasia's zenith. According to her admirers, she was the most beautiful woman ever seen. Apelles painted her and Praxiteles sculpted her—and both enlisted in the ranks of her lovers. One of Praxiteles' statues of her was even dedicated at Delphi as a religious monument.[7] With a fine feeling for effect, she veiled herself closely when she appeared in public—but disrobed completely in full view of all during the Eleusinian festivals, let down her hair, and waded into the sea to re-create the scene of Aphrodite's birth. Phryne had a sense of humor; she offered to pay for the rebuilding of the wall around Thebes if on it appeared this motto: "Destroyed by Alexander; restored by Phryne, the courtesan." The unamused Thebans refused the boon. At one point in her career, Euthias, an orator, became furious at her for some reason or other, and brought her to trial on charges of impiety. The orator Hypereides defended her, but sensed during his defense

[7] At least eight other hetaerae were similarly honored at various times.

speech that he was making no headway with the judges. He suddenly gambled on a different line of argument: with a dramatic gesture he tore open her clothing and bared her perfect bosom to the judges. In deference to such god-given beauty, they acquitted her.

But if men eagerly fell in love with hetaerae, it was a strange emotion they experienced. Few ever knew the unalloyed satisfaction that Pericles apparently found in Aspasia's company; most felt themselves caught by a passion that was delicious but painful, intoxicating but exasperating. For every word of praise of courtesans, there are two of condemnation. It was inevitable; the relationship was too commercial. Furthermore, a hetaera usually required the support of at least several lovers, and for each of them this meant that his relationship with her had built-in limitations and fatal flaws. And, of course, the drive toward love had to contend with the tradition of contempt of womankind.

The resentment of the hetaerae produced by all this emerged—as it often does in contemporary marriage—in the guise of money troubles. Men scolded hetaerae for their greed and their rapacity. "A courtesan," wrote Antiphanes, a comic poet quoted by Athenaeus, "is a calamity to the man who keeps her; indeed, he rejoices in keeping a mighty pest in the house." Numerous writers told of lovers who were plucked clean and then discarded, and of fine men who blindly squandered their wealth and reputations on insatiable hetaerae. "Not one of the wild beasts is more devastating than a harlot," snarled Anaxilas. Even a whole city might groan under the fiscal weight of love. According to Plutarch (who may have been writing with tongue in scholarly cheek) King Demetrius of Macedon levied on the Athenians a special impost of two hundred and fifty talents (about two million dollars) so that Lamia and her fellow courtesans could buy extra soap.

A vivid impression of the mingled love and hate, adoration and contempt, that men felt for the average hetaera may be gained from a court case of the fourth century B.C. concerning Neaera, whose life story survives in the speech against her written by Demosthenes and known as "Against Neaera." (Her defense is lost; we know only the prosecutor's view of her.) Neaera was accused of living with an Athenian citizen, Stephanus, as his legal wife; she being a noncitizen, this was a serious violation of the law, and severely punishable. The case against her was read to the jury of five hundred and one citizens from Demosthenes' script by one Apollodorus, an enemy of Neaera's husband.

As a young slave girl, Apollodorus told the jurors, Neaera was bought by a procuress in Corinth, trained in the courtesan's arts, and hired out. Two of the clients liked her well enough to buy her outright for thirty minae (three thousand dollars) and share her. Evidently they both felt some sort of friendship for her in addition to lust, for when they were both about to marry, they offered to let her buy her freedom at a reduced price rather than sell her profitably into a brothel.

Neaera put up part of the money herself and got the balance from a young Athenian named Phrynio in return for agreeing to live with him in Athens; she thus advanced herself to the status of free woman and full-time companion to one man. Unfortunately, Phrynio's treatment of her was hardly admirable. As Apollodorus told the jury: "He lived with her in a most indecent and reckless way, took her with him everywhere to dinners, where there was drinking; and she was with him at all his riotous parties, and he had connection with her openly whenever and wherever he pleased, making a display of his privilege to the beholders." Even allowing for the tendency of Athenian orators to exaggerate, Neaera's life as a companion was something less than ideal.

Eventually she ran away to Megara and set herself up as a self-employed hetaera. Stephanus met her there and slept with her; then he offered to bring her back to Athens, pass her off—illegally—as his wife, and claim her bastard children as his own legitimate ones. She accepted the offer with joy. Stephanus, however, was a professional *parasite* (the Greeks were first to use the word) and he soon persuaded her not to waste her talents, but to continue her practice in their home in Athens, while he drove hares into the net. The relationship seems sordid, to say the least. Yet Neaera was no vulgar whore; she must have had great personal charm as well as good looks, for wealthy men paid handsomely to spend time in her presence at the table, as well as in bed. Stephanus and she not only raised their children at home, but even gave her daughter, Phano, a dowry of thirty minae and got her properly married off.

Phano, alas, had learned her mother's ways, and the marriage failed when her husband got wind of her peccadilloes; he not only sent her home, but threatened to sue unless Stephanus forfeited the dowry. Phano came home and went to work with her mother. This, too, sounds rather crass; yet even under these conditions women could inspire feelings of loyalty and affection, for an elderly gentleman who was a lover of both of them voluntarily donated a thousand-drachma dowry to make another marriage possible.

However that might be, Apollodorus was unmoved and unsoftened by it. He pointed out in his summary to the jury that Neaera had been flagrantly guilty of pretending to be a citizen, and worse yet of pretending to be a legitimately married woman; he therefore appealed to the jurors to find her guilty, so as to show the world that "Women who have been carefully and modestly brought up . . . may not be ranked in the same class with one of loose and disgusting manners, who has repeatedly and day after day granted her favors to any number of men that solicited them."

Regrettably, we can never know the ending of the story; there is no record of the outcome of Neaera's trial. But one thing is perfectly clear from the events set forth in Apollodorus' speech, as well as the tone of his final plea: the dominant note in the love of Greek men for hetaerae was ambivalence. Though men were seeking a new love relationship with women, they were deeply influenced and limited by their cultural heritage of misogyny. They were able to love Love completely, but individual women only partly; they hungered for faithful love, but sought to obtain it by gifts, cash, and trickery; they stalked and preyed upon women, and were always dissatisfied with them; and when on rare occasions they actually fell deeply in love, they suffered, quarreled, and regarded it as a dreadful affliction.[8] Athenaeus filled the pages of Book Thirteen of *The Deipnosophists* with quotations to the effect that although moderate love is agreeable, powerful love is a heavy burden, a cause of toil, trouble, and frustration, a type of madness, an overpowering force that robs a man of self-control and wise judgment, a passion that makes the self-controlled man act wildly, a punishment by the gods for arrogance and pride, and so on and on. Elsewhere, Sophocles summarized it thus:

> . . . *Love is not love alone,*
> *But in her name lie many names concealed;*
> *For she is Death, imperishable Force,*
> *Desire unmixed, wild Frenzy, Lamentation.* . . .
> Fragment 678

[8] In many ways, this pattern is comparable to that of the adolescent or the emotionally immature adult in our own contemporary culture. One need not brand all Greek love relationships as immature—which would imply an absolute scale of values, apart from cultural context—but the similarities are unmistakable and illuminating.

And so Greek men, in experimenting with a new love relationship to women, were caught in a dilemma from which they could
find no escape. Love was either a mere pleasant game, an agreeable
diversion, a healthful exercise of body and mind; or it was a tragic
madness, an overwhelming force, and a ruinous disease. For if
woman were sadly imperfect, how could she merit ideal love, or
give it in return?

6

The Love of a Beautiful Boy

❊   ❊

❊

Man was more nearly perfect. It followed, therefore, that he
could be a more nearly ideal love object, particularly for
men of education and refinement who sought a mingling of minds
as part of love. The adolescent boy, with his immature, half-girlish
face and body, his unfolding mental powers, and his promise of
ultimate manhood, could inspire the Greek man with an emotion
still more intense and passionate than that aroused by the hetaera.
Far from being a purely genital deviation, it involved refined, aesthetic moods startlingly like those more usually felt by a romantic
man for a beautiful young girl. In his *Symposium*, Xenophon described the effect on a group of mature Athenian men when a beautiful boy entered the room. The men were dinner guests at the
house of an Athenian gentleman named Callias in 424 B.C., and had
all taken their places on the banquet couches when the youth Autolycus entered with his father:

Whoever had then observed what immediately took place would have thought that beauty was naturally something kingly, especially if a person possessed it in conjunction with bashfulness and modesty, as Autolycus possessed it at that time; for in the first place, as a brilliant light, when it appears in the darkness of the night, attracts the eyes of everyone towards it, so the beauty of Autolycus drew upon him the gaze of all on that occasion. . . . Some grew silent, and others composed themselves into a settled kind of attitude. . . . Such as are excited by the gentler influence of Love assume more affection in their looks, sink their voice in greater softness, and manifest in their gestures greater nobleness of soul. . . .

So deeply were they all stirred that when a professional jester entered and spun off a few jokes, he earned not so much as a chuckle, and fell into an acute depression, not realizing the source of their melancholy.

Plato describes similar scenes. His *Charmides* opens with a beautiful boy entering a public building followed by a troop of admirers; as he comes inside, all the men present turn and look at him, deeply affected, and when he sits down on a bench they push and shove to sit next to him until several fall onto the floor. Mature men, one gathers from numerous sources, were often enough in love with other mature men, but the ideal homosexual love affair was thought to be that between a mature man and a youth. The former was the "lover" and played the active (masculine) role, the latter was the "beloved" and played the passive (feminine) role. The outward expressions of the lover's infatuation for the boy were astonishingly parallel to those which, in more recent centuries, have been associated with love for a maiden. The lover made passionate declarations, wrote ardent petitions of devotion, swore solemn oaths, performed foolish errands at the boy's command, and slept all night, cold and miserable, on his doorstep. He blushed when the boy's name was mentioned, bored his friends with incessant praise of the beloved, and became dumb and stupid in the beloved's presence. "I like to see you blushing, Hippothales, and hesitating to tell Socrates the name," says Ctesippus in Plato's *Lysis*, "when, if he were with you but for a very short time, you would have plagued him to death by talking about nothing else." But however romantic the lover's conduct, or complete his success in the wooing, the relationship usually disintegrated when the lad's beard was fully grown (although some said a man could continue to love a boy until the latter was twenty-eight);

the boy himself, having become a mature man, and being discarded as a beloved, ceased to play the passive role and began in turn to stalk and seek out boys to love.[9]

The symptoms of the enamored lover were not inventions of homosexual men, but cultural traditions; fittingly enough, though, they first appeared in Greek literature in the poems of a homosexual woman. She was Sappho, of course, who caused the geographical label "Lesbian" to become a sexual one. Sappho lived in the sixth century B.C. at Mytilene on the Greek island of Lesbos, and ran a sort of finishing school where she taught girls poetry, music, and dancing. She fell madly in love with one after another of them, and expressed her love in delicate, but richly sensuous poems that won her, among later Greeks, the title of "the Tenth Muse." Her sexual preference did not prevent her from having a husband and rearing a daughter, and vengeful males even added to her history the apocryphal yarn that in later life she fell hopelessly in love with Phaon, a boatman, and, being repulsed, flung herself to death from the Leucadian Rock on the island of Leucas—first of the Lover's Leaps in Western tradition.

Sappho wrote a great deal of poetry (about twelve thousand lines, of which only five per cent survived the pious book-burning of Christian zealots), and had an immense influence on subsequent erotic literature. And on life, too: most of the symptoms from which lovers have suffered for nearly twenty-five centuries were first set forth by Sappho, and are perhaps as much a matter of cultural conditioning as of biology. Her most concise statement of the lovesickness syndrome appears in an ode she wrote to one of her favorites when the girl was about to leave her in order to be married.

> *Peer of Gods he seemeth to me, the blissful*
> *Man who sits and gazes at thee before him,*
> *Close beside thee sits, and in silence hears thee*
> *   Silverly speaking,*
> *Laughing love's low laughter. Oh, this, this only*
> *Stirs the troubled heart in my breast to tremble!*

[9] This general picture emerges from such Greek writings as Plato's *Phaedrus*, Xenophon's *Memorabilia* and *Symposium*, Demosthenes' *Erotic Oration*, Plutarch's *Of Love*, and others. It would seem, particularly in view of the reversal of roles at maturity, that Greek homosexuality was not strictly comparable to contemporary homosexuality. The family structure and child-parent relationships were rather different from ours, and it is not surprising, therefore, that Athenian deviation is not altogether explicable in the familiar terms of the rejection of masculinity, or the too close identification with a mother figure.

For should I but see thee a little moment,
  Straight is my voice hushed;
Yea, my tongue is broken, and through and through me
'Neath the flesh, impalpable fire runs tingling;
Nothing see mine eyes, and a voice of roaring
  Waves in my ear sounds;
Sweat runs down in rivers, a tremor seizes
All my limbs, and paler than grass in autumn,
Caught by pains of menacing death, I falter,
  Lost in the love-trance.

Ode to Atthis

This is something new, something not to be found in primitive life, poetry, or stories. This is the beginning of Western love; however unlike Sappho's love affairs those of modern men and women may be, the superficial symptoms of infatuation are still the same.

So great was Sappho's authority that Greek physicians accepted her symptom list as a diagnostic aid. About the year 300 B.C., for instance, Antiochus, son of Seleucus, King of Syria, fell secretly and violently in love with his father's young wife. Being an honorable young man, and seeing no hope of happiness, he decided to feign illness and die of starvation. Erasistratus, his physician, recognized the nature of the ailment, but could do nothing without learning who the woman was. As Plutarch tells the tale in his "Life of Demetrius":

> [Erasistratus] took notice that the presence of other women produced no effect upon him; but when Stratonice came, as she often did, alone, or in the company of Seleucus, to see him, he observed in him all Sappho's famous symptoms—his voice faltered, his face flushed up, his eyes glanced stealthily, a sudden sweat broke out on his skin, the beatings of his heart were irregular and violent, and, unable to support the excess of his passion, he would sink into a state of faintness, prostration, and pallor.

Happily, when the physician told all this to Seleucus, that excellent man handed over Stratonice to his son in marriage—making him symptom-free ever after. For such was the nature of love, at least as the Greeks celebrated it: if it culminated in a final and permanent union, the pains—and ecstasies—evaporated.

Homosexual love, with its intrinsic impediments to permanence, fitted the courtship and infatuation pattern perfectly, and ran no danger of permanent union and subsequent disillusion. As it gradually became a national institution, thoughtful Greek men sought to elevate it and justify it as the expression of the highest type of human emotion. Some argued that love between males should remain pure, involving only the mind and emotions, but their rapturous comments on the beauty of boys makes one suspect that such ideal conduct was difficult to maintain. Socrates was one of the few who could do so. Though he confessed to feeling a "flame" within him when he peered inside a youth's cloak, he remained pure. Alcibiades, at his youthful best, once wined and dined Socrates, tried to seduce him, and even slipped into his bed at night, but was astounded to be treated as though by a father. "I thought I had been disgraced," he later said, according to Plato's *Symposium*, "and yet I admired the way this man was made, and his temperance and courage."

Lesser men than Socrates often spoke of boy-love in clearly sensuous terms, praising the sexual satisfaction involved, while some others, relatively few in number, condemned it as degrading, unnatural, and ugly. The law made male prostitution punishable, but said nothing about unpaid voluntary connections. No Dr. Kinsey having been on hand, the frequency of actual sexual contact among Athenian males is unknown, but the literary evidence is clear: emotional liaisons among men were the fashion, nearly all of which involved flirtatious talk, kissing, and embracing, and in the majority of cases this led eventually to full sexual connection.[1]

Pederasty was hardly a Greek invention; it has been known and practiced in most human societies, sometimes widely, sometimes rarely. But in Greece it acquired a veneer of philosophy and was dignified as a superior relationship. And therein lies the reason, not merely the apology, for its prevalence in classic times. Even Aristotle, though he frowned on actual homosexual coition as a "morbid" abnormality, defended at length in his *Nichomachean Ethics* the proposition: "Love and friendship are found most and in their best form between men." Few others felt it necessary to draw so fine a line; they rejected indiscriminate pederasty, but felt that love for a youth of physical and intellectual appeal improved the character of both lover and beloved. Bravery, for instance, was said to result from such love, since both lover and youth would rather die than act cowardly in each other's sight; for this reason the famous

[1] Two major sources of Greek opinion on all this are the *Symposium* of Plato, and the *Symposium* of Xenophon. For summaries of other evidence from Greek writings, see J. Döllinger: *The Gentile and the Jew*, Vol. II, p. 254 et seq., and E. Westermarck: *The Origin and Development of the Moral Ideas*, Vol. II, ch. xliii.

Sacred Band of Thebes, a corps of shock troops, was composed entirely of homosexual pairs. In Sparta every trainee of good character had a mature lover who was a teacher to him and a model of manhood; it was deemed a military asset for them to fight near each other. Aristogeiton and Harmodius, a lover and his beloved, murdered Hipparchus, the tyrant of Athens, in 514 B.C., when he pestered young Harmodius sexually; later Athenians took this to mean that homosexuality was a force for democracy.

At the same banquet, described by Xenophon, where the guests were struck dumb by the beauty of a youth, one handsome young guest made a typical statement as to the beneficial effects of boy-love:

> We beautiful persons, since we produce a certain inspiration in those who are inclined to love, render them more generous with regard to money, fonder of enduring toil and gaining honor in hazardous enterprises, as well as more modest and self-commanding, since they are most bashful in regard to what they desire most. The people who do not choose handsome men for commanders of their troops are mad.

Even those who argued for pure love were apt to admit that the physical side of homosexuality was a good thing, though not the ultimate goal. Plato, for instance, wrote ecstatically of boy-love in his early dialogues; but he built upon it a towering edifice reaching toward spirituality, making of love a method of learning the superior reality of abstract ideas. In the *Symposium* he explained that love of a beautiful person enables one to recognize beauty in many persons, and so to extract the concept of beautiful types; likewise the beauty of knowledge in one boy or man leads one to recognize the beauty of all knowledge. Step by step, one can thus proceed to the love of ultimate reality—the pure, universal Ideas of beauty and virtue which, in Platonic metaphysics, are far more real than any individual or object. This early version of what he later developed into the full-flown theory of Ideas (which came to include all mathematical forms, all abstractions, and all generalized concepts) is the original meaning of Platonic love—a meaning which would surely have astonished many of those who have used the term in recent years. (In his later years, Plato changed his mind about some of this, and in Book Eight of his *Laws* condemned homosexual contact altogether as being contrary to nature and productive of intemperate habits and effeminacy.)

Most Greeks, however, criticized boy-love with obvious affection—saying that it was a fleeting kind of joy, that it was so powerful an emotion as to enslave a man, and that boys were cruel and tantalizing toward their lovers. Even these complaints smell somewhat of ink. The preponderance of the evidence indicates that homosexual love provided a considerable measure of intellectual and emotional satisfaction to many upper-class Greek men. But the most difficult aspect of this for modern man to comprehend is that the Greek man, loving a boy, could also enjoy sexual and love relationships with women; in switching from one to the other, he suffered neither from discomfort, guilt feelings, nor potency problems. Moreover, society—including women—accepted all this without hesitation. In the second Idyll of Theocritus, Simaitha, a lovelorn maiden, wonders why Delphis, an athlete, has deserted her bed. Finally an old woman brings her some news:

> After much other gossip she said Delphis was in love;
> But what desire has mastered him, for a woman or a man,
> She was not sure, but knew this only, that he was ever pledging
> His love in cups of unmixed wine, and at last rushed away
> Swearing he'ld crown with garlands the threshold of his dear.

Nor does Simaitha care which it is. Performing a magic fire spell, she says:

> O magic wheel, draw hither to my house the man I love.
> Thrice do I pour libation, Goddess, and thrice speak this prayer:
> Whether it be a woman lies beside him, or a man,
> Let such oblivion seize him, as on Dia once, they tell,
> Seized Theseus, when he quite forgot the fair-tressed Ariadne.

She is willing to have him back, in either case. For at that time in history a homosexual was not so much a neurotic or a pervert, but a man in search of love.[2]

---

[2] But those who therefore hold that Greek homosexuality was "normal" frequently assume that its social and psychological acceptability signify an overall normality. In the Greek culture, homosexuality may have been normal in some limited senses, but as always it reduced the interest and effort put by men into being fathers, and hence tended to put the human race out of business; such behavior, in any living thing, constitutes a biological abnormality. See discussion in Weston La Barre: *The Human Animal*, pp. 216–19.

7

The Limits and Fate of Greek Love

❀   ❀

❀

Western love began in classic Greece and early established a number of traditions that have never died out; yet in Greece it expressed itself principally as prostitution and sexual deviation. We have seen some of the reasons for this, but possibly the most basic of all was the condition of the Greek conscience.

In recent years, anthropologists have classified societies as "shame cultures" or "guilt cultures," according to their principal way of inducing self-control. In shame cultures, the main pressure toward good conduct comes from fear of public scorn. In guilt cultures, the rules of good conduct are "internalized"—they are absorbed from the parents during childhood, implanted in the unconscious, and form the conscience or the automatic "sense of right and wrong." Homeric society was clearly a shame culture: Homeric warriors did not desire a quiet conscience and a sense of rectitude, but sought public esteem and considered a broken vow or a piece of treachery not reprehensible but admirable—provided it succeeded. And even though the typical Athenian of six centuries later was a highly civilized man and could discuss ethics in a most elevated fashion, he was still much closer to being shame-guided than guilt-guided.[3]

He greatly admired and often cited the example of the dishonest heroes of Homer, and though he considered himself virtuous, he was notoriously tricky in business and crooked in politics. He praised

[3] Professor E. R. Dodds, in *The Greeks and the Irrational*, makes much of the change from Homeric times to the Golden Age, but admits that the internalizing of the rules of conduct and the creation of conscience appeared only late and uncertainly in the Hellenic world (pp. 36–7).

justice before the law, but voted for the thrilling oration rather than the just case. He spoke endlessly of friendship, but defined a friend as one who is useful. He talked of human dignity, but felt not a twinge at ordering a slave tortured to produce evidence for a trial. He swore loyalty to Athens, but easily forgave Alcibiades his treasons in order to borrow his talents.

This shame-guided man, in short, viewed other human beings as objects which either fitted, or failed to fit, his needs; as long as he did not run foul of society, he used them at his pleasure without suffering from guilt feelings. A wife, therefore, was a housekeeper, to be employed as effectively as possible for his own welfare; a courtesan was a pleasure-giving woman, to be enjoyed with as little strain on one's personal life as possible; and a beautiful boy was a delightful thing, to be loved for his body and his inspirational value until he was too mature to be useful any longer.[4] The Greek was not apt to identify his desires or goals in life with those of anyone else, or to subordinate his wishes to theirs; he was principally concerned with the richness of his own experience and the full utilization of his own capacities for enjoyment.

As long as personality remained so structured in the Greek culture, love would not fundamentally change. It did, of course, undergo continual refinement all during the Hellenic era following the Golden Age, but the refinements only devitalized and enfeebled it. Antiseptic shepherdesses and odorless shepherds appeared in love literature and became an enduring blight. In Alexandria, writers introduced into love tales such synthetic types as noble courtesans who sacrificed themselves for true love and passionate virgins who never quite lost their maidenheads, while the ideal male changed from the bearded warrior to milk-white curly-haired Daphnis, half-afraid of love. "A plague is Love, a plague!" groaned a hundred poets, but, strange to say, they seemed to have no fever; the plague had not really infected them. Eros was a naughty boy; life was short and death was long; lovers loved at first sight with never a word spoken. Artificial love-posturing reached what was perhaps a historic high with the epigram-writer Meleager, who produced such fancies as this:

---

[4] The egocentric nature of the Greek pederast is even sometimes spelled out in the form of blunt complaints by boys that their lovers merely use them for pleasure and give them none in return. See Xenophon: *Symposium,* viii, 21–2.

*Surely it was Love that made Heliodora's fingernail so
 long and sharp:
For does not her lightest scratching pierce me to the heart?*

Sometimes Greek romancers pretended that love was linked with
marriage or that lovers wanted to be married, but their tales were
always set in a context of make-believe and mythology, with lovers
becoming enamored of each other in dreams before ever meeting,
or naughty gods playing tricks upon stubborn parents by leading
lovers into marriage despite all obstacles. But actually the emotional
content of marriage changed little, even though women slowly
emerged from total seclusion. Even in the first century A.D., good,
decent Plutarch, in the midst of praising conjugal love and giving
advice on how to preserve it in his *Conjugal Precepts,* lets us see for
a fleeting instant what the relationship was still like:

> A young Lacedaemonian bride, being asked by an acquaintance
> of hers whether she had yet embraced her husband, made answer,
> No: but that he had embraced her. And after this manner, in my
> opinion, it behooves every honest woman to behave herself to-
> ward her husband.

And so the Greeks, though they invented love, neither connected
it with marriage nor endowed it with genuine ethical value, and
hence never solved the dilemmas it presented them with. For they
found love either a sensuous amusement that faded all too soon, or
a god-sent affliction that seemed to last all too long; they yearned
for inspiration and found it only in immature, impermanent boyhood, or longed for the love of woman and found it only in the arms
of whores.

Chapter III

BREAD AND CIRCUSES, LOVE AND GAMES

[53]

I

Two Views of Pagan Love

❄   ❄

❄

Lo, this is she that was the world's delight . . .
Lo, she was thus when her clear limbs enticed
All lips that now grow sad with kissing Christ.
                                                    Laus Veneris

S o speaks Swinburne's Tannhäuser in praise of Venus and of pagan love. Like him, many a modern man longs for the days of
Rome, when sensuous pleasure and exuberant sexuality were undiluted by the sense of sin, when Venus was joyously worshipped in
temples in every major city of the Empire, and when profane love
was as delicious as it was uninhibited. Modern love, an attenuated
version of what man once knew, is in contrast a passion tempered
by propriety and circumscribed by the mores of the suburb: one can
imagine Darby and Joan, but not Antony and Cleopatra, living in
Scarsdale, Forest Park, or Pasadena.

But perhaps like Miniver Cheevy, such people sigh for what was
not. Love in Rome was often viewed as an exhilarating game, but it
had a good deal in common with those other games at which thousands of spectators took delight in seeing one gladiator spill another's intestines onto the Colosseum sands. Love in Rome was lusty,
exuberant, and unclouded by the sense of sin, but it was strangely
blended with obscenity and hatred; it burned brightest between lovers who quarreled, tormented each other, and were flagrantly unfaithful. Love in Rome was cheerfully lecherous and expertly sensuous, but it was a malign symptom of a wasting ailment—the de-
composition of family life, and the over-all enfeeblement of the
hardy Roman character. For all its voluptuous appeal, and its
healthy appearance of guiltlessness, one can therefore also view

pagan love as a part of that syndrome of afflictions that resulted in the decline of Roman greatness. A grave charge, indeed; can love ever be so iniquitous and powerful a force in history? Let us look a little closer and see.

2

A Classic Roman Love Affair

❀   ❀

❀

O di et amo"—"I love and I hate": in those three words the greatest lyric poet of Rome epitomized his feelings for the woman in his life and summarized a typical Roman love affair of the first century B.C.

Gaius Valerius Catullus was his name, and he was born in Verona in 87 B.C., of a good family. That is practically all the information Latin historians recorded about him, yet we know him well, for the main events in his life and many of the intimate details of his love affair were recorded by Catullus himself in his poems. Though lyric poetry is, in general, not the most reliable form of social history or biography, the poetry of Catullus is something special. Most of his lyrics make no pretense at fictional invention and show few traces of the conventional terms of literary passion or bookish emotion; furthermore, they are sprinkled with names and allusions to events that correspond to, and are verified by, the reports of other writers on the same people and happenings. Scholars have therefore concluded that Catullus' poems form, in effect, a candid and literal autobiography.

Judging from what he tells of himself, his life was brief and rather uneventful. He came to Rome in his twenties (about 61 B.C.) to make his way in politics, but having an adequate income he chose to spend his time more agreeably, mingling in the patrician and literary circles of the city and playing the role of a poetic dilettante. It was an exciting time to be in Rome, even as a spectator: the city, brilliant and turbulent, was glorying in the Eastern triumphs of Pompey and the early Gallic conquests of Caesar; its people reveled in unwonted luxury, even while the power struggles of the conservatives and the First Triumvirate were destroying republican government. Unmoved by ambition, Catullus took no part in public affairs until he was thirty; then at last he secured an unofficial position as an aide to the provincial governor of Bithynia (northern Turkey). He stayed a year, failed to prosper in the role, and sailed back to Rome; shortly afterwards he died of unrecorded causes in 54 B.C., at the age of thirty-three.

In this brief unremarkable life there was only one experience of importance. When he was perhaps twenty-five years old, Catullus met Clodia, the wife of Caecilius Metellus Celer, governor of the province in which Verona lay, A wellborn lady of the Roman *haut monde*, she was a celebrated beauty and the center of attention of her circle. She was about eight years older than Catullus, but in the very prime of her beauty; her eyes were huge and black, her hands and feet were delicately tapered, her skin was pure white, and her manner was insouciant and provocative. She was the embodiment of sophistication and elegance, and Catullus was instantly infatuated.

Provincial though he was, he knew the customs and the ways of Rome. Such a lady, he was aware, could be pursued by a would-be lover without reproach or disgrace unless he were oafish or indiscreet; indeed, love of someone else's wife was thought far more desirable and more exciting than love of a courtesan or concubine. As a first step in his suit, Catullus translated for her Sappho's *Ode to Atthis*, thereby subtly declaring his feelings. He was able to see her fairly frequently thereafter; in that era the emancipated wives of Roman patricians could go about more or less freely in public, escorted by male friends and servants, and might be surrounded by admirers and hangers-on even in the presence of their husbands. So it was with Catullus; he even wrote that Clodia would scold him or talk to him scornfully in front of her husband so that Metellus would take him to be a youthful nuisance rather than a serious seducer. But Metellus was wrong.

Precisely what took place and in what order can be variously con-
strued by the sequence in which one reads the poems (they were
preserved in an arrangement clearly not intended by Catullus himself). According to the most generally received opinion,[1] however,
shortly after making the translation of Sappho he was daringly calling her his "girl," thinly disguising her with the name of "Lesbia"
because of the Sappho translation, and openly complaining of his
pain and his burning desire. He did not have to burn long. Allius, a
friend of his, lent Catullus the use of his house, and there he waited
in a fever until Clodia came to him alone, a "white goddess" who
paused for an endless moment on the threshold before flying into his
arms and completing their love. A happy period followed during
which no flaw marred the affair. They met again and again, and
Catullus wrote exultant boastful poems about their rapturous love-
making. In his various happy lyrics, he never indicated any troubled thoughts of her husband, or any plans for the future, and his
mood was uncomplicated by any philosophic speculations as to the
meaning or importance of their love. A typical lyric of this period,
as translated by Coleridge, says in part:

> My Lesbia, let us love and live,
> And to the winds, my Lesbia, give
> Each cold restraint, each boding fear
> Of age and all her saws severe.
> Yon sun now posting to the main
> Will set—but 'tis to rise again:—
> But we, when once our mortal light
> Is set, must sleep in endless night!
> Then come, with whom alone I'll live,
> A thousand kisses take and give!
> Another thousand! to the store
> Add hundreds—then a thousand more!
>
> No. 5

All too soon Catullus learned that such love is not quite so simple.
Clodia was vain and fickle, and saw no reason not to permit herself
the attentions of other men as well, and the provincial youth must
have annoyed her when he protested. Judiciously, he struggled to
adopt the sophisticated Roman viewpoint: "Although she cannot be
content with me alone," he wrote, "I'll bear my lady's rare, discreet
adventures, rather than seem to be a nagging busybody." But Metel-

---

[1] Gilbert Highet, in *Poets in a Landscape*, p. 251, briefly reviews the scholarly studies on which the usual version
of the affair is based.

lus, her husband, died in 59 B.C., leaving Clodia rich and free of the need for caution; from then on her affairs were neither rare nor discreet. Catullus was shaken when she accepted as a lover one of his close friends, Caelius Rufus, and embittered when she began to multiply her lovers almost at random. Soon she was holding feasts and entertainments in her house near the Tiber as openly as any Greek hetaera, and drunkenly lying with any guest who pleased her. Finally she even began to prowl the streets at night, accepting strangers in the darkness of alleyways. Catullus, in a puerile rage, threatened to defame her and to draw red phalli on the walls of her house, as on a brothel. He never could bring himself to do so, of course; what was worse, he could not stop loving her.

But what could he have loved in such a strumpet? Catullus was not explicit about it, but it seems, incredibly enough, that her very debaucheries were a cause of love.

> *Ah, then I loved you, not with passion wild,*
> *But as a father loves a trusted child.*
> *I know you better now, and here confess*
> *I love you more, though I esteem you less.*
> *"How can that be?" you say. Your ways, my dear,*
> *Make love more ardent but less kind, I fear.*
>
> No. 72

It was not the memory of a fine person who had degenerated, but the degenerate herself, whom he loved hopelessly and angrily:

> *I hate and love. You ask, perhaps, how can that be?*
> *I know not, but I feel the agony.*
>
> No. 85

When at last he told himself: "Wretched Catullus, play the fool no more," it was not that he could no longer stomach her, but because she would no longer accept him in her bed.

> *Now she refuses. You then must refuse, you too:*
> *Don't follow when she runs, don't live a poor fool's life.*
>
> No. 8 [2]

How much of his account of the affair was poetic license? How much of the portrait of Clodia's character is merely literary fancy? Not much; perhaps none. For not only did various other Roman writers mention similar details about her, but Catullus' description

---

[2] The poem listed as Number 8 in the traditional jumbled sequence was ob- viously written late in the course of the affair.

of her was practically duplicated in a Roman courtroom. Caelius Rufus, Catullus' close friend, had apparently broken off his affair with Clodia at his own pleasure rather than at hers, and she, furious for revenge, instigated a prosecution of him in 56 B.C. The counts included charges of lechery and adultery, but rested chiefly on the far graver charges that he had not only defrauded Clodia of money, but attempted to poison her. (Catullus, who would have been horrified and fascinated by the proceedings, was in Bithynia at the time, and had to get the details second hand.)

Caelius' defense counsel was the most distinguished court orator of the day, Cicero himself, who rightly judged that the best defense would be an unsparing attack. His defense speech was no great example of legal reasoning, but a *tour de force* of character destruction through rhetorical technique. "I would attack [Clodia] more vigorously," he told the court, for example, "if I had not a quarrel with her husband—I mean *brother;* I am always making this mistake." The jury and the onlookers must have roared with laughter. Clodia's brother, the radical politician Clodius Pulcher, was a notorious rake who, according to common talk around town, occasionally sampled the delights of his own glamorous sister's bed. The story was well known, and Cicero's "mistake" was sure to be relished by all except the Clodian faction.

Cicero was generous in the use of such sarcasm and insinuation, but toward the end of his speech he became more direct; he summed up Clodia's ways and days (without actually naming her) in one long rhetorical question:

> If any woman, having no husband, has opened her house to the passions of everybody, openly established herself in the way of life of a harlot, and been accustomed to frequent banquets of men to whom she is not related; if she does so in the city, in country-houses, and in that most frequented place, Baiae; [3] if by her gait, her style of dress, and the people who are seen attending her; by the eager glances of her eyes and the freedom of her conversation, by embracing men, by kissing them, at water-parties and sailing-parties and banquets; . . . if in all this she behaves so as to seem a very wanton and lascivious harlot, I ask you whether a young man who has been with her is to be called an "adulterer" —or a lover? [4]

And turning to Clodia a moment later, Cicero said, mockingly:

[3] A near-by summer resort, noted for its dissolute atmosphere.
[4] Cicero: "Pro Caelio," *Orations.*

> You are at liberty to suppose that all I said just now was not said about you.

One can hear, at the distance of two thousand years, the laughter in the courtroom; one can imagine the flushed face and burning eyes of the New Woman, the emancipated Roman lady, the practitioner of pagan love. Caelius was acquitted; history says nothing more of Clodia. Probably she continued her ways until time had stripped her of her charms and cooled her heat.

Yet if she was the most notorious woman of her circle, she was neither unique nor a rarity, but a representative of a trend. That same sickly combination of love and hate that Catullus felt for her —and she for her lovers—was far from unusual; indeed, Roman literature is full of it. Propertius, another autobiographical poet, described his affair with "Cynthia"—a love that could seemingly be kept alive only by the stimulation of particularly dangerous trysts, mutual infidelities, and terrible quarrels. The poet Tibullus doubled the mood by loving two women at the same time, both of whom were worthless, greedy, and hateful. The moralistic Virgil expressed the Roman male's viewpoint in the only love affair he ever wrote about: he had Aeneas abandon Dido in order to carry out his duty and get on with his destiny. Modern readers may weep for Dido and despise Aeneas, but Roman men understood him and enjoyed seeing him victorious over the power of love.

Victory over love—by the avoidance or repudiation of powerful emotions—seems, in fact, to have been the principal alternative in the minds of many Romans to the pain of love-plus-hate. At the very time when Catullus was in the toils of love agony, the philosopher-poet Lucretius was writing his all-encompassing poem, *De Rerum Natura*, in which, among many other things, he gave advice on the rationalistic Epicurean handling of love. Passionate sexual love should be carefully avoided, he said in Book Four; it is habit-forming, causes frenzied and irrational actions, and consumes the lover's strength and wastes his substance. Like Catullus, Lucretius viewed love entirely in terms of sexual activity; unlike Catullus, he considered it a snare and a delusion, a madness in which the lover longs unendurably to have complete union with another body although complete union is forever impossible:

> They cling greedily together and join their watering mouths and draw deep breaths pressing teeth on lips; but all is vanity, for they can rub nothing off thence, nor can they penetrate and

be absorbed body in body (for this they seem sometimes to wish and strive for). . . . At length there is a short pause for a while in the furious burning. Then the same frenzy returns, and once more the madness comes. . . . They can find no device to master the trouble; in such uncertainty do they pine with their secret wound.

And what remedy did this greatest Roman exponent of Epicurean philosophy suggest?—a measured dosage of physical disgust, and a judicious admixture of hatred: the same formula, really, at which poor Catullus arrived willy-nilly. The prudent man turns his thoughts away from love, knowing it to be a disease, said Lucretius; if he feels heat, he chooses to satisfy himself in the easiest connections, undisturbed by emotion. If, nevertheless, some woman begins to affect him with love, he deliberately studies her faults so as to see her plainly. Instead of foolishly admiring her for a delightful disorder, a Junoesque stature, or a sharp and nimble wit, he sees plainly that she is dirty, has sagging breasts, or uses a scolding tongue. He reminds himself, added Lucretius, that even the most beautiful woman does the same things as the ugly woman: she sweats, she eliminates, and she covers up her odors with perfumes. The rational man is not fooled.

It is significant that this excremental refrain, this linking of the loathsome with the lovely, appears not only in philosophizing and satire, but again and again in Roman love literature. Even Catullus— whom Tennyson once called the "tenderest of Roman poets"—set disgusting images next to beautiful ones. He wrote scurrilous poetry about Caesar's pederasty, sneered that one of Clodia's lovers, following an old Spanish custom, washed his teeth with urine, and declared in measured verse that another of her lovers had breath so foul that if he opened his mouth, bystanders would drop dead. And in his farewell poem to Clodia, he views her in thoroughly vulgar, purely genital, terms:

> *Give her my goodbye, her and all her lovers,*
> *Whom she hugs so close to her in their hundreds,*
> *Loving not one, yet with her constant lusting*
> *Leaving their loins limp.*
>
> No. 11

That is his final word about love: its most alluring feature is also its most disgusting. *Odi et amo.*

3

The Passing of the Old Ideal

❊   ❊

❊

Times always change, and men always lament the fact. Clodia and the liberated upper-class women of her type seemed glamorous to Catullus, but to conservatives who respected the old traditions they were dangerous revolutionaries.

The Roman woman had once been a figure of strength and moral integrity—a staunch, large-hipped child-bearer, spinner of wool, keeper of the household, and proper mate for the stern, tough, farmer-warrior of the early Republic. They were bound to each other by no such frippery nonsense as romantic preference, but by religious loyalties, clanship ties, and the urgent business of economic and military survival. Without such women, Roman men of the fifth and fourth centuries B.C. could hardly have left home so confidently on their long wars, or so persistently gone about that series of conquests that won them Italy and, in succeeding centuries, the entire Mediterranean, the Middle East, and almost all of Europe. The long-absent fighters demanded that their wives be dutiful and virtuous; they wanted to find neither ruined farms nor bastard sons when they came home. When Tarquinius raped Lucretia, she knew that her virtuous death would cause her husband less sorrow than her soiled life; she stabbed herself, and made him, relatively speaking, happy. But he and his fellow Romans, enraged at the ruling Tarquin clan, drove them out, founded the Republic, and began the conquest of Italy. The whole story is probably legendary, but it summarized ancient Roman morality: the home must be intact, the wife must be spotless, and men must fight, conquer, and die.

In all of Western history there is nothing quite like the patriarchal family of old Rome. It was cemented together by the formidable *patria potestas,* or power of the father. He owned and controlled all family property; priestlike, he directed the worship of family gods; and he himself was godlike in his absolute power to direct or dispose of the lives of his children. The Laws of the Twelve Tables, which date from about 450 B.C., stated that the father had the right during the entire lifetime of his children to imprison them, whip them, keep them to rustic labor in chains, sell them into slavery, or slay them, even though they might have attained to high state offices.

Where the male was drawn in such bold strokes, what was the picture of the female? As in Greece, she was a perpetual minor; even when her father died, she remained under the guardianship of some other male in her family. Marriage merely transferred her from the *patria potestas* of her father into the *manus* (literally into the hands) of her husband, who could then chastise, whip, and correct her as he pleased without external hindrance, put her out at labor like a slave and collect the proceeds, condemn her to death for a capital offense, and even kill her with his own hands if he caught her in adultery.

For all that, the formal law does not tell everything about how men and women treated each other. In actual fact the Roman matron was not a cringing slave, but a self-respecting subject of her lord. In the primitive era she labored alongside him in the fields, and was the nurse and teacher of his children, the provider of his clothing, food, and medicine, and the mainstay of his estate. In the era of expansion she could not, like Athenian wives, pass her time in idle seclusion; her husband might be away for years, conquering Sicily, Carthage, or Gaul, and she had to run things for him until he returned. Ideally she was unsmiling, stern, and hardworking. She considered it a disgrace to have anyone else suckle her children or weave her wool, and prided herself on seriousness, purity, and devotion to duty; lacking only Calvinism, she was the spiritual ancestor of the New England pioneer woman.

After the Punic Wars of the third century B.C. had cleared Carthage from Rome's way, imperialist expansion went ahead rapidly, and the patricians and the equestrians (the middle class) became far wealthier than before. Leisure and a growing taste for civilized refinements brought the affluent to Rome, or enabled them to make their own cities into little replicas of Rome. These upper and middle classes now began to live from the proceeds of wealth, land, and slavery, rather than by working, and there was no longer the need for the family, or for its women, to be what they had been. In addition, fathers were now able to give larger dowries to their daughters, but because they intensely disliked seeing their property pass into the hands of the son-in-law and his family, they began to avoid giving their daughters in *manus* in the older forms of marriage known as *confarreatio* and *coemptio*. Instead they married their daughters off by *usus*, a nonreligious civil marriage in which the girl remained under her father's guardianship. Her husband might enjoy the benefits of her dowry, but could not control it or inherit it; she herself controlled it through her father or through a male business agent. If she found her husband hard to live with, she could divorce him by merely sending him a written notice and return home with her dowry intact.

Conservatives tried to combat the change in woman's rights by turning the clock back. One of the most famous of them was Cato the Elder, an orator, consul, and censor during the second century B.C. In 195 B.C. he predicted disaster if women kept winning new privileges:

> If each of us, citizens, had determined to assert his rights and dignity as a husband with respect to his own spouse, we should have less trouble with the sex as a whole; as it is, our liberty, destroyed at home, is even here in the Forum crushed and trodden under foot. . . . Review all the laws with which your forefathers restrained their license and made them subject to their husbands; even with all these bonds you can scarcely control them. What of this? If you suffer them to seize these bonds one by one and wrench themselves free . . . do you think that you will be able to endure them? The moment they begin to be your equals, they will be your superiors.[5]

But he was sweeping back the tide with a broom; he lost and so did other conservatives, year after year, as woman moved out of the shadow of patriarchal domination. The actual issue in 195 B.C. concerned nothing more serious than the freedom to wear gold ornaments and varicolored garments, but a similar scene was played out a century and a half later, and again the women won—only by then the issue was one of taxation of their property. They had moved far from fighting for mere adornment.

With increasing control of her person and her money value, the Roman wife was changing radically and pre-empting much of the

[5] Livy: *Roman History,* Bk. XXXIV, Secs. ii–iii.

role the hetaera had in Greece. She was reasonably well educated, for as a girl she went to school with her brothers or was tutored at home, learning all the classical subjects and becoming well informed about current affairs. As a woman—if she held with the newer ideas —she moved freely in society, interesting herself in intellectual and social life; she was never sequestered in the home, as in Greece, and she was an ornament of social gatherings. If men jealously kept her out of political office or business life, she could at least seek to entertain herself, and when her husband helped conquer Greece and stole its statues, its plays, its ideas and customs, she found among them love, the best entertainment of all.

Though Roman love was imitative of Greek models, the differences were significant. Pederasty became popular, but remained candidly physical; Roman men had no interest in winning boys through spiritual and mental attraction, but preferred to seduce or buy them and get them into bed without intellectual bother. (Cato was outraged that a pretty boy might be sold for as much as a talent [$3,600], or more than enough to buy a farm.) Courtesans became popular, too, though they never captured the imagination of the hard-headed Romans, who preferred their sex unmixed with philosophy or significance. It was an appetite, the satisfying of which was delightful; what else need be said? A fool might let himself be trapped and hurt by it, like Catullus, but a more skillful hedonist would control its intensity by flitting easily from one bed to another. Sighed Horace:

> I am stricken with the heavy dart of Love, yea of Love who seeks to kindle me beyond all others with passion for tender boys and girls. . . . Affection for Lyciscus now enthralls me, he who claims to outdo any woman in tenderness. . . . Stern reproaches of my friends have no power to free me—I can be freed only by another flame, for some other fair maid or slender youth.
>
> *Epode xi*

Were such darts and flames really painful? Not very; reading through the Epodes, one soon senses that the beloved was not really a person, but any person—and not even that, but only an interchangeable set of lips, thighs, and buttocks, all of which served the same purpose.

In any case, Roman love as it emerged in the second and first centuries B.C. involved a variety of possible unions, all of them outside of marriage. The only illegal one was adultery, but up-to-date

Romans favored it above all others, regarding it much as modern man regards cheating on his income-tax return—a zestful wrong-doing that involves no sense of wrong or sin, but only apprehension lest he be caught. Adultery in Rome presented certain problems: there were no decent public lodgings to speak of, daytime trysts involved the danger of recognition, and nighttime trysts meant risky trips around the city alone, without a retinue of torch-bearers and gladiators. The most convenient place was the lady's home, but what peace of mind could a man know in another man's bed? Horace, a nervous fellow, had no moral compunctions against adultery, but objected to it for this very reason:

> A husband may rush back from the country, the door burst open, the dog bark, the house ring through and through with his knocking; the woman, white as a sheet, will leap away, the maid in league with her cry out in terror. . . . With clothes dishevelled and bare of foot I must run off, dreading disaster in purse or person or at least repute.
>
> *Satire i*

Many other upper-class Roman men disagreed. For them adultery was more delicious than whoring or boy-love precisely because of the extra risk; women played the game just as eagerly and with much the same motive. By the end of the first century B.C. adultery had become so fashionable that the ancient tragedy of Helen of Troy took on a new light; Ovid, writing typically upper-class opinions, viewed it thus:

> *Afraid of lonely nights, her spouse away,*
> *Safe in her guest's warm bosom, Helen lay.*
> *What folly, Menelaüs, forth to wend,*
> *Beneath one rooftree leaving wife and friend! . . .*
> *Blameless is Helen, and her lover too:*
> *He did what you or anyone would do.*
> *The means you offered made them misbehave;*
> *What did the wench but take the hint you gave?*
> Ars Amatoria, ii, 359–68

Under the impact of these changes, divorce grew ever more common and marriage came to seem so unimportant that it was broken for any trivial excuse—and in marriage by *usus* all one needed to do was send the spouse an announcement, via a freedman, saying: "*Tuas res tibi agito*"—"Take your things away." One Sempronius Sophus divorced his wife in this way because she went to the games without telling him first, and another man because his wife went onto the street without a veil. Women cast off their husbands for equally insignificant reasons, and men with political ambitions married four or five times in the process of self-advancement. Under such circumstances, child-bearing could hardly seem desirable to women, and the birth rate fell steadily. Abortion and contraception became common among the well-to-do, while the poor, using a cheap but time-honored device, deposited their newborn infants on the nearest dungheap, stairway, or hillside.

If the emotional flavor of the earlier moralistic patriarchy is not altogether agreeable, it is at least understandable to us; but that of the later Republic is so alien that few fictional or dramatic treatments of it have dared to be truthful. How many have ever visualized the great Caesar as a fop, a dandy, and a perfumed homosexual? Yet such he was, at least in his youth. His warm reception at the court of the King of Bithynia won him the nickname of "the Queen of Bithynia," an epithet thrown at him even on the Senate floor in Rome. He wore his clothing with a studied carelessness, kept his body plucked clean of hair, and fussed so endlessly with his thinning locks that Cicero once said: "When I see his hair so carefully arranged and observe him adjusting it with one finger, I cannot imagine that it should enter into such a man's thoughts to subvert the Roman state." [6]

The same man, however, could not only subvert the state, but also become an indefatigable lecher: the historian Suetonius indicated that his conquests included the wives of almost all his close friends, associates, generals, and the heads of state wherever he went. Partly in admiration, partly in resentment, Romans called him *"Omnium mulierum vir et omnium virorum mulier"*—"The husband of every woman and the wife of every man." His four marriages were all made for political or practical reasons; there is no evidence that love was responsible for any of them. He was past fifty and Cleopatra was twenty-one when they met; she deliberately offered him a queen's body for political reasons, and he found her person and her character alluring enough to keep him overtime in Alexandria, but it is doubtful whether the affair involved more than ambition and cunning on her part, and on his the powerful appeal of

[6] These and other seldom-taught details about Caesar were reported by such ancient historians as Suetonius, in his *Julius Caesar*, and Plutarch, in his "Life of Caesar."

having an exotic queen—and so young a one—as his mistress. The woman he was faithful to longest—in his fashion—was Servilia, a matron of a noble family; this affair, in some sense, may have helped undo him, for even in Rome a bastard might hate the man who begot him. Servilia's son, Brutus, was thought to look much like Caesar, and if Suetonius is correct the dying Caesar said to him not "You, too, Brutus?" but "You, too, *my child?*"

The avenger of Caesar's murder, Mark Antony, has for twenty centuries been upheld as the quintessential lover, driven by his passion for Cleopatra to gamble for an empire; the title of Dryden's play summed it up best—*All for Love, or the World Well Lost*. This most loving of lovers was, in actual fact, an unregenerate rake, whose long and gaudy sexual history included a period of adolescent homosexuality as the favorite of a Roman nobleman, youthful debauches with matrons and courtesans, the keeping of a harem of concubines (both male and female) in his house in Rome, and two marriages made for gain and dissolved when no longer gainful.[7] Cleopatra, according to tradition, created in Antony a truly grand passion; yet even while he was most in love with her, he was entirely amenable to the suggestion that he marry Octavia, sister of Octavian, his co-ruler of Rome, so as to create a firm bond between them. The marriage lasted until Antony decided to battle Octavian for the Empire. Then, divorcing the pregnant Octavia by mail, he married Cleopatra, fought Octavian for the world, and lost.

Tradition also says that in defeat he committed suicide after asking Octavian to spare Cleopatra, but that she, spurning Octavian's kindness, clasped the asp to her bosom rather than live without Antony; this too may be as wide of the mark as the usual "facts" of her life. She is always called an Egyptian; in truth, she was half Greek and half Macedonian, with no Egyptian blood whatever. She is said to have been a highly sexed voluptuary, yet there is no evidence from any source that she had any serious love affairs in her life other than those with Julius Caesar and Mark Antony. Even these were very likely somewhat cooler, inwardly speaking, than tradition says. Defying a hundred playwrights and a thousand poets on the basis of little-known Egyptian evidence about her, the learned Dr. W. W. Tarn of Cambridge University wrote in the *Cambridge Ancient History*: "Her two love affairs were undertaken quite deliberately

---

[7] The unpleasant facts about Antony were given by Cicero in his Second and Sixth Philippics, and by Plutarch in his "Life of Antony."

with the same purpose as all her actions. For the keynote of her character was not sex at all, but ambition." When the world slipped through her hands at Antony's final defeat, she was a woman past her prime and past further scheming for glory. Later ages have romantically imagined that she took the asp up with the same spirit that moved Juliet to snatch Romeo's dagger, but her suicide may actually have had more in common with that of Eva Braun in the bomb shelter under Berlin.

4

The Lex Julia *and Julia:*

A Roman Tragedy

❀   ❀

❀

A significant effort was made to restore family unity and sexual morality to Rome at about this time. It came from a man who, in his youth, gave no promise of becoming a great moralist, but neither did he seem destined to become the wise and all-powerful ruler of the entire civilized Western world. At eighteen he was nothing but a nervous, unprepossessing, somewhat sickly and routinely licentious youth named Octavian, whom Julius Caesar had named as his heir; as the years passed he underwent an astonishing metamorphosis into that calm, judicious, efficient dictator who ruled so well that the Senate granted him the title "Augustus" and made him in fact, if not in name, the first Roman emperor.

The metamorphosis was slow, but marvelously thorough. As a

young man, Octavian had lived the usual life of luxury; as Augustus he preferred simple garments, slept in a plain bed in a cubicle, ate little while his guests gorged themselves, and relaxed from his cares by doing nothing wilder than sailing quietly along the coast. As a youth, trying to inherit the world from Caesar, he ruthlessly exterminated his uncle's assassins and even abandoned his friend Cicero to Antony's blood lust; as the sole ruler of Rome after 30 B.C. (the year in which he finally defeated Antony), he became temperate, magnanimous, and forgiving, and cherished particularly a maxim given him by the philosopher Athenodorus: "Whenever you get angry do not say or do anything before repeating to yourself the twenty-four letters of the alphabet."

In his youth he had the same cavalier attitude toward love and marriage as other modern Romans. Suetonius, that classical scandalmonger, says he may have become his uncle's legal heir by granting the insatiable Julius the enjoyment of his body. Whether this was so or not, he certainly indulged in the usual amount of adultery. He married Antony's stepdaughter in a calculated effort to repair his first quarrel with Antony, but soon divorced her and took on the twice-divorced Scribonia, who bore him a daughter, Julia. In 39 B.C., when he was twenty-five, he fell mightily in love with Livia, compelled her husband to divorce her although she was pregnant, and married her himself as soon as the child had been born.

Since he needed a reconciliation with the aristocratic class at that time, and since Livia belonged to the noble Claudian clan, one might question how sincere his emotions were at the outset. But the marriage actually yielded a warm, mature, and abiding relationship. Augustus was genuinely attached to Livia and remained her devoted husband until his death more than forty years later. His occasional infidelities made no difference; they were routine and trivial, and she kept her peace and loved him just the same. All his life he confided in Livia, consulted her, and shared with her his burdens and his joys. She made him particularly happy by being an exemplar of the classic virtues—beauty, chastity, and devotion to hard work— and yet could mingle easily in glittering Roman society and play a quiet but significant role in affairs of state. Her only failure was that she never bore him any children.

It was a painful failure for Augustus; he wanted to be in every way the example of a good family man to his fellow citizens. Deeply concerned about the changing standards of his time, he read history, pondered long, and decided to restore morality by the force of law. Between 18 B.C. and 9 B.C. Augustus promulgated a series of "Julian Laws" (so named because he was, by adoption, a member of the Julian clan), which have been called the most important social legislation of antiquity.

The crucial law was the *Lex Julia de Adulteriis* which for the first time forbade a husband to kill an adulterous wife, but ordered him, under pain of severe fines, to bring her to court and accuse her. If he did not, her father was required to do so; and if he in turn failed, any right-minded citizen might accuse her, winning part of her property if she were convicted. Adultery, which had been a private wrong, thus became the state's business for the first time. The government was empowered to take away from an adulterous wife half her dowry and a third of her other property; what irritated Roman men even more, they too faced stiff penalties for adulterous connections with married women, though they could still freely use prostitutes. A whole series of other Julian Laws tried to prop up the birth rate of the upper classes: they made bachelors, spinsters, and childless wives ineligible to inherit, granted mothers of three or more children special legal privileges, gave political preference, between equal candidates, to the man with more children, and so on. It was a thoroughly imposing attack.

But although Augustus singlehandedly had brought about the beginning of the Pax Romana and made the civilized world prosperous and happy, he was vanquished on the moral battlefield; his fines and penalties could not genuinely restore disappearing family functions or provide new ones, and thus could not mend the social dissolution that had led to sexual license. To a greater or lesser degree, every one of the Julian Laws was a failure. Some people married merely to fulfill the requirements of his laws, and then were promptly divorced; some others adopted children to qualify for an inheritance and promptly "emancipated" them into the streets; some women gained the advantages of married status by legal unions with eunuchs or freedmen who gave them no trouble. In deference to law, men became discreet—and continued their adulteries; when evasion did not suffice, they challenged Augustus with a storm of protests and by open defiance of the harsher regulations.

Augustus temporized and shifted his tactics. He softened and modified the laws repeatedly, displayed children in his box at the games, gave money to parents of large families, and encouraged

Virgil to sing the praises of farm life in the *Georgics* and of ancient ideals in the *Aeneid*. It was all to no avail. Ten years after the final enactment of the laws in their modified form, they were in disrepair and disesteem. In the next century the historian Tacitus would write them off as a failure, without influence on marriage or fertility. Later emperors added to the laws and stiffened them; they were all equally unsuccessful. It was not legislation that would finally counteract and change the patterns of love and marriage.

To be sure, not all of upper-class or middle-class society was profligate. Augustus' own married life was undoubtedly paralleled in many a conservative home, but decency makes dull reading and historians tend to avoid it. Tombstone inscriptions indicate that there must have been a fair share of respectable and enduring unions. One inscription in particular, known as the "Laudatio Turiae" or "Praise of Turia," is noteworthy as a portrait of the good life. On two large marble slabs on a tomb outside Rome was chiseled a lengthy funeral eulogy written by the husband, telling the story of their marriage. It is a long recital of separations and tribulations caused by his fighting on the republican side in the civil wars against Caesar, and later against Antony and Octavian. Finally, however, the wars were over, he was pardoned, and the couple settled down to live in peace and harmony for many years. The wife proved to be barren, and in an excess of generosity offered to divorce her husband so that he might take a fertile bride. "I must confess," he said in his funeral address, "that I was so distressed by your proposal that I almost lost my mind." He made her give up the idea and they lived together, childless and loving, until her death many years later.

It is a touching glimpse of a warm Roman marriage, but it is almost unique. Most other funeral inscriptions are too brief or too traditional in style to be likewise meaningful, and most histories and letters include little similar evidence. Even the widower who wrote the "Laudatio Turiae" observed that long marriages such as his were quite rare. If Augustus personally knew the faithful couple, he must have felt that fate was unbearably ironic; a former enemy lived as Augustus wanted men to live, while Augustus' own daughter symbolized for all Rome the failure of his Julian Laws and his ideals.

Her name was Julia; she was his daughter by Scribonia, and his only child. She grew up in his home, and Augustus personally supervised her upbringing; he saw to it that she was taught to spin and weave, ordered her never to say or do anything that could not be

written in the household diary, and forbade her to have meetings or
conversations with strangers, even of noble rank and good character. Either in protest against this or against the criticisms of her upright stepmother, Livia, Julia developed an irresistible desire for
pleasure and folly. Her first husband having died when she was little
more than a child, Augustus married her off, when she was eighteen,
to Marcus Vipsanius Agrippa, his faithful deputy, general, and
builder of aqueducts, who was by that time wealthy, middle-aged,
and tolerant. Julia, in hot-blooded revolt against spinning and weav-
ing, took advantage of this to become the leader of the fast young
set, and made her home a center of gay parties and luxurious display.

Like a hetaera of Greece, she developed a sharp and witty tongue.
When a conservative friend urged her to avoid luxury, and to imitate the simplicity and frugality of her father, Julia replied: "If he
forgets that he is Caesar, I will not forget that I am Caesar's daughter." Livia advised Augustus to chastise her and told him about the
rumors of Julia's adulteries. Augustus did chide her (without effect), but as to the stories of adultery, he was reassured by the fact
that she dutifully brought forth no less than five children, all re-
sembling her husband. According to rumor, Julia herself had a frank
explanation of this flawless record: "I take on passengers," she is
supposed to have said, "only when the boat is full."

Agrippa died in 12 B.C. and Julia, a merry widow of twenty-
seven, stepped up the pace of her follies at the very time when her
father was laboring to complete and to enforce his Julian Laws. The
worried Augustus sought to tie her down by marrying her to Livia's
son, Tiberius, a dour young Stoic who relished neither her nor her
ways. Soon Tiberius found himself in a classically perfect dilemma:
the *Lex Julia de Adulteriis* required him to denounce his wife for
adultery, yet to do so would be to disgrace his stepfather, its author.
He solved the dilemma by resigning his posts and fleeing to Rhodes,
where he spent seven years in meditative, self-imposed exile.[8]

Julia meanwhile followed the trail blazed a generation earlier by
Catullus' love, Clodia. She went from adventure to adventure, her
jaded appetite requiring ever more startling feats of love, and her
premature gray hair driving her, in frenzy, to seize all possible pleasure while she might. She seemed impelled by a need to degrade her-

[8] His solution was a good one. Many
years later, after Julia's sons had died,
he was adopted by Augustus, and became his heir and the next Emperor.

self; from love affairs, she moved step by step toward harlotry, and all Rome knew it except Augustus. At last, in 2 B.C. when she was thirty-eight, friends of the self-exiled Tiberius let Augustus know that they would accuse Julia in court if he himself did not. The awakening was horrible. As Seneca recorded the story some decades later:

> Augustus learned that she had been accessible to scores of paramours, that in nocturnal revels she had roamed about the city, that the very Forum and the rostrum from which her father had proposed a law against adultery had been chosen by the daughter for her debaucheries, that she had daily resorted to the statue of Marsyas,[9] and, laying aside the role of adulteress, there sold her favors and sought the right to every indulgence with even unknown paramours.[1]

The aging Emperor was wild with grief and anger; he may have counted the letters of the alphabet, but it did not help. He summarily issued a decree exiling her to the barren island of Pandateria; there she lived in virtual house arrest, expressly denied the use of wine and other comforts and forbidden to have either company or callers except those specifically authorized by himself. Unendurably ashamed, Augustus wrote a letter detailing her crimes and had it read aloud to the Senate, seemingly as self-punishment. He forced one of her lovers to kill himself and banished the others, but even this brought him no relief. For years, whenever Julia's name was mentioned he would sigh and say he wished he had died childless. His accomplishments seemed vain to him, and the order and prosperity he had created were empty victories. Friends urged him to relent and let Julia return to Rome, even Tiberius adding his voice, but Augustus would only reply: "May you, too, be blessed with daughters and wives like her." Merciful and forgiving to many other wrongdoers and enemies, he could never forgive her; perhaps he sensed that she had not merely degraded herself, but used her sexuality as a weapon to strike down her own father.

Augustus eased her exile slightly after five years, by moving her to Rhegium (Reggio), and allowing her the freedom of the city, but there she was forced to remain, and died of tuberculosis at the age of fifty-four after sixteen years of exile. Coincidentally, in that same year her great father also ceased his efforts to remake the soul

[9] A place in the Forum where whores came to offer themselves.
[1] Seneca: *De Beneficiis,* vi, 32.

of man, and died, kissing his faithful wife, Livia. Rome deified and worshiped him, but rejected his ethics; Rome forgot Julia, but adopted hers.

5

The Tutor of Love,
and the Textbook of Adultery

❈   ❈

❈

Ten years after Augustus had exiled his only daughter, the aging, saddened monarch suffered another blow; he learned that Julia's daughter, also named Julia, was leading a life of adultery, heedless of her mother's fate. Once again the storm clouds rumbled and the lightning flashed on Olympus; Julia Minor was banished in A.D. 8 to the tiny island of Trimerus in the Adriatic, and there wasted away until her death twenty years later.

Among her friends was the sophisticated poet Ovid, a middle-aged but frolicsome favorite of the fashionable circles. He had reason to regret being a friend of Julia's, for in that same year he too was plucked up and flung far off to exile in Tomis (modern Constanta) on the southern shore of the Black Sea—a muddy, bitter-cold border town at the margin of the civilized world and a particularly cruel place of exile for an aging, soft-skinned sybarite.

The two banishments were not merely coincidental, but history does not say exactly what Ovid's crime was. He had not been the younger Julia's lover; this seems clear from the veiled remarks he made in the fawning letters of apology he wrote to Augustus, in which he referred to the crime of having "seen" something wrong, but having failed to say anything. Probably, say many scholars, he knew of, or aided in, the details of Julia's adultery. Perhaps he was even present at some wild party where she put on an indecent exhibition. In either case she could have learned her morals and gained her technical proficiency from Ovid's own writings—and therein, it seems, lay the real cause of his banishment.

For among his other works, the poet had written a long instructional poem called *Ars Amatoria—The Art of Love*—which was, in essence, the first textbook on methods of flirting, attracting lovers, and consummating adultery. It was no mere piece of vulgar obscenity: Ovid even patterned it (somewhat tongue-in-cheek) along the lines of philosophic and educational treatises, and called himself the "tutor" and "master" of the art of love. Romans agreed; it was said that Ovid had educated his entire generation in the techniques of love, although it would be more accurate to say that he in part educated them, and in part set forth didactically what they were already practicing. One must admire Augustus for withholding his wrath for ten years. Ovid had defiantly written the book in 2 B.C., though the Julian Laws had only recently been completed, and he specifically scoffed at the Emperor's hope of remaking Roman morality in an older style. "Let the past please others," he wrote. "I congratulate myself on being born into this age, whose ways are so congenial to my own." Ten years later, when Ovid played some part in Julia Minor's fall, the Emperor restrained himself no longer.

The tutor of illicit love was born in farming country east of Rome in 43 B.C., a year after Caesar's assassination. His father, a wealthy equestrian, sent Ovid to Rome to learn law, so that he might rise within the government and finally attain senatorial status. Ovid studied the law carefully, and the gay life even more so; he found he preferred the latter, and devoted his life to literature and the pursuit of cultivated amusement. His inherited wealth, his amiable manners, and his wit made him popular in the best circles, and the senatorial clan of the Fabii even gave him his third wife.

But his wives interested him little; he was intrigued by the women he wooed and won for pure sport. In his earliest poems, the *Amores*, he spoke of a lady called Corinna, but in succeeding poems he boastfully revealed that Corinna stood for many, or even any, attractive women. "It is no single she whose beauty calls forth my passion," he ambitiously proclaimed. "No, there are a hundred causes to keep me always in love." He listed the kinds of women he found appealing: modest ones, saucy ones, austere ones, flirtatious ones, literary ones, simple ones, tall ones, short ones— he loved them all, and all equally well. Many years later he would protest he had been speaking only of courtesans, but his own youthful words tell the truth of the matter:

> *About my temples go, triumphant bays!*
> *Conquered Corinna in my bosom lays;*
> *She whom her husband, guard, and gate, as foes*
> *(Lest art should win her) firmly did enclose.*
> *That victory doth chiefly triumph merit,*
> *Which without bloodshed doth the prey inherit.*
> *No little ditchëd town, no lowly walls,*
> *But to my share a captive damsel falls.*
>
> Amores, II, xii

When Ovid was forty-one his *Ars Amatoria* appeared. In it, though still lighthearted and laughing, he professorially set forth what he had learned in many years of practice, constructing a detailed guidebook for the playing of an elegant game. And game it was: in his work there is no hint of the genuine misery of Catullus, the studlike activity of Caesar, the psychopathic self-debasement of Julia. All those were extremes of Roman love; Ovid, cynically philosophic, offered a golden mean.

"If anyone among this people knows not the art of loving," he began, "let him read my poem, and having read be skilled in love." First, whom shall the would-be lecher pursue? Not married women; Ovid pretended to be on the side of the law. But this was only lip-service; he was talking about adultery, and made it perfectly clear again and again: "As to men, so also to women is stolen love the most pleasant."

One must first learn where to hunt for quarry, so he first suggested various fashionable public places in Rome. The Circus is particularly useful: the would-be lover can size up the woman first, then take a seat next to her and ask her whose horse is winning; this leads to friendly talk, and the chance to fix her cushion or fan her hot cheek. Now the chase is on. The adept hunter takes time out to befriend her personal maid—a useful ally who can carry messages, whisper his praises to her lady, and tip him off when her lady seems to be in the mood. "You will ask," Ovid said, "whether it profits to seduce the maid herself," for naturally if she is attractive the man will immediately want to do so. A seduced maid will be particularly helpful, out of fear of exposure; but on the whole, Ovid thought it a risky business, and not worth while.

After these early steps, the huntsman begins to use a variety of devices for breaking down the lady's coolness and reserve. They include the writing of flattering and earnest love letters (which must, however, include no learned words or allusions that might make her feel ignorant), intense covert looks and subtle gestures at the games or the secret touching of feet under the banquet table to convey burning desire while escaping the eyes of others, and such aphrodisiac deeds as seizing her cup and drinking greedily from the spot her lips had touched. The lover should hold a parasol for her against the sun, vigorously push aside the crowd when she walks, wait loyally at an appointed place though she fail to show up, and travel through night and storm to do errands that please her. He should be artful and generous with compliments on her gown, her hair, her face, but flattery will succeed best when coupled with some touching evidence of feeling:

> *If she appears in her negligé, cry out: "You inflame my passion!"*
> *Then add in anxious tones: "Take care! You'll catch a cold in*
>   *this fashion."*
>
> Ars, ii, 301-2

None of this will succeed if the lover is not impeccable: he must wear spotless, well-fitting clothes, keep his hair, nails, and nostrils well trimmed, and avoid body odor or halitosis.[2] Curling one's locks or scraping off body hair with pumice stone is too effeminate, but Ovid sanctions the use of tears, which, apparently, are not. The lover should weep, cultivate a pallor, and adopt a look of suffering. When all this finally wins him kisses, he may drop the fragile pose and be a bit more vigorous to gain the rest; she will struggle, for appearance's sake, but will consent. For all women will; it is only a question of the right approach: "Some fish are caught with spears, some are caught with the net, and some are taken by the hook." But all can be taken; and so to bed.

Having captured the quarry, the lover will want to keep her for

---

[2] Ovid also offers such notes on personal hygiene to women as this: "I hardly need warn you to let no rankness as of the goat be beneath your arms, nor your legs be bristling with rough hair" (*Ars,* iii, 193-4).

a while. This is not to be misunderstood as implying fidelity, as
Ovid hastily reassured his reader:

> Not that I'd doom you to a single flame:
> Preserve us! this a wife could hardly claim.
> Indulge, but o'er your lapses draw a veil,
> Nor of your peccadilloes boast the tale.
> Give nought another wench may recognize,
> Have no time-table for your gallantries.
> Lest any catch you in her favorite stew,
> Appoint for each a different rendezvous.
>
> Ars, ii, 387–94

In this, as in everything else in the *Ars Amatoria*, he has the air of
such a good-natured, well-intentioned rascal that it is hard to dislike
him. He did not write like a pornographer or a calloused thrill-
seeker; indeed, when he discussed sexual positions and techniques,
he so specifically insisted on patience and mutual satisfaction that
he might almost have been writing one of the modern books for
young married couples:

> Love's climax never should be rushed, I say,
> But worked up softly, lingering all the way.
> The parts a woman loves to have caressed
> Once found, caress, though modesty protest.
> You'll see her eyes lit up with trembling gleams,
> As sunlight glitters in pellucid streams;
> Then plaintive tones and loving murmurs rise
> And playful words and softly sounding sighs.
> But ne'er must you with fuller sail outpace
> Your consort, nor she beat you in the race:
> Together reach the goal: 'tis rapture's height
> When man and woman in collapse unite.
>
> Ars, ii, 717–28

But the patience and care of which he wrote were only a matter
of good tactics; the dominant attitude of the *Ars Amatoria* is that
the lover and his beloved are sly predator and wily prey, and the
nature of love is conquest. Despite the honeyed refinement of
Ovidian love, it is frequently given stronger flavor by judicious
infusions of sadism and masochism. An occasional charge of deliberate cruelty or repulse by either partner is, for example, essential to keep its fires burning, and Ovid highly recommended, as particularly delicious, making love to a woman who is in tears. Even
more pertinent is his suggestion that a gladiatorial combat is an ex-

cellent place to feel the first stirrings of passion. Ordinarily, one expects love and sexual excitement to be inhibited and sickened by the sight of cruelty and death; such a thought never occurred to Ovid when he suggested the "melancholy sands" of the Circus as a breeding-ground for tenderness:

> *Love oft in that arena fights a bout,*
> *Then 'tis the looker-on who's counted out.*
> *While chatting, buying a program, shaking hands,*
> *Or wagering on the match intent he stands,*
> *He feels the dart, and groaning 'neath the blow*
> *Himself becomes an item in the show.*
>
> Ars, i, 165–70

Yet the wounds below were real; human beings were stabbing and disemboweling each other, the victor asking the crowd whether to spare the fallen opponent or drive a sword through his throat. And while such games were being played out on the sand, fashionable men and women in the stands laughed to see their agony, munched nuts, plums, and pastries, and fell in "love."

The upright, serious Augustus found the *Ars Amatoria* offensive, but said nothing. But when Ovid was linked with the disgrace of his granddaughter, he could tolerate him no longer, and even ordered the book removed from public libraries. From distant Tomis, Ovid penned innumerable groveling letters. "I assure you," he wrote, "my character differs from my verse; my life is moral, my muse is gay. . . . A book is not an evidence of one's soul." But Augustus was not interested in these protestations; it was the book that had done the harm. Not for nothing did fashionable Romans refer to Ovid as "*praeceptor amoris*"—instructor in love; he had helped flout and wreck the Emperor's effort to restore goodness to society.

No letter ever arrived in Tomis to bid the aging poet bring back his upset stomach, his chilblained hands, and his aching heart. In A.D. 17, after nine years of exile, he died; only his bones returned to the warmth and comfort of Rome. Yet his book lived on, both as an instruction manual and a self-portrait of Roman lovers; like both Julias, the pitiful ex-sybarite was the victor over the emperor-god.

6

The Victory of Roman Love

✿   ✿

✿

"Wlithin my memory," wrote the philosopher Seneca in A.D. 55,
"the people in the Forum stabbed Tricho, a Roman equestrian, with their writing-styles because he had flogged his son to
death; Augustus Caesar's authority barely rescued him from the in-
dignant hands of fathers no less than of sons." The past was truly
dead. In the stabbing of Tricho (who recovered), a symbolic blow
was delivered to the *patria potestas* (which did not). Within a few
generations, emperors would formally take away most of the powers father nominally retained over their wives and children but almost never used, and would reassign them to courts established by
the state. The decline of man's supremacy, foreseen by Cato the
Elder in 195 B.C., would effectively be completed during the first
century A.D.

During that period, women acquired a number of new legal and
social freedoms. By Hadrian's reign (A.D. 117–38) jurists held that
the free consent of the female was necessary in marriage; although
she still had to use a man as her business agent, she was substantially
free to manage her property and to bestow her purse and her hand
where she chose. And still, despite their increases in freedom
during the century after Augustus' death, Roman women found
themselves strangely discontented and insatiable. They vainly
sought a new role, a new meaning to femininity to replace the
lost one. Some tried being literary and intellectual; some busied
themselves with religion, charities, and social events; some were
forever having their procurators whisper in their ears about business matters or offer them papers to sign; some preferred to meddle

in politics by cajoling and advising the men they slept with or were married to.

Many writings, monuments, and inscriptions attest to all this, but none more vividly than the sixth *Satire* of the poet Juvenal. His account is sensational, exaggerated, and bilious; yet allowing for all that, the types portrayed in it were, by the nature and standards of satire, intended to be easily recognizable to his readers, and hence have some reference to reality. Juvenal reflected his era's uncertainty as to what woman was; in his bewilderment, he knew only that she was terrible. The entire poem, in fact, is simply a catalogue of female faults in the year A.D. 116.

A wife is a tyrant—the more so if her husband is fond or loving. Cruelty is natural to women: they torment their husbands, whip the housekeeper, and enjoy having slaves flogged almost to death. Some women are silly and tedious in their newfangled addictions to religion; others are stupidly susceptible to astrology; still others make themselves ridiculous by donning armor and even taking part in mock combat. Their sexual lusts are disgusting—they prefer slaves, actors, and gladiators; their efforts to sing and play musical instruments are a bore; and their gluttonous eating and drinking are enough to make a man sick. Juvenal described the bibulous woman all too vividly:

> She drains a second pint before she tastes her food, to make her appetite ravenous; then, having washed her stomach, the wine returns in a cascade on the floor—rivers gush over the marble pavement. . . . Her husband, with eyes closed, smothers his rising bile.

But there is something even worse than this:

> And yet that woman is more offensive still who, as soon as she takes her place at the table, praises Virgil, and excuses the suicide of Dido; who matches and compares poets. . . . I hate her who is skilled in antiquarian lore, quotes verses I never knew, and corrects the phrases of her husband as old-fashioned.

Is this the clue? Did the singing, the astrology, and the vomiting really revolt him as such—or was it woman's appropriation of masculine privileges in her efforts to find her new role? One would suspect the latter, for many of the follies he was most aroused by were also committed by men, though he never said a word about that. And what drew his hottest fire was the assumption by women of sexual privilege, once completely the right of the male. Juvenal ranted about immorality—but only that of women; he was furious at their adulteries, but not at their adulterers. Nowadays, he wrote, if a husband scolds his wife for improper conduct, she says to him: "It was agreed that you should do what you pleased, and that I also might have full power to gratify myself. In spite of your outcry, confounding heaven and sea, I am mortal." She insists on her right to seek for diversion, as he does, and to call it love, as he does. Juvenal simply could not stomach this; the time was out of joint, but he knew not how to set it right. He could only be satirical and angry.

Yet if women were much given to adulterous love in Juvenal's time, it was in part because their many other freedoms and activities were little more than dilettantism and play-acting. The Roman woman tried to imitate man, and was not really allowed to. The only women who pursued useful careers came from the lower classes, or were of Greek and other foreign extraction. Highborn Roman women dabbled in literature, but did not become successful writers, and played at politics, but never voted in any senate except the *conventus matronarum*, a mock-congress that debated questions of etiquette and dress. They won financial and legal independence from men, but found themselves in a society which, living parasitically from its provinces, had no useful work for them to do. They imitated men as much as they were allowed to, but gained little sense of importance and little definition of their own value—except in the realm of love.

But their concepts of love were one with the general Roman concept of other pleasures—mere sensation, to be enjoyed until fatigue or boredom set in, and then to be enjoyed again with the help of novelty and change. In the middle of the first century, Seneca wrote a famous description of Roman banqueting:

> The food which their stomachs can scarcely retain is fetched from farthest ocean; they vomit that they may eat, they eat that they may vomit, and they do not deign even to digest the feasts for which they ransack the whole world.

About ten years later, he wrote concerning marriage in terms that are strikingly similar:

> There is not a woman left who is ashamed of being divorced, now that certain high and distinguished ladies count their years not by the number of consuls, but by the number of their hus-

bands; they are divorced in order to marry, and marry in order to be divorced.

Adultery, he said, was the greatest evil of the time, and although he may have exaggerated a bit, he claimed that a woman with only two lovers was, relatively speaking, a paragon of virtue.

In adopting this role, women were less and less interested in playing the role of mother. Among the patrician class, marriages became increasingly infertile. By the early part of the second century A.D., only one of the forty-five great senatorial families that had lived in Rome under Julius Caesar one hundred and sixty-five years earlier was still in existence. A psychological disease was exterminating the former upper class. The equestrians, or middle class, were following their lead: thousands of middle-class tombstone inscriptions were signed not by children of the deceased, but by their freedmen. From the forms of names in first- and second-century epitaphs, scholars have calculated that four-fifths of the population of Rome were emancipated slaves or their offspring—people of non-Roman origin who were filling up the vacuum left by those Romans who, having successfully disentangled sexual pleasure from considerations of permanent union or parenthood, were effectively discontinuing their own species.

Even when they did produce children, most Roman men and women were too lacking in the self-image of parenthood to guide and mold the growing characters of their children. Instead, as Tacitus glumly described it:

> The infant is committed to a Greek chambermaid and a slave or two chosen for the purpose, generally the worst of the whole household train and unfit for any office of trust. From the idle tales and gross absurdities of these people, the tender and uninstructed mind is suffered to receive its earliest impressions. . . . The parents themselves are so far from training their young families to virtue and modesty, that they set them the first examples of luxury and licentiousness.[3]

From parents who cared only for the stimulation of their own nerve endings, children formed their conceptions of Man, of Woman, and of Love, and grew up to repeat the pattern.

Yet there was another side to patrician society; there were still some anachronistic Lucretias, Cornelias, and Turias, and men to match them. At the very time when Juvenal was sourly castigating

[3] Tacitus: "Dialogue Concerning Oratory," Sec. 29.

the world, Pliny the Younger was admiring it and seeing good in it. Caius Plinius Caecilius Secundus, nephew and heir of the Pliny who wrote the famous *Natural History*, found life sweet, mankind decent, and fate kind, an attitude perhaps fortified by the fact that he was one of the wealthiest men of his time. Not content with a brisk legal practice and important governmental duties, he also wrote copiously, and among many other matters expounded upon noble and loving marriages, including his own. In an era of cynicism, he is the principal exponent of sweetness and light, but it is curious that his selection of loving wives seems to hang chiefly upon violent and suicidal acts of loyalty. Whom did he admire and write about?—Paulina, who had Seneca cut her wrists along with his own when Nero ordered him to die; another woman, unnamed, who, seeing an incurable lesion of her husband's genitals, leaped into a lake with him; and Arria, who, when her husband, Paetus, wavered at the Emperor Claudius' order to kill himself, stabbed herself in the breast and handed him the dagger with the words formerly known to every schoolboy: "*Paete, non dolet*"—"It does not hurt, Paetus."

Pliny himself enjoyed the love of a good woman, though she had no need to prove it with a dagger. When he was middle-aged he married his third wife, the young Calpurnia, and his love letters to her are among the very few that exist from antiquity. When he went down to Rome to plead a case and she remained at the country villa, he missed her sorely and wrote how he wandered disconsolately about the empty house. And when Calpurnia took a trip to the coast for her health, he worried continually and begged for word from her:

> As is the way of frightened people, my fancy paints most vividly just those calamities I most earnestly implore Heaven to avert. . . . I pray you, write to me every day and even twice a day; I shall be more easy, at least while I am reading your letters.
>
> (*Letters*, vi, 4)

But aside from a few genuine moments like this, his letters to her are rather artificial, and one gains a far more vivid and credible impression of their relationship from a letter he wrote not to her, but to her aunt, praising the girl:

> She is incomparably discerning, incomparably thrifty, while her love for her husband betokens a chaste nature. Her affection to me has given her a turn to books, and my compositions, which

she takes a pleasure in reading, are continually in her hands. . . .
When at any time I recite my works, she sits close at hand, concealed behind a curtain, and greedily overhears my praises. She
sings my verses, and sets them to her lyre, with no other master
but Love, the best instructor.   (*Letters*, iv, 19)

One may wonder whether Pliny's love was not somewhat a
literary invention. The style and content of his love letters makes
them seem clearly meant for publication; if so, his sentiments may,
in part, have been adopted for the benefit of his readers. But to a
friend, Fuscus, he described domestic routine at his summer villa in
Tuscany, and unwittingly revealed much about his marriage by saying almost nothing about it. He wakes (he wrote), lies abed thinking
about the day's writing, and then dictates to his secretary until
10:00 or 11:00 a.m.; then he meditates again for a while out on the
terrace. Next he takes a chariot ride alone, followed by a nap, and
then by some reading aloud to improve his voice; later he has a
rubdown, exercise, and a bath. At supper he finally see Calpurnia;
afterwards he walks in the garden and discusses philosophy and
letters—but with his favorite slaves, not his wife. In fact, in this entire recital, she seems no more important than a piece of furniture.
"We cannot avoid the conviction," concludes Jerome Carcopino,
a scholar of Roman social life, "that, taken all around, it [Pliny's
love] was gravely lacking in warmth and intimacy."[4]

And perhaps this was unavoidable, for in the last analysis, Pliny
still clung to the remnants of the older concept of marriage—the
patriarchal, land-based, economic view. Junius Mauricus, a friend,
asked him to help find a match for a kinswoman, and this is what
Pliny replied:

You ask me to look out for a husband for your niece. There is
no need to look far, for I know a man who might seem to have
been provided on purpose. His name is Minicius. He is well-con-
nected, comes from Brescia, which you know to be a good old-
fashioned place . . . is a man of active energy and has held high
office. . . . His father has ample means, and though perhaps your
family is not much concerned on that point, we have to remember that a man's income is one of the prime considerations in the
eyes not only of our social system, but of the law. (*Letters*, i, 14)

If sour Juvenal could not see the way to a healthier future, neither
could sweet Pliny. He let his wife write, sing, and take an interest in
his doings, but he treated her as an unimportant but agreeable

[4] Jerome Carcopino: *Daily Life in Ancient Rome*, p. 89.

household commodity, and viewed marriage in terms that had long since lost their power to bind people and create a stable social order. He was a decent sort of man, but he and Calpurnia, as models, were no more capable than Juvenal of arresting or modifying the course of social deterioration, or restoring the older ways of love.

7

Love as Symptom and Disease

✻   ✻

✻

I f Roman voluptuaries accepted the Ovidian concept of love without question, a number of Roman moralists were alarmed by it and considered it responsible for many of the social ills of the Empire. The Christians, moreover, who were beginning to become prominent in the second century, were of the same opinion, and vehemently so. By the fifth century, Saint Augustine and other Christian writers would state flatly that sexual sin was directly responsible for the crumbling away of the Empire, the afflictions of which were interpreted as the punishment visited upon mankind by a wrathful God.

The evidence of comparative anthropology, however, proves that many societies have permitted extramarital sexual activities and love affairs without major damage to themselves. Why, then, were they so hurtful in Rome? The historian need not invoke supernatural explanations. Roman love flourished in the context of the disintegration of family life, and even accelerated it; in that circumstance it produced a problem of utmost seriousness—the voluntary infertility of the native Roman stock. For it was when sex moved outside of marriage and called itself love, while marriage itself lost its values, that the long decline of population began which so worried Augustus, and which he was powerless to check.

By the second century, the Emperor Marcus Aurelius not only had to enroll criminals and gladiators in his army, but had to settle the conquered Marcomanni tribesmen within the Empire as land-holders and require them to supply soldiers to the Roman forces. In the third century, a long period of rebellion and civil war coin-cided with severe barbarian invasions and a prolonged plague to de-crease the Roman population still further, and the prevailing love pattern gave Roman society no chance to recoup its losses. Alex-andria gradually lost half its population and other great cities be-came deserted and ghostly, a large percentage of Roman farms were abandoned for lack of manpower, and later emperors resorted increasingly to the policy of settling conquered barbarians within the borders as farmers and farm-workers. Professor Richard Hay-wood even argues in his recent study *The Myth of Rome's Fall*, that the dissolution of the Empire was the inevitable result of its absorption of too many people with no cultural loyalty to an im-perial structure and no tradition of administrative control over a far-flung society.

But historians differ with the early Christians in assessing the role of love in the overall decline of Rome. To some extent, Roman love was indeed a contributing cause insofar as it produced in-fertility, but to a far greater extent it was only one painful symptom of a basic disease. What that basic disease was, legions of historians have sought to explain: they have named such factors as the squan-dering of resources, the indolence of the proletariat, the corruption and greed of the upper classes, the growing political power of the army, and so on; more generally, these are all related to the parasit-ism, excessive leisure, and purposelessness of imperial Roman life. Whatever the balanced and true explanation, Roman moralists and Christian reformers alike vigorously attacked the symptom, while the disease raged on unmolested and finally killed the patient.

Chapter IV
IT IS BETTER TO MARRY THAN TO BURN

I

The Dream of Spiritual Marriage

❀　　❀

❀

In the second and third centuries A.D. the Roman Empire, despite its infirmities, still gave the appearance of greatness and glory; indeed, in the great cities life continued to be as sybaritic and elegant as ever, and some of the greatest extravagances of construction and entertainment occurred in this very period. Yet in the midst of these glories, certain citizens were beginning to act in a bizarre and un-Roman fashion: in a world that offered them unprecedented luxuries and pleasures, they were unaccountably attracted to a new religion called Christianity which scorned the former and castigated the latter. Some of the patricians whose philosophy had long been based on the value of power, wealth, and practicality were succumbing to a new philosophy that stressed meekness, poverty, and mysticism. Although they lived in a society that was confirmed in the practice of Ovidian love and the indulgence of desire, they were inexplicably drawn to a faith that denied them the right to worldly love or sensuous enjoyments, and promised them instead a disembodied eternity.

One of these people was a young man named Ammon, who grew up in the latter part of the third century in Alexandria. Despite the buffeting the Empire had taken from civil wars and barbarian attacks for the previous fifty years, that city was still opulent, extravagant, and gorgeous during Ammon's youth; it was the Roman Empire's finest metropolis in the East, and combined the graces and sophistication of Hellenic culture with the pomp and pageantry of Rome. Most of its inhabitants lived just as Alexandrians had for the past two centuries, but a few, including Ammon, had begun to shun luxury and comfort in favor of poverty and pain, and in the very midst of life seemed to long for death.

What Ammon looked like or how he spent his boyhood and youth we do not know; all we are told by historians is that his parents were wealthy, and died when he was young, leaving him in the guardianship of an uncle. He evidently, however, lived in a fine house, was surrounded by servants, and had access to fine food, the baths, the games, the theater, and, of course, women. But Ammon was a Christian, and a devout one; at some point in his youth, taking seriously the words of Saint Paul and the early Fathers of the Church, he decided to remain chaste and to prepare himself for eternity.

The uncle held no such somber views, however, and having selected a proper bride for Ammon, he forced the youth to submit to a wedding. It was celebrated in the traditional Hellenic fashion by a joyous gathering of both families, followed by the usual banquet and then the procession to the nuptial chamber. Here the friends and relatives undoubtedly uttered all the worn amiable jokes, wished the bridegroom well with hearty platitudes, and finally left the two alone. Ammon closed and bolted the door, and turned to his bride, who was lying on the nuptial couch. There followed a remarkable scene, according to the account given by the fifth-century ecclesiastical historian, Socrates Scholasticus:

> He took a book containing the epistles of the apostles and read to his wife Paul's Epistle to the Corinthians, explaining to her the apostle's admonitions to married persons. [*1 Corinthians* vii: 1–9 are the particularly relevant verses, and include such crucial ideas as: "It is good for a man not to touch a woman. Nevertheless, to avoid fornication, let every man have his own wife, and let every woman have her own husband. . . . I would that all men were even as I myself. . . . I say therefore to the unmarried and widows, it is good for them if they abide even as I. But if they cannot contain, let them marry: for it is better to marry than to burn."] Adducing many external considerations besides, he descanted on the inconveniences and discomforts attending matrimonial intercourse, the pangs of child-bearing, and the trouble and anxiety connected with rearing a family. He contrasted with all this the advantages of chastity; described the liberty and immaculate purity of a life of continence; and affirmed that virginity places persons in the nearest relation to the Deity.[1]

[1] Socrates: *Ecclesiastical History*, iv, 23. The story was also told, with minor variations, by another fifth-century historian, Palladius, in his *Historia Lausiaca*, 8.

Ammon's young bride—her name was not recorded by Socrates—listened to this harangue with what very likely began as astonishment, but, according to the historian, ended as conviction. She and Ammon forthwith purified their marital union by jointly renouncing the world and taking a vow of celibacy. The last laugh was on the wedding guests.

The young couple lived as brother and sister, devoting themselves to contemplation and to the adoration of God, but after a while they realized that their life in Alexandria, surrounded as it was with fleshly comforts, was out of keeping with their aims. Abandoning all comforts, they moved south of Alexandria to Mount Nitria in the Egyptian desert country, installed themselves there in a rude hut, and took up an ascetic existence. Yet Ammon's wife, considering their way of life, found even this still too close to worldly ways. "It is unsuitable," she said to him one day, "for you who practice chastity to look upon a woman in so confined a dwelling; if it is agreeable to you, let us live apart." Ammon thought it a meritorious suggestion; they lived thenceforth in two huts, near enough for occasional visits, and observed identical rules of self-mortification, using neither oil nor wine, eating nothing but dry bread and water, and often fasting one, two, or three days at a time.

Even so, Ammon sensed that temptation lay always in wait for him. Considering that the sight of his own body involved danger, he took a resolve never to remove his clothing. "It becomes not a monk," he said, "to see even his own person exposed." Once he wished to cross a river, but was as unwilling to get his clothes wet as to remove them. In this dilemma, he besought the help of God; if one may believe the devout historian, He must not have considered the matter beneath His notice, for an angel promptly appeared, picked Ammon up, and deposited him on the other side, both dry and virtuous.

The fame of Ammon and his wife spread rapidly; not only did five thousand monks (according to the possibly wishful estimate of Palladius) gather about them within a few years to emulate their asceticism, but continent marriage became a Christian dream for several centuries thereafter. If it was never dominant statistically, it surely was intellectually. For centuries, while Christianity struggled against the flesh, continent marriage was praised as the highest form of union between man and woman. Genuine data do not exist, but innumerable allusions to cases of continent marriage appear in the patristic writings and ecclesiastical histories; even if we allow for the adverse effect of piety upon accuracy, it would seem that it existed with some frequency and was talked about to the point of obsession.

To be sure, one may doubt that many of the reported cases were altogether successful; even those ecclesiastics who most praise continent marriage admit its fragility, and tell of instances of failure. Saint Jerome, writing from Palestine in A.D. 408 to a wealthy young man named Rusticus in one of the outlying provinces, revealed just such a story. "Your former wife," he said, "who is now your sister and fellow servant in Christ, has told me that, acting on the apostolic precept, you and she lived apart by consent that you might give yourselves to prayer, but that after a time your feet sank beneath you as if resting on water and indeed—to speak plainly—gave way altogether." For Rusticus and his wife had moved together again and sunk back into wedded pollution; then, overwhelmed by a sense of guilt, the wife journeyed to Palestine to do penance, while Rusticus promised to follow as soon as he could settle his affairs, which were in tangled condition due to a threatened barbarian invasion. Time passed, but he did not arrive. So Jerome wrote him, urging him to come, but whether he ever did is not known; he may have feared the misery of continent marriage as much as life under barbarian masters. Yet even though Rusticus failed in his attempt to lead this purified kind of married life, the very fact that he and his wife tried to do so indicates the power of the new ideal; had he and his wife lived two centuries earlier, they would have regarded any such notion with derision and incredulity.

For several centuries—those very centuries when the once-firm structure of the Empire was weakening, and at last disintegrating—continent marriage was celebrated by Christians as a state scarcely less noble than dedicated celibacy; it seemed, indeed, to be one form of Christian reaction to the doom and destruction that first lowered, and then broke, upon the Roman world. Cases of it were reported and celebrated throughout the disintegrating Empire from its most civilized redoubts to its lost colonies, from indolent, decadent Alexandria to semibarbaric Gaul.

It was from Gaul, in fact, that there came one tale of continent marriage that sounded a new and important theme—that of chaste romance. Gregory, Bishop of Tours in the sixth century, told in Book One of his *History of the Franks* the story of Injuriosus, a wealthy young man of senatorial rank who had lived in Auvergne in southern Gaul in the early part of the previous century. Though the Visigothic invasions had disturbed and disrupted life in many parts of the Western Empire, Auvergne was relatively tranquil, and Injuriosus lived in a fine mansion, as befitted a Roman patrician, and got his income from his vast inherited domains. When he reached manhood, he paid a sizable price to obtain a bride of good senatorial stock, and married her. But when they retired that evening, his bride turned her face to the wall as soon as she got into bed, and began weeping bitterly. Injuriosus gently asked why she was crying. According to Bishop Gregory, she explained: "I had resolved to keep my poor body for Christ, pure from the contact of man. But woe is me, who am in such wise forsaken of Him that I availed not to carry out my desire." In place of unfading roses, she added, there would now be disfigurement and corruption. Would that she had died as a child! She abhorred the things of this world, including—for she was specific about it—Injuriosus' fine mansion and great estate.

The young man replied mildly that she was, like him, an only child, and that both their families would be made happy by the continuation of each line. This appeal fell flat; the world and its vanities, she argued at considerable length, were worthless, and the only real bliss lay in the eternal life. Injuriosus, having listened to her long harangue, at last found himself strangely freed of his desires and uplifted in spirit. "Through thy sweetest eloquence," he said, "eternal light hath shone upon me, as it were a mighty radiance." To her great delight, he thereupon vowed to abstain from fleshly desires; husband and wife then made a solemn pact of virginity, clasped hands, and at once fell asleep peacefully.

For many years they slept chastely in the same bed and led a good life, managing their property and serving God. When both of them died, the servants built tombs for them against different walls of the building, but in the middle of the night the tombs moved together until they rested side by side. "Which thing shows," concluded Gregory, "that when two are united in heaven, the tomb that holds their bodies buried may not keep them asunder. The people of that place have chosen to call these twain 'The Two Lovers' until this day." He was much impressed, as always, by a physical miracle; the modern reader may think the emotional miracle by far more impressive.

Even stranger than continent marriage was a somewhat similar arrangement between men and women known as spiritual marriage that existed in the early days of the Church. Unmarried virgins known as *agapetae* (from the Greek, *agape*, spiritual love) would become spiritual sisters or spiritual wives (the two terms being used almost interchangeably) of the clergy, with whom they lived in household intimacy. Their relationship ostensibly involved no unchastity, but they had not even the tie of marriage to excuse them from sin in case their feet (to borrow Jerome's phrase) were to sink beneath them. The agapetae must have been numerous and widespread from the second through the sixth century. Tertullian and Hermas, among other early writers, praised them; what is more significant, such ecclesiastical writers as Irenaeus, Jerome, Saint John Chrysostom, Epiphanius, and Eusebius all complained about them, and, at least from the historian's point of view, one complaint is better evidence of their prevalence than ten hosannahs.

Many of the religious leaders and sects which permitted agapetae and spiritual marriage later came to be regarded as heretical. Perhaps the Church was wise to recognize that the arrangement would fail in the long run. Only in a disintegrating society, when men and women were transfigured by their search for an eternal and better world, might they be able to maintain such a relationship; and even then it was often suspect. Paul of Samosata, Bishop of Antioch at the end of the third century, was sharply scolded by a group of fellow bishops for having two "blooming and beautiful" spiritual sisters who traveled everywhere with him. Other heretical clerics such as Alexander the Montanist and Apelles the Marcionite maintained companionships they claimed were pure, but the orthodox doubted the wisdom of their efforts and the truth of their claims. Since the orthodox destroyed the writings of most of the heretics, one can hardly come to an impartial conclusion on the question.

But agapetae were also found within unimpeachably correct churches as well. No diaries or letters of these women or their male friends have survived, but one can glean some vivid details about the companionship from the outraged polemics of the righteous. "From what source has this plague of 'dearly beloved sisters' found its way into the church?" fumed Jerome in A.D. 408. "They live in the same house with their male friends; they occupy the same room, often the same bed; yet they call us suspicious if we think that anything is wrong." The early Christians were, after all, Romans; they tried to carry out the tenets of a new faith within a framework of old customs. Even a celibate cleric and his spiritual sister might still wear senatorial garments and live in a mansion; similarly their sexual patterns might be a composite of old and new, confusing to observers and themselves alike. In the search for chastity, for instance, they evidently arrived at a kind of compromise that consisted of intimate love play stopping short of actual sexual connection; such is the picture one gets from a troubled letter written in A.D. 249 by Cyprian, Bishop of Carthage, to a fellow church-leader who had consulted him on the subject.

> We have read, dearest brother, your letter which you sent to Paconius, our brother, asking and desiring us to write again to you and say what we thought of those virgins who, after having once determined to continue in that condition and firmly to maintain their continency, have afterwards been found to have remained in the same bed side by side with men (of whom you say that one is a deacon); and yet that the same virgins declare that they are chaste. . . . We must interfere at once with such as these, that they may be separated while yet they can be separated in innocence, because by and by they will have become firmly joined by a guilty conscience. . . .
> And do not let any of them think to defend herself by saying that she may be examined and proven a virgin, for both the hands and the eyes of the midwives are often deceived, and even if she be found to be a virgin in that particular in which a woman may be so, yet she may have sinned in some other part of her body which may be corrupted and yet cannot be examined. Assuredly the mere lying together, the mere embracing, the very talking together, and the act of kissing, and the disgraceful and foul slumber of two persons lying together, how much of dishonor and crime does it confess! [2]

Some of the more earnest practitioners of this relationship considered that great merit lay in this "trial of chastity," and sought to expose themselves to the maximum of temptation so as to gain virtue by resisting it. According to the legend recorded by a medieval scholiast, a certain Irish holy man of the sixth century named Scuthin always slept in bed with two beautiful virgins. When Saint Brendan the Navigator chided him for taking such risks, Scuthin challenged him to prove himself equally capable of virtue. Brendan tried it and managed to resist temptation; he found himself, however, quite unable to sleep, and cut the experiment short.

[2] Cyprian: *Epistle lxi* in the Ante-Nicene Library edition; same as *Epistle iv* in Oxford edition.

By diligent opposition, the Church slowly eradicated agapetism. It persisted longest in monastic life; in the Irish Church, for instance, monks and nuns shared monastic houses until late in the sixth century. "They did not scorn to administer and live together with women," wrote an old ecclesiastical historian, "because being founded upon the rock, they did not fear the wind of temptation." But the Church felt the rock could stand some buttressing, and the practice was condemned by the sixth-century Irish Rules and Penitentials. In Spain, three separate synods in A.D. 589, 590, and 633 recognized the inability of conscience permanently to master such temptation, and ordered the housekeepers and female companions of the clergy to be sold as slaves. As for the central Church itself, from the Council of Nicaea on (A.D. 325), the clergy were forbidden to have women in their houses; the custom must have been difficult to stamp out, for the penalties grew ever stricter as time passed. Leontius, Bishop of Antioch, gave the only convincing answer to those who doubted that a man and his agapeta could be wholly blameless: faced with an order to rid himself of his female companion, he castrated himself and kept her. It was not an answer most men cared to give.

2

The Sources of Asceticism

❀   ❀

❀

At first it seems incredible that asceticism should so rapidly have become the ideal of a large part of Hellenic and Greek society, since the love and sex patterns of those cultures had been firmly and completely established in the other direction for many centuries. Everyone knows how long and painfully the Christians fought to evangelize the pagan world; everyone is familiar with the repeated persecutions by which that world fought back and expressed both horror and detestation of the new religion; and yet it gradually and inexorably captured the loyalty of a large segment of the population, and with the conversion of the Emperor Constantine in A.D. 323 became effectively the dominant state religion, its ascetic ideal being progressively embodied in law and rigorously enforced. In view of that protracted and difficult struggle against social ideals so unlike those of Christianity, one wonders why asceticism had so powerful an appeal and so inexorably conquered the violently resisting Romans.

The answer is bound up with the whole question of the victory of Christianity, a subject beyond the scope of this book. Yet within the area of love itself, the triumph of asceticism is neither as surprising nor as paradoxical as it first seems. Pagan eroticism had, over the centuries, worn itself down in excess and over-refinement, producing a jaded appetite and weariness on a national scale; meanwhile, the disintegration of family life had left people without a satisfying system of affectional ties, and with a disturbing feeling of isolation and emotional frustration. These matters were obviously bound up with sexual practices, and when the Roman world still knew of Christ only that He had been a minor Jewish troublemaker, certain pagan philosophers had already begun to argue in favor of sexual restraint and even asceticism. Musonius Rufus, a first-century philosopher, held that sexual acts outside marriage were impermissible, and Apollonius of Tyana argued that even married love was impure. Precursors of Neoplatonism such as the Stoics took Plato's doctrine of Ideas and paralleled his metaphysics with an ethic in which flesh and the world were held to be transient and impure, while spirituality and ideality were timeless and good. (Saint Paul himself was deeply influenced by this early Neoplatonism, and so were many Church Fathers, both heretical and orthodox.) Meanwhile, among the non-Christian pagans there also appeared in the second century a popular religious-philosophic movement known as Gnosticism, mystical in nature, which stressed the need for salvation from sins, and relied on the intervention of a savior.

By the third century, many Stoics and Neoplatonists lived and acted much like Christians, even though not believing in the Christain God. Even when Julian the Apostate succeeded to the throne of the Eastern Empire in 361, bringing to a temporary end the reign of Christian emperors, there was no real change in palace life or official attitudes. True, Julian had deserted Christianity in favor of paganism, and during his short reign strove to reopen the pagan temples and revive the glories of Greek philosophy; yet he lived in celibacy after his wife died, ate food as plain as any monk's, wore his beard uncut and full of lice, and shunned soft beds, the theater, and the races. The Christians never rejoiced at having Julian on the throne, but he was no great threat to them after all.

The most glamorous woman of the age was Hypatia, the beautiful and brilliant lecturer in philosophy at the Alexandrian Museum. Students from far lands came to study with her; many ended by falling in love with her. Although Christian monks finally murdered her, they might better have reverenced her for her attitude toward the body. As lovely as she was, Hypatia chose to remain a virgin, and when one student professed his passionate love for her, she hoisted her dress to the waist and contemptuously said: "This, young man, is what you are in love with, and not anything beautiful."

The Christian influence on love and sex life was not, therefore, so much a revolution as an alliance with sympathetic forces. A growing current of asceticism and antifeminism had already manifested itself within pagan society in the Hellenic part of the Empire as early as the time of Christ. By the third century these trends had become far stronger, and were accompanied by an increasing cynicism and weariness that affected the Western Empire as well as the Eastern, maturing into widespread soul-sickness by the time of the major fifth-century invasions.

It was within this context that Christian morality made such notable conquests and so effectively displaced the traditional Greco-Roman patterns of sexuality. In a society in which asceticism was already so powerfully on the increase, the Jewish Old Testament seemed to offer an excellent explanation of the source of evil and a thorough justification of antifeminism and celibacy. The primal transgression of man against God, it said, was instigated by woman, resulted in the creation of the sense of sexual shame, and brought about the permanent misery of mankind. God Himself explicitly stated that a permanent antagonism would thenceforth exist between the sexes. "I will greatly multiply thy sorrow and thy conception," He told Eve. "In sorrow shalt thou bring forth children;

and thy desire shall be to thy husband, and he shall rule over thee."
To Adam He said: "Because thou hast hearkened unto the voice of
thy wife, and hast eaten of the tree, of which I commanded thee,
saying, Thou shalt not eat of it: cursed is the ground for thy sake;
in sorrow shalt thou eat of it all the days of thy life" (*Genesis*
iii: 16–17).

Yet the connection between sex and the Fall, which so intrigued
and even obsessed the early Christians, had not really been central to
the thinking of the Jews. Men in the Old Testament were patriarchal and powerful, and often guiltlessly enjoyed the services of
several wives and concubines (as, for instance, Jacob, in *Genesis*
xxix). Women were sometimes portrayed as scolding or conniving,
but more often as loyal, diligent, and devoted (as was Abigail, in
Samuel xxv, or the good wife delineated in *Proverbs* xxxi: 10–31).
Even when women were portrayed as an aggravation to man, they
were not said to have caused the pollution or corruption of his soul.
And though the Jews, unlike the pagans around them, were sternly
opposed to whoredom, adultery, fornication, and all forms of sodomy and homosexuality, their attitude towards sex within marriage
was essentially lusty. The *Song of Solomon* is far from the only
case in point; there are countless passages which refer to "laying
with," "begetting," or "going in unto" without the faintest over-
tone of sin or dirtiness.[3]

It was not until Paul was carrying out his mission in the first
century that the Temptation, Original Sin and Fall began to seem
the central tragedy of mankind, or that Eve's guilt appeared so
great as to justify woman's subordination in life. The earlier Jews
had considered marriage and procreation a holy duty, looked down
on childlessness, and even excluded castrates or eunuchs from their
congregations (*Deuteronomy* xxiii: 1); in contrast, Christ—though
His strictures against easy divorce seemed to indicate concern for
family integrity—spoke approvingly of those "which have made
themselves eunuchs for the kingdom of heaven's sake."[4] Paul went

---

[3] *Leviticus* xv: 16–24 does prescribe
ritual purification for the "uncleanliness" resulting from intercourse, but if
this is read in context (the chapter also
deals with several forms of nonsexual
uncleanliness), it assumes no great significance.

[4] The quote is from *Matthew* xix: 12.
It is now generally agreed that He

meant voluntary abstinence rather than
actual castration, but early Christians
interpreted His words in both senses.
Thousands mutilated themselves in the
early centuries (Origen being the most
famous case), but the Church slowly
concluded that this was absolutely impermissible, and forbade it.

further, urging all men to be abstinent if they could; and a little more than a generation after Paul's death, the author of *Revelation* saw, in chapter fourteen of his vision, 144,000 virginal men who had never been "defiled" with women, standing next to the Lamb on Sion.

Within the next two centuries, Christianity developed a fanatical fixation about the glory of virginity, the evilness of woman, the foulness of sexual connection, and the spiritual merit of denying the flesh and repudiating love. To be sure, these were not the only concerns of Christianity, which also warred against the riches, selfishness, war, usury, and cruelty of the Roman world. Yet even these evils were always linked with sexual sin; in *Revelation* and much other early Christian writing, for instance, the terms "fornication," "lust," and "whoredom" were used symbolically to refer to any and all sins against God. So essential did asceticism seem to the early Church that when a maverick monk named Jovinian came to Rome in A.D. 385 to argue that marriage was superior to celibacy, he drew the concentrated fire of the Church's top thinkers and writers, and Pope Siricius personally excommunicated him for heresy and blasphemy. Bishop Gregory of Nyssa and other Christian thinkers, facing the thorny question of how Adam and Eve—had they never sinned—could have blamelessly obeyed God's injunction to produce offspring, laboriously concocted theories about a "mode of transient generation" by which they could have reproduced more or less like pollinating plants, without contact or pleasure.

Although sin was equated with love of man for woman, the love of man for man was attacked with particular ferocity. The Council of Elvira denied pederasts communion even *in extremis*. Constantius and Constans, sons of the Emperor Constantine, made homosexuality a capital offense, and the Emperor Valentinian borrowed in the name of Christianity a technique of its persecutors and burned homosexuals at the stake. Why all this? Possibly because homosexuality was an indulgence in pleasure without the excuse of child-getting; this made it not merely sin, but heresy.

Yet whatever methods Christianity finally employed, it was not really by legal sanctions that it managed to create in a happy mankind an overwhelming sense of guilt and the equating of sexual love with transgression against God. If these attitudes became dominant, it was because they coincided with and expressed larger, more pervasive social forces. And those were the changes in the Empire itself—the erosion and deterioration of a once impregnable world. From the middle of the second century on, the Empire was almost continually under barbarian attack. At first the barbarians were thrown back, although the imperial mechanism creaked and groaned ominously under the strain. Then during the third century, a series of civil wars, plagues, and Teutonic invasions greatly strained and weakened the economy, and caused genuine alarm about the condition of the imperial defenses and growing pessimism about the future. The fourth century saw some respite from some of these pressures, but no improvement in the Empire's basic internal problems—the abandonment of farms, the decline of commerce, the falling birth rate, and other indices of social necrosis. Fear and gloom lay always close behind the façade of gaiety and splendor; Rome was brilliant still, but the firm earth shook, and men trembled to see the Empire changing and perhaps dying.

Even Christians, their thoughts directed toward the eternal world, and their personal affections more engaged by the intense family-like society of the early Church than that of the Empire, wept for Rome. When it fell in A.D. 410 for the first time, taken by Alaric the Goth, even that most ardent evangelist, Saint Jerome, wrote from Bethlehem: "Who would have believed that Rome, victorious so oft over the universe, would at length crumble to pieces? . . . In vain I try to distract myself from the sight by turning to my books; I cannot fix my thoughts on them." A little more than a century later, when the process of disintegration had gone much further, Pope Gregory was in still deeper despair. "Everywhere we see mourning and hear groans," he wrote. "Cities are destroyed, strong places are cast down, the fields are depopulated, and the land is become desert. . . . Moreover, the scourge of God's justice resteth not, because men's guilty deeds have not been corrected, even under this scourge."

There *was* evil on earth, and people hungered for an explanation and a justification of it; the angry God of Christianity furnished better ones than the philosophies of even the most ascetic pagans. While imperial armies, once invincible, now sometimes lost their battles, and while emperors temporized and let barbarians into the Empire unchallenged, men and women made sense of their fears and miseries by calling themselves the very source of evil. To do so was to find a way one could deal with it personally. Voluntary suffering and self-denial would earn spiritual credit and pay off, in part, a debt that would be due eventually. In this process of propitiating the Deity by self-denial, it was inevitable that the love life of mature adults, being the most intense of all satisfactions, should be the most severely attacked.[5]

3

The Struggle against Lust

❀   ❀

❀

In the latter half of the fourth century, enthusiasts reported, perhaps with more zeal than accuracy, that in Egypt alone at least twenty-two thousand men and women had quit civilized communities to lead monastic and ascetic lives in the desert along the upper Nile. Some lived in huts or caves, but the more devout preferred dry wells, the deserted dens of beasts, and tombs. Most refrained altogether from washing, and prized their crusted, malodorous state. A monk named Arsenius wove palm leaves, and refused to change the nauseous water in which he steeped them year after year, so as to add stench to his other discomforts; the monk Macarius ate nothing but raw desert herbs for seven years; and the monk Besarion did not lie down while sleeping for forty years. The most famous was Saint Simeon Stylites, who, it is often pointed out, spent thirty years on top of a sixty-foot pillar; it is less often mentioned (though equally true) that he also accumulated spiritual credit by allowing himself to become a mass of clotted and ulcerated filth, and that he

---

[5] The Roman-Christian experience was far from unique; many other peoples have tried to propitiate angry gods by sexual self-denial. See Havelock Ellis: *Sex in Relation to Society*, pp. 1415–17.

bound a rope around his waist so tightly as to produce a maggot-infested putrefaction. Worms filled his bed, and fell from him as he walked; sometimes he replaced them, saying: "Eat what God has given you!"

All this seems a long way from love, but it was not. In the *Verba Seniorum*, a collection of anecdotes and maxims of the desert fathers, a young monk tormented by sexual daydreams asks a wise old monk: "I entreat thee to explain to me how thou hast never been harried by lust." The old man replies: "Since the time that I became a monk I have never given myself my fill of bread, nor of water, nor of sleep, and tormenting myself with appetite for these things whereby we are fed, I was not suffered to feel the stings of lust." To judge by other accounts in this ancient work, few other monks were so easily able to be rid of their desires; they endured the same penances, but suffered continually from sexual fantasies. Indeed, it becomes clear as one reads these scores of brief tales that the monks had no genuine wish to be free of tormenting desire; their heroism and spiritual satisfaction lay in defeating the powerful urge, and without it their desert life would have been hollow and meaningless.

For these practitioners of asexuality were, in fact, more totally preoccupied with sex than any pagan debauchee. They credited themselves with immense concupiscence and very fragile will power; not by thought, but by desperate deeds, did they stay pure. In lower Egypt, according to the *Verba Seniorum* again, a prostitute hired by some practical jokers tried to seduce one desert-dwelling solitary by coming to his cell at evening, weeping that she was lost, and pleading fear of the wild animals. The monk let her in, and was immediately seized by overpowering desire. Realizing the gravity of his situation, he lit the lamp and held a finger in the flame, "and when it burnt and scorched he felt it not, for the flame of lust that was in him." Nevertheless it kept him busy; by morning all his fingers were gone, but he was still pure.[6]

The intensity and obsessiveness of such temptations are nowhere more vividly recorded than in a letter written by Saint Jerome to a

[6] Many other celibate men also possessed—or thought they possessed—extraordinary strength of desire. In sixth-century Italy a priest took orders, and parted from his wife although he loved her. Forty years later, when he lay in a coma, dying of ague, his aged wife visited him and bent over his bed. "In great fervor of spirit," noted Pope Gregory the Great in his fourth *Dialogue,* "he burst out, saying: 'Get thee away, woman, a little fire is yet left; take away the straw!'" What non-celibate man could claim as much?

female follower, recalling for her his own desert sufferings of A.D. 375. It is an awesome confession of the struggle against lust.

> How often when I was living in the desert and the solitude that affords hermits a savage dwelling-place, parched by a burning sun, how often did I fancy myself amid the pleasures of Rome! I sought solitude because I was filled with bitterness. Sackcloth disfigured my misshapen limbs, and my skin had become by neglect as black as an Ethiopian's. . . . Yet I, who from fear of hell had consigned myself to that prison where I had no other companions but scorpions and wild beasts, fancied myself amongst bevies of dancing maidens. My face was pale and my frame chilled with fasting; yet my mind was burning with the cravings of desire, and the fires of lust flared up from my flesh that was as that of a corpse. So, helpless, I used to lie at the feet of Christ, watering them with my tears, wiping them with my hair, struggling to subdue my rebellious flesh with seven days' fasting.[7]

Again and again that same thinly disguised note of inflamed eroticism appears in the writings of the holy men. Among the several biographies of saints written in the fourth century, that of Saint Mary the harlot exemplifies, even better than the more familiar story of Thaïs, the strong brew of sex and piety on which the early monks became intoxicated. In a desert region near Edessa in Mesopotamia (modern Iraq), a girl, Mary, was brought up by her uncle, Abraham, a devout Christian solitary, whose entire contact with her took place through a tiny aperture between the two rooms of their hut. When Mary was a beautiful girl of twenty, a stranger lured her into opening her door to him, and promptly defiled her. In shame she fled to the city of Assos and became a harlot in an inn. The grief-stricken Abraham sought her for two years and finally learned where she was. Dressing his aged body in military disguise so that Mary would not take flight, he pretended to be a client and roundly praised her charms before her and the innkeeper. They drank wine together and she fondled him; then he gave the innkeeper a gold piece and said: "Now, friend, make us a right good supper, so that I may make merry with the lass, for I am come a long way for love of her." After the supper Mary enticed him to her room, and locked the door. He sat on her bed, and she knelt before him, smiling, and began to pull off his shoes; not until then did he reveal his identity. This, of course, brought on the predictable sequence of tears, repentance, and forgiveness; they then made their

---

[7] Saint Jerome: *Epistle xxii* (to Eustochium), 7.

escape, fled the city, and returned to the old happy life in their twin
cells. The ending is moral, but the tale itself is dangerous stuff: it
skirts hard by the forbidden heights, the blasphemous act, the incestuous abomination.[8]

The struggle against lust produced an explosive state of mind;
the personality could be held together only by the tenacious cement
of irrationality. The desert fathers saw and worked little miracles
every day. In themselves, these sound harmless enough, but the
same intellectual orientation could lead further, and did; not by
mere coincidence, it was a towering figure of asceticism, Tertullian,
whose formula for finding the truth of Christianity was *Credo quia
absurdum* (I believe because it is absurd), while Pope Gregory—
later sainted and called "the Great"—burned the Palatine library because he considered it a hindrance to Bible study. Asceticism led
thus to intolerance, obscurantism, and overt aggressiveness. The
ascetic was not content to master himself; inevitably his route led
him to try to master other men's flesh, and their minds as well.

His greatest assault was launched against the female half of humanity. He constantly dinned in her ear such words as: "She
[woman] was created as a helpmate for her husband, yet brought
only ruin upon him," and: "You are the gate of hell, the unsealer of
that forbidden tree, the first deserter of the divine law." [9] A bishop
soberly offered for debate at the Council of Mâcon in A.D. 585 the
proposition that woman did not even have a mortal soul, but after
earnest discussion the Council decided she did. In the opinion of
some Fathers of the Church, however, heaven would be spared the
indignity of ever having women on the scene, for at the Resurrection they would, by God's grace, become sexless.

A second ascetic attack on woman was to desert her. Continent
marriage itself was a form of partial desertion; in addition, literally
thousands of marriages were completely broken up because of the
earnest desire of the husband (or occasionally the wife) to lead a
dedicated life. Saint Abraham (the uncle of Saint Mary the harlot)
and Saint Alexis both fled from their brides on their wedding nights;
Saint Nilus persuaded his wife to permit him to leave her and their
children in order to live on Sinai; and Saint Melania talked her husband into letting her go seek a monastic life. But these are only

---

[8] Saint Ephraem of Edessa: "Life of Saint Mary the Harlot," *Vitae Patrum*, I.
[9] Clement of Alexandria: *Paedagogus*, iii, 2; Tertullian: *De Cultu Faeminarum*,
i, 1.

names and events, and tell us nothing of the feelings of the people behind them. What was the actual emotional condition of these zealots? What feelings could make a man fly from marriage and love as though they were a loathsome infection?

In A.D. 370, when Saint John Chrysostom, the greatest orator and writer of the Eastern Church, was still a young man, his friend Theodore fell in love with a maiden named Hermione and made plans to marry her. Chrysostom salvaged him for celibacy by writing him an impassioned letter which changed his mind completely, and of which this is a significant segment:

> The groundwork of this corporeal beauty is nothing else but phlegm and blood and humor and bile, and the fluid of masticated food. . . . If you consider what is stored up inside those beautiful eyes, and that straight nose, and the mouth and cheeks, you will affirm the well-shaped body to be nothing else than a whited sepulchre. . . . Moreover, when you see a rag with any of these things on it, such as phlegm, or spittle, you cannot bear to touch it even with the tips of your fingers, nay you cannot endure looking at it; are you then in a flutter of excitement about the storehouses and repositories of these things? [1]

This attitude was translated into doctrine in diverse ways. Montanus and his followers advocated the separation of husbands and wives, the adherents of Tatian the Syrian attributed the invention of marriage to the devil himself, and comparable views were held by Marcionites, Basilidians, Saturninians, Gnostics, Manicheans, and other early Christian and semi-Christian sects.[2] Eventually the Catholic Church labeled them all heretical; yet the Church itself incorporated much of the same point of view in its own doctrines. In the writings of the Fathers of the Church nothing is more highly praised than celibacy, while marriage is only grudgingly permitted. For over seven centuries the Church waged a bitter fight to impose celibacy on its clergy, and finally won; at the same time, monasticism for each sex grew from a few tiny communities to a vast organized institution throughout Europe. So profoundly was the orientation against all sexuality built into the Church that many centuries later, even under the attacks of Protestantism, the Catholic Church did not retreat; rather, the Council of Trent in 1563 went one step further and finally condemned with anathema the

[1] Chrysostom: "Letters to Theodore," i, 14.
[2] The Gnostics, referred to above as a non-Christian sect, became increasingly allied to Christianity as time passed.

doctrine that the married state was as good as, or superior to, celibacy.

The third and worst attack on woman consisted of convincing her to renounce her own sexuality and all it meant as lover, wife, and mother. Nearly every great writer and preacher of the early Church wrote voluminously in praise of virginity. Among female martyrs, the favorites were virgins who preferred burning pitch, the rack, and the hot iron, to sexual intercourse. Such virginity was said to have miraculous powers; typically, when a hungry lion was turned loose upon Thecla in the arena, he stopped short and then licked her feet in humble admiration of her purity.

The most notable exponent of virginity and cultivator of saved women was the gifted Saint Jerome, who so graphically described his own torments in the desert. After receiving a thorough education in Rome and spending several years in the desert, he entered the priesthood and became secretary to Pope Damasus. Still affecting the brown robe of an anchorite, he spent much time winning to the holy life a number of wealthy Roman women, whom he persuaded to live in dirt, tears, and austerity in the midst of luxury and self-indulgence. From his many letters of guidance and encouragement to them, one can extract a dismal picture of the only way of life a Christian woman could, at that time, pursue with self-respect and dignity. Its absolute prerequisite was the renunciation of sexual pleasure—virginity for the unsoiled, self-denial for those who had already sinned. To one of his virgins, a young woman named Eustochium, he wrote a letter in A.D. 384 that became a classic description of the Christian virgin's life.[3] "I need not speak of the drawbacks of marriage," he began—but then immediately listed them in full: pregnancy, the crying of infants, the torment caused by a rival, the household chores, and so on. "I praise marriage," he added piously, "but only because it gives me virgins. I gather the rose from the thorns, the gold from the earth, the pearl from the shell."

He told Eustochium, in commendably specific terms, how to remain a virgin and avoid all temptation and danger. She must shun wine as though it were poison, and eat only the simplest and smallest meals, for "the rumbling of our intestines . . . the emptiness of our stomach . . . [and] the inflammation of our lungs . . . [are] the only way of preserving chastity." She must not visit wealthy

[3] Jerome: *Epistle xxii.*

homes or look upon the ways of luxury. She should read much, fast often, wear the meanest clothes, remain at home, and weep for her sins every night. Yet she must not be vain in her sufferings or publicly display her devotion: "Do not lower your voice on purpose, as though you were worn out by fasting; nor yet lean upon a friend's shoulder, imitating the gait of one who is completely exhausted." Yet, wonder of wonders, for all her self-denial she will still have a love life of sorts—the only one a decent woman may have:

> Let the seclusion of your own chamber ever guard you; ever let the Bridegroom sport with you within. If you pray, you are speaking to your Spouse: if you read, He is speaking to you. When sleep falls on you, He will come behind the wall and will put His hand through the hole in the door and will touch your belly. And you will awake and rise up and cry: "I am sick with love." And you will hear Him answer: "A garden inclosed is my sister, my spouse, a spring shut up, a fountain sealed." [4]

4

The Transformation of Marriage

O nly a small percentage of Christians actually succeeded in sublimating their drives and leading lives of abstinence; the rest continued to lust and love, fornicate and marry. But all these activities were undergoing major changes in form and in spirit, and none more so than marriage. And since love seems so full of

[4] The Biblical echoes are from the *Song of Solomon*. iv:12, and v:2, 4.

paradoxes, perhaps we should not wonder that Christianity affected marriage in two seemingly irreconcilable ways: it at once ennobled it and debased it, strengthened it and poisoned it.

The Christians criticized and fought against the wanton customs of marriage and divorce that had long existed in the Roman Empire, but their own beliefs and practices long remained unformulated, and were crystallized only in the course of several centuries. The process was slow partly because of the immense discrepancy between long-established Roman habits and Christian doctrines—and even, to be truthful, because of internal quarrels as to what Christ Himself had thought about divorce. (In *Matthew* xix:9 He recognized "fornication"—the word means "adultery" in Biblical usage—as grounds for divorce, but in *Mark* x:11–12 He recognized no grounds whatever.) For centuries it was held by some Christians that a second marriage was equal to adultery; others would allow two but not three, others three but not four, and so on. But after the conversion of the Emperor Constantine the trend was unmistakable: civil divorce regulations grew ever tighter, and religious opinion became ever more strict. Gradually marriage came under clerical domination. By the fifth century it was rare for any wedding not to include an ecclesiastical benediction, and the notion that marriage was a sacrament—a holy act, not dissoluble by private or personal wish—steadily gained ground, although it was not authoritatively defined until the Middle Ages. The sixth-century Code of Justinian (which was chiefly effective in the still-flourishing Eastern Empire but influenced the West during the brief period of Justinian's reconquest of Italy) made divorce almost impossible and listed adultery as a capital offense; simultaneously, however, it revoked the ancient penalties placed by Augustus against celibacy and childlessness. Marriage, in short, had become indissoluble, but sexual self-denial stood above all else as the ethical way of life.

When Italy was again inundated by the Lombards, beginning in A.D. 568, the Code of Justinian ceased to be enforced, and Italy's connections with the Emperor in the East were effectively ended. Western Christianity, cut off from continued imperial influence, faced the difficult task of adapting itself to, and amalgamating itself with, the primitive customs of the Teutonic tribes. This retarded the progress of its moral ideas for some centuries, but in the end they prevailed: Roman monogamy became the pattern in the barbarian lands, thoroughly modified by Christianity into a serious lifetime contract made under religious auspices and not to be dissolved lightly, if at all.

Most authorities agree that this was a major contribution to the sexual and marital life of Western man. But since life is rarely simple and history seldom logical, Christianity also worked in precisely the opposite direction: it both reversed the partial emancipation of woman and thrust her firmly back under male domination. Oriental, Jewish, and barbarian ideas were mingled and fused with the Christian contempt for women; the concept of the wife was that of an inferior and sinful creature who should be confined, dominated, and chastised according to need—a viewpoint which contradicted, but coexisted with, the vaguely romantic ideals of continent marriage.

"What cause have you for appearing in public in excessive grandeur?" wrote Tertullian, scolding wives for putting on fine clothes and jewels. "You have no reason to appear in public except such as is serious. . . . Submit your heads to your husbands, and you will be enough adorned. Busy your hands with spinning; keep your feet at home; and you will please better than by arraying yourselves in gold." The *Apostolic Constitutions* of the fourth century summed up the early Christian view of woman's place in marriage: "O wife, next after the Almighty . . . and after His beloved Son, our Lord Jesus Christ . . . do thou fear thy husband and reverence him, pleasing him alone, rendering thyself acceptable to him in the several affairs of life. . . . Ye wives, be subject to your own husbands, and have them in esteem, and serve them with love and fear, as holy Sarah honored Abraham. For she could not endure to call him by his name, but called him Lord. . . ."

But this was only part of the change; the Church Fathers invaded the very marriage bed with their ukases, exhortations, and pronouncements. In his *Paedagogus* (in effect, a third-century Christian version of Xenophon's *Economist*), Clement of Alexandria told married people when it was permissible to lie with each other —not during the day or even after coming back from the market place, for such times should be devoted to reading or praying, but only after supper. Even then, married love-making would remain sinless only if delight were confined and restrained. The moral man is required to practice self-control, he warned, but there is no self-control in enjoying something intensely pleasurable. Two centuries later, when the evils of the world were much more advanced, Jerome restated the point in far harsher terms:

It is disgraceful to love another man's wife at all, or one's own too much. A wise man ought to love his wife with judgment, not with passion. Let a man govern his voluptuous impulses, and not rush headlong into intercourse. . . . He who too ardently loves his own wife is an adulterer.

He went even further: each experience of marital intercourse, he argued, constituted a temporary separation from the holy spirit, for such was the nature of sexual love—even within marriage—that just after it neither prayer nor communion was possible.

This startling doctrine became Church dogma. The seventh-century *Penitential* of Archbishop Theodore of Canterbury (a manual for priests) set down what must even then have been an old established rule in the Western Church: "Those who are joined together in matrimony should abstain from cohabitation three nights before receiving communion." The Church had made marriage a holy act—and yet considered this part of it an unholy, almost abominable, lapse from grace. The resulting frame of mind in which man and wife embraced each other was surreptitious, hasty, and guilt-ridden—somewhat, says Bertrand Russell, like drinking during the Prohibition.

No personal confessions of those blighted intimacies remain, but a good idea of their emotional content can be gained, inferentially, from the tone in which Tertullian, one of the great married clerics, addressed his own wife in a letter. Though Tertullian turned away from the Catholic Church in his later years and headed the Montanist sect in Africa, he was the first truly great Church writer of the West. Born about A.D. 160, the son of a Roman centurion of Carthage, he received an excellent classical education both there and in Rome itself, in the latter of which he then practiced law. In his early forties Tertullian underwent conversion to Christianity, returned to Carthage, married a Christian woman, and became a presbyter. Using his immense rhetorical powers, he began to turn out a veritable flood of influential writings on Christianity; it has even been said that Christian literature in the West sprang from him full-grown. When he was about forty-seven, he wrote his wife a long letter on marriage and widowhood which became one of the standard Christian tracts on these subjects, and which is particularly intriguing for the tantalizing glimpses it gives of his relationship to his wife.

"I have thought it meet, my best beloved fellow servant in the

Lord," he began, "even from this early period to provide for the course you must pursue after my departure from the world, if I shall be called before you." Tertullian directed her not to remarry, likening second marriage to outright adultery. Widowhood was God's call to sexual abstinence; he explained at great length that though marriage is permissible, God would much prefer that men and women practice celibacy. A widow is really getting a chance to please God. In any case, if Tertullian did die first, he wanted his wife not to grieve, for his death would be only the early ending of an enslavement to a disgusting condition which, under any conditions, they would have to give up to enter heaven:

> To Christians, after their departure from the world, no restoration of marriage is promised in the day of resurrection, translated as they will be into the condition and sanctity of angels. . . . There will at that day be no resumption of voluptuous disgrace between us. No such frivolities, no such impurities, does God promise to His servants.[5]

It is one of the most remarkable consolations ever addressed by any man to his wife.

To most Romans this must have seemed thoroughly demented, but harmless. It was then only A.D. 202; the Empire still seemed to flourish on all sides, in Carthage, Spain, Italy, Gaul, and of course in the East. It was but three generations since Hadrian had finished beautifying Rome, and only one generation since the reign of the benevolent Stoic, Marcus Aurelius. Plotinus, the greatest of the pagan Neoplatonists, was still unborn, the vast Baths of Caracalla were yet unbuilt, the sensual excesses of Elagabalus were not even dreamed of. Tertullian must have seemed a foolish fanatic, who would soon be forgotten. As it turned out, his was the voice of the future. By him, and by Saint Paul—the source of so much of his thinking—morals and love would be influenced for many generations; indeed, he and Paul would still speak within the consciences of many people in the twentieth century.

---

[5] Tertullian: "Ad Uxorem," i, 1–3.

5

Saint Augustine: The Victory of Guilt

❊   ❊

❊

F ar more influential even than Tertullian was a man who, living
two centuries later, saw the first fall of Rome and became the
first definitive voice of the medieval mind. He was Saint Augustine,
nominally only the Bishop of Hippo, a small African seaport,[6] but
in actual fact a master theologian who exerted an immense influence on all of Christendom by pouring forth a flood of brilliant
commentaries and speculations which were multiplied by copyists
and carried throughout the Empire by messengers. Augustine wrote
two hundred and thirty major works, many hundreds of letters,
and a vast quantity of sermons; engaged in protracted warfare with
Donatists, Manicheans, and Pelagians (all of whom considered
themselves good Christians, and all of whose doctrines he considered pernicious); and elaborated upon every major Christian
theological idea, including original sin, free will, election, predestination, monism, idealism, the state of grace, salvation, the Trinity,
and the nature of the sacraments. "Theology in Western Christianity," a scholar has said, "has been a series of footnotes to Augustine."

With most of this we are only tangentially concerned; what interests us directly is that Augustine's *Confessions* are the first
autobiography in Western literature, and contain an intimate record
of the love life of a man who has profoundly affected other love
lives for more than fifteen hundred years.

He was born in A.D. 354 in Tagaste, a minor city in Numidia,
North Africa, where his father was a sort of local magistrate. Ac-

[6] At that time, in Africa, the term "bishop" meant something roughly equivalent to parish priest.

[117]

cording to Augustine's evaluation of his parents, Patricius, his father, was a quick-tempered, domineering, and unfaithful man who
wanted his son to be a pagan; Monica, his mother, was submissive,
meek, and virtuous, but fanatically determined to make her son a
Christian. The struggle for Augustine's soul was fought on more
than one battleground.

Augustine received a good schooling at Madaura and later at
Carthage, and proved to be an excellent pupil; even so, he found
time in his teens to be a monstrously wicked young fellow.

> And what was it that I delighted in, but to love, and be be-
> loved? but I kept not the measure of love, of mind to mind, friend-
> ship's bright boundary; but out of the muddy concupiscence of
> the flesh, and the bubblings of youth, mists fumed up which be-
> clouded and overcast my heart. . . . I was tossed about, and
> wasted, and dissipated, and I boiled over in my fornications.

This is how Augustine saw his youth many years later; yet the facts
he himself scattered throughout the *Confessions* oddly bely the
continual self-accusations of dissipation. For when he was seventeen, he moved to Carthage to continue his studies, and there acquired a young concubine (whose name he never recorded), to
whom he was completely faithful for the next fifteen years, and
who bore him a son he reared and cherished, calling him Adeodatus,
or gift of God. It is hardly a picture of moral abandonment.

Yet if it felt so to Augustine, it may have been because the short,
thin, rather feeble youth was already struggling to resolve his own
feelings about his manhood, pulled one way by the pleas of his
mother to avoid fornication and adultery, and the other way by his
desire to emulate his virile pagan father. The Oedipal conflict was,
in his case, perfectly aligned with the conflict between the dying
order and the new one. "In effect," wrote Dr. Charles Kligerman of
the Chicago Institute for Psychoanalysis in a recent study of the
Confessions, "Monica demanded that Augustine relinquish sexuality in favor of the Church, which meant, at an unconscious level,
that he should belong to her forever . . . but the events at the
time show vividly how desperately he struggled for his manhood."

In Carthage, Augustine became a successful professor of rhetoric;
meanwhile, in his own continuing search for truth, he allied himself with the Manicheans, but remained unbaptized. At twenty-
nine he decided to move to Rome, and when his mother tearfully
begged him either to remain or to take her along, he lied about the

departure date, left her praying in a dockside chapel, and sailed without her. Dr. Kligerman interprets both the choice of a heretical sect and the escape by ship as desperate efforts by Augustine to resist his mother's attack on his sexuality, for she, now widowed, daily wept and prayed for his salvation, and was gradually gaining control over him.

After teaching in Rome for a year, Augustine won the post of public professor of rhetoric in Milan. There he heard Ambrose lecture, was deeply moved, and grew a little closer to Catholicism; there, too, Monica eventually found him, moved in with him, and took over control of his house. She convinced Augustine that at last he must make a proper marriage, and selected for him a twelve-year-old child whom he would not be able to wed for two years; meanwhile, however, she used the betrothal as a potent argument for ousting his faithful mistress from the household. Augustine spinelessly agreed to this heartless act, although it apparently caused him genuine pain:

> My concubine was torn from my side as a hindrance to my marriage; my heart which clave unto her was torn and wounded and bleeding. And she returned to Africa, vowing unto Thee never to know any other man, leaving with me my son by her.

This admission of affection seems real, but Augustine hastened to disparage it, claiming that it had been nothing much but sexual need after all, as proven by his actions a few weeks later:

> Not being so much a lover of marriage as a slave to lust, I procured another, though no wife, that so by the servitude of an enduring custom the disease of my soul might be kept up and carried on in its vigor or even augmented, into the dominion of marriage.

Yet he felt more wretched than ever, desperately wanting what he desperately wished to avoid. "Give me chastity," he prayed, "but not yet."

In the summer of 386, when he was thirty-two, he was sitting one day, "soul-sick and tormented," in the garden with his friend, the celibate youth Alypius. Suddenly Augustine was seized by a paroxysm of weeping and fled to the end of the garden; there, after a while, he heard a childlike voice saying: "Take up and read; take up and read." He seized a copy of the writings of Paul and opened it at random, finding the words: "Not in rioting and drunk-

enness, not in chambering and wantonness, not in strife and envying: but put ye on the Lord Jesus Christ, and make not provision
for the flesh, in concupiscence." At once his heavy soul-sickness
disappeared, and he felt joyous, serene, and certain. He hastened
back to tell Alypius, who read on in the passage and found the
sentence: "Him that is weak in the faith, receive." They went in-
doors together and informed Monica they were ready to be baptized; hearing this, wrote Augustine, "she leaps for joy, and triumpheth, and blesseth Thee." It is no wonder the psychoanalyst
finds the *Confessions* so rewarding and revealing; the single word
"triumpheth" is worth chapters.

On Easter Sunday, 387, Augustine, Adeodatus, and Alypius were
baptized by Ambrose, with Monica standing proudly by. The *Confessions* say nothing more of the second mistress or the fiancée;
all of Augustine's conflicts, on all fronts, had been resolved. He
gave up the comfortable Roman life not long afterwards and returned to Africa, where he founded a religious community of celibate men—the Augustinian order, oldest monastic fraternity of the
West. In 396 he was chosen Bishop of Hippo and remained in that
post for thirty-four years until his death, sending out from that
minor post words that shaped the future of the Christian world.

The outcome of the struggle between love and asceticism in him
was embodied in many of the doctrines he gave to Christianity.
Trying to solve the dreadful question as to where evil came from,
in a world made by a good God, Augustine reasoned that although
man does have a free will, it is permanently inclined to choose the
bad by an indelible stain of original sin. Original sin included not
just Adam's and Eve's specific defiance of God, but their concupiscence, or sensuous desire. Though Augustine did not invent the
idea of original sin, it was he who first held that it attached to virgins, to celibates, and even to newborn infants; he argued that
since parentage and new life come about only by means of the
pleasurable sexual act, all flesh is inherently depraved, and all mankind is necessarily a "mass of perdition."

Some of Augustine's opponents protested that in effect he had
denied the sanctity of marriage by so coloring it with depravity,
and he tried to rebut the charge. "Marriage and fornication are
not two evils, the second of which is worse," he wrote, "but marriage and continence are two goods, the second of which is better."
Yet he belied his own words, for he also argued that the earlier in

life a married couple could begin to refrain from intercourse with each other, the better they would seem in God's eyes, and he repeatedly maintained that the evil of lust—even married lust—was justified only when it had the sole and immediate aim of begetting children. In brief, Augustine set up a permanent barrier between personal affection and sexual expression, and gave formal theological structure to the confused ideal of continent marriage and asexual love. The Oedipal conflict had at last been enshrined in a religion, and enlarged into a lifelong struggle for salvation.

Most revealing of all is Augustine's attempt to figure out how children might have been purely propagated, had Adam and Eve remained free of original sin. Augustine devoted many chapters of *The City of God*, his magnum opus, to solving this problem. He started by candidly agreeing that the sexual act "is the keenest of all pleasures on the level of sensation. . . . At the crisis of excitement, it practically paralyzes all power of deliberate thought." The flesh takes command over man, defying his will as he defied the will of God. Augustine was by then so used to ascetic thinking that he simply took it for granted that any good and reasonable person "would prefer, if this were possible, to beget his children without suffering this passion." And in Eden it would have been possible: "Even if there had been no sin in the Garden, there would still have been marriages worthy of that blessed place and . . . lovely babies would have flowered from a love uncankered by lust."

How would this have been achieved? The imagination balks at the task, Augustine admitted. But he would not shirk his duty; he would try to portray as best he could the method of propagation in Eden.

> In Paradise, then, generative seed would have been sown by the husband and the wife would have conceived . . . by deliberate choice and not by uncontrollable lust. After all, it is not only our hands and fingers, feet and toes, made up of joints and bones that we move at will, but we can also control the flexing and stiffening of muscles and nerves. . . . Some people . . . can make their ears move, either one at a time or both together. . . . There are individuals who can make musical notes issue from the rear of their anatomy, so that you would think they were singing. I knew a man myself who could raise beads of perspiration at will. . . . Human organs, without the excitement of lust, could have obeyed [the] human will for all the purposes of parenthood. . . . At a time when there was no unruly lust to excite the

organs of generation and when all that was needed was done by deliberate choice, the seminal flow could have reached the womb with as little rupture of the hymen and by the same vaginal ducts as is at present the case, in reverse, with the menstrual flux. . . . Perhaps these matters are somewhat too delicate for further discussion.[7]

It is an astonishing piece of fantasy, scarcely surpassed by the myths of primitive men, or the hallucinations of schizophrenic ones.

6

The Dark Ages of Love

❀

❀

I t is the latter part of the sixth century. Mighty Rome has been repeatedly ravaged and looted. Her people have died off or slunk away to country towns and semi-fortified villages not so attractive to the endless armies. Where once half a million to a million people lived in imperial magnificence, perhaps fifty thousand now exist in a deserted city whose great buildings are burned ruins, whose streets are filling with rubble and growing over with grass, whose aqueducts are broken, whose ancient swamps, long drained, are filling again with stinking ooze, and whose once-glorious Senate has finally ceased to meet because it cannot muster enough qualified men to make a showing. The Eastern Empire has lost all but the merest toehold on southern Italy, and Western Europe is committed to going its own way: breaking down into semi-barbaric kingdoms, dukedoms, towns, and manors, forgetting how to read or write,

[7] *City of God*, Bk. xiv, Ch. 24 and 26.

and abandoning the hygiene, science, and culture of the Romans for the myths, terrors, and tribal customs of the Germans.

Infinitely complex, infinitely painful is the fusion of the rotting Roman sophistication with the vigorous primitive cultures of the Franks, Normans, Goths, Burgundians, and others. The result is what history calls the Dark Ages—A.D. 600 to A.D. 1100 will do as well as any dates for it—out of which the emergence of medieval feudalism will look like the very dawning of day; and just as learning, health, economics, and government are on a semi-primitive level during the Dark Ages, so too are love and morals.

The Roman Christians had dissociated love from sex, the former being God's business, the latter being the Devil's. The Teutonic savages were unwilling to accept ascetic ideals at first; they could agree that sexual activity was mere lust, but saw nothing bad in that fact, and no reason to refrain from it. Their earthy sexuality might have been given sophistication or refinement by contact with Periclean Greece, but gained only a base and gloomy coloring from Christian Rome. For some centuries, Teutonic sexuality was not so much inhibited by Christianity, as soured by it; what had been unromantic and lusty became unromantic and ugly. The sex life of the Dark Ages was grossly sensual, harsh, and sinful—with penance easily and cynically performed as often as required.

Few accounts exist of the loves of real men and women in this period, but occasional scraps remain, embedded in histories of wars and dynasties, which tease the imagination and grant us a tantalizing instant of vision. One such scrap can be found in the *History of the Franks*, where Gregory of Tours mentions some details in the private life of Lothar (Clotaire) I, King of Gaul. In the middle of the sixth century, Lothar married a lady named Ingund and, wrote Gregory, "loved her with all his heart." What, precisely, did that phrase mean to Lothar, or to Bishop Gregory who wrote it down? We read on, and learn. Shortly after their marriage, Ingund told Lothar that she was well pleased to have been chosen for his bed, and had only one favor to ask of her husband: he should find a good husband for her sister, Aregund. Lothar, listening to her praises of Aregund, found himself instantly inflamed; he traveled to the sister's domain, married her, and then returned to explain things. "I sought a man wealthy and of good wit whom I might give to thy sister," he told Ingund, "but I found none better than myself. Know, therefore, that I have taken her to wife, which I believe will not displease thee." "Let my lord do that which seemeth good in his sight," replied Ingund, "only let his handmaid live in the enjoyment of his favor." Seven hundred years' worth of gains by Roman women had thus been wiped out; woman was once again a useful, desirable, domesticated animal, and love was much as it had been in the days of the primitive Homeric warriors who either fought over captive women or gave them to each other as presents.

Two centuries after Lothar, the mighty Charlemagne briefly reconquered an empire in the West and almost rescued Europe from the barbaric doldrums. By the standards of the eighth century, he was both learned and enlightened, and he adored women. He could hardly get enough of them, in fact; he married four times, had five known mistresses, and indulged in a multitude of brief encounters. He was patriarchally fond of his six daughters and ordered them not to marry so that they might remain in his household; this was not due to paternal jealousy, however, for when at times one or another grew suspiciously fat and retired to give birth, he indulgently smiled and accepted the situation. In short, for all that he was crowned Emperor of Rome by Pope Leo III and tried to play the part of a second Augustus, he too was still basically a Frankish chieftain.

Gradually, however, the persistent clerics, laying heavily about them with their ascetic doctrines, changed things. The primitive customs did not suddenly alter, but they took on the color and odor of sin. From the top of society to the bottom, men heard themselves and their actions described in the same harsh terms Saint Boniface used in 756, when he wrote a letter of bitter castigation to King Ethelbald of England, saying in part:

> Your contempt for lawful matrimony, were it for chastity's sake, would be laudable; but since you wallow in luxury and even in adultery with nuns, it is disgraceful and damnable. . . . We have heard that almost all the nobles of the Mercian kingdom, following your example, desert their lawful wives and live in guilty intercourse with adulteresses and nuns.

Perhaps things were not quite as bad as all that; the only literate people from the sixth century to the thirteenth were clerics, trained to see the Devil lurking in every shadow, and we have no one else's evidence. Nevertheless the emotional tone of the Dark Ages is unmistakable. What had been a guiltless habit became a guilty one;

appetite was renamed lust; men and women did not all become ascetic, but learned to be ashamed of what they did.

The status of woman resulted from a blending of Church and Teutonic views. Woman became, once again, a piece of property, and lost her status as a real person in the eyes of the law. A Kentish law of the early seventh century stated that "If a man forcibly carries off a maiden, he shall pay fifty shillings to her owner and afterwards buy from the owner his consent." The Franks excluded women from the courts, barred them from the inheritance of certain ancestral lands, and even kept them out of family councils. Adultery in a wife was punishable by death; for men there was no penalty whatever.[8] Free-born women required the consent of their parents, and later of their overlords, to marry, and eventually women became attached to land, both person and title going as a package to purchase military loyalty. What women thought of the disposal of their persons was of no consequence; Charlemagne, that light in the darkness and admirer of women, is said by legend to have married off in one mass ceremony all the widows of his barons, killed in the war in Spain, to young noblemen of his own choice.

Even the clergy, who were supposed to rise above the sordid lusts of ordinary men, clearly showed the effects of the fusion of barbarian morality and ascetic values. Though Eastern anchorites and despairing Romans had been capable of renouncing the flesh, the clergy of the Dark Ages lacked any such sophisticated character. The more the Church fought against clerical marriage, the more the clergy turned to simple concubinage. Bishop Boniface and the Venerable Bede in the eighth century, Bishop Ratherius of Verona in the tenth century, and scores of others have left their written complaints about the widespread failure of the clergy to live up to the celibate ideal. A canon in England specifically ordered that the property of dead priests should go to their churches and not, even by testament, to their concubines; another canon said, in part: "Let not sons be instituted in their fathers' benefices, unless someone succeed between them." These conditions were

[8] In a well-known passage, Tacitus praised Teutonic morality early in the second century A.D. But the conduct he admired was neither moralistic nor ascetic; it restricted woman's sexual freedom because it gave man a property-right in his wife, and this typically primitive idea appealed to the Roman historian since it harked back to the early days of the Republic.

common until the Lateran Council of 1059 and the decrees of Pope
Gregory VII in 1074 inaugurated an all-out fight; even so, it took
three more centuries before it was won.

Meanwhile, the papacy itself had been the scandal of Christendom
all through the tenth and half of the eleventh century. In 904,
Marozia, daughter of a high official of the papal palace, got her
lover made Pope (Sergius III); her mother secured the job in 914
for *her* lover (John X); and in later years Marozia's son and
grandson took their turns, the latter being the notorious Pope
John XII, who was tried before an ecclesiastical council and
charged by his own cardinals with incest, and adultery with his
father's concubine. This spectacle continued with only brief inter-
ruptions until the middle of the eleventh century, when Pope
Leo IX began a thorough reform of the Church.

The reform coincided with other notable changes in Western
civilization: the emergence of medieval culture, of knighthood, of
feudal chivalry—and the discovery of a new meaning to love.

7

The Heart's Paradox

❋   ❋

❋

The influence of Christianity upon love and marriage is thus an
impossible tangle of opposites—purification and contamina-
tion, the rebuilding of the family and the total flight from the
family, the glorification of one woman and the condemnation of
womankind. But the paradoxical is not meaningless, for it is a reflection of a basic mechanism of human personality; in the human

heart paradox has its equivalent in the form of the paired and warring drives of love and hate, selfishness and altruism, submissiveness and rebelliousness. It is, in a word, ambivalence—the ability to feel two ways about one thing: the most perplexing, best-hidden, and most pervasive aspect of human nature.

Christianity accentuated ambivalence in the area of love far beyond any previous social system. Formerly, men and women accepted sex as a human appetite, considered love a pastime and sometimes a torment, and viewed marriage as an inescapable social duty. They had some conflicting feelings about each, but not too many, and consequently felt at ease about taking their several satisfactions jointly or separately. Christianity forbade the separate gratification of the desires for sex, love, and marriage, but made it impossible to enjoy them together. Sex became so sinful and disgusting that even within marriage, as an act allowed by God, it seemed shameful and more ignoble than elimination. Men and women hungered for it and hated the hunger, enjoyed it and felt guilty for the enjoyment. Marriage itself was the only state in which the body's yearnings could legitimately be satisfied, and through which God's commandment to be fruitful was realizable, yet it was expressly said to be an inferior condition, and one suited for weaklings. The more elevated emotions of love, since they could hardly be linked with the shameful act of sex, were limited to the painful and dangerous artifice of continent marriage. An ever-larger fraction of the European population, unable to find any tolerable solution to these dilemmas, voluntarily deprived themselves of sex and marriage, and fled to a celibate life in monasteries and convents; there they could love God, the saints, and the Pope without complications.

Saint Augustine epitomized the Christian conflicts in a single terrible sentence: "Through a woman we were sent to destruction; through a woman salvation was sent to us." In comparison, the "*odi et amo*" of Catullus looks almost puerile, and the inner conflicts of Greek men concerning women seem like childish make-believe. Yet paradox has the final word, after all: out of ambivalence, out of sexual restraint, out of the virgin-mother image of woman, man would first fashion that new notion of romantic love that has seemed so enormously valuable to him ever since.

Chapter V
THE CREATION OF THE
ROMANTIC IDEAL

I

Courtly Love:
A Game That Became a Reality

❀   ❀

❀

Toward the end of the eleventh century A.D., a handful of
poets and noblemen in southern France concocted a set of
love sentiments most of which had no precedent in Western civilization, and out of them constructed a new and quite original relationship between man and woman known as *l'amour courtois*, or
courtly love. *Cortezia, courtesie,* or *Frauendienst,* as it is also called,
began as a game and a literary conceit, but unexpectedly grew into
a social philosophy that shaped the manners and morals of the
West. It started as a playful exercise in flattery, but became a
spiritual force guiding the flatterers; it was first a private sport of
the feudal aristocracy, but became finally the ideal of the middle
classes; and with wonderfully consistent inconsistency, it exalted at
one and the same time adultery and chastity, duplicity and faithfulness, self-indulgence and austerity, suffering and delight. Although satirists have slain and buried it in the tinsel costume of all
its follies a thousand times over, it has not stayed interred for one
night, and men and women throughout the Western world still
live by and take for granted a number of its principal concepts.

Scholars, historians, and religionists, according to their special
bents and personalities, have interpreted it in startlingly diverse
ways. Some have seen it as a mere passing foolishness and an
amusement of the aristocracy; others have found it a diabolically
clever disguise of the undying Manichean heresy.[1] Some have

---

[1] The Manichean sect, which became
particularly prominent beginning in the
third century A.D., was one of those
semi-Oriental religions which became
closely allied to early Christianity, but
was finally stigmatized as heretical by
the Catholic Church; see chapter four.
Augustine, it will be recalled, was a
Manichean before becoming a Christian.

viewed it as a quaint but unimportant chapter in social history; others as a poisonous ethic that has corrupted morals and marriage ever since; and still others as the origin of modern romantic love and a huge forward stride in human relationships that has set our millenium and our part of the world permanently apart from the Western past and the Oriental present.

2

The Service of Woman

❀   ❀

❀

On Sunday, April 25, A.D. 1227, crowds gathered at every crossing along a road on the Italian mainland near Venice, to watch an extraordinary procession pass by. It had been thoroughly advertised in advance by a messenger bearing an open letter to all the knights of Lombardy, Austria, and Bohemia. The letter stated that on April 24 the goddess Venus would arise from the sea near Venice and start the next day to travel north to Bohemia, breaking lances with every warrior who would meet her in the lists. Whoever tilted with her would gain a gold ring and great honor with ladies; whoever failed to meet her would henceforth be shunned by all lovely ladies; and whoever first unhorsed her would win all the horses of her retinue.

The cavalcade of the putative deity, when it finally hove into view, was worth the wait. First there slowly rode by a dozen squires, extravagantly dressed in white; then came two maids-in-waiting, also gorgeously got up, followed in turn by half a dozen musicians, festively sawing and blowing away; finally there ap-

peared on a luxuriously caparisoned horse a husky man-sized figure,
attired in an outrageously ornate white gown, a heavy veil, a pearl
headdress, and waist-length pearl-bedecked braids. Even in the
credulous Middle Ages, none but fools and louts supposed this to
be a real goddess, nor even a real woman; indeed, it was an open
secret, not particularly meant to be kept, that inside the finery, the
pearls, and the braids, was none other than Ulrich von Lichtenstein,
knight-errant, jouster of great prowess, *Minnesinger* of some talent, and devoted admirer of an unnamed lady for whose love he
was undertaking this superb, arduous, and all but impossible task.
The curious poor watched and cheered, noblemen saluted gravely,
the ladies, informed by gossip of Venus' real identity, hastened
to kiss him warmly at every halt, and impatient knights-at-arms
sent their men to him with invitations to combat.

Ulrich accepted every challenge, and by his own reckoning
(which may, of course, represent some degree of hyperbole),
broke the incredible total of three hundred and seven lances as he
fought his way to Vienna in the course of the next five weeks. In
those combats, he succeeded in unhorsing four of his opponents,
and was never himself unhorsed. It was a notable performance;
throughout the world of Austrian chivalry his name and fame
spread greatly, and lords and ladies spoke admiringly at many a
dinner table of the magnitude of the love that could have inspired
such service and produced such a record of performance in the lists.
And what was the purpose of these immense exertions and this very
considerable expenditure? To win for Ulrich the unutterable joy
of being allowed to see and speak to the nameless lady face to face,
and possibly be favored with a kiss.

To understand this singular state of affairs, let us learn something of Ulrich's life up to that point. He had been born about A.D.
1200 in the hilly, fertile Austrian province of Steiermark, or Styria.
His father must have been a member of the lesser nobility, for
although Ulrich never possessed any great titles or vast fiefs, he
grew up within castle walls, was knighted after a suitable ap-
prenticeship, and led an active life in the service of his feudal overlords. His signature on certain existing documents indicates that for
his successes as a knight-errant and jouster, he eventually won the
position of high steward of Steiermark, and later on also became a
marshal and a justice of the province. At the height of his fortune
he owned not only the castle of Lichtenstein, from which he took

his name, but two others and considerable land. According to a fairly recent scholarly German monograph, these and other documentary details indicate that he was a reasonably clever, energetic, and purposeful medieval politician and landowner.

But of all this Ulrich never bothered to say anything in his autobiography, which is the principal source of information on his life. It runs to a wearying thirty thousand lines of narrative verse plus numerous added lyric poems, which is surely room enough for everything, but he devoted it entirely to the only subject that seemed important to him—courtly love. Its very title is the story of his life: *Frauendienst*, or the service of woman. *Frauendienst*, dictated by the illiterate knight in later life to a scribe, is not a work of fiction, even though the aging man-at-arms may have yielded to the delights of exaggeration or been tricked by the distortions of memory. Nor is it a work of satire, though *Don Quixote de la Mancha*, not written until more than three centuries later, could have been directly patterned upon it. *Frauendienst* is one man's personal testimony—the actual record of his life as he lived it under the domination of courtly love.

When he was a mere lad of five, says Ulrich, he first heard older boys saying that true honor and happiness could come only through serving a noble and lovely woman; he was deeply impressed, and began to shape his childish thoughts in that direction. Even at that tender age it was perfectly clear to him that such service, the keystone of courtly love, could be undertaken only for a woman one could never marry. True love had to be clandestine, bittersweet, and beset by endless difficulties and frustrations; by virtue of all this, it was spiritually uplifting, and made a knight a better man and a greater warrior.

The subject evidently dominated the thoughts of the boy, for by the age of twelve he put away childish things and consciously chose as the lady of his heart a princess. In every way, it was a perfect choice: she was far too highborn for him, considerably older than himself, and, of course, already married. He became a page in her court, and conscientiously cultivated his feelings of love until they commanded his whole being. He adored her in total secrecy, and trembled (inconspicuously) in her presence. When he saw her hands touch the petals of flowers he had secretly placed where she would see them, he was all but in a faint. And when she washed her hands before dinner, young Ulrich would sometimes filch the basin, smuggle it off to his room, and there reverently drink the dirty water.

Five years of this went by; his love affair progressed no further, however, since being totally unworthy of the lady he dared not even tell her of his feelings. At the age of seventeen he therefore took himself off to the court of the Margrave Henry of Austria, to raise his status; there he studied knightly skills for five more years, and at last was made a knight in 1222, during the wedding festival of the Duke of Saxony. By a marvelous coincidence, his ladylove, whom he had not seen but religiously dreamed of during those years, was one of the guests at the wedding, and the very sight of her so moved him that he immediately took a secret vow to devote his newly won knighthood to serving her. This decision filled him with melancholy and with painful longings, a condition which apparently made him very happy.

That summer, feverish and flushed with his infatuation, he roamed the countryside fighting in numerous tourneys and winning many victories, all of which he ascribed to the mighty force of love within him. At last, having compiled an impressive record, and feeling worthy to offer the lady the tribute of his devotion, he persuaded a niece of his to call on her and privately tell her of his desire to be an acknowledged but distant, respectful admirer of hers; he even got his niece to learn and sing for the Princess a song he had written (Ulrich was already a competent *Minnesinger*—the German equivalent of the troubadour—as were many young noblemen of breeding).

The heartless lady, unmoved by his ten years of silent devotion and his recent feats of valor, sent back a cruel and pointed reply: she considered him presumptuous, was scornfully critical of the high-flown language of his quite inappropriate offer, and for good measure, took the trouble to let him know he was too ugly to be considered even in the role of a very distant admirer. For it seems (and the lady was specific) that the unhappy young knight had a harelip. Undaunted—perhaps even inspired by this obvious proof that she had actually noticed him—Ulrich promptly undertook a journey to a famous surgeon and had his lip repaired. Considering the techniques of medieval surgery, this must have been both excruciatingly painful and quite dangerous; indeed, he lay feverish on a sickbed for six weeks. News of this, plus a new song he wrote for her, softened the lady's heart, and she sent word that he might attend a riding party and enjoy the rare privilege of speaking with her for a moment, if the opportunity should arise. And it did, once, when he had the chance to help her down from her horse, and could have uttered a sentence or two of devotion; unfortunately he was tongue-tied by her nearness and could say nothing. The lovely lady, considerably put out, whispered to him that he was a fraud, and gracefully indicated her displeasure by ripping out a forelock of his hair as she dismounted.

Not in the least angered by this, Ulrich reappeared the next day, this time found his voice, and humbly begged her to permit him to be her secret knight and to allow him to fight for her and love her. She accepted his service, but under the very minimum conditions, granting him no "favor" whatever—neither embrace, kiss, nor word of promise, and not so much as a ribbon to carry in his bosom. Ulrich, nevertheless, was filled with joy and thankfulness for her kindness, and sallied forth, tilting about the countryside with anyone who would break a lance with him, and composing many a song to his ladylove, which his secretary set down for him since writing was not a knightly accomplishment. The messages and letters that passed between him and the Princess at this time conveyed, in the one direction, his endless, burning, worshipful feelings and, in the other direction, her condescension, coldness, and criticism. But this was exactly what was expected of her in the situation, and he found each new blow a delicious pain; it even sounds somewhat as though a large part of his pleasure lay in observing his own noble constancy under duress. If so, he must have had a thoroughly agreeable time for the next three years.

At the end of that period, Ulrich petitioned her forthrightly through a go-between to grant him her love, at least verbally, in return for his faithful adoration and service. The Princess not only sharply rebuked the go-between for Ulrich's unseemly persistency, but expressed her scorn that Ulrich had falsely spoken of losing a finger fighting for love of her. Actually, he had suffered a finger wound which healed, but an incorrect report had reached her. When the go-between related her scornful message, Ulrich paled for a moment, then resolutely drew out a sharp knife and ordered his friend to hack off the finger at one blow. This done, the knight had an artisan make a green velvet case in which the finger was held by gold clasps, and sent her the mounted digit as a keepsake, together with a special poem about the matter. Deeply impressed by this evidence of her power over him, she returned word that she would look at the finger every day from thenceforth, a message which, incidentally, he received as he did all other communiqués from her—on his knees, with bowed head and folded hands.

Determined now to earn her love by some stupendous feat, Ulrich conceived the scheme of the jousting-trip from Venice to Bohemia in the disguise of Venus. He went to Venice and there had seamstresses make a dozen white gowns to his own measurements; meanwhile he sent off a messenger with the open letter announcing the event. The northward march began on schedule on April 25, and concluded five weeks later, during which time Ulrich shattered an average of eight lances every day, made the notable record already mentioned, and acquired great glory and honor, all in the cause of love and for the sake of the Princess he so faithfully adored.

All this being so, it comes as something of a shock when one reads Ulrich's own statement that in the midst of this triumphal *Venusreise* he stopped off for three days to visit his wife and children. For the fact is that this lovesick Galahad, this kissless wonder, this dauntless knight-errant, had long had a wife to lie with when he had the urge, and a family to live with when he felt lonely. He himself speaks of his affection (but not his love) for his wife; to love her would have been improper and almost unthinkable. Like the other men of his class and time, Ulrich considered marriage a phase of feudal business-management, since it consisted basically of the joining of lands, the cementing of loyalties, and the production of heirs and future defenders. But the purifying, ennobling rapture of love for an ideal woman—what had that to do with details of crops and cattle, fleas and fireplaces, serfs and swamp drainage? Yet, though true love was impossible between husband and wife, without it a man was valueless. Ulrich could therefore unashamedly visit his wife during his grand tour, proud of what he had been doing and certain that if she knew of it, she too was proud, because *Frauendienst* made her husband nobler and finer.[2]

Having completed his epochal feat of love service, Ulrich waited for his reward, and at long last it came: the Princess sent word that

---

[2] Ladies, too, were increased in value by being loved. In a fictional counterpart of Ulrich's relations with his wife, a lady in an old Provençal romance, reproached by her husband for having a lover, proudly replies: "My lord, you have no dishonor on that account, for he is a noble baron, upright and expert in arms, namely, Roland, the nephew of King Charles." (*Gesta Karoli Magni ad Carcassonam et Narbonam*, p. 139)

he might visit her. Yet he was to expect no warm welcome; she specified that he must come in the disguise of a leper and take his place among lepers who would be visiting her to beg for alms. But of course this monstrous indignity fazed the faithful Ulrich not in the least; nor did he falter when she knowingly let him, disguised in his rags, spend that night in a ditch in the rain; nor was he outraged when the next night he was finally allowed to climb a rope up the castle wall to her chamber, only to find it lit by a hundred tapers and staffed by eight maids-in-waiting who hovered about her where she lay in bed. Though Ulrich pleaded urgently that they all be sent out, she continued to be coyly proper, and when she began to see that this patient fellow really was getting stubborn at last, she told him that to earn the favor he would have to prove his obedience by wading in a near-by lake. She herself assisted him out the window—and then, bending to kiss him, let loose the rope, tumbling Ulrich to the ground, or perhaps into a stinking moat. (It is worth remembering at this point that this painful incident was not recorded by any enemy or satirist of Ulrich, but by himself, his purpose being to make clear the extent of his suffering for love and his fidelity in the face of trials.)

Even such torments cannot go on forever. The cruel Princess next ordered Ulrich to go on a crusade in her service, but when she learned that he joyfully and obediently received the direct command from her, she suddenly relented, bade him rather stay at home near to her, and finally granted him her love. What an outpouring of thankful verse then! What a spate of shattered lances, dented helmets, broken blades, humbled opponents! For having won her love, Ulrich was puissant, magnificent, impregnable; this was the height of his career as a knight. Regrettably, it is not clear in the *Frauendienst* just which of her favors she so tardily vouchsafed after nearly a decade and a half, but in the light of other contemporary documents concerning the customs of courtly love, one can be fairly sure that she permitted him the kiss and the embrace, and perhaps even the right to caress her, naked, in bed; but if she gave him the final reward at all, it was probably on extremely rare occasions. For sexual outlet was not really the point of all this. Ulrich had not been laboring nearly fifteen years for so ordinary a commodity; his real reward had always been in his suffering, striving, and yearning.

The proof of this is that it took him nearly fifteen years to win her love and to become idyllically happy—but that condition, once achieved, lasted only a brief two years. For at the end of that time, the Princess wounded him in some fashion so cruel that he could not bring himself to name it, even long after. Perhaps she had accepted the service of some other knight, or even granted her love to another; what is probably more to the point, Ulrich's quest had ended when he won her, and in the peculiar psychology of courtly love, most of the magic had vanished with the pain. Whatever the cause of his break with her, at any rate, he formally quitted her service after all the years of loyalty, wrote a series of bitter songs against womankind, and permitted his affair and his break with her to become a matter of aristocratic gossip.

But for him the absence of love was an intolerable spiritual impoverishment. Soon he discovered another perfect lady; in her service he made another mighty tour, this time in the get-up of King Arthur; the new lady, too, eventually granted her love and was a source of increasing spiritual power. And then she, in turn— well, let us be brief about it: Ulrich continued this kind of thing for most of his long life. Even in his reflective years, looking back with perspective on all of it, he could write of his harelip, his torn-out forelock, his chopped-off finger, his transvestite mumming, his leper's rags, his tumble into the moat, all in a tone of self-admiration. For, to the end, he considered that love, the finest thing in his life, had made him a true Christian and a model knight.

3

The New Love in Theory and Practice

❀   ❀

❀

Admittedly, Ulrich's case is an extreme one; yet its very exaggerations serve to highlight the originality of the beliefs embodied in *l'amour courtois*. Whether many other real persons acted out these beliefs in as extreme a form as Ulrich is doubtful, but it is perfectly certain that nobles of France, Germany, Italy, and other countries spoke and wrote eloquently of them, and listened raptly to countless poems and romances based upon them. Many stalwart French fighting men, long accustomed to take what they wanted by warfare and to consider women little better than serfs, were beginning to think that a man should act reverent, stupefied, and suppliant before the all-perfect lady of his heart. Hundreds of songs written by these lords and sung by their hired *jongleurs* (or *Singerlein* in Germany) echoed the theme sounded by Bernard de Ventadour, one of the most notable twelfth-century troubadours:

> *I stand in my lady's sight*
> *In deep devotion;*
> *Approach her with folded hands*
> *In sweet emotion;*
> *Dumbly adoring her,*
> *Humbly imploring her.*

In the resounding vaulted chambers of hundreds of baronial castles, ladies and gentlemen were beginning to enjoy the reading aloud or reciting of long verse romances after dinner, telling the legends of King Arthur, of Charlemagne, and of Greece and Rome. The actions of the knights in these romances, though fanciful, are indicative of what twelfth-century lords and ladies were interested in. They bore somewhat the same relationship to history as do our modern historical novels; one can learn more about the 1940's from *Forever Amber* than about the eighteenth century, and more about the twelfth century from Arthurian romance than about King Arthur.

When, in medieval romances, the Count de Nevers faints dead away at the mere sound of his lady's name or Parsifal falls into a love swoon of several months' duration, we need not suppose such things really happened to knights under the influence of courtly love; what does intrigue us is that such representations of knightly conduct seemed neither objectionable nor laughable to the real lords who loved real ladies. Whether fiction followed life, or life patterned itself upon fiction, sometimes they were fairly close to each other. The troubadour Peire Vidal was being autobiographical when he wrote of the extremity to which love had driven him: in his misery he had dressed himself in a wolf's skin and lived for some time in the woods like a beast.

Less bizarre, yet perhaps just as significant, was the change in manners coming first over the medieval noblemen of France and then those of adjacent nations. Rather suddenly—in a mere handful of years—these fierce semi-primitive chieftains had begun to culti-vate the arts of singing, dancing, and composing, in order to please the ladies of their courts. They put on finer clothing, started to use handkerchiefs, and began to bathe more often; they practiced gen-teel discourse and sophisticated argumentation; and they took love vows in secret (though the secrets were discreetly told) and squan-dered both money and health on endless jousts and harrowing pilgrimages designed to gain merit in their ladies' eyes. By dint of such continued "service," plus unswerving fidelity and thorough self-abasement, they traveled the long course of love, rising slowly from the initial stage of the mere aspirant to love (*fegnedor*) to that of the suppliant (*precador*), the recognized suitor (*entende-dor*) and finally the accepted lover (*drut*).

Yet even in the final stage the behavior of the lover and his lady was, by most standards, curious, if not altogether improbable. For they were very likely to indulge repeatedly in protracted sessions of sex play, unclothed and in bed, without yielding to the imperious drive toward completion. This seems a trying undertaking for mature men and women, and at first one may wonder if he has misread or misunderstood the evidence; but the many testimonials that remain as to the existence of the practice of *amor purus*, or "pure love," make it very clear that adult, healthy, normally sexed

lords and ladies frequently, and perhaps most of the time, managed
to limit themselves to this kind of dalliance in their courtly love
affairs—and considered it a finer form of love than the completed
act. "He knows little or nothing of the service of women who
wishes to possess his lady entirely," wrote the troubadour Daude de
Pradas, and scores of rhapsodists of *l'amour courtois* scorned the
culmination of the sex act as "false love" while extolling as "true
love" the "pure" kissing, touching, fondling, and naked contact of
the lovers.

Some students of the subject have doubted that such conduct
could be, and have assumed that the relationships of the troubadours and their ladies were generally completely adulterous. Even
on literary grounds, one might disagree with them; there is an almost endless amount of praise of looking upon the body of the beloved, or holding her, or touching her, but there is practically never
any expression, even implicitly, of the ideas of satisfaction, climax,
or weary peacefulness. On the basis of circumstantial evidence, too,
one might doubt that the relationship was fully consummated most
of the time; although bastardy was quite common in the Middle
Ages (nine per cent of the villeins of a typical English manor in
the time of Edward III were known bastards), references to
children born of courtly love affairs are practically nonexistent
both in romance and in historical writing. But above all we can believe that this curious sexual pattern did exist, for it, at least, was
one part of courtly love that was not quite new; it had had a
precursor in the form of the spiritual marriage experiments of the
early Christian centuries and the agapetae cults of the heretical
sects. Those mutations of sexual behavior were the result of the
violent separation of love from sex in the teachings of the early
Church. When the lusty Frankish barbarians overran the Empire,
they resisted the ascetic influence for centuries, but it was perhaps
inevitable that in time they should yield to it too. Out of the same
teachings, therefore, a sexually inhibited form of love again appeared in the eleventh century, this time richly surrounded by sentiments and observances which coalesced into a coherent new relationship.[3]

[3] Many scholars, however, have assumed that courtly love almost always
involved sexual consummation; see, for
instance, Robert Briffault: *The Mothers,* Vol. III, pp. 474–5. But the bulk of
medieval writing on the matter says

And it *was* a new thing in Western history. The relationship of the agapetae and their spiritual brothers had been innocent of the theory that moral and ethical improvement was the major purpose of being in love. Among the troubadours, however, ceaseless desire, unending yearning, and unsatisfied passion were thought to illuminate and elevate the character. "No man is of value without love," said our dumbly adoring, humbly imploring troubadour, Bernard de Ventadour, and many a man who could ride all day without fatigue, fight in armor for hours, or spend two years in going to Jerusalem for his soul's good, was able in all seriousness to kneel before his lady and thank her for having made him a better knight and Christian by causing him suffering and rarely fulfilled desire. One could overstress the role of *amor purus;* even those who believed in it and preached it sometimes admitted that lovers might easily lapse into "false love" unless they consciously thought of the higher values. But whatever the extent of such lapses, pure love was the ideal many professed to believe in, and which they were impelled to follow as best they could.

Such emotions and practices could thrive only on separation and denial; they were wholly inappropriate for, and unsuited to, the intimacies and necessities of married life. And since lust and love could not be combined in the same person, marriage inherited only lust, and was totally denied the possibility of love. Not surprisingly, therefore, the high arbiter of courtly love—Marie, the Countess of Champagne—issued the following proclamation to all interested persons in the year 1174:

> We declare and we hold as firmly established that love cannot exert its powers between two people who are married to each other. For lovers give each other everything freely, under no compulsion of necessity, but married people are in duty bound

otherwise, and so important a source as the *Tractatus de Amore* of Andreas Capellanus (see below, pp. 156–61) refers to "mixed love" (consummated love) as a dangerous practice into which some slip, but which most of the judicious carefully avoid. G. R. Taylor has summarized evidence against consummation in *Sex in History*, pp. 87–93. Even Father Alexander J. Denomy, a Jesuit scholar who has analyzed troubadour love as a grossly sensual heresy, concluded from painstaking study that "it was a love that yearned for, and at times was rewarded by, the solace of every delight of the beloved except physical possession of her by intercourse . . . [namely] the delights of kissing and embracing, the sight of the beloved's nudity and the touching and lying beside her nude body." ("Fin' Amors," *Mediæval Studies*, Vol. VII (1945), p. 139f).

to give in to each other's desires and deny themselves to each other in nothing.[4]

All in all, courtly love, as it appeared during the first century or so of its existence, was a human relationship with only the faintest of precedents in Western culture. Plato, Ovid, and Saint Augustine, though they might have recognized traces of the loves they knew, would all have been astonished and even mystified by it. Only in Greece had love been even vaguely allied to the ennoblement of character—but there the relationship was a special type of latent or overt homosexuality. Only in Rome had secrecy and adultery been so systematically studied and practiced—but there it was purely for sensuous pleasure, without the faintest coloring of real "service" or praise of purity. Only among the early Christians had the emphasis on sexual restraint and pure love appeared—but there it was without any admixture of the adoration of woman, the abasement of man before her, or the theory that in suffering, desire, and doled-out dalliance there was Christian virtue. *L'amour courtois* borrowed and blended components from the past, yet was something distinctly new in the history of love.

[4] Quoted by Andreas in *Tractatus de Amore*, Bk. One, Ch. vi, Seventh Dialogue.

4

A New Plant Grows in an Odd Soil

❀   ❀

❀

In many ways, it would seem as though there could have been no less propitious time and place for romantic love to appear than France of the late eleventh century. When Charlemagne's brief monarchy had disintegrated, Western Europe had been plunged into two centuries of semi-barbarian warfare; out of this chaos the feudal hierarchy had only begun to emerge. Despite vows of fealty and vassalage, petty nobles were still constantly warring upon one another without pretext other than the bald hope of gain. Though powerful rulers began to limit the right of private baronial warfare, fighting and hunting remained the basic interests of the noblemen. They accepted tourneys in place of actual combat, but even these long continued to be bloody and ferocious affairs. Such men would hardly seem to have been candidates for gentle emotions and silent suffering.

Noblemen and ladies alike still used their fingers at the table (the fork being unknown), and they customarily wiped their knives on the bread and their hands on the tablecloth. For lack of dinner dishes, they ate their meat on trenchers (large thick slabs of bread), which they flung under the table afterwards, together with the leftovers, to quarreling dogs. The bones and dog dung remained there undisturbed; even in the fourteenth century an Italian artist, describing the making of fine plaster for frescoes, advised his readers to begin by collecting the oldest and driest chicken bones lying about the floor. Castles were being built in somewhat lighter and grander style than in the Dark Ages, but carpets were nearly unknown and the rushes sometimes strewn over the floor in the homes of minor lordlings were changed only when, after collecting spittle, vomit, and the urine of dogs for a number of months, they began to smell intolerable.

The Franks had always regarded woman as a useful piece of property, and protected her accordingly; in the ninth century, the penalty called for by the *Leges Alamannorum* for killing a free, mature woman was the payment of six hundred *solidi* to her master, while if she were a young unskilled girl the price was only two hundred *solidi*. Such an evaluation of woman was clearly far removed from the spirit of chivalry. Similarly, clerical writers of the canon law had long given husbands express permission to beat their wives, and civil law often followed suit. A notable thirteenth-century statute of the town of Villefranche in Gascony granted every man the right to beat his wife, "provided death does not ensue." A woman's word could not be admitted in court because of her "frailty," she could not represent herself in any legal action, and her husband assumed full authority over the property she owned at the time of marriage. Divorce was, until later centuries, simple enough for a husband discontented with her personality or the yield of her lands; whatever his real reasons for wanting to be rid of her, he had only to "discover" that he and she had a single great-great-grandparent in common (a relationship known in canon law as "consanguinity in the fourth degree") in order to cast her off with Church approval and marry more profitably elsewhere.

Despite the gradual influence of Christianity, the early Middle Ages were an unthinkably crude era—not as licentious as Ovidian Rome, but infinitely more vulgar. Noblemen considered that they had a natural right to ravish any peasant woman they happened to meet in a lonely spot, and did so without compunction or hindrance. Prostitution was so candidly accepted that many European towns and cities legalized it under municipal supervision. The *jus primae noctis* theoretically entitled the lord of a manor to deflower the bride of a vassal, and scattered but reliable reports indicate that this custom was actually practiced in several European countries, even in the period when chivalry was becoming the guiding philosophy of the aristocracy. For the chivalrous could also be thoroughly boorish: on the first crusade of the pure-souled King Louis IX (who later became Saint Louis), the King's barons openly set up brothels around his royal tent. So could the pious: in 1311 even the Vatican, according to Durand, Bishop of Mende, permitted brothels to operate near by for a consideration. Possibly the ultimate in blasphemous lewdness is an incident referred to by the knight, Geoffrey de La Tour Landry, who claimed to know of people fornicating within the very walls of a church.

Teutonic primitivism in sexual matters was made still harsher by the teachings of ascetic clerics. Traditionally the clergy were woman-haters, and as the Church slowly succeeded in enforcing priestly celibacy, their misogyny became ever more virulent. Preachers systematically thundered at woman from the pulpit, a typical medieval sermon containing endless fulminations of this type:

> In the woman wantonly adorned to capture souls, the garland upon her head is as a single coal or firebrand of Hell to kindle men with that fire. . . . In a single day, by her dancing or her perambulation through the town, she inflames with the fire of her lust perhaps twenty of those who behold her, damning the souls God has created and redeemed at such a cost.[5]

The Church considered marriage a precious sacrament and stoutly defended it, but by the Middle Ages, Jerome's statement that "he who too ardently loves his own wife is an adulterer" had become the general ecclesiastical opinion. Confessors' manuals and penitentials ordered that marital sexual connection be performed only in one position, and not at all during penance, or on Sundays, Wednesdays, and Fridays, or during a number of holiday seasons; indeed, all sexual intercourse within marriage, except when specifically undertaken in order to beget a child, was considered by confessors a venial offense.

Yet it was out of this unlikely compost of feudal barbarism, male domination, and religious asceticism that courtly love suddenly burst into flower. Scholars have long wondered why and unearthed many answers, most of them not individually very satisfying. Some, for instance, have stressed the role of socio-economic factors. They point out that the increasing leisure and wealth of the nobility gave them time to develop love as an amusement; more particularly, the marriage system and the suppression of private war made for a large number of propertyless younger sons who had a great deal of time to idle away at the courts of powerful nobles, and who were inevitably attracted to the women they themselves had been unable

[5] From a sermon by a fourteenth-century English preacher named John Bromyard, quoted in G. R. Owst: *Literature and Pulpit in Medieval England*, p. 392f.

to win in marriage. Yet by itself this explanation is clearly insufficient; though economic conditions might have allowed time and place for adulterous amusement, why should it have been endowed with such ethical and philosophic value—and why should it have put such emphasis on incompletion and technical chastity?

The worship of Mary has often been suggested as an answer. Though churchmen regarded woman as the primal temptress, theologians were beginning to title Mary "Mother of God" in the fourth century, and thereafter slowly but inevitably deified her. By the eleventh century, Mariolatry was creating an ideal image— sacred Mary, as opposed to profane Eve—that may have prepared men for a new feeling about women. Troubadours, indeed, often addressed their ladies as "Madonna," and even Saint Bernard de Clairvaux, the great monastic reformer and a bitter foe of courtly love, made God Himself sound like a mooning knight-errant. In a sermon on the Annunciation, Bernard portrayed God asking Mary if she wanted to have a child by the Holy Ghost. "He, the King and Lord of all things," said Bernard, "waits for the word of your consent, by means of which He has proposed to save the world, inasmuch as He has approved of your graces. He whom in silence you have pleased, you will please still more by speech, since He cries to you from heaven: O fairest among women, let me hear thy voice. If then thou doest this, He will cause thee to see our salvation." Yet for all the similarities between Mary-worship and troubadour love, the former reached its high point some time *after* the appearance of troubadour love, and it is hard to know which influenced which the more; one might suspect that both stemmed from, and were twin effects of, some still more fundamental causes.

Others have explained courtly love as a heresy in disguise. In the very area of southwestern France where troubadour love began, a type of deviant Christianity became popular during the eleventh century, its principal body of adherents being known to history as the Albigenses. The Albigenses were dualists who thought the world of the flesh was evil, and ruled by Satan, while God ruled only the world of the spirit, which was good. Logically enough, they placed great value on abstaining from procreation, which would only make more creatures for the Devil's domain. Many of them therefore gave up sex relations with their wives; they thus plainly resembled the Manicheans and those other early heretical

Christians who had practiced spiritual marriage and praised the chaste love of the agapetae. Certain scholars therefore say that courtly love, with its idealization of chaste love and its disinterest in procreation, was only a poetic disguise for the Manichean heresy.

But the Manichean attitudes toward sex, love, and celibacy were really very close to those held by the Catholic Church itself at various times. Furthermore, courtly love was just as appealing to the orthodox as it was to the heretical; the French armies which made a bloody crusade into Provence at the behest of Pope Innocent III were led by knights of unshakable loyalty to Rome—but they too had been captivated by courtly love, and saw nothing heretical in it. Throughout Europe, in fact, courtly love rapidly caught on among the unimpeachably orthodox without subverting their religion.

Evidently, there were still deeper forces at work. And in fact they had been implicit in early Christianity, which established the diametrical opposition between sexuality and love. For it is true in all monogamous family life that children must repress the sexual impulses they feel toward the parents they love; but it was early Christianity that made a philosophy of the situation and turned it into a life-long problem, rather than a problem of childhood alone.

It was, in sum, an institutionalized incest-fear, setting up nearly impassable barriers between sexual desire and the emotions of love, which made simultaneously for the ill-concealed voluptuousness of Mary-worship and the partial impotence of *amor purus*, and which led men to treat women as chattel and sexual beasts of burden and at the same time regard them as goddesses and sovereign rulers. But powerful as the incest-fear was, it successfully produced the pattern of courtly love only when many other forces coincided and contributed their shaping and enriching influences. Courtly love *did* catch on first by no mere coincidence in a heretic-dominated area of France with a tradition of chaste love, and appropriately enough offered the orthodox a genteel way to defy the misogynist clergy. It undoubtedly drew upon the growing cult of Mary-worship, borrowing its moods, its mystical transports, and its emphasis on humble supplication. It spread and throve wherever feudal order had emerged from barbarian chaos, for feudalism provided both leisure and wealth enough to permit the new game and make it welcome; moreover, it ideally met the need of that society to find duties which would refine and tame men's manners. Finally, it also met the unsatisfied need of individuals for affection—the result of a marriage system which took no account of love.

All in all, despite the barbaric past, the residuum of primitivism, and the ascetic tradition of Christianity, it would seem that the unpromising ground had actually been fertile; it had needed only someone to plant the seed.

5

The Founders and Exponents

❀   ❀

❀

Guilhem was his name: William IX, Duke of Aquitaine and Count of Poitou, born in 1071, and first of the troubadours. When one puts aside all speculations about the origins of courtly love, there remains the concrete fact that the first of the new-style love lyrics, and manners to match, were the creation of William, and seemingly from that single point of origin set a fashion which swept through Provence where he maintained his court, and went on later to conquer Europe. Lyricist or no, this was no mincing rhymester; William was a powerful ruler, and a full-blooded, fierce, independent warrior. He became the feudal overlord of nearly a third of France when he was scarcely more than a boy, and ran it well enough. He went along on the First Crusade and played an active part in its trials and fierce battles. At home he defied and flaunted mighty churchmen in matters political and social, protected the Albigenses in his domain, was excommunicated for his unyielding spirit, and long refused to yield to the Church.

One day he happened to meet the Bishop of Poitiers and demanded absolution, threatening otherwise to kill him; the Bishop offered his neck and told him to strike, but William, intractable as ever, changed his mind. "No," he said irritably, "I do not love you well enough to send you straight to Paradise."

Despite his arrogance and belligerence, he was in many ways the model for all future courtly lovers. According to an old Provençal chronicle: "The Count of Poitou was one of the most courteous men in the world, and a great deceiver of ladies; and he was a brave knight and had much to do with love affairs; and he knew well how to sing and make verses." So there it is: abruptly and without evident preparation, courtly love had begun. From William, the fashion of flattering and celebrating one's ladylove in delicate verse spread rapidly throughout the castles and courts of southern France. Probably thousands of knights followed suit, for despite the fragmentary remains of medieval literature, we know the names of four hundred and sixty troubadours and possess twenty-five hundred of their poems. Many were minor nobles, but there were even several kings among them, of whom Richard Coeur de Lion, great-grandson of William IX, was the best-known.

Though William was said to be "a great deceiver of the ladies," he paid lip service to fidelity and spirituality, and courtly lovers after him seized upon and emphasized these aspects of the new manners. Many of the troubadours dwelt at length on the sensuous aspects of *amor purus*, but others exaggerated the ascetic element in the relationship until love assumed an extremely rarefied form. Within a few years, the troubadour Gaucelm Faidit could tell his lady: "Nor kiss I ask, nor sweet embraces, lest I were blaspheming," and Sordello, an Italian who lived and wrote as a Provençal, could set down this extraordinary love sentiment:

> *Thus, lady, I commend to thee*
> *My fate and life, thy faithful squire;*
> *I'd rather die in misery*
> *Than have thee stoop to my desire.*

But whether the lady was totally untouchable, or whether she could be touched within specified bounds, courtly love as practiced by the troubadours remained a matter of devotion to an almost inanimate object; the lady was an inert, icon-like figure, and one cannot find in Provençal writing anything about what she said, felt, or did. She simply was loved. When the new idea spread to northern France, however, it became allied to chivalry—the social and military philosophy of feudal knighthood—and the knight lover, instead of limiting his adoration to self-humbling verses, began also to perform deeds and services called for by his lady. She thus ceased to be a graven image for worship and started to enter into the process; she became an actual participant in an interaction of personalities. Courtly love acquired elements of mutuality and reciprocity, and very likely this was one major reason for the mysterious appeal it so clearly exerted from then on.

In 1122, when middle-aged William's ideas were already flourishing among the Provençal nobility, his granddaughter Eleanor was born. It was her fortune to become one of the most famous and powerful of medieval women and, among many other accomplishments, bring courtly love from Provence to the royal courts of both France and England and help it grow from a literary fad into a seriously practiced way of life. Oddly enough, although Eleanor was ideally fitted for this task, she did the chief work of propagandizing for courtly love when she was a disillusioned middle-aged woman and the mother of ten royal children. Perhaps a love that could, in many cases, remain chaste and purely verbal was well suited to her circumstances.

When Eleanor was fifteen and already thoroughly imbued with troubadour ideas, her father, the son of William IX, died; the young girl thereupon became Countess of Poitou and Duchess of Aquitaine, and thus the major marriage prize in Western Europe. Her feudal overlord, Louis the Fat, King of France, instantly dispatched southwards his son and heir apparent, a seventeen-year-old youth named Louis Capet, to wed her. Eleanor had nothing to say about this, since it was King Louis's undeniable legal right to dispose of her in marriage; in any case, she understood perfectly that marriage was an instrument of political policy, and that love was no consideration.

Two weeks after the marriage, Louis the Fat died, and the teen-aged girl found herself the Queen of France. It was the beginning of a long, turbulent, and unique life. She struggled to bring some of the poetry and charm of her ancestral home into the drab royal court at Paris, but her husband was a sober, religious youth who was uninterested in these matters and pious beyond all expectation; Eleanor later remarked that she had married a king only to find him a monk. When Louis decided to go on the Second Crusade in

1147, the bored young Queen accompanied him on the long terrible expedition in order to see new sights and escape the tedious routines of Paris. She saw more than he expected her to. In Byzantium, where they remained for a while, she was overcome by admiration for the sensuous, indulgent way of life the Eastern Christians practiced, and chroniclers alleged later that during the crusade she began the first of many amours. Some even said, improbable as it seems, that she made love to the great Saladin, archenemy of all Christians. But a rather more likely story holds that she fell in love with her uncle, Raymond, Prince of Antioch, at whose Syrian court the French royal party rested and recouped its forces after a military disaster in Asia Minor. King Louis, belatedly realizing this, suddenly seized his own wife prisoner and spirited her hastily out of the city under guard. After prolonged adventures and misadventures they came back to Paris, but by 1152 Louis was ready to let her go her own way, for in fifteen years of marriage she had provided him with only two daughters and no sons. They were divorced on the excuse of consanguinity, under an agreement which returned to Eleanor her lands and titles and made her Louis's loyal vassal instead of his disloyal wife.

So thin was that loyalty, however, that within two months she married young Henry Plantagenet, Duke of Normandy, eleven years her junior, and Louis's most dangerous political rival in northern France. Faced by this threatening alignment of Normandy and Aquitaine, Louis promptly invaded Normandy, only to be beaten back by Henry and his men. This safely accomplished, Henry left Eleanor in charge at his castle at Angers, in Anjou, while he went to England to press his own claims to that throne.

Eleanor, now relatively free to lead that kind of life she had long dreamed of, gathered knights, ladies, and poets around her and began to create an elegant court. Among the poets who soon paid homage to the thirty-year-old Duchess was Bernard de Ventadour himself, imported by Eleanor from his Provençal homeland. "She had understanding in matters of valor and honor," says an old chronicler, "and cared for a song of praise; and the songs of Bernard pleased her; she received and welcomed him cordially. He was a long time in her court and he fell in love with her and she with him." One cannot judge how intimate or complete the relationship between the poet and the beautiful young Duchess became, but Henry, probably hearing about it, soon summoned her away to

London, and she left Bernard behind—very likely at Henry's order. He had been putting his time and energies to good use, meanwhile, for in 1154, on the death of King Stephen, he became Henry II, King of England. Eleanor thus became a queen, at the age of thirty-two, for the second time in her life. Again she introduced her new fashions and ideas into a royal court, and apparently had considerable success; so one may conclude from the fact that within five years of her coronation, John of Salisbury, a scholastic philosopher, devoted a whole book to the follies and extravagances of courtiers in London.

For the next fifteen years Eleanor led a busy life; the times were filled with complex power-struggles among Henry of England, Louis of France, their various insubordinate vassals, and the lords of the Church. Also filling her time was the almost nonstop production of Henry's children—eight in fifteen years. This output indicated no love between the King and Queen; their personal relations had long since progressed from a workable partnership toward unendurable mutual dislike, particularly when Henry built a retreat for his mistress, Rosamond Clifford, and openly flaunted his affair to the shame of the Queen. In 1169 or 1170 Henry sought to end their strife. He divided the succession to his lands among his sons, and allowed Eleanor to retire to her own county of Poitou, in control of her former French domains; their second son, Richard, who went with her, was guaranteed the eventual inheritance of both Aquitaine and Poitou.

At this time Eleanor was still under fifty. Despite her many *accouchements*, she was said to be still beautiful, and her death-effigy in the abbey at Fontevrault, near Le Mans, shows a woman of graceful figure, with a straight fine nose, an oval face, and a full ripe mouth. She had seen much of the world in high places, and possessed poise and learning unusual for her time. Mistress of her own affairs, she chose the recently enlarged castle at Poitiers as her official seat, and gathered around herself there a brilliant new court, thronged with poets, philosophers, and young knights and ladies who came to learn the ways of wit, courtesy, and graciousness. To this court, too, came her own daughter, Marie, the Countess of Champagne (the child of Eleanor's first marriage to Louis of France), to be in effect *maitresse d'école* to the court and the principal tutor of the new manners and morals. Music and games, chivalry and knight-errantry, dialectic and love-making, table manners and courtesy, literature and philosophy, were all part of the way of life demonstrated by Eleanor and Marie to a culture-thirsty retinue of young lords and ladies who came here from northern France, England, and even from the farthest of Eleanor's own southern domains.

Among the methods Eleanor and Marie employed to teach the concepts of courtly love was a formal piece of play-acting known as the "Court of Love." In mock-legal proceedings, an anonymous lover or his lady—speaking through representatives—could present a complaint or defense in a disputed question of love behavior. Hearing the case and handing down the decision might be a single judge—a great lady such as Eleanor herself—or an entire panel of noble ladies acting as a jury. This idea may have come from Provence and Gascogny where, a few years earlier, debates on the new manners were an exciting after-dinner amusement. But in the hands of Eleanor and Marie, such debates became more than after-dinner talk; they grew to be a semi-serious pedagogical device for perfecting the new relationships, codifying and clarifying them, and promulgating them among the nobility at Poitiers.

And it is even possible that the Court of Love at Poitiers had greater stature than this: it may have been a pseudo-legal hall of justice where pronouncements on love questions were seriously sought and honestly obeyed. But whether it really was this, or simply an artful way to examine a growing code of behavior, there is one significant fact about it: men and women met in the Court of Love on terms of mutual respect to explore the propriety, the ethics, and the aesthetics of their relationships to each other. This is the importance of the Court of Love, and a measure of the profound alteration beginning to take place, at the top level of European society, in the kind of feelings existing between the sexes.[6]

[6] Whether the Court of Love actually considered cases and exercised quasi-judicial powers is a question that has vexed generations of scholars. At first they accepted the medieval evidence at face value; later they rejected it completely and considered all Courts of Love a fictional device used by poets. Today there is a tenable middle ground held by such scholars as Amy Kelly, the most recent and thorough student of Eleanor's life and times. The above and succeeding sections generally follow the viewpoint expressed in chapter fifteen of her book, *Eleanor of Aquitaine and the Four Kings.*

6

Courtly Love in the Court of Love

❀   ❀

❀

There are scores of fictional and poetic representations of the Court of Love, but happily for the historian, one man who lived in Eleanor's castle at Poitiers observed the Court of Love in session there and later wrote a more-or-less reportorial account of what he had seen. He was a cleric named André; later he became the chaplain at Countess Marie's court at Troyes, and is known to history by the way he then signed his name and title: *Andreas Capellanus*, i.e., André the chaplain. At Marie's urging Andreas wrote a *Tractatus de Amore et de Amoris Remedio* (*Treatise on Love and Its Remedy*), the only straightforward exposition of the theory and practice of courtly love which exists from that period.[7] From the title and the overall structure, it is clear that Andreas thought of himself as the twelfth-century equivalent of Ovid, whose mantle he expected the book to drape around his shoulders. If it seems strange that a clergyman should undertake so secular a work, that only indicates the astonishing ambivalence inherent in medieval man and the ability of the orthodox to hold seemingly heretical beliefs; a medieval chaplain of the Church of Rome could believe both in the Church and in profane love without too great a sense of strain.

To judge from his side remarks in the *Tractatus*, Andreas was a vain, shallow, and yet likable man. His learning is inconsiderable, his quotations from classic writers are often secondhand and inaccurate, and his arguments have none of the wit of his master, Ovid. But there is something disarming about his simple egotism when he

[7] This is one of several medieval titles for the work, which is also sometimes called in English *The Art of Courtly Love*.

calls himself "Andreas the Lover," and says without false modesty: "We consider ourselves very expert in the art of love." This he excuses in himself by pointing out that, though the clergy should refrain from sin, hardly any are actually able to do so. In fact, he spends quite some time trying to prove that clerics are better lovers than knights because they are more prudent and have better judgment. Nevertheless, Andreas admits that no clergyman can win high Church honors if it is known that he indulges in love, so, after spending most of his space explaining and extolling it, he hastily adds a brief and unconvincing retraction of the whole thing. The gist of it is that to win greater recompense from God for refraining from love, one must first know all about it. Andreas was no fool: later manuscript copies of his book call him "chaplain of the royal court," from which it would appear that his retraction cleared the way for his advancement from Troyes to Paris.[8]

For all the limitations of Andreas's character, his *Tractatus* has been called by Robert Bossuat, a French scholar, one of those rare works which "explain the secret of a civilization." The greater part of it consists of specimen dialogues between lords and ladies of differing rank, showing the arguments they might be expected to use with each other in requesting love on the one hand, and specifying the service that will earn it on the other hand. But the actual forms of argument and speechmaking are much less interesting than the insight we get into the emotional content and the actual practices of courtly love. For this, like Ovid's book, is no fictional dream or poetic exaggeration, but a guidebook; this is a manual of sound advice on how people should, and did, practice courtly love.

And it is all here, in somewhat more down-to-earth form than we find it in the poets, but here nevertheless. The unswerving loyalty of a lover to his beloved; the emphasis on pleasing habits, courteous conduct, and personal attractiveness; the subservience, in the courtship stages, of the man to the woman; the gentleness and considerateness required in actual love-making; the spiritual benefits of being in love; the techniques of *amor purus* and the dangers of "mixed love" (love that proceeds to consummation); and, behind the tedious talkiness of the arguments, some brief indications of mutuality and reciprocity in the entire process:—all this is documented, blueprinted, and reported from real life. We might

---

[8] It is also true that he was only further imitating Ovid, who placed after his *Ars Amatoria* a *Remedia*.

have supposed from the poems and romances that they existed, but now we know.

Andreas thought he was emulating Ovid, but the difference between them is extraordinary. The *Tractatus* is always dead serious; the *Ars Amatoria* was always amused. The Roman spoofed at the exaggerated effects of infatuation and urged men to simulate them in order to succeed at seduction. Andreas never dreams of spoofing; love is an earnest and virtuous exercise of the soul, and simulated passion is unthinkable, sincerity being a *sine qua non*. Andreas shows the woman not as the prey, but the predator, and man not the conqueror, but the conquered; as for the nature of the conquest, Ovid was candidly and plainly speaking of intercourse, the sooner achieved the better, while Andreas carefully and specifically urged his readers to control their lusts, and avoid the completion of the process. The change that has come about is enormous—and Andreas does not seem especially aware of it.

Nothing in Andreas's book makes such absorbing reading as the brief section on the Court of Love (Book II, Chapter VII). Andreas tells us that as many as sixty ladies formed the panel on one important case; in others, individual opinions were rendered by Queen Eleanor, Countess Marie, Countess Isabelle of Flanders, Countess Ermengarde of Narbonne, and so on. Most likely they convened in the large ceremonial hall that had recently been added to the castle at Poitiers. The ladies sat on a dais, while the courtiers assembled on the stone benches lining the walls. Advocates for the anonymous plaintiff and defendant would present their arguments, and the ladies would then ponder the case and pronounce judgment on it.

Andreas cites a total of twenty-one such cases, probably a sampling of those he had seen. The complex mores of courtly love are caught with astonishing sharpness in these little abstracts. Here, for instance, is one complete case just as Andreas records it:

> A certain knight loved his lady beyond all measure and enjoyed her full embrace, but she did not love him with equal ardor. He sought to leave her, but she, desiring to retain him in his former status, opposed his wish. In this affair the Countess gave this response: "It is considered very unseemly for a woman to seek to be loved and yet to refuse to love. It is silly for anybody disrespectfully to ask of others what she herself wholly refuses to give to others."

The knight's vows of fidelity, in other words, would not permit him to desert his cold mistress without her permission, but the Countess Marie denied that the mistress had a right to such consideration because of the one-way nature of the affair. The wording of Marie's dictum is somewhat airy, yet it clearly means to say that love should not be an unequal relationship, but an interplay of mutual emotion; for the twelfth century, this was a daring and even a radical idea.

Some of the cases, to be sure, are seemingly so artificial that we cannot easily project ourselves into the situations or take them seriously. A knight presented this complaint in court: his lady had been vowed to another, but gave him the promise of her love if she ever lost her present lover; later on she married her lover, whereupon the knight demanded she make good her promise, since marriage cancelled her lover's status. Adele, Queen of France, heard the case; she ruled that since love cannot exist between husband and wife, the lady had indeed lost her love and hence must honor her vow to give her love to the plaintiff. It seems like an empty charade; one wonders what kind of love could be summoned up by edict in this fashion. And yet there is something interesting and fresh even here: this equality, this responsibility of each party to carry out the promises of love, is something drastically different from the domination-submission pattern of medieval marriage.

Another lord wanted to prove the constancy of his lady by asking her for permission to make love to another woman. A month later he returned and told her he had only been testing her, and had not actually been unfaithful to her. At that point she angrily rejected his love, out of pique and disbelief. He appealed to the Court, claiming no wrongdoing. Queen Eleanor herself made the following pronouncement:

> We know that it comes from the nature of love that those who are in love often falsely pretend that they desire new embraces, that they may the better test the faith and constancy of their co-lover. Therefore a woman sins against the nature of love itself if she keeps back her embraces from her lover on that account or forbids him her love, unless she has clear evidence that he has been unfaithful to her.

Such pranks and tests seem rather juvenile and game-like; yet games often provide the pattern by which one learns about, and prepares for, the real world. Is it possible, then, that behind the foolish details of this case there was a twelfth-century man who seriously sought loyalty and devotion in a love relationship, but tried to make certain of it by a childish means?

And even with its background of secrecy and adultery, the growing code of courtly love was developing values that would seem fully applicable to legitimate relationships. In one case a knight who was totally lacking in chivalric virtues asked a lady's love, and she granted him the hope of it if he became a worthy knight. This apparently stiffened his spine, improved his manners, and added to his general manliness, with the result, as Andreas noted, that "by her teaching she developed in this lover so good a character that she gave him a kiss and an embrace and through her he was brought to the highest excellence of conduct." At this point, unhappily, he became enamoured of another and perhaps less demanding lady, and abandoned the first. She complained to the Court, asking the return of her rightful property. The Countess of Flanders ruled that the first lady had a right to reclaim her lover, since "she has a just and reasonable claim upon a man whom she, by working with him, had made worthy, after he had been worthless." Andreas wrote nothing more about this case, but is it not evident that the courtiers and the ladies of the Court of Love were trying to define loyalty and responsibility? Is it not possible that beneath the artificiality of the mock judgment there is a plea for love that is not mere amusement, love that endures despite disappointments and errors, love that achieves value by considering the loved one's desires as well as one's own?

Finally, Andreas codified the thirty-one basic rules of courtly love, which were the foundation of "law" upon which the cases had been tried, and upon which all other rules, forms, and manners must be based. Some of them reflect simply the conflict of adultery with the marriage system:

> When made public, love rarely endures.
> The easy attainment of love makes it of little value; difficulty of attainment makes it prized.

Others seem merely like the vacuous play-acting of idle nitwits:

> He who is not jealous cannot love.
> Every lover regularly turns pale in the presence of his beloved.
> A slight presumption causes a lover to suspect his beloved.

But certain others have a quaint, if unsophisticated, sound of seriousness, and a hint that conscience is entering into love relationships:

> That which a lover takes against the will of his beloved has no relish.
> A true lover does not desire to embrace in love anyone except his beloved.
> A true lover considers nothing good except what he thinks will please his beloved.

No doubt many of the important lords of the twelfth century were too busy to spend their time in castle halls playing at love, and too proud to reshape their ideas of right and wrong to this tamed and civilized pattern. No doubt the admiring young noblemen, the subsidized and hired troubadours and trouvères—and Andreas too —were acting in earnest only in part, and in part pretending to emotions they did not altogether feel. No doubt, finally, the ladies of the court were in part dreaming aloud of a vague ideal not genuinely possible in their own time. But in part, says Amy Kelly, they were doing more—they were attempting to "rationalize a conduct that [had] outburst the rigid feudal scheme for women." The *Tractatus* was not just a guidebook to a complex amusement; it was the manifesto of an emotional revolution.

7

The Spread of the New Doctrine

❀   ❀

❀

The gay civilized life at Poitiers lasted only four years and then came to a sudden halt. Eleanor, ever a meddler in politics, had been intriguing with powerful French lords on behalf of her sons, Richard and Geoffrey; this posed a threat to Henry II, her estranged husband, who thereupon crossed the channel and swept down upon Poitiers in the spring of 1174. He routed her court and captured Eleanor herself on the road, fleeing in man's disguise, but failed to catch his own sons, who escaped and sought asylum with the King of France. Eleanor was hauled off to England and imprisoned in various castles for fifteen years until Henry's death. Even then the dauntless woman was not done. She acted as regent of England while the King, her son, Richard Coeur de Lion, was off crusading; she went to Austria to ransom him after his capture; and she remained endlessly busied by the continuing struggle between the Plantagenets and the Capets. Not until 1204, at the age of 83, did she finally give over; since then she has lain in the abbey at Fontevrault alngside Henry, the husband who used her, shamed her, imprisoned her, and who broke up the one perfectly happy period of her life.

Meanwhile, courtly love was not snuffed out with Eleanor's imprisonment. When the court at Poitiers was broken up, Marie of Champagne, Eleanor's daughter, returned to her own court at Troyes, county seat of Champagne, and there re-established just such a circle and such practices as Eleanor had sponsored. And she did much more—she patronized writers who would explain the system of courtly love and spread it to the rest of the civilized Western world. One of her writers was Andreas, and it was at her court, and at her request, that he wrote the *Tractatus*. And here Marie also caused the code of courtly love to be embodied in a work of romance that had immense influence and became the very master pattern after which all future stories of knights in courtly vassalage to ladies were modeled. Although it is only a romantic fiction, its purpose is avowedly didactic, and it had as great an importance as the *Tractatus* in conveying instruction in the new form of love throughout Europe.

The author of the romance was the most important poet of medieval France, but almost nothing is known of him except his first name, Chrétien, to which he added the further identification "de Troyes" to show that he was Marie's resident versifier. His work, *Le Chevalier de la Charrette* (*The Knight of the Wagon*), was a story of Lancelot and Guinevere, and one of the first long romances in French to use the newly popular Arthurian legendary background. So great was its success that long romantic narratives rapidly became the reigning literary style, displacing troubadour lyrics and acting for centuries as the chief vehicles of ideals and sentiments among the ruling class.

Marie had not only directed Chrétien to write it, but quite specifically told him how to make it a demonstration of courtly love. Chrétien had to obey, though he seems not to have approved, for he tried to wash his hands of the results by saying in the prologue: "Matter and meaning of it the Countess gives and delivers unto him; and he undertakes to direct his thinking so that he may add nothing to it except his own effort and understanding." [9] And no wonder Chrétien was uncomfortable; he was attributing to a noble lord a host of actions that violated or conflicted with feudal masculine beliefs. Lancelot, for instance, starts out to rescue Guinevere, but loses his horse. Along comes a tumbril of a type used to carry common criminals, and the dwarf driving it offers Lancelot a ride. Though it was a dishonor to a mighty lord to ride in such a wagon, the power of love and lady's service conquers, and Lancelot climbs in. Later, after Lancelot has found Guinevere and is about to fight in a tournament for her, she secretly commands him to show his obedience by letting himself be unhorsed again and feigning cowardice and fear in combat; he does all this to her order. And though

[9] Chrétien was over-generous in so crediting her; Lancelot had already appeared in other writings which Chrétien probably had seen. But in none of them was he Guinevere's illicit lover; this innovation, plus some of the details of Lancelot's service, may have been Marie's contribution.

a knight's proper business might seem to be war, the increase of his land, the service of justice and the Church, and the like, Lancelot has little to do with such matters, except as they happen to fall in with his ceaseless efforts to please Guinevere.

For thousands of lines he and she undergo suffering and misery, perform noble deeds, enjoy trysts and meetings, concoct artful ruses to deceive the rest of society, and triumph over all mundane obstacles to their illicit love. It is the archetypal story of knightly service in the name of love. It is the fiction upon which men like Ulrich patterned their real lives. Similar ideas and actions, carried throughout Europe by the irresistible appeal of the Arthurian legends, would appear for centuries, elaborated, varied and reshaped in hundreds of different ways. They would be told and retold by historians and *Meistersinger* alike; they would preoccupy Chaucer and obsess Sir Thomas Malory; they would be allegorized by Edmund Spenser and ridiculed by Cervantes; they would be blended with the burning religiosity of the Grail legends and diluted by the endless dull details of sentimental romances. They would appear in forms as diverse and far-flung as as Dante's *Commedia*, Rousseau's *Nouvelle Héloïse*, and the operas of Richard Wagner. The seed sown by William IX, Duke of Aquitaine, and carried north by his granddaughter Eleanor, would indeed flourish.

The growth of courtly love between 1100 and 1400 is indicated by a remarkable production of romances, poems, and didactic works dealing with its ideas, but there are even better proofs of its influence scattered throughout the pages of history and the chronicles of men's lives. To begin with, various medieval historians recorded public celebrations in honor of love which would have been unimaginable before the days of Eleanor of Aquitaine. The Florentine historian Villani, for instance, gives us this glimpse of thirteenth-century upper-class life:

> In June of the year 1283, at the festival of St. John in Florence . . . a social union was formed, composed of a thousand people who, all clad in white, called themselves the Servants of Love. They arranged a succession of sports, merrymakings, and dances with ladies; nobles and bourgeois marched to the sound of trumpets and music in wild delight to and fro, and held festive banquets at midday and at night. This Court of Love lasted nearly two months, and it was the finest and most famous that had ever been held in Florence, or in all Tuscany.[1]

[1] K. Vossler: *Medieval Culture*, Vol. I, p. 323.

The last phrase reveals that the collective celebration of love in this elaborate fashion was not uncommon. As for mock-legal trials of love suits, they continued, and we find them recorded as late as 1389, when King Juan of Aragon and his wife held hearings before a Court of Love in Barcelona, using the *Tractatus* as a textbook.

But as early as 1159 the English scholastic, John of Salisbury, painted a picture in a work called *Polycraticus* of what to him was the newly degenerate society all around him. He complained that young knights were "sleeping until daylight," "postponing honorable duties to fornication," and becoming far too fond of "the cithern, the lyre, the tambourine and the note of the organ at the banquet." He regretted the passing of roughhewn warriors and scolded the new-style courtiers for showing no marks of duty on them; "bristling beard and hardened skin," he lamented, "are now in disrepute as being unmeet for works of wantonness."

Was this really widespread? Even if one makes liberal allowance for the fault-finding habitual with spiritual leaders, the details he gave are convincingly realistic. And he specifically added that this was not confined to petty lordlings, but that the infection had attacked even the mighty and the proud: "The singing of love songs in the presence of men of eminence was once considered in bad taste, but now it is considered praiseworthy for men of greater eminence to sing and play love songs which they themselves with greater propriety call *stulticinia*, follies."

So it was no limited fad, but a spreading habit; moreover it was no mere affectation of new manners, but a major motivation in life and a force shaping character. In 1409 a biographer of the heroic fighter and statesman, Jean le Meingre, le Maréchal Bouciquaut, wrote his life story expressly to demonstrate that chivalry and courtly love were guiding lights of the Maréchal's entire life. Another chronicler, writing the life of Duke Louis of Bourbon, pithily summed up the two sources of the Duke's sterling character as follows: "He was a very amorous knight, first towards God and then towards all ladies and highborn girls." Jean Froissart, a leading chronicler of fourteenth-century chivalry, likewise recorded the acceptance of courtly love ideals by many of the historical figures of whom he wrote, and took for granted the beneficial effects on their character.

Even the literature that scorns, criticizes, or ridicules courtly love—and there is plenty of it—indicates by its very intensity the appeal and threat of the new ideas. Geoffrey de La Tour Landry, a fourteenth-century knight of Angers, wrote a curious book whose purpose, he said, was "to teach my daughters the conventions of love"; actually, it is a series of admonitions against straying from strict virtue, and so carefully did he point out the pitfalls and temptations of love talk, kissing, and the like, that it is perfectly clear courtly love had become a dominant fashion, and one that worried a conservative father.

Beyond being a danger to the chastity of girls, courtly love also looked subversive to many, since it tended to mock religion and the marriage system, and to loose the controls that both of them exerted on society. The ladies of the Court of Love at Poitiers, and Andreas Capellanus after them, had specifically discredited marriage and extolled adulterous love instead. Troubadours, in addressing their ladies as "Madonna," trod dangerously close to impropriety, and Aucassin, in the tale of Aucassin and Nicolette, bluntly said he would prefer hell with his beloved to heaven without her. Chrétien de Troyes, finally, had the temerity to portray Lancelot coming to Guinevere's room, spending some hours in bed with her in "agreeable and sweet sport," and then bowing and genuflecting at her door as he leaves, precisely as if before a shrine. The code of courtly love had become practically blasphemous, and churchmen were bound to fear and fight it. Saint Thomas tried to combat *amor purus* by specifying that to kiss or touch a woman with delight, even without completing the act of fornication, was to commit a mortal sin, and confessors' handbooks listed specific questions designed to uncover the practices of courtly sex play. In 1277 the Bishop of Paris condemned the entire *Tractatus* of Andreas; in one century, the merry chaplain's codification of love had ceased to be a permissible piece of folly, and been reassessed as an instrument of heresy and social disorder.

The more conservative feudal noblemen likewise often disliked and resented the notions of *l'amour courtois*. When the Countess of Flanders returned to her own city of Arras after the court at Poitiers had been dispersed, she brought with her a taste for the fashions she had seen; one of her husband's vassals obligingly sighed and mooned, Poitiers-fashion, in her presence, but Count Philip, her husband, had no stomach for it and ordered the fellow to be beaten half-dead and then suspended head downward in a sewer. King Henry II may even have seized Eleanor and dissolved the court of Poitiers partly because of what he sensed to be pernicious and dangerous doctrines coming out of that gay gathering.

Malicious satirical writings mocking courtly love were subsidized and enjoyed by high-ranking noblemen, and gained in popularity along with courtly romance itself. About the year 1237, for instance, the poet Guillaume de Lorris began a work called *Le Roman de la Rose;* it was intended as an extravagant tribute to courtly love, but Guillaume died and left only 4,266 lines finished. Forty years later the poet Jean de Meung completed it by adding another 18,000 lines—but these were filled with cynicism, ribaldry, and satire. The poem ends with the victory of the God of Love, but this is mere pretense; Jean was transparently contemptuous of women and romance, and what had started out as a super-romantic poem ended by being alloyed with frivolity and cynicism. It could hardly have become the most famous single poem of the Middle Ages had there not been so great a desire for levity and reassuring cynicism about the whole subject of noble love.

For throughout medieval society, even as courtly love was making its greatest gains, the symptoms of the ancient ambivalence toward sex and love were becoming ever more distinct. The "quarrel of women"—the pro-and-con discussion of courtly love, and of the excellence or vileness of the female sex—was growing in volume and intensity from the eleventh century to the fourteenth, and would become still more violent in the Renaissance. While poets and knights were celebrating the beauty and the spotless purity of their ladies, there existed simultaneously a contrasting hunger for bawdiness and vulgarity. Pious volumes and books of spiritual edification were often decorated with crudely sexual, and even excremental, illustrations; even church decorations embodied these themes in the frankest way. (And why not? Even so revered a Father of the Church as Augustine, expressing his lowly opinion of the procreative process, had said forthrightly: "We are born between feces and urine.") In direct opposition to the refinement of the courtly romances and lyrics, there was an undiminished, and perhaps increased, market for vulgarity in literature; one might point, merely by way of example, to the ribald Goliardic poems of the wandering medieval scholars, and to the bawdy sexuality, somewhat later on, of Boccaccio's *Decameron* and such fabliaux as Chaucer's "Miller's Tale." More ominously, during the 1300's there began to appear a new and spreading interest in witchcraft, and a growing belief in the evil powers of women who had formed pacts with Satan—an explanation of womankind totally at odds with that of courtly love.

The dilemma of medieval love therefore offered two alternatives —courtly love, with its tantalizing and often incomplete sexual expression, or loveless fornication, with its ugliness and weight of sin. The more men tried to ally noble and ethical qualities to love, the wider grew that split, and the more outlandish grew their concept of love itself. One of the most extreme forms of adaptation to the ambivalent fear of love lay in the direction pointed out earlier by those Provençal poets who had fervently begged their ladies not to grant them sexual favors under any conditions. Not only did this bizarre attitude not die out after the crusade against the Albigenses, but it came to have great historical importance. In the thirteenth century, the Tuscan poets of Italy seized upon the theme and intensified it, finding in it a way to obey Saint Thomas, to emulate Plato, and yet to preserve something of the worship of sensuous beauty in woman that they found in troubadour poetry. They were living exemplars of the ambivalent human soul: they sought sexual outlet in marriage and in brothels, but adored ladies for years at a time without even letting them know about it, and were content to love without even desiring so much as a kiss, certain that they were the better for it.

The most famous and influential example of this is Dante's celebrated love for Beatrice. In the *Vita Nuova* he tells how he first saw her in the year 1274, when he was only nine years old, and immediately began to worship her with a pure and inspiring love. He never spoke one word to her, and scarcely hoped to; he made no efforts to meet her and saw her only at rare intervals. As for intimacies, even to think of them would have been totally impossible. Beatrice was perfect, goddess-like, and a source of spiritual guidance, rather than a flesh-and-blood female.

Actually, Dante had come to the point where he was no longer concerned with exploring the nature of human love; he was interested in divine love, as revealed through human experience. Beatrice was really only an instrument through which he felt uplifted and inspired to seek the divine heights; in the *Commedia*, it is therefore Beatrice's spirit that guides Dante to Paradise. This, in a general way, is the kind of evaluation literary scholars have given to Dante's love for Beatrice. To the psychologist or the historian of love, however, there is something else to be said. Dante did love Beatrice (he *says* so) though she neither knew of, enjoyed, nor was influenced by his distant worship. His writing on the subject of his love, whatever religious implications or value it had, was taken by his contemporaries and by subsequent generations down to the Victorian period to be a true picture of how man and woman should love each other.[2] It will not do to argue that Dante merely used Beatrice as a symbolic way to explore divine love: she was nearly all the love he was capable of feeling for actual woman. He had a wife and several mistresses, but in all his writing he said practically nothing about them; the impulse toward love was directed toward his remote ideal, and for the other women in his life there remained only the gratefulness he felt for their seeing to his sexual needs and his household requirements. His wife and mistresses might have had much to say about what it was like to share so sublime a lover with a hypothetical ideal; unfortunately for the history of love, they left us not a word.

[2] As late as 1884, Violet Paget ("Vernon Lee"), a British scholar and essayist, wrote that Dante had made sexual desire "burn clear towards heaven," and purified it of lust; this, she held, could even benefit marriage: "If the old lust-fattened evil of the world is to diminish rather than to increase, why then every love . . . should tend, to the utmost possibility, to resemble that love of the 'Vita Nuova.'" (*Euphorion*, Vol. II, p. 205)

8

The Outcome of Courtly Love

❀   ❀

❀

I t began as a game, but it ended as a way of life. Yet "ended" is not
the right word; it has never ended since the eleventh century,
for its influence has been paramount in Western love ever since—
minimized at some times, emphasized at others, absent from none.

But attitudes toward the influence of courtly love have ranged,
for eight centuries, from complete approval to total condemnation.
We will see, as we proceed, how various succeeding centuries continued and modified the romantic tradition, and how many a generation has considered that love was heightened and purified by the
troubadour influence, and particularly by the contribution of
Dante. A contrary view exists, however. The Swiss scholar, Denis
de Rougemont, maintains that courtly love was bad to begin with
and worse in its development; he holds that it has exerted a wholly
baleful influence by making Western man believe that to love means
to be mastered by emotion, overcome by it, powerless, unhappy,
and tragic because of it. "Why does Western Man wish to suffer
this passion which lacerates him and which all his common sense re-
jects?" he asks, and answers: because it represents a repressed
longing for death. He sees the kind of love immortalized in the lives
of Héloïse and Abélard and the legend of Tristan and Iseult as
having cast upon love a permanent blight—the desire for passion,
suffering, and death. Some psychiatrically oriented writers have
even seen in these same love stories clear allegories of the medieval
incest-fixation: when one loved where one lusted, the guilt feelings
that resulted could only produce a desire for the ultimate punish-

ment. Tristan had to die, for did he not both adore Iseult and possess her rapturously?

But we have already so often seen unexpected and incongruous values within any one variety of love that we might well look for them here too. Consider the elements that courtly love introduced for the first time into the emotional relationships between men and women. For one thing, it brought into them tenderness and gentleness, exaggerated and sometimes absurd in form, but important nevertheless. It operated within a framework of adultery, yet it stressed as never before the importance of the fidelity of one man and one woman, each to each. It expressed itself via the artificialities of love debates and Courts of Love, but introduced the revolutionary notions that love must be a genuinely mutual relationship, involving respect and admiration. Perhaps all this only proves the incestuous overtones of *l'amour courtois,* since all of it is copied from good parent-child relationships; whether so or not, love which incorporated these elements has proved to have an undying and unkillable appeal ever since, despite the great changes in manners, religion, and social structure. And since few courtly lovers desexualized their feelings as thoroughly as Dante, it was courtly love through which erotic or semi-erotic emotions began to be wedded to moral achievement. "Oh, what a wonderful thing is love," exulted Andreas, "which makes a man shine with so many virtues and teaches everyone, no matter who he is, so many good traits of character!"

Those who, like de Rougemont, claim that courtly love and the romantic ideal damaged marriage have ignored the fact that medieval marriage was no joining of personalities, no merging of desires; it was a master-and-servant, owner-and-property connection. Until woman's status was drastically altered in society, the marriage relationship would hardly become more emotionally satisfying. And it was courtly love, with all its shortcomings, absurdities, and neurotic components, that began to change the position of women. By the end of the fourteenth century, says the historian Sidney Painter, "woman had edged her way into the mind of feudal man and had elevated and enlarged her place in society as he recognized it. No longer was she merely a child-bearer and lust-satisfier—she was the inspirer of progress." In short, by still another of those paradoxes that occur so often in the history of love, the adulterous flirtation and illicit infatuations of the Middle Ages were the very instrument that began to enhance woman's status, and hence eventually to alter marriage. But before all that could happen, man would have to solve the major problem of love: he would have to decide whether woman was really a madonna of heaven, or a witch serving Satan, or possibly a bit of each.

Chapter VI
THE LADY AND THE WITCH

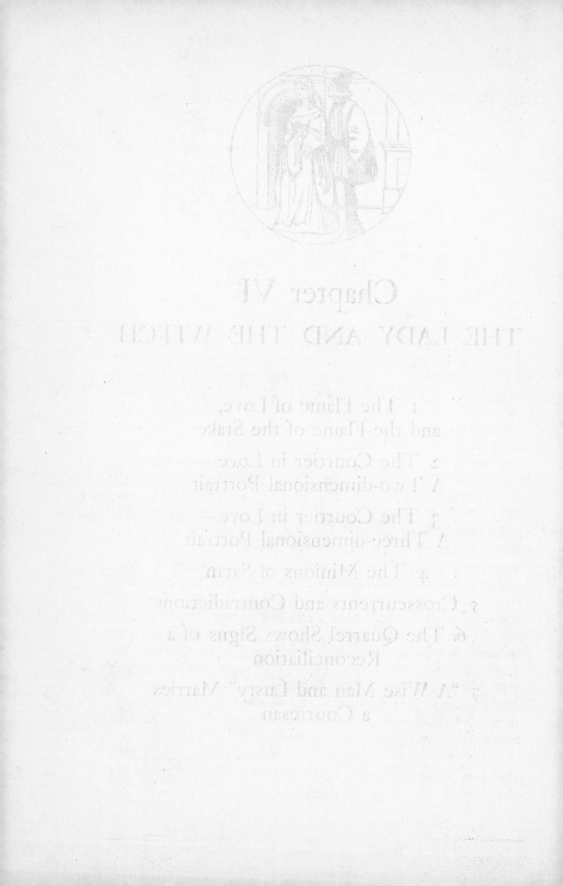

Chapter VI
THE LADY AND THE WITCH

I

The Flame of Love,
and the Flame of the Stake

✿   ✿

✿

In the three centuries after the death of Eleanor of Aquitaine, the
European world acquired a very different look. Cities swelled
and spilled out over their medieval walls. Commerce and manufacturing flourished, and princes learned to befriend the bankers
and merchants who financed their wars and intrigues. Gunpowder
made castle walls obsolete, and printing did the same thing to medieval obscurantism. Scholars, poets, and courtiers reveled in their
rediscovery of Cicero, Plato, and Sappho, and the arts became consciously imitative of ancient classic models rather than the Gothic
and Christian ones of recent centuries. By 1500 the bright sunlight
of the Renaissance shone over Italy and was beginning to reach the
North, dispelling the fogs and glooms, and dissolving demons and
dungeons like so much morning mist—or so we often think.

The past, however, is no such insubstantial vapor, and its shadows
tend to persist. In the Renaissance, one of the longest of them was
still cast by the figure of Saint Augustine. It was eleven centuries
since he had said: "Through a woman we were sent to destruction;
through a woman salvation was restored to us," but at the end of the
fifteenth century his dictum seemed even more compelling than
ever. The concept of woman had gradually become completely
dualistic: she was not Woman—she was either Lady or Witch,
Blessed Virgin or sinful Eve, object of adoration or vessel of abominable lust.

In the year 1507, for instance, at the ducal palace in Urbino, a
group of elegant lords and ladies spent four spring evenings de-

[175]

bating the manners, ideals, and love life proper for courtly persons. Their comments, later set down by one of them, became the very gospel of aristocratic conduct. One of the nobles present apotheosized the Lady as follows:

> Who does not know that without women we can feel no content or satisfaction throughout this life of ours, which but for them would be rude and devoid of all sweetness and more savage than that of wild beasts? . . . [They] alone banish from our hearts all vile and base thoughts, vexations, miseries, and turbid melancholies. . . . It is impossible for vileness ever again to rule in a man's heart where once the flame of love has entered.[1]

It is still the voice of the twelfth century, speaking through the lips of the sixteenth century. And even though the nobleman does not frown too darkly on actual sexual union, he refuses (like any Provençal troubadour) to suppose that it is in any way the product of woman's desires. Instead, it is due entirely to seduction by the male:

> What day, what hour, ever passes that the persecuted girl is not besought by the lover with money, gifts, and all things that must please her? When can she ever go to her window, but she shall always see her persistent lover pass, silent in word, but with eyes that speak, with sad and languid face, with those burning sighs, often with most abundant tears? . . . What wonder is it if . . . [she] is finally brought to love him by continual wearing (as water wears the hardest marble), and, conquered by this passion, contents him?

Renaissance noblemen not only idealized beauty in woman, as had their medieval predecessors, but having rediscovered in Plato arguments that made Beauty identical with the Good, they viewed it with quasi-religious awe. A Polish ambassador, upon being presented to the striking Queen of Navarre, stated in heartfelt terms: "Never do I wish to see such beauty again. Willingly would I do as do the Turks, pilgrims to Mecca, where the sepulchre of their prophet, Mahomet is . . . [who] burn their eyes out with hot irons, saying that nothing more could be seen as fine, and therefore they would see nothing."

Yet at the very same time, other men in Western Europe were studying, applying, and imitating the words of another immensely influential book dealing with women—a manual of witchcraft which had been written near the close of the fifteenth century, at

---

[1] Castiglione: *The Courtier*, Bk. III.

the request of the Pope. Its authors were two German Dominican theologians, but their opinions were not wholly derived from bookish studies; as Inquisitors for northern Germany, they had personally interrogated hundreds of women. Their conclusions about the sex were unmarred by qualifications or hesitation:

> A woman is beautiful to look upon, contaminating to the touch, and deadly to keep . . . a foe to friendship . . . a necessary evil, a natural temptation . . . a domestic danger . . . an evil of nature, painted with fair colors . . . a liar by nature. . . . [She] seethes with anger and impatience in her whole soul. . . . There is no wrath above the wrath of a woman. . . . Since [women] are feebler both in mind and body, it is not surprising that they should come under the spell of witchcraft [more than men]. . . . A woman is more carnal than a man. . . . All witchcraft comes from carnal lust, which is in women insatiable.[2]

Like the courtier, the Inquisitors had an explanation for consummated love affairs, but they reversed the roles of hunter and hunted:

> These women satisfy their filthy lusts not only in themselves, but even in the mighty ones of the age, of whatever sort and condition, causing by all sorts of witchcraft the death of their souls through the excessive infatuation of carnal love.

Their reaction to female charms was rather different from that of the Polish ambassador: making no talk of blinding themselves in ecstasy, they preferred to hoist women aloft by the thumbs, twist ropes around their heads, hammer needles under their fingernails, and pour boiling oil on their feet, in the devout hope of eliciting confessions of iniquities. Even after a suspect confessed her abominations, the pious investigators were wary of her physical seductiveness; to protect the judge, they caused her to be shaved bare at the head and crotch, and dragged backwards into court naked, so her eyes could not bewitch him.

It is an astonishing fact that the schism in men's feelings about women appeared to be most extreme not in the early Christian era nor in the Middle Ages, but during that golden Renaissance that we think of as almost modern, almost enlightened. The burning of witches was never more prevalent than at the very time when woman was being glorified by Botticelli, Giorgione, and Titian. Love and sexual feelings had become hopelessly entangled in the struggle between medieval religion and Renaissance humanism, be-

[2] Sprenger and Kramer: *Malleus Maleficarum*, Pt. I, Quest. 6.

tween the power of the Pope and the power of the emerging nations of the West. Caught in this intense struggle, sexual neurosis
might look like satanic skulduggery and lead to the stake, while
romantic love could become an issue over which a king might break
his ancient ties to Rome.

2

The Courtier in Love —
A Two-dimensional Portrait

❀   ❀

❀

At the beginning of the sixteenth century, there was no more
civilized court in Italy than that of Guidobaldo di Montefeltro, Duke of Urbino. Guidobaldo's tiny principality, nestled on
the slopes of the Appenines in north-central Italy, was prosperous,
well-administered, and peaceful, and his father, Federico, having
ruled it excellently for forty years, had left a legacy of love for the
Montefeltro name. Guidobaldo should have been a happy man, but
he was not. Gaunt and fragile, he tried like other Renaissance
princes to be both a warrior and a man of culture, but was able to
succeed only at the second; his feeble body had been plagued by
various ills from his earliest teens, and by twenty was crippled by
gout. Nor was this his severest affliction. At sixteen he had married
Elizabetta Gonzaga, the gentle, gracious young sister of the Marquis of Mantua, and almost at once discovered himself to be impotent.

Fortunately, the young Duke and his Duchess were steeped in the literary traditions of Dante and Petrarch, both of whom had exalted the disembodied form of courtly love. Moreover, the young couple were also students of Neoplatonism, which provided such love with a properly classical rationale.[3] Guidobaldo and his young wife therefore comforted themselves with lofty discussions on the superiority of chaste love, and Elizabetta showed him a devotion and loyalty that would have honored any marriage. In 1502, for instance, when Duke Guidobaldo was thirty, the treacherous Caesar Borgia made a surprise descent upon Urbino while the Duke's artillery was away helping Caesar's father, Pope Alexander VI. Guidobaldo and Elizabetta fled, and Caesar added Urbino to the Pope's possessions. Seeking to stabilize the conquest, the Pope then offered Elizabetta an annulment and a potent French husband, while Caesar Borgia added the promise of a pension. Though she was living on Venetian charity in ignominious exile with her ailing husband, Elizabetta refused all. In 1503 malaria killed the Pope. Caesar Borgia's power swiftly crumbled, the people of Urbino drove out his soldiers, and the Duke and his faithful Duchess were joyfully welcomed back. They celebrated their happiness by surrounding themselves with the leading poets, painters, musicians, and writers of Italy, and conducting endless discussions about life, ethics, manners, poetry, and love.

All these topics, as examined and demonstrated at Urbino, were talked about throughout Western Europe, and the ways of Urbino were diligently copied; wherever wealth had made for increased leisure, and the concentration of power had produced important capital cities and princely courts, such things were becoming all-important. It was expected that every lord and lady would know Latin and a touch of Greek, be able to write sonnets and compose a tune, and discourse gracefully on philosophers, gods, and lovers. The medieval trouvères, jesters, and jugglers, entertaining in dank baronial halls, were succeeded by chamber orchestras, troupes of players, and elegant banquets, presented in well-lighted palaces which had glazed windows and hence were often warm and comfortable.

Courtiers and merchants alike bought and avidly studied large

[3] Neoplatonism of the Renaissance was a Christian reinterpretation of Plato's doctrines, and not identical with the philosophic-religious system called Neoplatonism which arose in Alexandria in the third century (see chapter four, p. 101). In the present chapter, the terms "Platonic," "Platonizing," etc. will be understood as referring neither to the original Platonic doctrines nor to Alexandrian Neoplatonism, but to Renaissance Neoplatonism.

numbers of "courtesy books" in which the manners of gentlemen
were set forth in detail, although to the modern age some of the subject matter seems curiously elementary. One of the most famous
courtesy books (the *Galateo* of Giovanni della Casa, first published
in 1559) advised, for instance, against yawning, sneezing, scratching in public, smelling someone else's meat, or making bad puns.[4]
Though the economic basis of feudalism and feudal warfare had
largely disappeared, there was a keen renewal of interest in the
romantic aspects of chivalry. Tourneys became popular again and
were more splendid than ever in the sixteenth century, even though
armored knight and wooden lance were nearing obsolesence and
jousting had lost much of its military and political importance.
Above all, the courtiers cultivated the art of *bel parlare*, or fine
conversation, and practiced it immoderately: the poet Bembo told
of a single discussion of love that lasted for three days. Extensive
lists of love questions, the raw materials of such heroic exercises,
were published continuously from the fourteenth to the seventeenth century and contained such fertile problems as these: Can a
man love more than one woman at a time? Is love noblest which
never possesses the body of the beloved in any way, or is the kiss
permissible? Which is more agreeable—to speak to the beloved
without seeing her, or see her without being able to speak to her?
(By 1566 a French writer was able to fill sixteen pages with his discussion of the latter question.)

Such were the principal leisure distractions of Renaissance courts,
of which the one at Urbino was a leading example. Among the
noblemen attached to that court was Baldassare Castiglione, a
gentle, meditative, well-born young man from Mantua, who had
entered Guidobaldo's service first in 1503 as a soldier, remained to
serve him also as ambassador and court intellectual, and soon became
deeply enamored of the Duchess. Luckily, he too could attune himself to Platonic love, and although he wrote sonnets to her and was
fairly outspoken in his admiration, he lived for many years in blameless amity with her and Duke Guidobaldo in what seemed to him
the best of all possible worlds.

[4] If such advice seems unnecessary, it
is worth noting that as late as 1611 an
English traveler remarked with astonishment upon an Italian custom he had
seen nowhere else in Europe: they used
forks at the table while cutting meat off
the main joint. "The reason of this curiosity is," he explained, "because the
Italian cannot by any means endure to
have his dish touched with fingers, seeing all men's fingers are not alike clean."
(Thomas Coryat: *Coryats Crudities*,
1611)

That world, he felt, should be preserved and offered as a model to all other men, and he did so in the form of a book entitled *The Courtier*, which is an account of four evenings of conversation among several dozen lords and ladies at Urbino in March 1507.[5] One can assume that much of the wording is of Castiglione's own invention, but the people named were all real and the opinions of several key speakers tally with what they themselves wrote in other books. *The Courtier*, though no stenographic transcript, is therefore very likely a faithful portrayal of what was actually said at Urbino, either during that four-day series of talks or at other times. As a clear exposition of aristocratic ideals, it was immensely influential, and was translated into French, German, and Spanish. In England it was considered required reading for every gentleman. One Italian lady, as she lay dying, recited not a prayer, but favorite passages from *The Courtier*.

A large part of *The Courtier* deals with the characteristics of the ideal gentleman. He must, of course, be of aristocratic birth. He must be learned in the classics, and possess both literary and conversational style. Arms are his true profession, but in order not to become brutalized, he must cultivate refinement; the book therefore intimately inquires into his clothing, his grammar, his manners, and even the types of practical jokes he plays on others. The ideal court lady is likewise anatomized; significantly, she is not at all the remote, rarely approached goddess of medieval troubadour lyrics, but a real person who must be witty, well read, active in social gatherings, skilled in writing and conversation, and capable of handling worldly and political matters.

The most important segments of the book are concerned with Renaissance concepts of love, courtship, and sexual conduct. Many of the statements, like the quotations from *The Courtier* with which this chapter began, are essentially repetitions of the principles of courtly love somewhat modified in flavor by the passage of time, but throughout the book there is also a strong overlay of Platonism, a distinctly new element. The fundamental theme is that love is the source of all sweetness and moral virtue, since it leads men to concentrate on beauty, and beauty leads the mind toward the contemplation of divinity. It was therefore clear that the lover and the

---

[5] Castiglione wrote that he himself had not been present and was only repeating what he had been told, but the dates of some of his letters prove the opposite; the statement is a graceful pretext for omitting himself from the dialogue. His manners were always impeccable.

lady had to see and converse with each other frequently (there would be none of those interminable medieval quests away from the lady in the name of serving her), but their love, to be finest and most ennobling, had to remain chaste and free of actual physical union. Although they would talk of love a great deal, it was up to the lady to preserve their purity by refusing to let the talk heat her blood. Giuliano de' Medici (the third son of Lorenzo, and brother of the later Pope Leo X), explained how a lady should handle this, and it is reasonable to suppose that he was really portraying the Duchess Elizabetta herself.

> If the gentleman shall be pert . . . she will give him such an-swer that he may clearly understand he is causing her annoyance. Again, if he shall be discreet and use modest phrases and words of love covertly . . . the lady will feign not to understand and will apply his words in another sense, always modestly trying to change the subject. . . . If, again, the talk is such that she can-not feign not to understand, she will take it all as a jest, pretend-ing to be aware that it is said to her more out of compliment to her than because it is true, depreciating her merits and ascribing the praises that he gives her to the gentleman's courtesy.

One may wonder whether this bloodless feinting was intended to go on indefinitely. Lord Giuliano was quite clear on that point:

> I would have her yield her lover nothing but her spirit; nor ever let her show him any clear sign of love (either by words or by gestures or by any other means) by which he may be sure of it.

What intrigued this particular assemblage of Renaissance cour-tiers and ladies was not sexual conquest, but the prolonging of chaste raptures and exaltations, the artful playing of conversational games, the indulging in purified courtship. But they did not con-sider this a mere amusement or trivial pastime; philosophy dignified it with a high and worthy goal, without the tiresome mechanics of good deeds or knightly service. Pietro Bembo, a poet and minor cleric who later became a cardinal, made the definitive closing speech on love in *The Courtier*, eloquently expounding the Platonic theory of chaste love in terms compared to which even the medieval talk of *amor purus* seems almost hot-blooded and sensual: [6]

> Beauty seen in bodies and especially faces . . . is an effluence of divine goodness. Beauty is good, and hence true love of beauty

[6] The ultimate origin of his ideas was, of course, Plato's *Symposium*, though Bembo's Renaissance mind reinter- preted what he said there and ignored the homosexual context. See above, chapter two, p. 47.

is most good and holy . . . but whoever thinks to enjoy the beauty by possessing the body deceives himself, and is moved, not by true perception through reasonable choice, but by false opinion through sensual appetite. . . .

The true courtier who wishes to possess beauty in a perfect and lasting way (Bembo continued), and who uses it as a guide along the ascent toward divinity, permits himself only the two least fleshly senses—sight and sound. He enjoys seeing his lady's beauty, her grace, her actions; he revels in the sweetness of her voice and the concord of her words. Using these perceptions of beauty in one body, he strives step by step to learn to love the beauty of human nature; thence he proceeds to the recognition of the beauty of the universal intellect.

Let us, then, direct all the thoughts and forces of our soul to this most sacred light, which shows us the way to heaven. . . . Let us lay aside the passions wherewith we were clothed at our fall, and by the stairway that bears the shadow of sensual beauty on the lowest step, let us mount to the lofty mansion where dwells the heavenly, lovely and true beauty, which lies hidden in the inmost secret recesses of God.

With this, the fourth evening of discussions at Urbino in March 1507 was concluded; there was really nothing more anyone could say.

Such theorizing about love was especially welcome at Urbino, in view of the Duke's sexual difficulty, but it also became highly fashionable at courts throughout Western Europe. Neoplatonism gave a pleasant classical dignity and a philosophic aura to the pure love that had been invented in Provence, developed in Poitiers, and perfected by Dante and Petrarch; it offered the Renaissance humanists a way to blend the highest pagan thinking with their own version of Christianity. For the most part, they studiously ignored the fact that Plato thought of the first step toward the divine as the love not of a woman, but of a beautiful boy.

For some men, Platonic love seems to have been entirely satisfying. Castiglione himself, despite his mother's pleas that he should marry and perpetuate the line, remained a pure-minded bachelor at Urbino for nearly a dozen years. During the latter eight of them Elizabetta was a widow, but there is no hint of impropriety between her and Castiglione. She was at least six years older than he, a semi-invalid with a heavy pale face and listless eyes, but perhaps that has nothing to do with it; he might have remained pure in any case.

In 1516 Pope Leo X deposed Guidobaldo's nephew from the ducal throne and put one of his own on it instead. Castiglione had to leave, and returned at last to Mantua where, when nearly forty, he faced up to his familial responsibility and married a teen-aged girl. To his great surprise, he found considerable happiness in marriage and learned that he could love in a new way, quite unlike that he had thus far practiced. But his happiness lasted only a few years, for his young wife died after bearing their third child. Castiglione turned back to his long-neglected manuscript and thrust aside the meaning of his recent experiences; the finished form of *The Courtier*, published at last in 1528 after circulating privately for some time, reflected only the ideas expressed at Urbino and nothing learned in his actual marriage. For him, the make-believe was important, after all, and reality was not.

3

The Courtier in Love —
A Three-dimensional Portrait

❀   ❀

❀

Castiglione's portrait of Platonic love in the year 1507 is, really, only a silhouette—a simplified and idealized likeness, drawn from life in a court with a special problem. Platonic love of the Urbino variety was a highly fashionable subject of discussion in the other courts of Western Europe, but most men and many women were not completely attuned to the ascetic and spiritualized form of love. They strove to be Platonic, but often satisfied the hunger of the flesh in shameful places and with lowly persons; they talked Platonism and sometimes practiced *amor purus* with their Platonic loves—and sometimes lost their grip on Platonism altogether.

Many clues indicate that the ancient separation of sex from love still dominated the emotions of Renaissance men. To a considerable extent, they were able to love ladies purely while seeking their relief elsewhere. Petrarch himself, the best-known of pure lovers and the pattern upon which Italian men, and then French and English ones, modeled themselves, had shown just the same clear-cut schism in his feelings. He had grown up a couple of centuries earlier, when Dante was still alive, and had been deeply influenced by Dante's love for Beatrice. Following this lead, Petrarch had a famous long-range love affair with a lady he called Laura; his sonnets on the subject set the mode for centuries, and like him countless lovers admired their ladies from a distance, wrote poems to them, sighed, wept, and prayed for the tiniest favor. The real Laura, meanwhile, sturdily bore her husband eleven children, none of them Petrarch's; he would never have dreamed of real intimacy. On the side, however, he took a mistress while writing his sonnets, and sired two bastards before abandoning both sex and Platonic love in favor of scholarly studies. Any number of later Petrarchans followed the same route, up to but not including the final abandonment.

But as in the time of Andreas, many of those who professed spiritual love were tantalized by desire, and drawn on to experiment, sometimes gingerly, sometimes zestfully, with the physical embodiment of their love. Sometimes we gather this indirectly, as when a writer scoffs at Platonic-Petrarchan posturing for going on too long and being too prissy. One Melchiorre Zoppio, writing a *Treatise of Love* in 1587, portrayed a pale and sighing youth standing before the bed of his ladylove, who asks what troubles him. "Only what you see, that you should wish me well," he says.

"I do," she answers.

"And that you know I wish the same to you."

"I know it."

"And that you hold it dear."

"I hold it dear. Do you wish anything else?"

"Only that you wish me well and know that I wish you the same."

Having had about enough of this, the lady finally says: "Since you wish me well and I wish the same to you, leave me to sleep by myself as I will leave you to sleep by yourself. Good night." And she rolls over. Such love, Zoppio said, is really only friendship; true love should end in embraces—"and most lovers will be found of the same opinion."

Yet this is only an imagined scene, and Zoppio may have been indulging in some wishful thinking. Although a good deal of true love undoubtedly ended in embraces of one sort or another, it is also true that the double standard kept many ladies pure out of fear of the consequences. Some of the great ladies of the Renaissance, for whom men felt celebrated Platonic affections, remained perfectly virtuous and found in Platonic love an intellectual and emotional recompense for their husbands' erring masculine ways.

Such motives may explain why Platonic love was so important in the life of Marguerite of Navarre, sister of King Francis I, who preached it to French courtiers and ladies for thirty years in the early part of the sixteenth century. Married for political reasons at seventeen, she could find nothing to love in her first husband; her second, Henri, titular King of Navarre, was eleven years younger than she, and treated her amiably but with little pretense at fidelity. Marguerite, as the arbiter of fashion and leading female intellectual of the court of King Francis, and later as the co-ruler of her husband's courts at Nérac and Pau in southwestern France, diligently encouraged and fostered Platonic love discussions and customs among the courtiers, poets, intellectuals, and mystics who gathered about her. She also encouraged the practice in a personal fashion: nearly a dozen men are said to have been in love with her, and she loved them all in return, sincerely, intensely, and chastely. It was the safe course for a lady, and one that neatly complemented the dominant male view of woman as either a hallowed saint or vulgar sinner.

But at all levels of Platonism, including the most rarefied and elevated, Renaissance men and women candidly recognized the less exalted practices of love and sex that existed side-by-side with professedly divine love, and were not in the least shocked by the contrast. Marguerite's own brother had the morals and tastes of a stud bull, but she never found fault with him for it, and though she was the champion of spiritual love, she willingly befriended his various unspiritual mistresses. All around her she saw and heard stories of licentious and vulgar conduct, and though her own habits were so exemplary, she found the opposite amusing and put much of her laughter into the *Heptameron,* a collection of seventy-two tales she wrote in frank emulation of Boccaccio. The Abbé Brantôme, a dilettante historian of the latter part of the century, claimed that a key existed to the stories, identifying its scapegrace characters as real persons; if so, French morals were no better in the sixteenth century than in the twelfth. But whether the Abbé was right or not, it is astonishing that Marguerite, a sweet, intelligent, inspiring, and religious queen, could permit herself to write stories as bawdy and ribald as any in the *Decameron.*

Some of them, to be sure, contain lofty Platonic sentiments. "No man loveth God," says one of her characters, "who hath not loved with a perfect love one of His creatures." But side by side with this are stories of bed-partners switched in the dark, incestuous mix-ups, insatiable priests, and cuckolded husbands. One is hard put to know just how the most Platonic lady in France felt about these unedifying yarns or the persons in them. Evidently, along with her intense Platonism she had an equally intense feeling for vulgarity and brazenness—a Renaissance combination that is often called re-freshing frankness or healthful realism by those who like to view the past with nostalgia and longing. "What!" exclaims one of Marguerite's characters, "you mean that if no one is advised thereof, all things are lawful to lovers?" "In good faith," is the typically Renaissance answer, "there is but one crime I have seen punished, and that is folly; for your murderers, thieves, and adulterers are neither over-taken of justice nor blamed of men, if they be but as crafty as they are wicked."

Such candor contrasted oddly with the sublime ethics of Plato-nism, but in the same way, Renaissance men could exhibit both an ultra-refined adoration of female beauty, and a startling frankness about sexual functions and marriage. In Italy, men charged with impotence by neglected wives had the legal right, as late as the sixteenth century, to disprove the allegation before witnesses either in a brothel or at home. Vincenzo Gonzaga, Duke of Mantua, is said to have so proved himself in the presence of a group of ambas-sadors and dignitaries of the Church. At the very time when Bembo and others were penning tributes to woman as the first step of the stairway to divinity, King Henry VII of England sent three gentle-men of his court to study the young Queen of Naples, widow of

Ferdinand II, as a possible match for himself. Some of the points on
the detailed directive he gave them are wonderfully enlightening:

> *Item,* specially to mark the favor of her visage, whether she be
> painted or not, and whether it be fat or lean, sharp or round.
> *Item,* to mark well the fashion of her nose and the height and
> breadth of her forehead.
> *Item,* to mark her breast and paps, whether they be big or small.
> *Item,* to approach as near her mouth as they honestly may, to
> the intent that they may feel the condition of her breath, whether
> it be sweet or not.
> *Item,* . . . [to] make inquisition and ensearch what land or
> livelihood the said young queen hath or shall have after the
> decease of her mother.[7]

The young woman was apparently satisfactory on all counts except
the last, but it was the most important; Henry VII, neither Pla-
tonist nor hot-blooded youth, decided to remain a widower.

For in the earlier part of the Renaissance, marriage was treated
with utter candor—not only as to its physical aspects but its financial ones. Love, Platonic or otherwise, was neither the basis for
making a marriage, nor any essential part of it, once made. As it had
been for many centuries, marriage was still fundamentally a genetic
device, with household and welfare functions among the lower
classes, and economic and political values for the propertied classes
and the aristocrats. Throughout Renaissance Europe the principal
questions asked by parents of both the girl and the boy concerned
dowry, income, and property guarantees. Marriage was a financial
transaction and a lifelong business; raptures and adorations would
either be hurtful to it, or simply perish in its mundane soil. "I would
not counsel ye to marry her with whom thou hast been in amours
withal," wrote Juan Luis Vives, the leading educator of the early
sixteenth century.

But few had the chance to try illicit amours before marriage,
and so they tried them afterwards; most marriages took place when
the girl was between fourteen and sixteen, and the boy but little
more, while many children and even infants were espoused in
church ceremonies at the desire of parents who had struck a bargain.
Such an espousal was effectively a marriage, for though it had to
be ratified by actual marriage later on, only a few of the children,
when they grew up, dared to appeal for a release from the contract.
In 1477, Anna Sforza, aged three, was affianced to Alfonso d'Este;

[7] *Historia Regis Henrici Septimi,* p. 223–39.

she walked in the ceremony, but he, being newborn, had to be carried by a chamberlain. Not only the mighty arranged such marriages for benefit. A study made of the records of the English diocese of Chester in the middle of the sixteenth century shows a number of similar marriages among the children of obscure burghers. John Somerford and Jane Brerton, three and two years old respectively, were held in arms by adults who spoke the words of the ceremony for them. In another such espousal, John Rigmardon, aged three, was coaxed by a priest to repeat the matrimonial vows aloud; halfway through, the child said he would do no more, to which the priest replied: "You must speak a little more, and then go play you."

Though many an economic marriage may have resulted in some degree of affection, the feelings were apt to remain strongly colored by the money value of each partner. Messer Donati Velluti, a fourteenth-century Italian gentleman, wrote in his diary these telltale phrases: "Bice, my first wife, was a little woman and not pretty, but sagacious, good, kindly, well-mannered, and full of every virtue. . . . She lived with me in blessed peace and got me favor, honor, and possessions enough." The effect of money considerations on the emotional aspects of courtship is revealed still more clearly in several of the Paston Letters, a wonderful collection of the papers of a family of well-to-do gentry in fifteenth-century England. John Paston, a younger son, wrote to his older brother, Sir John, in July 1474, concerning certain prospects for his marriage:

> Right worshipful sir, I recommend me to you, praying you to remember, before ye depart out of London, to speak with the wife of Harry Eberton, the draper, and to inform her that I am proffered a marriage in London which is worth 600 mark and better. . . . If so be that Mistress Eberton will deal with me, ye should not conclude in the other place,[8] even though Eberton would not give so much with Mistress Elizabeth, his daughter, as I might have with the other, for such fantasy as I have in the said Mistress Elizabeth Eberton.[9]

But fantasy did not impress the Ebertons, for John Paston had too little property of his own; and probably for the same reason, the deal in "the other place" also fell through. Three years later, still single, he met and wooed Margery Brews, daughter of a Sir Thomas Brews, and apparently managed to inspire some tender

[8] He was at the same time dickering for the daughter of someone named Stockton.

[9] *Paston Letters*, Vol. III, no. 739.

sentiments in the girl. But a message of hers to him mingles fiscal and tender sentiments in a fashion never seen in anthologies of love letters:

> Right worshipful and well beloved Valentine . . . ye be pur-
> posed to come to Topcroft in short time . . . to have a conclusion
> of the matter between my father and you; I would be most glad
> of any creature alive if the matter might grow to effect. . . .
> [If not] then should I be much more sorry and full of heaviness.
> And as for myself, I have done and understood all in the matter
> that I can or may, as God knoweth; and I let you plainly under-
> stand that my father will no more money part with in that behalf
> but an hundred £ and fifty marks, which is right far from the ac-
> complishment of your desire. Wherefore, if that ye could be con-
> tent with that good, and my poor person, I would be the merriest
> maiden on ground.[1]

Happily John Paston saw the light and the marriage took place on those terms; it is also possible that he may have been influenced by the fact that still another marriage prospect his older brother was looking into for him had just proven fruitless.

For all these reasons—the continuing schism between noble love and sexual function, the financial involvements of upper-class mar-riage, the medieval tradition that placed romance outside marriage, and the preciosity of the Neoplatonic conception of love—the average Renaissance husband looked upon his wife with eyes which appraised rather than adored. Yet he was equally capable of look-ing with adoration elsewhere, for although Platonic love was only a pose for some people, the qualities it praised in the Lady were real and existed in many Renaissance women. Vittoria Colonna, Lucrezia Borgia, Catherine de' Medici, Beatrice d'Este, Margaret More, Mary Stuart, Queen Elizabeth—history is studded with their names. And there were even more whose names are practically forgotten, but who still live in remote bits of biography. Here, for instance, is a vignette written in the seventeenth century, limning a typical six-teenth-century virago,[2] Elizabeth Nevill, daughter of Baron Lati-mer:

> . . . Prodigious parts for a woman. I have heard my father's
> mother say that she had Chaucer at her fingers' ends. A great
> politician; great wit and spirit, but revengeful. Knew how to
> manage her estate as well as any man; understood jewels as well

---

[1] Ibid., no. 784.
[2] A woman who was a man's equal; in the Renaissance, a term conveying only admiration.

as any jeweler. Very beautiful, but only short-sighted. To obtain pardons for her sons she married Sir Edmund Carey, cousin-german to Queen Elizabeth, but kept him to hard meat.[3]

Even courtesans occasionally managed to capture something of the intellectual glamor and high status the Renaissance Lady had attained outside her marriage. This was particularly true in Rome, where the glittering papal court was nearly devoid of married ladies. The courtesan Imperia was celebrated by a hundred poets and honored with burial in the chapel of San Gregoria. Tullia d'Aragona's salon was crowded with philosophers, courtiers, and cardinals, and no one laughed when she wrote a book praising Platonic love. Guglielmo, Duke of Mantua, was honored rather than embarrassed when Veronica Franco dedicated a book of verses to him.

These latter details are reminiscent of the hey-day of the hetaera in the Athens of Pericles. Yet except in the cities of Rome and Venice, the high-grade courtesan was not particularly important in the Renaissance, and neither was the homosexual lover. For although both of them could offer sexual satisfaction, when it came to the rich spiritual and emotional content that love had acquired they were simply no match for the Lady.

[3] John Aubrey: *Brief Lives*, p. 42.

4

The Minions of Satan

✿   ✿

✿

Meanwhile, another version of woman—the Witch—had simultaneously been taking clear and frightening shape in Western Europe. So novel and distinct was this phenomenon that churchmen and inquisitors concluded a new race of malefactors, not heretofore known, had appeared on earth. Prior to the fourteenth century, according to their studies, blighted crops, storms, diseased cattle, and deformed children had been the work principally of male sorcerers and devils; now, inexplicably, the Inquisitors found these and other forms of *maleficium* (evil-doing) being performed chiefly by women. At the same time it appeared to them that *maleficium* had become dominated by sexual matters. The most common deeds of witches were the stealing of semen from sleeping men, the causing of impotence, sterility, and miscarriages, and the afflicting of the private parts with diseases and deformities. This being so, nightmares, dreams of forbidden activities, sexual reveries, and waning powers all began to assume a new and more terrifying aspect; they were the work of Satan, carried out by his new hordes of female vassals.

All this was in sharp contrast to the earlier Church attitude. Even though Saint Augustine and other Church Fathers had written about the existence of succubi, or evil female spirits, the Church had long discouraged the belief that the average woman could voluntarily join the legions of the Devil and be granted magical powers. The Synod of Paderborn stated in 785 that such a belief was in itself a deception produced by the Devil, and set the death penalty for anyone who burned a woman on the grounds that she was a witch. Charlemagne confirmed this ordinance. Various councils and canons from the ninth to the thirteenth century commanded bishops to combat the popular belief in witchcraft, and stated that witches' night journeys and marvelous powers were pure illusion.

Then the change came. Beginning in the 1300's, the belief in witchcraft spread rather rapidly through the clergy, particularly in Germany, France, and the Lowlands, and news and reports of cases reached all ranks of society in Western Europe. A series of papal pronouncements and bulls starting in the early 1300's advised ecclesiastical courts on the activities of witches and urge their extermination. Theologians wrote impassioned appeals to the public, and preachers terrified their congregations with lectures on the dangers and symptoms of witchcraft. By 1400, civil courts began to recognize that actual copulation with the Devil was not only possible, but should be cause for capital punishment, since it constituted the ratification of the witch's pact with Satan. By 1450 it had become accepted dogma that witches could fly by night. Witch trials and burnings grew increasingly common even in the most civilized centers of Western Europe; Catholics and Lutherans, Inquisitors and humanists, accepted them as a normal facet of life, and those few who raised their voices against the mania were at once accused of being in league with the Devil himself.[4]

And is this dismal aspect of Renaissance life a part of the history of love? Alas, yes. Many centuries earlier, as we have seen, the separation of woman into two aspects was becoming a reality in the mind and life of Christian man. By the Middle Ages, his conflicting feelings about woman had finally caused him to decompose his notion of her into two clearly opposed halves—the all-good, tender, passionless goddess (the Virgin-Mother, and the Lady of the troubadours), and the evil-doing, seductive, lascivious sorceress (Eve, and all sinful or physically desirable women).

But why should this dichotomy have become intensified just as men's minds were turning toward worldliness, rationalism, and the rediscovery of joyousness? Why should the Witch have flourished in the same soil as the Renaissance Lady? The subject is extremely complex; let us be content merely to note a few suggestions. Courtly love, as we saw in the previous chapter, was somewhat of

---

[4] The change from the early Church attitude to the later one is documented in J. Hansen: *Zauberwahn, Inquisition und Hexenprozess im Mittlelalter;* Henry C. Lea: *History of the Inquisi-* *tion of the Middle Ages;* Ernest Jones: *On the Nightmare;* G. R. Taylor: *Sex in History;* Lynn Thorndike: *History of Magic and Experimental Science;* and others.

a disturbing force, running counter to feudal patriarchalism and Catholic ideology; it had already met opposition and occasionally found itself linked with heresy. But all this was before the real trouble arose. For it was the Renaissance, and the concomitant social, economic, and intellectual changes in European society, that seriously disturbed the equilibrium of the Church and upset the stability of the order it had long maintained. Sensing its own illness, the Church began to fight back without clearly knowing what was ailing it; it hazily saw all the new influences as one common enemy, and identified heresy, nationalism, humanism, and Renaissance love as one interconnected plot.

The two views of women became standards of the two sides in the impending conflict. Cultured courtiers saw women as ladies, the clergy and the poor still saw them as nuisances or worse; humanists were interested in love, theologians in sin. But economics and geography cut across these alignments: in Italy, where there was no doubt about the Pope's powers and control, witchcraft hysteria took hold for the most part only in a few Alpine valleys; in northern Europe, where economic development was making for dissatisfaction with Vatican control and the Pope's power was in danger, Inquisitors were inclined to see spooks and witches everywhere.

The most important document about the witches of northern Europe was written by two men who not only saw them, but interrogated, tortured, and burned them, and wrote down their findings for the good of mankind. The two were Jacob Sprenger and Henry Kramer, Dominican brothers and professors of sacred theology at the University of Cologne in the latter half of the fifteenth century. Both were Germans, but about their family backgrounds, personal appearance, or habits and tastes, we know nothing; we know only that for many years both of them were active Inquisitors in Germany (Sprenger was named to the task by Pope Sixtus IV in 1475, and Kramer was named later as his associate), and that they traveled widely in Germany, took part in many trials, and were unsparing of their own energies in pursuing their important work.

After some years, Sprenger and Kramer appealed to Pope Innocent VIII to help them overcome the opposition and reluctance of local clerics and princes to aid them in their efforts. In December 1484, Innocent issued a famous bull, *Summis Desiderantes Affectibus.* "It has indeed lately come to Our ears," began the Pope, "that in some parts of northern Germany . . . many persons of both

sexes [5] . . . have abandoned themselves to devils, incubi, and succubi." Having done so, they have obtained magical powers, he said,
by which they have been producing stillbirths, killing calves, destroying crops, causing disease, creating impotence, and doing other
sundry acts of *maleficium*. The Pope said he was shocked that Inquisitors Sprenger and Kramer had not received co-operation from
some lay people and clerics; indeed some of these people had even
brazenly denied that witchcraft was being practiced within their
provinces. His Holiness decreed that Sprenger and Kramer should
proceed without let or hindrance, and that all persons in all towns
and provinces of northern Germany should aid them.

Armed with the Bull, which gave a crucial stimulus to the witch-
hunting movement, Sprenger and Kramer intensified their activities
and their research, and reaped a rich harvest of burnings. Within
three years they were able to produce a monumental study of
witchcraft they called *Malleus Maleficarum* (*The Witches' Hammer*—i.e., a hammer to strike witches with). Officially endorsed by
the University of Cologne and avidly studied throughout Western
Europe, it was scarcely ever out of print for the next two centuries.
It went through nineteen separate editions by the eighteenth century, inspired the publishing of scores of similar works in other
languages, and influenced the direction and content of nightmares,
neuroses, accusations, trials, and burnings for at least two hundred
years.

From actual testimony of witnesses and confessed witches,
Sprenger and Kramer had learned that, by means of their incanta-
tions and brews, evil-doing women could summon plagues of lo-
custs to destroy a harvest or bring a hailstorm to ruin it, make men
impotent or women frigid, induce abortions or dry up a mother's
milk. They could see at a distance, fly at night, and leave a dupli-
cate body behind to fool people; sometimes they could turn themselves into cats or other creatures; some of them turned men into
animals and kept them at hard labor; and some kidnapped children,
and roasted and ate them.

But the dominant concern of the *Malleus Maleficarum* was with
the sexual problems caused by witches—principally infertility, impotence, nocturnal emissions or sexual dreams, painful coitus, nym-
phomania and satyriasis, and the like. Sprenger and Kramer were

[5] Sprenger and Kramer later corrected this impartiality by amassing evidence to show that the great bulk of
acts of witchcraft was done by women.

such good reporters that despite their attribution of these and other ailments to supernatural causes, their descriptions often permit the modern doctor to make an unequivocal diagnosis of psychosexual disorder. A typical case is that of a woman with a phantom pregnancy which seemed real in every way, but was only the result, they said, of a quantity of wind in the bowel; modern doctors immediately recognize the ailment, but diagnose it as a form of conversion hysteria, probably due to an intense, frustrated desire to conceive, rather than a digestive disturbance. Also very likely of neurotic origin was such a case as that of the young man on whom an angry witch cast a "glamor" (a type of spell) which made it seem to him as though his penis had disappeared from his body; even the Inquisitors pointed out that it had not really come off, and that this was only an illusion she had created.

Impotence was a problem of deep concern to the Inquisitors, and they recorded some case histories with almost journalistic flair. A count living in the diocese of Strasburg had enjoyed an illicit relationship with a mistress, but broke it off in order to marry a young noblewoman. On the wedding night, he found himself completely impotent with his wife. This distressing condition continued unchanged for three years, until one day the Count happened to meet his old mistress as he was walking in the streets of Metz on business. For old times sake, he stopped to chat with her. She asked after his health; he smiled and lied, saying that it was fine. Seeming a bit surprised, she asked about his wife and then about his children; he said his wife was fine, and they already had three splendid children. Her perplexity and distress were obvious, and the Count asked: "Why, my dear, do you make such careful inquiries? I am sure that you congratulate me on my happiness." "Certainly I congratulate you," she said, "but curse that old woman who said she would bewitch your body so you could not have connection with your wife!" She told him in detail how she had paid to have a pot containing bewitched objects placed in his well. "But see," she concluded, "it is all in vain, and I am glad!" The Count hurried home, drained the well, and burned the contents of the pot, and according to Professors Sprenger and Kramer he immediately recovered his virility and consummated his marriage.

The Inquisitors explained at length why witchcraft was far more common among women than among men. Basically, woman is a weak, inferior creature; moreover, she is afflicted with insatiable carnal lust. This makes her easy prey to the advances of the Devil, who offers to satisfy her desires. "It is common to all [witches] to practice carnal copulation with devils," they stated; indeed, only after doing so with Satan himself, in person, did each witch gain her extraordinary powers.

The sexual union with Satan took place during the travesty of Christian Mass known as the Witches' Sabbath. The first report that such a ceremony existed was made in 1335 at a witch trial in Toulouse; prior to that, it was unheard of, but in the century after it, the Witches' Sabbath became a central feature of the trials. The details that gradually accumulated were so vivid and thorough that at least one recent scholar has maintained that in late medieval and Renaissance times, there must have been a widespread pagan religion whose adherents worshipped a horned deity, met in "covens" or clans, and practiced orgiastic rites. But in the opinion of several eminent psychiatrists who have intensively and independently studied the evidence, the descriptions of the Witches' Sabbath bear the unmistakable characteristics of abnormal sexual fantasies, which the celibate Inquisitors eagerly, even hungrily, seized upon and accepted as objectively real.[6]

Certainly, there was an ample cultural tradition on which, whether they realized it or not, both inquisitors and suspects could draw in piecing together their versions of the wicked celebration. In earlier medieval times, the inferior clergy in many European countries had practiced an annual New Year's revel called the Feast of Fools which was basically a vulgar burlesque, full of genial nose-thumbing at all moral and religious standards. Although various popes criticised its excesses, the Feast of Fools was allowed to continue because of its great popularity; both clergy and townspeople found in it a welcome temporary release of pent-up feelings and restrained emotions. In 1445, members of the Faculty of Theology at the University of Paris described it as follows:

> Priests and clerks may be seen wearing masks and monstrous visages at the hours of office. They dance in the choir dressed as women, panders, or minstrels. They sing wanton songs. They eat black puddings at the horn of the altar while the celebrant is saying Mass. They play at dice there. . . . Finally they drive about the town and its theatres in shabby traps and carts, and

[6] Ernest Jones: *On the Nightmare,* pp. 203–6, 210–12, 226; Gregory Zilboorg: *Medical Man and Witch during the Renaissance,* pp. 144–6; Walter Bromberg: *The Mind of Man,* p. 51.

rouse the laughter of their fellows and the bystanders in infamous performances with indecent gestures and verses scurrilous and unchaste.[7]

From such materials, it was easy for theologians and suspects alike to construct a picture of the Witches' Sabbath that became clearer with each passing decade.[8] In general, it would start with a summons blown on a trumpet that only witches could hear. They would gather at night, riding through the air to some remote glen or ruin. There the ceremony began with a long formal processional of witches, both male and female; at last the Devil appeared in a cloud of stinking smoke, and each witch paid him homage by kissing his buttocks or "filthy parts." A burlesque of Christian ritual followed, in which the most beautiful witch present was baptised in the Devil's urine while he made the sign of the Cross backwards with his left hand; then she lay prone while the host was prepared, her bare buttocks being the altar and the dough being composed of feces, menstrual blood, urine, and the like. After the entire coven completed the Black Mass by eating the host, the orgy began; during this part the Devil personally had connection with each witch in turn, while the rest continuously performed a lascivious dance.

The neurotic element of the Witches' Sabbath revelations is nowhere more obvious than in the frequent claims that sexual relations with the Devil, so eagerly sought by the witches, were at the same time horribly painful, a fantasy which, Dr. Ernest Jones has pointed out, is characteristic of many guilt-laden anxiety dreams. Hundreds of witnesses testified that witches howled in pain during the process and came away bleeding. Jeanette d'Abache, a thirteen-year-old girl, swore that the Devil's penis was covered with fish scales which wounded his partner with each movement. Other girls and women supplied different but equally frightening details.

Like these witnesses, the investigators saw things they unconsciously both wanted and feared to see. In examining a suspect, they would strip her naked and closely scrutinize her whole body

---

[7] The document is quoted in E. K. Chambers: *The Medieval Stage*, Vol. I, p. 294.

[8] The *Malleus Maleficarum* itself spent relatively little time on it, but fuller descriptions were given in such other Renaissance witch-studies as: J. Bodin: *De la Démomanie des Sorciers* (1593); P. de Lancre: *Tableau de l'Inconstance des Mauvais Anges et Dé-* mons (1612); James VI (King James I of England): *Daemonologie* (1597); etc. What follows is a synthesis of these and other Renaissance sources, as made by Jones, op. cit., Bromberg, op. cit., and M. Garcon and J. Vinchon: *The Devil*,

for the Devil's mark. Finding none, they would often search the body, particularly the genitals, with sharp probes or long needles, poking repeatedly in the effort to locate a numb or insensitive spot, supposedly a telltale sign of a witch. Generally, they found what they sought, but only after long and satisfying searching. They did not, incidentally, consider that such procedures constituted torture.

Such was the spirit promulgated by the *Malleus Maleficarum* and its offspring. According to an officer of the Inquisition named Paramo, writing in 1554, the Holy Office had by then burned at least thirty thousand witches in the previous century and a half, save for which the world would have been destroyed. That spirit had been sanctioned by popes who themselves admired the viragoes and court ladies of Italy, but saw witches rampant in far-off northern Germany. So it was that the Renaissance perfected the Lady at Urbino and the Witch at Cologne, and paraded the images of both across Europe in the complex struggles of the Reformation.

5

Crosscurrents and Contradictions

❀   ❀

❀

At this point, one can construct a beautifully orderly set of dicta, to wit: the Lady was perfected by the modern Renaissance spirit and the Witch by the reactionary medieval spirit; the former was the ideal of the aristocrats and the rich, the latter the specter seen by the clergy and the poor; the one was Woman as seen by liberals, the other as seen by defenders of the Church. But it is all simply too neat, too pat, too comfortable; it must be wrong. Human beings are not that logical and consistent.

Pope Alexander VI, for instance, who followed Innocent VIII, thoroughly admired the female of the species; he surrounded himself with them, had a twenty-year liaison with Vanozza de' Catanei who bore him four children, and in his aging years acquired a teen-aged blonde mistress named Giulia Farnese. Nevertheless he felt no compunctions about writing new bulls on witch-hunting to add to the effect of Innocent's *Summis Desiderantes Affectibus*.

Humanists were supposedly liberated persons, relatively free from medieval superstitions. Pico della Mirandola, a precocious youth who flared briefly across the philosophic sky during the pontificates of Innocent and Alexander, wrote and argued in favor of a temperate, liberal, and emancipated religion made up of the best parts of all religions; but he also stated that he personally knew one priest who, for forty years, had been having relations with a succubus named Hermeline, and another who for thirty years had had a demon mistress named Fiorina.

Humanists, furthermore, were generally fond of life, literature, and learned women, and Sir Thomas More, the outstanding English humanist in the early sixteenth century, had an appropriately warm home life, educated his daughters excellently, and envisioned in his *Utopia* a communist state in which women might even be priests, and priests might marry. It is confusing, therefore, to learn that he also wrote deeply devotional works, wore a hair shirt under his clothing for a long time, and believed implicitly in the actuality of witchcraft. He loved his wife and daughters, but in a thoroughly old-fashioned, patriarchal way. Sir William Roper called on him early one morning to propose he marry one or the other of More's daughters. More ushered Roper into the room where the girls were both asleep and whipped the covers off them; both lay on their backs, their smocks up under their armpits, but awoke and rolled over in a pretty confusion. "I have seen both sides," said Sir William, satisfied; then he patted the older girl on the rump and announced: "Thou art mine." One must presume that since this method of mate selection was Sir Thomas More's own idea, it seemed perfectly adequate to him.

Perhaps no one included in his own person so many of the contradictions of the age as Henry VIII of England—scholar and despot, lover and hater of women, enemy of the Pope and of Martin Luther. Without reviewing Henry's well-known history here, we must still pause to note one or two aspects of his love life which spell out the remarkable change of the era and the equally remarkable persistence of old ways of thought.

Literature has done little for Henry; few people remember that he was a wonderfully handsome golden-haired youth who excelled at tennis and jousting and adored the study of the classics. These graces disappeared in the later and more dramatic part of his life; the image that remains is that of a fat, irascible tyrant, immensely vain, repulsive of person, and coldly capable of beheading his friends (including More) and two of his six wives. Love, its frustrations, and its ailments, played a large part in the metamorphosis.

In 1509 the youthful Henry had married his late brother's widow, Catherine of Aragon. She was six years older than he, and only moderately attractive; but Henry took her as his Queen because he felt, first, a due regard for treaty obligations with Spain, and second, a sense of obedience to his dying father's wish. Gallantly, however, the young King wore his own wife's favors in the lists, linked their initials on his sleeve, and poetically proclaimed his devotion to her. For a few years, the marriage seemed to go along well enough, but it had been made primarily for state reasons and Catherine was unable to fulfil the most important state function of all: she could not produce a live son. Whether she could or not, he was not tied to her emotionally in any fashion that made him faithful, and after several years of marriage he began to dally with various mistresses for amusement. He found amusement and something more—a continuing illness, probably syphilis, that slowly ruined his body, sapped his potency, and helped bring about the shocking change in his character.

When he was thirty-six, Henry's eye was caught by the fresh charm and winning insouciance of Anne Boleyn, a lady of the court; for the first time, he was genuinely infatuated. As everyone knows, he belabored Pope Clement VII with demands for an annulment of his marriage to Catherine on canonical grounds; the Pope dawdled and temporized until Henry eventually broke all ties with Rome and became head of a nationalized English Church; and Henry got his divorce at last from compliant English clerics, and married Anne.

Was it all for love? Historians say that Henry had been thinking of an annulment long before the infatuation began in 1527, because of the clear political value of having a son to whom he could pass on the throne. But not any woman would do. Cardinal Wolsey had a French princess in mind for whom, he thought, the Pope might grant Henry an annulment; Henry wanted no one but Anne. Cardinal Campeggio, the papal legate who sat on the annulment proceedings with Wolsey in 1528, was astonished. "He sees nothing, he thinks of nothing but his Anne," he wrote to the Pope. "He cannot be without her for an hour, and it moves one to pity to see how the King's life, the stability and downfall of the whole contry, hang upon this one question."

The point is that Henry VIII wanted love and wanted a son, and sought to have them in the same place; otherwise his need for a male heir and the Pope's obstinacy might not have made history. Even more remarkable is the fact that although Anne Boleyn slowly and judiciously parceled out her favors to the King, she could not withhold them long enough to insure marriage—and yet he married her. In one of Henry's early letters to her he speaks of "the pang of absence" and "the hope of your unchangeable affection." Because Anne, though not a virgin, skillfully held back, Henry was soon writing: "Assuring you that henceforward my heart shall be dedicated to you alone, with a strong desire that my body could be also thus dedicated." A while later he is saying: "I trust within a while to enjoy that which I have so long longed for. . . . I think it long since I kissed you." After nearly two years, toward the end of 1528, matters had come very slowly to the following state:

> Mine own sweetheart, this shall be to advertise you of the great ellingness [9] that I find here since your departing, for I ensure you, me thinketh the time longer since your departing now last than I was wont to do a whole fortnight. . . . Wishing myself (specially an evening) in my sweetheart's arms, whose pretty duckies I trust shortly to kiss; written with the hand of him that was, is, and shall be yours by his will,
> H. R.

Henry wrote only one more letter, though he did not marry Anne until January 1533; from this, and the fact that he and she had adjoining apartments in Greenwich, it seems fair to conclude that she had not been able to hold the line for six years. Yet the striking fact is that Henry, having bedded Anne, still wanted her to be his wife, and forced his quarrel with the Pope until the break was past mending and Anne was Queen. The example had immense force; marriage for love became a living issue in England, and since most men faced far smaller obstacles than Henry had surmounted, it seemed a not-impossible idea after all.

[9] Loneliness

But Henry was both kinds of Renaissance man, where woman was concerned. In less than three years of marriage, he wearied of Anne's temper and her incessant demands, and when she failed to produce a son, and his own declining sexual powers infuriated him, he began to re-evaluate his whole romance; it even seemed to him sometimes that he had been seduced into marriage by the dark machinations of witchcraft (after all, did Anne not have a rudimentary sixth finger on her left hand?). He might have chosen this charge as his avenue to freedom, but possibly because waning potency bred jealous thoughts he turned instead to suspicions of misconduct and obtained evidence of it, if a confession extracted by torture deserves that name.[1] Anne and five supposed lovers of hers lost their lives. Six years later Henry passed a law making it a felony to practice conjurations or sorcery, including any such acts as would "provoke a person to unlawful love." Perhaps that was his final opinion of the whole question.

---

[1] In addition to the tortured witness, a number of toadies swore to improbable evidence, saying what they knew Henry wanted to hear. Sixteen persons testified to Anne's incest with her brother, George Boleyn, swearing that they had all clearly and at the same time seen her "alluring him with her tongue in the said George's mouth and the said George's tongue in hers." (Indictment of May 15, 1536)

6

The Quarrel Shows Signs of a Reconciliation

In 1558 Anne Boleyn's daughter, Elizabeth, ascended the throne; the child of love triumphed after all. In Elizabeth—virago of viragoes, virgin and lover, humanist and autocrat, queen and woman —the Renaissance Lady had reached her ultimate exemplar. Yet even in her presence, Bishop John Aylmer could still sound the ancient theme of woman's dual nature—with his emphasis being on the evil side. "Women are of two sorts," he intoned from the pulpit one day, duly deferring to the omnipotent woman sitting before him. "Some of them are wiser, better learned, discreeter, and more constant than a number of men." Then he gathered his energies, filled his lungs, and thundered:

> But another and a worse sort of them, and the most part, are fond, foolish, wanton, flibbergibs, tatlers, triflers, wavering, witless, without council, feeble, careless, rash, proud, dainty, nice, tale-bearers, eavesdroppers, rumor-raisers, evil-tongued, worse-minded, and in every way doltified with the dregs of the Devil's dunghill.

Queen Elizabeth probably smiled at Bishop's Aylmer's fulminations, knowing them to be the saber-rattling of an obsolescent warrior. For although the "argument of women" reached its greatest volume in the sixteenth century, it seemed to mean less than it said. Woman's status was changing and people had to talk and think about it, but even as the quarrel waxed loudest, it lost some of its genuine virulence. In 1541, for instance, an all-inclusive anti-female diatribe

[204]

called *The Schoolhouse of Women* had been written by a hack journalist named Edward Gosynhill. It drew several stinging pro-female replies of which the first, printed in 1542 and entitled *The Praise of All Women*, was written by none other than Gosynhill himself. Writing about women, pro or con, was in other words already less a matter of conviction than of good business. In the 1560's a writer named Pyrrye even published *The Praise and Dispraise of Women*, trying to be sure of capturing the entire market. The tone of pamphlets on the subject remained intemperate,[2] but that was characteristic of all Elizabethan pamphleteering; actually, the ambivalence of men's feelings about women began, little by little, to be somewhat of a pose and not so much of an agonizing reality. Evidently something was happening to the dualist view of women; a process of fusion was beginning, and her two aspects were starting tentatively to merge.

Occasional signs and hints of a fusion had appeared even earlier in Italy. Pinturicchio painted Giulia Farnese, Pope Alexander's mistress, on the walls of a Vatican chamber and surrounded her with angels; Palma Vecchio painted a courtesan as Saint Barbara; Filippo Lippi had his own mistress model for none other than the Blessed Virgin. Was it blasphemy? Or did these men no longer find it impossible to see both aspects in one and the same person? Pietro Bembo, who had delivered the ultimate speech on Platonic love in Castiglione's *The Courtier*, became papal secretary in Rome some time after the Urbino conversations, and took to Roman ways; when he was fifty, he acquired a mistress, Donna Morosina, a lady of Venetian origin. Far from keeping his sexual functions separate from his high concept of love, Bembo proceeded to develop a tender attachment to her and had three sons by her. When she died, the aging cleric wrote to a friend in terms quite remote from his former brand of love talk:

> I have lost the dearest heart in the world, a heart which tenderly watched over my life, which loved it and sustained it neglectful of its own; a heart so much the master of itself, so disdainful of vain embellishments and adornments, of silk and gold, of jewels and treasures of price, that it was content with the single and (so she assured me) supreme joy of the love I bore it. This heart, moreover, had for vesture the softest, gracefulest, daintiest of

[2] A very successful 1615 pamphlet was typically entitled: *The Arraignment of Lewd, Idle, Froward and Unconstant Women*, and one of the replies was: *The Worming of a Mad Dog, or A Sop for Cerberus, the Gaoler of Hell.*

limbs; it had at its service pleasant features, and the sweetest, most graciously endowed form that I have ever met with in this country. I cannot forbear lamenting.

Bembo, being in orders, had been unable to marry the lady during their long friendship, but elsewhere Platonists were beginning to introduce even wedlock into their thinking. In a work on Platonic love first written in about 1540, an Italian writer named Alessandro Piccolomini stated: "Love is a reciprocity of soul and has a different end and obeys different laws from marriage. Hence one should not take the loved one to wife." By the time he rewrote his book twenty years later, he had changed his mind and argued that Platonic love is not a separate entity but a prelude and accompaniment to marriage, inspiring the highest feelings, creating the desire for the joining of lives and bodies, and sweetening and purifying the sex act. Perhaps Piccolomini had merely grown practical; more likely, he had sensed and given voice to a new direction in human relationships.

At the same time, there began to appear in anecdotal historical writings of the time various stories in which the romantic impulse culminated in marriage. In their raw form, lacking the transfiguring treatment given love stories by the dramatist, they are often tedious and pedestrian—but perfectly believable. In 1554, for instance, a handsome Florentine youth named Ludovico di Neri Capponi fell in love with a girl named Maddalena Vellori. Maddalena's stepfather, who had married her mother for her wealth, hastily tried to marry the girl to his own son, while at the very same time, the Medici Duke of Florence, Cosimo I, tried to appropriate the heiress for one of his own favorites. The imperiled Maddalena fled to a convent while her mother pleaded, plotted, and maneuvered to change the Duke's mind. After many routine incidents, Cosimo agreed to talk to each of the lovers separately. Each pleaded ardently for the right to marry where love called, and Maddalena, on her knees, swore she would rather die than marry anyone but Ludovico. Disturbed and confused, the Duke finally laid aside his seignioral privileges, dismissed the stepfather's suit, and gave the lovers their will. It is hardly a great narrative, but it is a clear sign of changing attitudes.[8]

Against this background, we can be somewhat more certain that romantic marriage, as sometimes portrayed in the imaginative literature of the era, had a counterpart in reality. Two famous examples

[8] G. E. Saltini: *Tragedie Medice e Domestiche, Narrate Sui Documenti*, pp. 8–31.

are worth mentioning—Spenser's *Faërie Queene*, Books III and IV of which are an allegory of the defeat of courtly love and its replacement by romantic marriage; and Shakespeare's *Romeo and Juliet*, which is essentially a tale of Renaissance love, with marriage as its goal, frustrated by old-fashioned familial and political traditions.

Shakespeare, to be sure, took another stand on the husband-wife relationship in *The Taming of the Shrew*, and Spenser's allegory is muddy at best. But Spenser was less ambiguous elsewhere. One of his shorter poetical pieces is an enraptured tribute to a young lady, in which, like any good courtly lover, he praises her beauty, admires her soul, and pants for the shelter of night:

> *Ah when will this long weary day have end,*
> *And lend me leave to come unto my love?*
> *How slowly do the hours their numbers spend?*
> *How slowly does sad Time his feathers move?* . . .
>
> *Now welcome night, thou night so long expected,*
> *That long day's labor does at last defray,*
> *And all my cares, which cruel love collected,*
> *Hast summed in one, and cancelled for aye:*
> *Spread thy broad wing over my love and me,*
> *That no man may us see.*

But totally unlike the courtly lover, he concludes with a prayer for plentiful offspring—for the lady in question was Elizabeth Boyle, his fiancée, and the poem ("Epithalamion") was a bridal hymn, written before their wedding but published a year after it. The distance from Castiglione is immense, though less than a century has passed; one can hardly visualize an ideal Italian courtier printing a love song to his wife.

Not only were aristocrats and intellectuals beginning to think about the allying of romance and marriage, but so was a much larger group, soon to become important in history. The slowly growing middle classes had long been envious of the romantic love conduct of the nobility, but since the average bourgeois and his wife could afford neither the time nor money for extramarital courtly love affairs, they had traditionally frowned upon it and used Christian morals as the justification of their views. But romantic ideals blended with marriage were something the middle class not only could accept, but secretly hungered for. The prosaic domestic-conduct books of the middle class therefore began to reveal signs of a change from the mid-sixteenth century on. Writer after writer, for instance, discussed whether marriages should be arranged by the parents or by the personal inclination of the young people; even though many writers still held out for the former, it is obvious from the amount of talk that they were dealing with a perplexing situation and an unsettling new phenomenon. Roger Ascham, tutor to Elizabeth when she was a princess, observed it with alarm just prior to 1570:

> Our time is so far from that old discipline and obedience as now, not only young gentlemen, but even very young girls dare without all fear though not without open shame, where they list and how they list marry themselves in spite of father, mother, God, good order, and all.

The subject was hashed and rehashed endlessly, for it had become genuinely important. Shakespeare might please the ancient prejudices of men by having Petruchio tame Kate—yet in the very same play he held Kate's father up to ridicule for auctioning off Bianca to the highest bidder.

The middle class yearned to emulate the love-making manners of the courtiers, but always in a purified and moral context. In 1632, for instance, an unknown scribbler wrote a handbook of amorous conversations entitled *Cupid's School*, from which the uncouth could learn the refined manner of love-making, and at least in the preface the author managed to sound like a properly devilish fellow:

> He that thinks to win affection by telling a maid in plain terms that he loves her is much deceived, for when she hears you begin so plainly, she will start back from you, and think you to be some ignorant Corydon that know not Cupid's language; when on the contrary, he that can deliver his mind in amorous words doth seem to keep the keys of their maidenheads, of which he can take possession when he list.

But it was all only a bourgeois affectation of sin, without seriously sinful intention; each and every specimen dialogue in *Cupid's School* was directed specifically toward convincing maidens to yield to respectable matrimony.

More important still, the many books advising men on the proper control and management of wives were increasingly filled with statements to the effect that man and wife should not be tied to each other only as co-workers and begetters of offspring, but ought to experience with each other companionship, friendship, and the tender, intense, delights of passion just as lovers do. A work on marriage written in 1604, as typical as it is forgettable, stated the matter in limping verse:

> *Marriage is God's indenture which he draws*
> *'Twixt man and woman: 'tis life's obligation;*
> *It is love's pillar: this the chain of laws;*
> *'Tis the good evil, the bitter delectation.*
>
> *Wedlock's hell is when the husband throws*
> *His frowns, his brawls, his curses and his blows,*
> *On his wife's head: yet spends the amorous charms*
> *Of smiles and kisses in a strumpet's arms.*

And thus within the very century when lady-worship and witch-burning reached their greatest intensity, a partial rapprochement of the two attitudes became evident. The Renaissance enlightenment, with its pagan echoes, had made sex seem not so sinful and disgusting after all; men and women could therefore begin to associate it with love. But sex and love combined might have meant only adultery; instead, it began to imply, or at least infiltrate into, marriage. In addition to the reasons for this which we have already seen, there was one other of major importance—the changing nature of family life. In the Middle Ages, most noblemen and many merchants had regarded the family as a kind of depot at which one stopped occasionally to pick up fresh gear and to deposit one's seed. But in the Renaissance, aristocrats spent less time in petty skirmishings and more in cities and princely courts, while merchants were able to transact business by letter and bank draft, and could insure their goods with no need to defend them in person. In both cases, men spent more time in or near their homes, and the selection of a desirable and well-matched mate assumed new importance. A tiny clue tells much of the new emotional significance of marriage: late in the sixteenth century we find, for the first time, the suggestion that young married couples should live apart in a dwelling of their own.

All this may make one suppose that something like modern marriage was beginning to appear by the year 1600. Like it, but not *very* like it. Although the status of the wife as a human being and love object was rising, her status as a legal person remained little better than in the Middle Ages. Her identity was submerged in that of her husband when she married him; he had the right to make all contracts for her, to bring suit or to plead, and to run her affairs in every way. The law's position was summed up in the apothegm: "Husband and wife are one, and the husband is the one." Wife-beating was still a husband's legal right, against which the wife had no redress, according to an English legal manual for women published in 1632. Some lawyers maintained otherwise, but the domestic-conduct books and pulpit orations so continually criticized wife-beating that it must have been common.

Even more important, along with her growing value as a companion and a love partner, the wife was still thought of as an economic acquisition—not only a worker and manager, but one who brought property with her. In England, in the sixteenth and seventeenth centuries, a woman's personal belongings (money, furniture, linens, and the like) still became the *absolute* property of the husband at marriage, and he did not have to pass them on to her designated heirs. As for dowry, though that did pass to her heirs, the husband used and enjoyed it during her lifetime; if she died first, he could continue to use her land until his own death. The law in other Western countries, though varying in details, was generally similar.

The romantic value of a bride did not mix any too well with her cash value, though Renaissance men made continuous efforts to blend the two. In the legal manual for women just cited, the anonymous seventeenth-century author quaintly opined that the dowry "is the condiments of love. . . . Good meats are the better for sauce; venison craveth wine, and wedlock hath certain condiments, which come best in season at the wooing time." But as long as a man thought of his wife as a bringer of dowry and a preserver of his wealth, the generous ardor of the lover was apt to be held in check by the critical scrutiny of the economist. Even so romantic a figure as Sir Walter Raleigh, a good lover and later a good husband, urged his son to love his wife—and to put limits upon that love:

> Have therefore ever more care that thou be beloved of thy wife rather than thyself besotted on her; and thou shalt judge of her love by these two observations: first, if thou perceive she have a care of thy estate, and exercise herself therein; the other, if she study to please thee, and be sweet to thee in conversation without thy instruction, for love needs no teaching.

Yet having duly noted all this, we can still agree that between the early and the later phases of the Renaissance, a notable change had begun to show itself. As the power of medieval repressions abated, men began hesitantly to see women as complex creatures who united within themselves both good and bad attributes. If a real woman was somewhat less divine than the Lady, she was also considerably less vile than the Witch. Men could begin to feel the emotions of affectional love where they also felt animal heat, and to envision in the ideal wife the qualities that produced both.

7

"A Wise Man and Lusty" Marries a Courtesan

❁   ❁

❁

Just how far things had gone in the direction of uniting the sundered aspects of love by the early seventeenth century can best be seen in the form of a famous (and, in its own time, infamous) love affair of the period. Sir Kenelm Digby, the hero of the piece, was born in 1603. The son of a conspirator executed for his part in the Gunpowder Plot of 1605, he grew up despite the stain to be a splendid specimen of the cavalier—handsome, swashbuckling, and learned; a poet, a fashion plate, and a philosopher; a man as willing to brawl for honor's sake as to spend long nights at chemical experiments. In his youth, Digby met and was infatuated by Venetia Stanley, a girl of adequate, though unimportant, family. When his intentions toward her became too serious, he was shipped off to Europe. Digby himself later wrote that his affair with her was broken off because of old disagreements between his family and hers, and that he went to the Continent to forget his woes; it seems more likely, from other historical evidence, that Venetia was already known to have been seduced by one or two wealthy noblemen, and that Digby's mother sent him away to break up the unfortunate attachment.[4] In Europe he heard that she had moved to London and become the mistress of several important men; he suffered, hated her, and sought to forget.

He returned to London three years later in 1623 and almost at once saw her by accident, riding past in her carriage, elegant, utterly lovely with her oval face, delicate coloring, and rich dark hair, and yet strangely sad of countenance. Overcome and softened by the sight, he called upon her and paid his respects. It was a highly successful reunion; each greeted the other with quivering politeness, and their warmth rapidly grew as they told each other of the events of the intervening years. When Digby hesitantly mentioned the ugly rumors he had heard, Venetia was able to explain them all away and made him thoroughly happy by convincing him of her virtue, or so he says; the subject is somewhat confused, since he concluded that first reunion by making an all-out attempt to seduce her. Venetia wisely repelled him and he fell more in love than ever.

Nevertheless his friends and his mother soon told him that Venetia was generally thought to be the favorite of the Earl of Dorset and to have had one or two children by him; she was also said to entertain and receive support from several other noblemen. In Digby's mind all was bewilderment. Considering himself to be hopelessly in love, he tried to believe in her purity, but somewhat inconsistently he bribed the servants to let him into her house one morning while she was asleep and crawled into her bed stark naked. The excellent Venetia awoke and drove him away with maidenly indignation; Digby's love thereupon became boundless, and despite the strong opposition of his friends and his mother, he determined to marry her.[5]

That, at least, is what he wrote; actually, he must have known that the rumors were based on fact. Perhaps it made no difference to him; he is said to have remarked on various occasions: "A wise man, and lusty, can make an honest woman out of a brothel-house." Pos-

---

[4] Digby wrote an autobiography which he called *Loose Fantasies*, first published in 1827 as *Private Memoirs of Sir Kenelm Digby*. In it he used pseudonyms for all persons, and altered some of the facts so as to put the best complexion on the affair. Other sources of information, however, have enabled literary historians to identify the principals, and to spot the improvements on truth; see Notes.

[5] This and certain other incidents were expurgated from the 1827 edition, but were published in 1932 in E. W. Bligh's *Sir Kenelm Digby and his Venetia*, pp. 285–300.

sibly he was also fortified by financial considerations; shortly before he decided Venetia was good enough to marry, she had put up her jewels as security and made him a very considerable loan. Later in the century John Aubrey, the writer of brief biographies, recorded a story that the Earl of Dorset, who had settled £500 per annum on Venetia, cut it off when Digby married her and that Digby promptly sued him for it. In actual fact, Dorset died before the wedding; probably what happened was that he earlier cut off some stipend when he saw Digby replacing him, and Digby pestered him about it. It would seem highly likely that Digby knew exactly what Venetia was, and that his friends knew he knew. Perhaps the final clue is a statement of Digby's, in his autobiography, that a woman's honor does not consist in chastity alone, and that in some cases it is justifiable for a man to consent to his wife's pollution.

In any case, Sir Kenelm married Venetia in 1625, and from then on no scandal attached to their name or way of life; she bore him three sons and a daughter, conducted herself as an admirable wife, and there is reason to think they were well satisfied with each other. Such notables as Ben Jonson and Thomas Carew were frequent visitors at their home, and Jonson paid tribute to her sterling qualities in verse. After eight years of marriage, she died of a sudden illness. Digby was nearly unhinged by grief; he immersed himself for a time in chemical studies at Gresham College in London, and what with his long mourning cloak, untidy beard, and piercing eyes, assumed the look of a latter-day alchemist. He eventually recovered from his depression, but remained an eccentric the rest of his life, dabbling in politics, conniving with Cromwell (although a Catholic) during the Civil War, playing at chemistry, and writing several inconsequential books.

The love story of Sir Kenelm Digby and Venetia Stanley is a curious one, blurred by the distortions in his autobiography and somewhat self-consciously modeled upon patterns of fiction and drama. Yet its basic outlines are clear enough. If the affair hardly represents the usual or the ideal concept of love and marriage in the early seventeenth century in England—for few men were able to fuse the Lady and the Witch to such an extent as Digby—it is nevertheless a valuable bench mark: it was no fiction, but a real love affair, with a not very pure woman, that led to a happy marriage. Much talked about in its own time, it would have seemed impossible and even unthinkable only a century or two earlier.

Chapter VII
THE IMPURITANS

I

Puritanism Revisited

❋ ❋

❋

The Puritans, as everyone knows, were against love; indeed, the very word Puritanism has long been used as a synonym for disapproval of sexual passions, of sensuous enjoyment, and of all but the most circumspect emotions of love. Let us eavesdrop across the centuries for a moment, and hear how these formidable and depressing people spoke.

It is a rainy Sunday in London, in the spring of 1620; we take our seats, in imagination, in the church at Rotherhithe to hear the eminent Puritan preacher Thomas Gataker. His sermon today is upon marriage; at the moment he is discussing marriage-by-arrangement versus marriage-for-love. We listen, and wonder if we have got into the wrong church or the wrong century, for this pious sobersides is saying things that are sentimental and even romantic—and linking them to heaven:

> As there is no affection more forcible [than love], so there is none freer from force and compulsion. The very offer of enforcement turneth it oft into hatred. . . . Things fall out many times so unexpectedly, such strong liking taken to some [one] suddenly not once thought on before, and such strange alienation of affections where there hath been much laboring to link them . . . that even a natural man's dim eye may easily see and discern a more special providence of God oft carrying things in these cases.

The words have a Puritan seasoning but their substance is almost neo-pagan, for it was a Greek conceit that love was a gift—or curse —given by the gods, holding mortals helpless in its power. What has this to do with Puritanism? Let us leave the church and look further.

[217]

We move on, and stop at a bookstall in St. Paul's Churchyard, in
the year 1642. London is noisy and bustling as usual, but not far outside it armies are fighting; the opposition between King Charles
and Parliament, between the aristocratic way of life and the middle
class, has finally come to bloodshed. Love, though not the crucial issue, is at stake too; the fashionable Neoplatonism, the love literature,
and the amours of the courtiers are all abominable to the Round-
heads, who have vowed to uproot them from English life. The Puritans, it is clear, are the enemies of love. We pick up a brand-new
book called *Matrimonial Honor* by Daniel Rogers, the son of a notable Puritan preacher and himself one of the same, and flip through
it; we find not one, not a dozen, but two hundred rhapsodical pages
on love. A typical sentence strikes the eye:

> Husbands and wives should be as two sweet friends, bred under
> one constellation, tempered by an influence from heaven, whereof
> neither can give any great reason save that mercy and providence
> first made them so, and then made their match.

All very well, but what does Pastor Rogers think of the physical
side of love? Is it a disgusting necessity, a shameful weakness of the
flesh? We turn the pages, and find the answer; here is a passage in
which he says that "marriage love" is "a sweet compound" of spiritual affection and carnal attraction, and that this blend of the two is
the "vital spirit and heart blood" of wedlock. Can this really be a
Puritan speaking?

Thoughtfully replacing the book, we decide to search for the
real, undiluted Puritans, and whisk ourselves across the Atlantic to
the colony of Massachusetts in the 1670's. Surely in this harsh, grim-
faced theocracy, the desires of the flesh have been put in their proper
place; at the very least, those weak mortals who yield to pleasure
must suffer the inner hellfire of guilt and remorse for their sins. In
a small comfortless courtroom, the Justices of the Middlesex Court
are seated in hearing on a bastardy case, and a clerk is about to read
aloud a letter that had been written by the unwed mother. Let us
steal in and listen:

> Dear Love, I remember my love to you, hoping your welfare,
> and I hope to embrace thee, but now I write to you to let you
> know that I am [with] a child by you, and I will either kill it or
> lay it to another and you shall have no blame at all, for I have had
> many children and none [of their fathers] have [to support] none
> of them.

In some confusion, we seek reassurance in a visit to that bulwark of probity, good, gray Judge Samuel Sewall, who nearly thirty years ago sat on the trial of the Salem witches, and whose record of devoted service to the Puritan ideal is unsurpassed. We hurry to him on an October evening in 1720, unmindful of the fact that Judge Sewall, now a widower, is paying a social call upon Widow Winthrop. We approach the drawing room, but pause in alarm; the Judge is acting more like a Cavalier than a Roundhead. Having stolen a kiss a few nights ago, he is getting still bolder tonight; at the moment he is holding Mrs. Winthrop's hand and saying: "Will you acquit me of rudeness, Madam, if I draw off your glove?" The lady archly asks why he need draw it off, and he replies in handsome, if rather homespun, fashion: " 'Tis great odds, Madam, between handling a dead goat and a living lady." The widow tries to blush, the glove comes off, and we depart hurriedly to return to our own times and reconsider our notions about the Puritans.[1]

2

The Anti-Augustinian

❀   ❀

❀

Protestants like to think of the Reformation as a progressive outgrowth and enlargement of the Renaissance; Catholics prefer to think of it as a reactionary repudiation of the Renaissance and a retrogression from it. In order for us to see the Puritans whole, we

[1] The several quotations in this section come, respectively, from: Thomas Gataker: *A Good Wife God's Gift—A Marriage Sermon;* Daniel Rogers: *Matrimonial Honor* (1642), pp. 200 and 151; a letter in the files of the Middlesex Court, quoted in *The New England Quarterly,* Dec. 1942, p. 602; and Samuel Sewall: *Diary,* Oct. 11, 1720 (Vol. III, p. 267).

must first agree to an awkward assumption: namely, that the Reformation was both things. Historians may simplify, but history itself is always complex.

The Renaissance, for instance, had unfolded and blossomed in the good earth of increased trade and accumulating wealth, yet the Catholic Church, so closely identified with it and so prone to adopt its luxuries, still taught Aquinas's view that pursuing money beyond one's bare needs was "sinful covetousness," and continued to treat business as a somewhat shameful activity. The Reformation, which likewise flourished in that same soil, praised financial effort, removed the stigma from the charging of interest, and regarded business success as a sign of God's special blessing—yet the Protestants disapproved of the very luxuries that their new wealth could buy them. The Renaissance revival of learning weakened the hold of medieval theology on men's minds, but although the Reformation was indebted to this, in its revolution against Rome it rejected much of the enlightened thinking of the time, immersed itself once more in theology, and temporarily disrupted university education. The Reformation broke up the antiquated feudal systems of economics, politics, and religion, but in the process also destroyed much of the beauty, the joy of living, and the rationalism that had lately come into Western life.

The Protestants' feelings about sex and love were similarly complicated and contradictory. They devalued celibacy, praised marriage without qualification, and argued that marital sex was wholesome and free of taint; nevertheless they continued to examine, condemn, and execute witches very much as the inquisitors had, often exhibiting in these activities the same morbid sexual fantasies. In 1597, after eighty years of liberalizing Reformation influence, the Protestant King of Scotland, James VI, could still personally inform his subjects and the world at large that the Devil, in order to leave his mark on witches, "doth lick them with his tongue in some privy part of their body," and a century later in Salem, Massachusetts, a jury of Puritan women would still eagerly jab pins into the genitals of one Bridget Bishop, ostensibly by way of searching for a telltale dead spot or Devil's mark.

No man was a more bewildering mixture of the liberal and the reactionary than the first reformer, Dr. Martin Luther himself. Often he spoke like one who had come to liberate the body altogether from guilt-induced asceticism: "If our Lord God may make excellent large pike and good Rhenish wine," he said, "I may very well venture to eat and drink. Thou mayest enjoy every pleasure in the world that is not sinful." He lustily and vigorously battled against the Catholic tradition of asceticism, and specifically prescribed small doses of deliberate enjoyment as the best antidote for temptation:

> Satan has so spoiled and besmirched our nature that we don't want to let ourselves be comforted. Therefore, whoever feels such devilish thoughts and is tempted by them, I advise to drive them out quickly—think of something merry, take a good drink, play, and amuse yourself.

Yet Luther often spoke like a monk of the despairing early Christian centuries. "We are the children of wrath," he maintained, "and all our works, intentions, and thoughts are nothing at all in the balance against our sins." "Works"—including gifts to the Church—could not buy one's way out; faith alone could save, but God allowed few that salvation and most would burn for their sins. God, said Luther, "seems to delight in the tortures of the wretched." [2]

In the course of his long fight against the Catholic Church, Luther often found himself confronted by the Devil in person, and many times argued violently with him and fought against his subtle temptations. As improbable as it seems, however, those struggles were marked less by weeping and suffering than by a mood of healthful exertion and an exuberant appetite for vulgarity. Everyone knows that Luther once flung an inkhorn at the Devil, but it is more indicative of his peasantlike sense of humor that he specifically advised throwing a handful of dung in the Devil's face, or breaking wind at him, or even saying to him, as Luther himself once did: "Lick my ass!" (On that particular occasion, Luther noted with gratification: "He said no more. A good way of getting rid of him!")

Luther found in sex an ideal weapon in his war against Rome. He early sanctioned the marriage of priests and hotly argued that celibacy had been invented by the Devil as a source of sin; after a while he advanced to the radical view that marriage was not a sacrament at all, but a civil matter, subject to city and state regulations rather

[2] In contrast, Friar Johann Tetzel, whose peddling of papal indulgences angered Luther into posting his ninety-five theses on the church door, had an almost jolly view of sin, and is said to have offered to relieve sinners of their burdens with the following cheerful formula:
As soon as cash in the coffer rings,
The soul from purgatory's fire springs.

than to canon law; and still later in life (1532) he held that Christ had probably committed adultery with Mary Magdalene and other women so as to partake fully of the nature of man.[3]

But to arrive at such a point of view had been no easy matter for him. The son of a stern German peasant who became a miner, Luther was brought up under harsh Teutonic discipline. Both parents beat him mercilessly for small boyish errors, gave him a vivid sense of his own wickedness, and filled his head with medieval notions of demons, witches, and miracles. When he went away to school, a natural zestfulness asserted itself, and he sang, played the lute, and learned to love good company. But he had not resolved his inner conflicts, and during a thunderstorm one day in 1505 when he was a twenty-two-year-old law student, he was struck with terror at the thought of death and decided he had received a warning from God; he abandoned the study of law forthwith and entered the Augustinian Eremite cloister in Erfurt. There he fasted, prayed, and so strictly observed the ascetic regime of his order that he very nearly killed himself. After a while, he learned to moderate his austerities, became a priest and an instructor in the Augustinian monastery at Wittenberg, and slowly attained a degree of clerical stature. In October 1517, when he challenged anyone to debate his ninety-five theses on the nature of sin, contrition, forgiveness, and the inefficacy of bought indulgences, he still considered himself a devout Catholic and completely loyal to the Pope. Carried away by forces beyond his imagining, within the next several years Luther was inevitably led into open defiance of the Pope's direct orders, was excommunicated and branded heretic, stood before Emperor Charles V and the Diet at Worms and defended his position, and saw the Reformation he had touched off sweep across Northern Europe like a grass fire.

Under the immense pressure of these events, Luther came to defend (somewhat reluctantly at first) the breaking of monastic vows and the marriages of priests, and in 1521 he wrote that the sexual impulse was both natural and irrepressible. Yet not until another four years had passed did he himself marry, and even then the event was produced neither by romance nor by urgent desire. In 1525, Luther, then forty-two, recommended to a group of nuns that they leave their convent and helped them find husbands. Katharina von Bora, a woman of twenty-six, was the last of the lot; Luther tried

[3] This last startling statement appears in Luther's *Table-Talk* (*Tischreden* 1472, Weimar ed.).

to pair her off, but the proposal fell through and she was forced to go to work as a domestic. Meanwhile the Peasants' War was raging, threatening the entire Reformation. It occurred to Luther that the war was the Devil's attack on him, and to spite the Devil—and only incidentally to solve Katharina's problem—he married her.

Enthusiasts have sometimes said that Luther was carried away by her beauty, but her portrait belies the story. She was buxom, strongly made, and distinctly lumpish of feature—no Iseult, nor even an avant-garde Anne Boleyn. By no means in love when he married, Luther was soon plagued with misgivings and feared that his marriage had cost him the respect of some of his followers; then, happily, he saw that this was only more of Satan's work, and accepted his marriage cheerfully. After a year he wrote to a friend: "My Käte . . . is well and, by God's grace, is submissive to me, obedient in all things, and more agreeable than I had dared to hope." Not only was she agreeable, but productive, useful, and efficient; she ran the farm, bore Luther six children, fed and housed all of them plus eleven of his nieces and nephews (luckily, their home was the many-roomed former Augustinian monastery at Wittenberg, by then emptied of monks), and did all this on the modest salary paid Luther by the Elector Frederick of Saxony.

As the years passed, Luther saw his wife in many lights—and always with blithe inconsistency. After half a dozen years of marriage, he once said in an expansive mood: "My wife is more precious to me than the Kingdom of France and all the treasures of Venice," but the following year he sourly grumbled: "Get you a wife and then your mind, however fuzzy it is, will become straight as a ribbon; it will be reduced to one idea: Do and think as *she* wishes." Like a mooning young swain, he could say: "I love my Käte, and know that I love her more than she loves me," and like a henpecked husband, he could say: "If I were to marry again I would carve myself an obedient wife out of stone, for to find one of flesh and blood is not conceivable."

Luther evidently found the sexual side of marriage satisfactory, for having experienced it he continued to argue that sexual love was as natural and necessary as eating; he retained the medieval notion that it was somehow sinful, but felt that within marriage "God covers the sin," leaving the act untainted. But if he had no qualms about married sex, he was hardly ecstatic. "Had God consulted me about it," he said in one of his many dinner-table pronunciamentos,

"I should have advised Him to continue the generation of the species by fashioning human beings out of clay, as Adam was made."

Luther loved his Käte, but he had very firm old-fashioned ideas about woman's role in life. Every woman, he said, should—like Käte—be a good housewife and mother. "Take women from their housewifery and they are good for nothing," he remarked, ignoring the evidence of the Renaissance ladies even then shining in all their glory in Italy, though not in Wittenberg. Woman's proper sphere was the bearing of children and the providing of household comforts to her husband, to whom she should be meekly obedient; a husband was a fool who, because of love, let her rule the household, but he should be gentle and considerate, recognizing that she was but a frail vessel. This consciously biblical attitude fitted Luther's theological position; even more to the point, it was ideally suited to the habits and needs of the very class to which Protestantism appealed for other reasons.

Through Luther's personal life and public actions, most of the major attitudes of the Reformation toward women and love were clearly, if contradictorily, established. Little remained of the Renaissance idealization of woman or of exaggerated and gallant courting. Not only was the average Protestant a more practical and business-like person, inclined to prefer Old Testament patriarchalism, but he regarded the elegant courtier's religion of beauty with suspicion and fear as something typically Roman. But as for sexual frigidity, repression of sensuous enjoyments, or the prudish avoidance of biological facts, these had been no part of Luther's make-up and were not inherent in Protestantism. They appeared, rather, only among the extremist factions of those who followed him.

3

The Bluenoses

❀   ❀

❀

If Luther was inherently genial but chronically inconsistent, John Calvin, a young Frenchman he inspired, was inherently dour, and chronically consistent. Calvin wrote his epochal work, the *Institutes of the Christian Religion*, when he was only twenty-six, and never changed his mind on any salient point; in it, he rigorously drew together all the most severe elements of the Old Testament, the patristic writings, and Lutheranism, and derived from them by selection and extension a ferocious theology built upon total human depravity, the implacable wrath of God with man, and the concepts of absolute predestination, the election of the very few, and the certain damnation of all the rest.

Had Calvin been a happier or healthier man, Puritanism might never have been puritanical, and the thinking of the Genevans, the Dutch, the Scotch, the English, and the Americans ever since might have been different. Historians reassure us that it is not so, and that larger forces were responsible for the rise of Calvinism: his democratic, primitive church structure appealed even more to the bourgeoisie than Lutheranism, which was controlled by princelings; his disapproval of frivolity and luxury was ideally suited to the temperament of those whose aim was to work and accumulate; and so on. Yet it may be that trivial forces also have mighty effects. Unlike Luther, Calvin did not enjoy playing the lute or flute, eating broiled fish, or downing a flagon of beer; unlike Luther, he was small and thin, dyspeptic and ailing, intense and unhumorous. Conceivably, the ascetic and repressive features that mark Puritanism at its unloveliest and have given it a bad name owe as much to one man's glandular shortcomings as to the social goals of the bourgeoisie.

[225]

Calvin was born at Noyon, in Picardy, in 1509. His father, a lawyer, wanted the boy to be learned, and from the first Calvin proved an excellent student. For unknown reasons (possibly because he grew up under a harsh stepmother), he was so censorious and moralistic even in his boyhood—and so excellent at Latin—that fellow students called him "the accusative case." He studied law and the classics as earnestly as though seeking his salvation, poring over his books until midnight and arising with the dawn to begin again. Headaches, indigestion, and fits of anger plagued him, but he would not slacken his efforts. Later on he added to these ailments ulcers, stones, and pulmonary tuberculosis; it is little wonder he could consider life of no value and God a pitiless tyrant.

In 1532, when Calvin was a budding humanist scholar of twenty-three, he happened to read some of the sermons of that bold ex-monk Martin Luther and underwent a conversion. Almost at once he saw his destiny and, mustering all his learning and his legal training, began to write his epochal study of the original nature of the Christian Church and the Catholic additions to it; the result, the *Institutes*, was a blueprint for a neo-biblical, primitive Christian life. A year after it was published, Calvin became an evangelizing Protestant preacher in the city of Geneva, and there, already famous at twenty-seven, he began to play a role in the affairs of that city which eventually made him its virtual dictator. In its developed form, the government of Geneva became a model theocracy: the Council (civil government) chose a Consistory or Presbytery (religious government) of five pastors and twelve elders, which was given dictatorial powers over the religious observances and morality of every citizen. Calvin, as head of the Consistory, was thus, in effect, a complete dictator of morals, and his views on sex, love, and other pleasures became the code by which Genevans lived for the next century.

The most depressing features of that code are familiar to everyone who has read any history. It was punishable by fine or imprisonment to sing, to dance at weddings, to curse, to serve too many dishes at dinner, or to wear clothes of too extravagant a cut. Plays were banned, jewelry and other adornments discouraged, and elegant hair-styles made grounds for jailing.[4] Sexual transgressions,

---

[4] Probably echoing Luther, Calvin had written: "We are nowhere forbidden to laugh, or to be satisfied with food . . . or to be delighted with music, or to drink wine." (*Institutes*, III, xix, 9) Nevertheless, in one two-year period, 414 people were prosecuted for crimes such as singing or wearing ex-

however, were something else again—they merited as severe punishments as heresy: fornication was cause for exile, and adultery deserved death, sometimes by drowning, sometimes by beheading. Some sinful Genevans actually met such fates, although many sexual offenders were let off with steep fines and jail sentences. Even legitimate love was astringently regulated. Engagements were limited to six weeks' duration, for one did not dally or play at romance, but got down to cases. Having done so, if either the bride or groom arrived late for the wedding, they were to be sent away again; there would be no nonsense in Geneva. As for the wedding itself, it would be grave, correct, and simple; the law expressly forbade revelry, minstrelsy, dancing, or the use of tambourines.

What kind of person could cram such regulations down the throats of ordinary human beings by the force of his personality and his arguments? His portrait shows a middle-aged man with a thin intent face, domed forehead, and penetrating eyes. We can read into it genius, tremendous drive, a terrible persuasiveness, but we cannot easily imagine his personal feelings. Unlike Saint Augustine he left no intimate record of his inner torments and sufferings over sex and love; the scanty details given by his contemporaries leave room for many interpretations.

Calvin had been a bachelor, and almost certainly celibate, until the age of thirty-one; he left no word as to whether he suffered temptations and lusts in all this period of youth, and perhaps in itself that is a valuable clue. During a brief period of exile from Geneva (1538–41), he lived in Strasbourg, was minister to a small church, and took in boarders. Finding this burdensome, he asked friends to find him a wife, and provided us with one clue to his nature when he specified: "I am none of those insane lovers who, when once smitten with the fine figure of a woman, embrace also her faults. This only is the beauty which allures me, if she be chaste, obliging, not fastidious, economical, patient, and careful for my health." A poor widow named Idelette de Bure filled this bill of particulars, and he married her in 1540. She served him faithfully until her death nine years later; Calvin wrote kindly words about her after she was gone, but remained a widower thereafter.

Some light is shed, too, by his official statements on married love. Like the Catholics before him, Calvin spoke of marriage as having

travagant clothing. Calvin said, however, that he wanted his people to be happy, and encouraged them to play quoits.

two main functions: the production of offspring and the remedying of incontinence. Like the most antifeminist of the early Fathers of the Church, he had nothing to say about its involving companionship, affection, passion, or adoration. He condoned married sex, and in fact insisted on it (in Geneva a woman could sue for divorce if her husband became impotent); but he was obsessed by the subject of adultery and defined it so broadly as to include even immodest gestures or words. Both attitudes, it would seem, could logically grow out of the same conception of sexual love as a purely animal activity.

Like many another reformer before him, this first Puritan was quite sure that his actions would make people good; like others before him, he overestimated their wish to be good. Although various visitors remarked that Geneva was orderly, decent, and sober, the records of the Council show that beneath the surface of that rigidly conformist life, much was going on: how else can one explain the numerous entries relating to illegitimate children, abandoned infants, forced marriages, and death sentences? (Ironically, even a step-daughter and a son-in-law of Calvin himself were condemned for adultery.) He must have known of these shortcomings; to some extent he comforted himself and his followers with the thought that almighty God had sent syphilis to earth to punish those who escaped the law.

Few men are of so stern and severe a character, but surprisingly enough Calvin's ideas and practices took hold in a number of countries of northern Europe; in each, the more extreme and dogmatic leaders of Calvinist thought were responsible for giving Puritanism a name for intolerance, hard-working asceticism, and lovelessness. If most Puritans and Puritan life in general were quite unlike the ideal of Calvinism, it is nevertheless true that many of the vocal and identifiable Puritans did sound almost inhumanly joyless to the Renaissance peoples all around them.

In England, from whence American Puritanism sprang, the movement was at first diffuse and moderate in character. In part it consisted of extreme Calvinists inspired by John Knox, who had made Scotland over along more or less Genevan lines by the 1560's; in part it consisted of a variety of Englishmen still within the conservative official Church of England who disagreed with certain forms and ceremonies reminiscent of Catholicism, and wished to "purify" it of them. (As one witty preacher later said about the Church of

England: "King Henry the Eight brake the Pope's neck, but bruised not the least finger of Popery.") But the Puritan label rapidly acquired a Calvinist flavor and became a term of opprobrium. "I find many that are called Puritans," noted Owen Feltham several decades later, "yet few or none that will own the name. Whereof the reason sure is this, that 'tis for the most part held a name of infamy."

The English Puritans grew increasingly Calvinistic and severe as the cleavage widened between the aristocracy and the middle class, between the Renaissance tradition and the Reformation zeal. All during Elizabeth's reign and the Shakespearean era, Puritan critics of the stage, the court, and upper-class life were growing ever more outspoken. Elizabeth's successor, James I, thought to quiet the Puritans by persecuting them, but only drew them together; in a still worse blunder, he drove some of them to emigrate to New England beginning in 1620 and thus made them the inheritors of the New World. In the reign of Charles I the schism in English life continued to widen; the King and Parliament were locked in a struggle over the King's rights of taxation and certain other powers, with the Puritan elements aligning themselves against the royal party. The Anglicans at court so loved ritual and pageant as to seem practically Catholic to their opponents in Parliament; coincidentally, the growing licentiousness and dissoluteness of the courtiers, who affected Neoplatonic words but practiced wantonness, gave the extremists among the Puritans an excellent target.

In the autumn of 1642 King Charles and the Commons finally took to the field to settle the issues between them; by 1646 Puritanism of the Calvinist variety was triumphant, and by 1649 Charles lost his head. Like Calvin, the extremists closed the theaters, enforced church attendance, passed strict laws limiting the elegance of clothing, and made fornication punishable by three months' imprisonment, and adultery by death. But it was one thing to pass such laws and another to make them work in England, where there had been so long a time for Renaissance ideas to become absorbed into the culture. English juries and justices, for example, even when Puritan in sentiment, felt little sympathy with the harsh laws against sexual misconduct, and very few persons were actually convicted; by 1657, in fact, the law had become practically inoperative.

In any case, the extreme Calvinist measures were soon swept into oblivion, for in 1660 the Commonwealth government disintegrated and Charles II, son of the beheaded king, was summoned home from

France. Meanwhile, however, thoroughgoing Calvinism was getting a far better trial in New England; there the Cavalier influence was negligible, and the terms of the charter maintained the Calvinist theocracy in power from 1629 until 1691.[5] It is there that we may see Puritanism at its severest, except for Geneva and Scotland. Even though some of the "Blue Laws" of Massachusetts and Connecticut never existed (having been concocted by an unfriendly historian in 1781 and perpetuated by the unwary ever since), it is perfectly true that there were numerous restrictions on smoking, drinking, gaming, Sunday amusements, fancy clothing, and unchaperoned meetings of the unmarried. No Puritan church had an organ ("the Devil's bagpipe"), sermons ran two to three hours long, and tithing men switched those who fell asleep or let their attention stray. A New England gentleman could attend a funeral and seriously say afterwards, that it had been "an awful, yet pleasing, treat."

Public whippings, brandings, and duckings were handed out for such offenses as riotous conduct or scolding. Sexual offenses were treated more strictly: prior to 1650, adultery was a capital offense in Massachusetts, and some adulterers are known to have been actually executed. After 1650 the law required less—or was it more?—in the form of a whipping and the lifelong wearing of the scarlet letter. Repression of pleasures in general, and of sexual pleasure in particular, undoubtedly played a part in the two outbreaks of witchcraft hysteria in New England; the earlier one began in 1647 and resulted in the execution of fourteen witches in Massachusetts and Connecticut, while the Salem frenzy of 1692 brought about the execution of twenty persons and two dogs.

Yet to sense the leaden atmosphere of Puritan life at its most oppressive, we need to step into a real home. It is January 13, 1696, and this is the house of good Judge Samuel Sewall in Boston. His young daughter Elizabeth, who has recently heard a sermon on the text: "Ye shall seek me and shall die in your sins," has been dejected and sorrowful all day. The family finishes eating, and then, as Judge Sewall later noted in his diary, "a little after dinner she burst out into an amazing cry, which caused all the family to cry too." Mrs. Sewall questions the girl and at last the reason comes out: the child "was afraid she should go to Hell, her sins were not pardoned." Such a spell of childhood terror was not unique. Seven years earlier

[5] The charter expired in 1684, but the new non-theocratic charter was not granted until 1691, after some interim uncertainties.

Judge Sewall had lectured his ten-year-old son Sam one day on the need to prepare for death, and afterwards noted disconsolately: "He seemed not much to mind, eating an apple." But Sam did mind, for later, when saying his prayers, "he burst out into a bitter cry and said he was afraid he should die. I prayed with him and read scriptures comforting against death, as 'O Death, where is thy sting,' etc." [6]

And that is the stern, bloodless portrait of Puritanism that hangs in the hall of historical caricature. But like all caricature, it is incomplete and exaggerated; moreover, this particular one is far from a good likeness. All the things we have described were true of Calvinist Puritanism, but like the Neoplatonism of Castiglione's friends at Urbino, it was a faith more sworn by than lived by, a goal men and women could not quite reach. A complete and realistic portrait of the early Puritan would have a stern expression thinly masking two ill-controlled moods: one of mischief, and the other of romance.

4

The Puritan as Sinner

To redraw the portrait so as to make it more than caricature, let us use as our model not England, for there Puritan control was brief, the country was divided in sentiment, and the records of morality under the Commonwealth are fragmentary; instead let us draw it from life in New England, where the ideals of the Puritan churches were the law of the land for nearly three quarters of a

[6] *Diary*, Jan. 13, 1696 and Jan. 12, 1689.

century, where the population was almost entirely Puritan, and where documentary materials are relatively abundant.

The easiest thing to observe about a man is his clothing; yet even in so obvious a thing the caricature differs significantly from the reality. It is commonly believed that Puritans all dressed in drab-hued clothing of a plain, functional cut, and certainly they appear so in countless statues, murals, and book illustrations. But Puritan Governor John Winthrop knew better. In his *History of New England* he reported that in 1638 a court had directed the elders of all churches to curb extravagant dress, but Puritan dandies defiantly continued to sport ruffles, capes, and roses and silver buckles on their shoes. The next year a law was passed expressly forbidding these follies; it, too, must have been ineffective, for other laws continued to be passed on the same matter again and again.

Many a seventeenth-century preacher heaped verbal fire upon those New England men and women who affected wigs and peri-wigs, and by 1675 a law was passed banning such follies; yet peri-wigs gained ground and in 1685 Judge Sewall noted in his diary with evident annoyance that two people just received into the Church wore wigs. By the end of the century many men and women were wearing them without prosecution; in 1704 Judge Sewall scolded a young man who had just cut off his hair and taken to a wig, but it was a personal scolding, not an official one, and had no effect. After the turn of the century still more outrageous finery could be found in Boston and elsewhere—slashed sleeves, fine gloves, lace, jewelry, satin doublets, and the like. If most Puritan dress in the early years was somewhat dull, it was as much due to pioneer frugality as religious conviction; as conditions improved, the basic instinct to preen re-emerged.

Even before the close of the seventeenth century, Boston had its first fencing-master and soon afterwards several New England towns had granted licenses to dancing-masters. Though children sometimes wept for fear of God and death, there were toys and dolls on sale in shops in Boston and Salem. In a number of homes there were guitars, virginals, and celli; the picture of the Puritan family spending all its leisure studying the Word is, like all partisan propaganda, thoroughly untrustworthy. Still more surprising, the court and church records of early New England are filled with case histories of men and women who gamed, swore, fought, and got drunk—but who were Puritans.

So, too, with the practice of sex and love. If one but looks into the faded, crumbling archives of county courts and of churches, he may catch momentary glimpses of normally libidinous, moderately sinful men and women caught and made immortal not by poetry or art, but by a line or two of legal jargon. Here, for instance, is one John Smith of Medfield, Massachusetts, leaving his wife and going off about 1670, brash as you please, to live with Patience Rawlins; the Suffolk County Court purifies him with thirty lashes and a fine of £10, and orders him home. Here are Elizabeth Wheeler and Joanna Pierce both being severely admonished for sitting in the laps of men other than their husbands. Mrs. Edmond Maddock is charged with sitting up late by the fireside with two male friends while her husband is asleep. A Mr. Clark is ordered by a court to stop keeping company with Mrs. Freeman, "concerning whom there is a strong suspicion of incontinency." Abigail Bush of Westfield, a shrewish young woman, is censured in church in 1697 for using bad language about her elderly father's remarriage: to wit, she has said that his new wife is "as hot as a bitch." Can this be a Puritan woman speaking, and can she really be describing another Massachusetts female in the year 1697? But conditions in Connecticut are no better. In 1660, Jacob Minline and Sarah Tuttle of New Haven are summoned to court for an offense described in fond detail: in the presence of others these shameless people "sat down together, his arm being about her, and her arm upon his shoulder or about his neck; and he kissed her and she kissed him, or they kissed one another, continuing in this posture about half an hour." The court fined and scolded Miss Tuttle with a strangely honorable term of condemnation—it found her to be a "bold virgin." [7]

The very wording of the laws which thus interfered with private conduct is often an excellent indication of the real state of affairs. The legislators of Massachusetts, for instance, unwittingly documented an all-but-forgotten aspect of Puritan life when they set down in 1647 the justification of a new law to control and regulate courting: "It is a common practice in divers places," they explained, "for young men irregularly and disorderly to watch all advantages for their evil purposes, to insinuate [themselves] into the affections of young maidens, by coming to them in places and seasons un-

[7] These and many similar cases have been extracted from church and court records by Professor Henry W. Lawrence in *The Not-Quite-Puritans;* Edmund S. Morgan in "The Puritans and Sex" (*The New England Quarterly,* Vol. 15, Dec. 1942); and Emil Oberholzer in *Delinquent Saints.*

known to their parents. . . ." And so they made a law; but eight
years later the General Court noted with alarm an increase in fornication, and still three years later remarked on the large number of
bastards in the colony. In Plymouth Colony, similar controls had
had a similar lack of success; Governor William Bradford, recording in his *History of the Plymouth Plantation* a veritable epidemic
of sexual misdemeanors in 1642, speculated for a moment along surprisingly advanced lines:

> It may be in this case as it is with waters when their streams
> are stopped or dammed up; when they get passage they flow with
> more violence, and make more noise and disturbance, than when
> they are suffered to run quietly in their own channels.

And for all the emphasis on the sinfulness of fornication and adultery, the early Puritans were definitely not against sex as such. Not
only did they breed large families and take pride in so doing, but
their spiritual leaders praised married sex and roundly condemned
the "Popish conceit of the excellency of virginity." The congregations themselves acted from the same point of view. At the First
Church of Boston, for instance, the congregation considered action
against one James Mattock for several offenses, one of them being,
of all things, sexual abstinence. Mattock, it appeared, had denied his
wife conjugal relations for two years on the grounds that he was
punishing himself for his sins; the congregation voted that this was
unnatural and unchristian, and expelled him from membership in the
church.

It was only sex outside of marriage that the early Puritans attacked. The churches, punishing more sinners than the courts, employed a public form of confession far more painful than the Catholic confessional they had repudiated. Church elders would investi-
gate allegations of fornication, adultery, or other serious sins, and
require the accused, if guilty, to make a written confession which
was read aloud to the congregation on Sunday. The congregation
would then vote to accept it, restoring the member to grace, or to
reject it, leading to suspension or excommunication from membership. All this sounds revoltingly autocratic and severe to the modern
mind. But Dr. Emil Oberholzer, a diligent historian, recently read
all the 1,242 confessions of fornication, or reports of such confessions, that exist in church records from 1620 to 1839, and concluded
that what is most remarkable about them is how unremarkable they
seemed to the Puritans; the vast majority were recorded in a per-

fectly matter-of-fact manner without comment, as though they were nothing but routine business.[8]

The 1,242 confessions are not a valid reckoning of the incidence of illicit love-making in New England, but only a small sampling. For one thing, only those who got caught had to confess; for another, many of the church records are missing or imperfect. Yet there *is* one exceedingly important statistic to be gleaned from these records. Dr. Oberholzer tabulated by type all disciplinary cases of every sort mentioned in the records of the Massachusetts churches he visited, and discovered that a plurality of them concerned fornication. It was, in other words, the most prevalent and most popular sin in Puritan New England.

5

The Puritan as Lover

❋ ❋

❋

If it is somewhat surprising to learn that Puritans could be so impure, it is still more so to find that some of them were tenderly romantic, and that both English and Colonial Puritanism absorbed various love concepts from the Renaissance tradition.

It is true, of course, that English Puritans were opposed to the dandified worship of beauty and the adulterous follies of the court

[8] Op. cit., p. 150. Another indication of that attitude can be found in the civil law in Plymouth where, under the Revised Statutes of 1671, fornication was conceded to be a fairly natural impulse; at least, one may so interpret the fact that ordinary fornicators were fined £10, but if engaged to each other at the time (which would ostensibly heighten the impulse and decrease the inhibitions), were fined only half as much.

of Charles I; it is true furthermore that much of what they said
about love was a justification of marriage along patriarchal biblical
lines. They lavished an enormous amount of rhetoric, via pulpit and
printing press, on the justification of the God-appointed subordination of woman to man. A fair sample of the mood of such writing is
this brief passage from William Whately's *The Bride-Bush* (1617):
"Whosoever therefore doth desire to be a good wife, or to live comfortably, let her set down this conclusion within her soul: Mine husband is my superior, my better; he hath authority and rule over me,
nature hath given it to him . . . [and] God hath given it to him."
For via family and congregation, the Puritans desperately sought to
shore up the changing and shifting society of their time. William
Gouge, who wrote a full seven hundred pages entitled *Of Domesti-
cal Duties*, linked housekeeping with divinity: he set forth a theo-
cratic pecking order that ran from child to mother, and thence to
husband, magistrate, king, and God. "A family is a little church
and a little commonwealth," he stated, "a school wherein the first
principles and grounds of government and subjection are learned."

But the Puritan idea of the patriarchy was quite different from
that of earlier systems of female subordination. Unlike Greek wives,
Puritan women were supposed to be good companions to their husbands; unlike early Christian and medieval wives, they were not
subordinated because of their vileness and frailties, but because of
their adaptation to child-rearing and home-making. Puritan writers
stressed the importance of emotional harmony between man and
wife, and Gouge wrote that they should be closer and more nearly
attuned to each other than to any other people on earth. Whately
sounded practical and unromantic when he advised young men to
pick and choose carefully, weighing the health, wealth, skills, position, and temperament of various girls; but once he got beyond the
subject of courting and into marriage, he slipped into another vein:
"For him to think her not only more comely, handsome, beautiful,
but also more loving, more dutiful, more submissive, more trusty,
than perhaps she is . . . by looking through the spectacles of love
. . . is doubtless a praiseworthy blindness." A Puritan view, this—
yet indebted ultimately, to the medieval troubadors and to Castiglione, for no Western people before the eleventh century had said
that man should unrealistically exaggerate the excellence of his beloved.

The romantic elements in a Puritan love affair can best be illustrated by the story of Lucy Apsley and John Hutchinson, an account of which is contained in Mrs. Hutchinson's *Memoirs of Colonel Hutchinson*. Lucy Apsley was born in 1620 in the Tower of London, of which her father, a faithful servant of the Crown, was then lieutenant-governor (Puritans were not all boorish tradesmen and ink-stained merchants). The Apsley home life was a blend of pious and worldly influences. At one time young Lucy had eight tutors—several teaching her languages, music, and writing to make a gentlewoman of her, others teaching her needlework, sums, and other housewifely skills. From her parents she acquired a serious moral outlook and used to deliver childish lectures on good conduct to the maidservants, but at the same time she read omnivorously, and enjoyed nothing better than romances and love poems.

In 1637, when the Apsleys had a house at Richmond, near London, a handsome youth named John Hutchinson was spending the summer in Richmond with friends. He was the son of a country squire and mingled easily in aristocratic company, but like his Puritan father he was serious, studious, and moral. During the summer, Hutchinson happened to visit the Apsley home at a time when seventeen-year-old Lucy was in London; while there he saw some of her Latin books, asked what sort of girl took such interest in learning, and was deeply intrigued by what he heard. The young ladies of Richmond told him, with much artful giggling, that Lucy was studious, conceited, and dull, but the more they mocked, the faster his pulses beat. One evening someone played a song Lucy had written, and young Hutchinson said he would simply have to meet so gifted a lady. "Sir," answered a gallant youth, "she is of such a humor she will not be acquainted with any of mankind. . . . She shuns the conversation of men as the plague." Tristan never felt the magic potion take more violent effect than did John Hutchinson.

Evidently it showed, for several days later his friends took the trouble to play a practical joke on him. They arranged for word to be brought during dinner that Lucy had been married in London. The results were noteworthy: young Hutchinson, though he had not yet met her nor even seen her picture, turned pale, broke into a sweat, and nearly got sick at the table. Excusing himself, he fled to his room and sank into a depression, wondering how such a thing could have happened to him.

Lucy soon returned from her trip to London, the joke was exposed, and Hutchinson finally met her. She was struck by his good looks, quiet manners, and serious personality; for his part, he found her earnestness and her disregard for feminine frills and manners quite lovable. Best of all, he did not worship her in the foppish courtly style, but stood ready to guide and command: "Never was there a passion more ardent and less idolatrous," wrote Lucy many years later. "He loved her better than his life, with inexpressible tenderness and kindness . . . [but never] suffered the intrusion of such a dotage as should blind him from marking her imperfections" —which, she adds, he patiently and gently corrected. (If Hutchinson had heard of William Whately's *Bride-Bush*, he failed to see the need for "praiseworthy blindness.")

After six weeks of courtship (almost all of which consisted of walking in the garden and discussing intellectual matters), they were ready. Friends met to conclude arrangements—and that same day Lucy fell ill with smallpox. Then, indeed, was Hutchinson put to the test. He passed it nobly, insisting on marrying her as soon as possible even though, as Lucy wrote, "all who saw her were affrighted to look on her." Lucy reported that her deformed face gradually improved and that she regained all her beauty; we would like to believe it was so. Whether it was or not, they succeeded in having a warm, solid, rewarding marriage for the next twenty-five years.

Hutchinson devoted his time to his estate, and to the study of divinity; gradually he became involved in the Puritan cause and during the Civil Wars was a colonel in the Puritan army, a member of Commons, and one of the judges who signed the death sentence of Charles I. After the Restoration, he was arrested as a regicide, and died while in prison. Lucy Hutchinson wrote her memoir to moderate her grief and preserve her love, and we may be thankful she did; no other such intimate Puritan autobiography exists from that period.

The courtships of less well-to-do and less well-educated Puritans were not so perfumed with learning and rather more influenced by the immediate domestic values to be gained by the union. This was particularly true in colonial New England, where each man urgently needed a wife to satisfy many imperative needs—clothing, food, medical care, companionship, sex, and, not least of all, status.[9]

[9] In many a New England town the bachelor was suspect. Hartford taxed bachelors twenty shillings a week for living alone, and Massachusetts and Plymouth permitted them to live only in homes approved by the selectmen, who kept them under constant surveillance.

It was common for a man to meet a girl, appraise her, propose to her, and publish the banns all within a few weeks or less. In 1675, Thomas Walley, living in a town some distance from Boston, decided to go to Boston as soon as spring came in order to find a wife. Just then some friends mentioned to him that a Mrs. Clark had moved to town and was available. Walley hustled off and called upon her without ceremony, and within a day or two they had agreed to wed. Walley was much relieved, and wrote to his friend, John Cotton: "God hath sent me a wife home to me and saved me the labor of a tedious journey."

Yet one can exaggerate the extent of such primitivism. Even in New England, seventeenth-century Puritans far more frequently were servants of Eros than either their religion or the hard necessities of colonial life would lead one to suppose. The wonderful diary of Judge Sewall is full of vignettes of human beings who, though they do not resemble the inhibited, self-torturing Puritans of Hawthorne's novels, nor exhibit the sweetly Victorian ways Longfellow ascribed to John Alden and Priscilla Mullens, have the merit of being real and genuine. Timothy Dwight, for instance, a young servant in the house of Samuel Sewall's father, fell down in a frenzy one day in 1676, kicking and banging the floor, and talking incoherently even after being put to bed. Sewall's father questioned him when he grew calm. The youth would say only that he had a reprobate nature and was spiritually disturbed, but the younger Sewall observed the case more closely and recorded what he saw:

> Notwithstanding all this semblance (and much more than is written) of compunction for sin, 'tis to be feared that his trouble arose from a maid whom he passionately loved: for that when Mr. Dwight and his master had agreed to let him go to her, he eftsoons grew well.

One of the better-known Puritan love letters, written by the Reverend Michael Wigglesworth to a Mrs. Avery in 1691, is often cited as evidence of the arid and unemotional nature of Puritan relationships. It lists, for instance, ten logical reasons why she should marry him, Point Three being: "I have not been led hereunto by fancy (as too many are in like cases) but by sound reason and judgment." Yet the evidence is unfair; Wigglesworth was sixty at the time, and elderly people, even in romantic times, have often had to make practical arrangements. Moreover, as evidence it can be used for the other side—for perhaps the real clue lies in the Reverend's statement that he is not led by fancy *"as too many are in like cases."*

What the modern person may especially dislike in Puritan love letters is the now-unfashionable mixture of romance and righteousness. Yet if one carefully analyzes that mixture, he must at least admit that the original Puritan was not altogether frigid; he simply felt, or tried to feel, that the love of God came first, and that of woman right afterwards. The opening sentence of a letter from Edward Taylor, a minister in Westfield, to his fiancée may have a distinctly unpleasant flavor for the contemporary palate:

> My Dove, I send you not my heart, for that I trust is sent to Heaven long since, and unless it hath woefully deceived me, it hath not taken up its lodgings in anyone's bosom this side of the Royal City of the Great King.

But Taylor went on to praise conjugal love in orotund tones above all others on earth and to say that the only limit on it is that it must be subordinate to God's glory. One cannot be sure whether the young lady was flattered or irritated, but since she probably had different vision from ours, she could perhaps see through the fog of piety and perceive the minister's meaning.

Often, too, God won first place in men's affections only by a narrow margin. The wife of one Thomas Shepard nearly died in childbirth; when she had passed the crisis, Shepard stopped to reflect on the experience, and commented thoughtfully in his diary:

> As the affliction was very bitter, so did the Lord teach me much by it, and I had need of it for I began to grow secretly proud and full of sensuality, delighting my soul in my dear wife more than in my God whom I had promised better unto.

Many another man, not so providentially warned, very likely found mortal love sweetest of all and delighted himself in it as much as any Renaissance courtier, even though the circumstances and the coloring of it were so very different.

Finally, it is worth noting that even that Devil-wrestler, that soother of demon-possessed girls, that champion of a dying theocracy, Cotton Mather himself, once suffered from a painful romantic yearning for a slightly tarnished young lady. God won, but nearly at the cost of Mather's reason. This strange episode is not what one thinks of when Mather's name is mentioned: what comes to mind, rather, are the less amiable recollections—Mather preaching against

plays, card games, and Christmas festivities; indulging in fasts and
bouts of weeping, and telling of his visions from the pulpit of his
Second Church in Boston; portraying for his flock the way to
Heaven as a wilderness filled with fiery flying serpents, dens of
lions, and droves of devils; helping to ignite the fires of the Salem
witchcraft hysteria of 1692 by "investigating" supernatural phenomena and publishing several credulous reports on possession by
demons and other matters; and proudly writing the official, self-
satisfied report of the Salem trials under the title, *Wonders of the
Invisible World*. By all these things one may know Mather, and by
a very tiny detail one may know him still better: one day, having
just relieved himself, he pondered what a great deal of time he had
wasted in life in all his evacuations—time that might be put to God's
use—and quite seriously wrote down a resolve "to make it an opportunity of shaping in my mind some holy, noble, divine thought
. . . that may leave upon my spirit some further tincture of piety."

Yet even this man wept and suffered for love, and confided his
agonies to his diary. It began in December 1702, when Mather's
wife died, leaving him with a brood of nine children. Mather was
still only thirty-eight, physically attractive, and at the height of his
career. Shortly he began to receive notes from a "young gentlewoman" (he never named her in the diary), who offered sympathy,
and asked to call on him. Early in February, 1703, she first came to
his study, a handsome girl a little over twenty, well educated, and
with considerable wit. But she had not come to be witty. According to Mather's account of the meeting, she forthrightly spoke of
having always admired him; now that he was a widower, she felt
herself free to "confess herself charmed with my person to such a
degree that she could not but break in upon me with her most importunate requests that I would make her mine. . . . I was in a
great strait, how to treat so polite a gentlewoman." He offered her
a number of discouraging facts, including the probable opposition
of his congregation, but she was undaunted, and by the time she
left Mather was half entranced, half fearful. "I know she has been
a very airy person," he wrote. "What snares may be laying for me,
I know not."

The snares soon became evident: her airiness had won her a
somewhat doubtful reputation, yet at the same time Mather felt
himself deeply attracted. "I am in the greatest straits imaginable,"
he jotted in his diary on February 12. "Nature itself causes in me

a mighty tenderness for a person so very amiable." Nevertheless, he wrote her a note asking her to leave off lest the strain of it kill him (he used that very word). "Yet such was my flexible tenderness," he added less than a week later, "as to be conquered by the importunities of several [1] to allow some further interviews."

By March 6, however, Mather began to perceive the Prince of Darkness beginning to meddle in the affair, hoping to wreck his ministry.

> There is a noise, and a mighty noise it is, made about the town. . . . Satan has raised an horrid storm of reproach upon me, both for my earliness in courting a gentlewoman, and especially for my courting of a person whom they generally apprehend so disagreeable to my character. . . . My spirit is excessively broken.

Concluding that his congregation would never accept his marriage to someone young, saucy, and possibly tarnished, he decided after an agonizing soul-struggle to follow duty and break off the affair, but suffered intensely from the decision.

> I set myself to make unto the Lord Jesus Christ a sacrifice. . . . I struck my knife into the heart of my sacrifice by a letter to her mother. . . . Should I tell in how many forms the Devil has assaulted me, it would strike my friends with horror. Sometimes temptations to impurities; and sometimes to blasphemy and atheism and the abandonment of all religion as a mere delusion; and sometimes to self-destruction itself. These, even these, O miserable Mather, do follow thee with an astonishing fury.

The girl herself seems to have been just as upset, but she and her mother doggedly continued the suit, even going to see his father, Increase Mather. By late spring, however, Cotton Mather discovered that a suitable young widow, Mrs. Elizabeth Hubbard, lived only two houses away, and he called upon her. In a single evening he appraised her as being agreeable, civil, appropriate, and full of veneration for himself. "I see," he wrote in his diary that night, "she will be a great gift of Heaven unto me." When the "young gentlewoman" heard of this new interest, she was outraged and threatened to cause the minister public embarrassment or disgrace, but nothing came of her threats. In August he married the widow Hubbard, having by then come to regard her as "a most lovely creature and such a gift of Heaven to me and mine that the sense thereof

[1] Her mother and, probably, friends.

. . . dissolves me into tears of joy." We may as well believe him, since he is the only source of evidence on the matter.

The point of the story, in any event, is perfectly plain: even if one wishes Mather had had the courage to follow his heart and marry the saucy young thing, the affair and his feelings about it thoroughly belie the accepted image of the Puritan with his stony heart, his ice-cold blood, his repressed and unuttered desires. Even this Devil-fighting fanatic was capable of feeling both heat and tenderness; as for keeping quiet, that was the furthest thing of all from his character. He published four hundred and fifty titles in his lifetime, and his desires, far from being unutterable, were to him another excellent source of literary and hortatory material.

6

"Hail Wedded Love"

No survey of Puritan love would be complete without a look at the central figure of seventeenth-century Puritanism—John Milton, the man whose personality, thoughts, and writings are the perfect expression of that movement.

It has long been fashionable to praise Milton's poetry and to dispraise his personality, to admire his technique and dislike his content. Studious, unsmiling, virtuous, and devoid of winning graces, he is genuinely difficult to like. Samuel Johnson called him "an acrimonious and surly republican," and most critics and historians have thought him tough-minded, unsociable, egotistical and priggish. As for his feelings about love, Robert Graves wrote a novel showing

Milton as an abominably tyrannical husband, and a contemporary scholar referred to him, typically, as "a sore, angry, intolerant, and arrogant critic of women." All this is certainly true, but it is not all there is to say. If he was priggish and virtuous, he also expressed a completely healthy view of sex—at least of married sex; and if he was not a very loving husband, it may be because his expectations of married love had been excessively idealistic and romantic.

Milton, born in 1608, was from early youth a studious and serious boy. Partly this was the result of his father's special efforts, for the elder Milton, a scrivener (a writer of legal contracts and a money-lender), had literary ambitions for his son. Partly, too, it fitted in with the fact that young Milton was physically slight and somewhat retarded in bodily maturation ("I do notice a certain belatedness in me," he once observed.) At Cambridge, his smooth-cheeked immaturity and his dislike of bawdy talk or sexual adventures led some students to nickname him "the Lady." "Why do I seem to them too little of a man?" Milton later complained; then, contemptuous of their inferior morals, he answered the question: ". . . Perhaps because I have never showed my virility in the way these brothellers do."

During his early manhood, Milton wrote a handful of exquisite poems which abound in ravishingly sensuous imagery, but these were a triumph of art over personal habits. Charles Diodati, his closest friend during his college years, once gently scolded Milton for his cloistered ways in a letter:

> Why do you despise the gifts of nature? Why inexcusably persist in hanging over books and studies all day and all night? Live, laugh, make the most of youth and the hours; and cease studying the zeals and recreations and indolences of the wise men of old, wearing yourself out the while. . . . Farewell, and be joyous.

Diodati's mood intrigued Milton, and sometimes he would write as though he were considering taking the advice to heart:

> *Alas! what boots it with uncessant care*
> *To tend the homely shepherd's trade,*
> *And strictly meditate the thankless Muse?*
> *Were it not better done as others use,*
> *To sport with Amaryllis in the shade,*
> *Or with the tangles of Neaera's hair?*
> > Lycidas, 64–9.

But it was all talk. John Milton, Puritan and puritanical, and dedicated to becoming a great poet, sported in no shades and tangled no girl's hair. To the best of anyone's knowledge, he lived in complete chastity; as for romance, he felt love only twice before his marriage —once for an unknown girl he saw for a fleeting moment in a London crowd, and once for an Italian lady with whom, in Petrarchan fashion, his connection was limited to the writing of some sonnets. Yet he had no intention of spending his life in bachelor chastity, and industriously read about married life, expecting it some day to yield him a very special kind of human relationship.

In the summer of 1642, when Milton was thirty-three and deeply involved in writing polemic tracts on behalf of the Puritan cause, he went to Oxfordshire on vacation and visited the Powells, a family he had known for some years. Mary Powell, who had been only a child when last he had seen her, was now a blooming girl of sixteen. Some June madness came upon him, and when his month's vacation was over, he brought her home to his house in London as his wife.

It was an astonishingly poor choice. The Civil War was imminent and the Powells were Royalists. Milton, furthermore, was a quiet, settled man, dedicated to scholarly studies, while Mary was a mere girl, high-spirited, ignorant of learning, and unable to appreciate his poetic aims. Great love and great understanding on his part might have made the marriage work, but in the emotional dealings between man and woman Milton was still an unfledged adolescent. He expected everything in her, and found almost nothing. Even the long-deferred pleasure of physical love was soured for him by the boredom, the shallowness, and the petty bickering of the marriage; later he referred to sexual connection under such conditions as "a displeasing and forced remedy against the sting of a bruit desire."

The situation must have been as painful for Mary as for him. Within a few weeks she asked Milton for permission to visit her family for the balance of the summer. Probably he hoped the separation would ease the tension and let them start afresh, for he agreed, but set Michaelmas, in September, as the date of her return. In late August, however King Charles unfurled his royal banner at Nottingham and rallied his army. Oxford became his headquarters, and the Powells found themselves in the very thick of events. Only great love could have brought Mary back to her scholarly Puritan husband under such circumstances; not surprisingly, she made no attempt to do so. Milton wrote letters asking her to return, but she ignored them; he sent a messenger, who was brusquely turned away from the Powell home. But why did Milton want her back at all? Because even if he had chosen ill, it was his only chance. The divorce law of England consisted of the conservative canon law of the official Church of England. Milton, who wanted love, could not get rid of one wife for another, and would not seek love outside marriage; he therefore longed to try again with his adolescent wife, and being rebuffed again and again, grew bitter and full of hate.

A year after Mary had left, he published what was in part the product of this experience—a forty-two-page pamphlet addressed to Parliament and entitled *The Doctrine and Discipline of Divorce*— to which, within the next two and a half years, he added three more similar tracts. His aim in all of them was plain: he urged the Puritan Parliament to revoke canon law, authorize divorce on the radical ground of "contrariety of mind," and "with one gentle stroking to wipe away ten thousand tears out of the life of man."

The divorce tracts are full of bilious hatred for woman, yet they rest upon an idealistic, quasi-romantic concept of married love, as magnified by the imagination of an unusually chaste, inexperienced, and serious man. Milton distinguished between two kinds of sexual expression—a noble one, growing out of a beautiful and natural desire, and the other a venomous burning, incontinent and vulgar, which he equated with illicit love or with lustful connection between a husband and wife who do not love each other. Chaste and puritanical though he was, Milton insisted that the former kind of sex was natural and healthful. For normal persons to remain unmarried in the effort to attain continence was, he said, "a diabolic sin" and he held the Catholic views on celibacy to be the work of the very Antichrist.

But the most important goal of marriage, he argued, was not sexual outlet; there was a higher goal—loving "conversation" (i.e., loving companionship). Milton even reinterpreted Saint Paul; when the Apostle said that it was better to marry than to burn, the word "burn" must have referred not to sexual desire, he said, but to a "pure and more inbred desire" to join with "a fit and conversing soul"—this was "that rational burning that marriage is to remedy." Half religious, half humanistic, Milton took not an anti-sexual, but a supra-sexual view of married love:

> Conjugal love [arises] from a mutual fitness to the final causes of wedlock: help and society in religious, civil, and domestic conversation, which includes as an inferior end the fulfilling of natural desire and specifical increase. . . . God, in the first ordaining of marriage, taught us to what end he did it . . . [namely] to comfort and refresh [man] against the evil of solitary life, not mentioning the purpose of generation till afterwards. . . . He who affirms adultery to be the highest breach affirms the bed to be the highest [goal] of marriage, which is in truth a gross and boorish opinion.

Repeatedly he stressed the importance of nonsexual factors in love, and sometimes his personal experience shows through:

> For all the wariness can be used, it may yet befall a discreet man to be mistaken in his choice. . . . Who knows not that the bashful muteness of a virgin may oft-times hide all the unliveliness and natural sloth which is really unfit for conversation?

From all this, Milton derived the sweeping conclusion that divorce should be granted where there was a deep-seated inability of a man and wife to be happy together. The just ground of divorce, he wrote in a famous sentence, is "indisposition, unfitness, or contrariety of mind, arising from a cause in nature unchangeable, hindering and ever likely to hinder the main benefits of conjugal society, which are solace and peace." [2]

But the divorce tracts were not merely an outlet for Milton's personal unhappiness; the postulates on which they rested had all been expressly contained in the earlier writings of Puritan divines. Milton, being a deep thinker and a tormented man, simply carried them to their logical extreme. It was a profound shock to him, therefore, when various Puritans preached against his views, wrote stinging answers to his tracts, and sometimes even labeled him a heretic. Parliament did far worse: it ignored his recommendations completely. Years later, when Cromwell became Lord Protector, the divorce law was modified, but scarcely a tenth of the way toward Milton's position. [3]

Long before Cromwell's changes, however, Milton was no longer an abandoned husband. The King's cause had suffered a mortal blow at the battle of Naseby on June 14, 1645; the Powell family,

[2] The sentence is from *Doctrine and Discipline of Divorce*, as are most of the quotations and opinions cited above; some, however, are from *Tetrachordon*, another of the divorce tracts.

[3] The "Barebones" Parliament of 1655 gave civil magistrates the power to grant divorce, but only on the usual limited Calvinist grounds—desertion, impotence, or adultery.

tacking desperately, sent Mary down to London to a relative of
Milton's, who stationed her in a side room one day when Milton
was expected. He came and was unwittingly steered into the room
where he suddenly found her on her knees before him, weeping
and begging for pardon. A passage in *Paradise Lost* seems almost to
be his memory of this very scene:

> *She ended weeping, and her lowly plight,*
> *Immoveable till peace obtained from fault*
> *Acknowledged and deplored, in Adam wrought*
> *Commiseration. . . .*
> *As one disarmed, his anger all he lost,*
> *And thus with peaceful words upraised her soon.*
>   (X, 937–46)

Life is usually a little less than poetic; a nephew of Milton's wrote
that Milton softened only after considerable talking and urging by
friends and relatives who were also present. But in the end he
relented, and Mary returned to his home after a three-year absence.

One aspect of their marriage functioned at least adequately, for
Mary produced four children in the next seven years. But time had
neither made her better-suited to him, nor him more flexible and
undemanding. He wrote no more on the divorce question, but he
felt neither joy nor fulfilment in his marriage. Less than two years
after Mary returned, he wrote to Carlo Dati, a dear friend, as follows:

> Those whom the mere necessity of neighborhood, or some-
> thing else of useless kind, has closely conjoined to me . . . sit
> daily in my company, weary me, nay, by Heaven, all but plague
> me to death whenever they are jointly in the humor for it. . . .
> Those whom habit, disposition, studies, had so handsomely made
> my friends, are now almost denied me. . . . I have to live well-
> nigh in a perpetual solitude.

Mary died in 1652, leaving Milton with three living children. He
was by then Latin Secretary to the Council of State, a job which involved his writing official letters and papers for the Puritan government. Having children to rear, and official chores to perform, and
having, furthermore, become completely blind in 1652, Milton cast
about for another wife and remarried in 1657. This second wife
died in a year, and he married once more in 1663, his third wife
caring for him until his own death eleven years later. Very little is
known about either of these later marriages except that they were

matters of absolute necessity to Milton—and both worked, albeit in a fashion different from that of his early expectations.

During his third marriage Milton completed and published *Paradise Lost*, the noblest effort of the Puritan movement to sum up its cultural and religious philosophy. Though the Commonwealth had foundered, Puritanism was a continuing force in English and colonial life, and *Paradise Lost* was long a favorite work with the humbly pious, who took Milton's portrayal of Adam and Eve almost as a doctrinal guide to the relationships between the sexes. Though in part it surely reflects Milton's personality, it is still more an expression of the Puritan tradition and a guide to Puritan conduct. It perfectly summarizes in a few lines the improbable Puritan compound of romanticism, sensuousness, and pious patriarchalism:

> . . . Both
> Not equal, as their sex not equal, seemed;
> For contemplation he and valor formed,
> For softness she and sweet attractive grace;
> He for God only, she for God in him.
> His fair large front and eye sublime declared
> Absolute rule. . . .
>
> (IV, 295–301)

The happy pair had neither doubt nor guilt in their love-making; conjugal sex was beautiful and pure:

> . . . Into their inmost bower
> Handed they went; and, eased the putting off
> These troublesome disguises which we wear,
> Straight side by side were laid; nor turned, I ween,
> Adam from his fair spouse; nor Eve the rites
> Mysterious of connubial love refused. . . .
> Hail wedded love, mysterious law, true source
> Of human offspring, sole propriety
> In paradise of all things common else!
> By thee adulterous lust was driven from men. . . .
>
> (IV, 738–53)

When Eve ate the apple, Adam followed suit not so much to gain forbidden knowledge, but for love of Eve, saying:

> . . . With thee
> Certain my resolution is to die:
> How can I live without thee! how forego

Thy sweet converse and love so dearly joined,
To live again in these wild woods forlorn!
                                                    (IX, 904–10)

Eve, being woman above all else, was so flattered that she referred
to Adam's impending Original Sin as a "glorious trial of exceeding
love."

   Adam ate, and he and Eve were then overwhelmed by a new kind
of desire—hot, lascivious, and guilty. Milton thus precisely denied
the entire view of Saint Augustine. Concupiscence did not cause
Original Sin, but was its result; sexual union was not the product of
eating the apple, but existed prior to it and was blighted by it. But
in Milton's view, Adam and Eve then recovered the purity of
wedded love after a bitter quarrel during which Adam bade Eve
go from him, and she, repenting of her ways, begged forgiveness
and reassumed that fitting subservience the laying-aside of which
had caused their Fall:

Forsake me not thus, Adam! witness heaven
What love sincere and reverence in my heart
I bear thee, and unwitting have offended,
Unhappily deceived; thy suppliant
I beg, and clasp thy knees. . . .
        Both have sinned, but thou
Against God only; I against God and thee. . . .
                                                    (X, 914–931)

It is, after all, just a masculine daydream; but it is also the kind of
advice Puritan parents gave to their daughters, assuring them that in
such dulcet female accents lay the secret of lasting love.

7

The Meaning of "Puritanical"

W hat, then, did the Reformation and in particular its Puritan
outgrowth, do to love?

The feminists of two generations ago (and less) were inclined
to see it as a retrogression to stern patriarchalism, a dethroning of
woman from her status as Lady to the lesser one of housekeeper, and
a blighting of love by repression and joyless piety. There is some
truth in all this, but much distortion and omission; though Puritans
shunned amorous verse, high-flown compliments, and the elegant
techniques of adulterous upper-class flirtation, they borrowed
some of the ideals of romantic love, accepted the normality of sex
and tried to fuse the two within marriage.

Nevertheless they seemed dismal, joyless people to their contemporaries. In part, they had turned their backs upon the enlightened mood of the Renaissance. In part, they came mostly of a
class which valued money more than leisure, and success more than
culture. In part, they were reformers who threw out the baby
with the bath water, for while repudiating both Neoplatonism and
illicit love, they flung away much of the magic, tenderness, and
intimacy of romantic tradition. It took a Puritan (William Gouge),
writing in 1622, to soberly urge wives not to use terms of endear-
ment upon their husbands, specifically cautioning them against such
unseemly familiarities as *sweet, sweeting, heart, sweetheart, love,
joy, dear, duck, chick,* and *pigsnie (sic)*; none of these would do,
and neither would the first name or nickname. The only proper way
for a woman to address her mate was *Husband*.

Yet in some practical ways, woman's status continued to improve
under Puritanism. In Puritan New England a woman whose hus-

band beat her could win legal separation, and sometimes divorce; in the Southern colonies, where the influence was Anglican and Cavalier, the law made no such provision. In Salem, in 1682, a man named Daniel Ela was fined forty shillings for having told his wife in front of neighbors that "she was none of his wife, she was but his servant." Property rights and inheritance laws continued to improve slowly in woman's favor. Marriage in Protestant countries (except for England) became in general a civil contract, and divorce with the right of remarriage was established firmly, if on limited grounds. And finally, if early Puritans were collectively intolerant of love and sex outside of marriage, they were all in favor of both within it.

How can all this be equated with the standard image of Puritanism? Perhaps the discrepancy lies in the fact that the picture of early Puritanism has been distorted by the later phenomena that took its name. Seventeenth-century Puritanism was tight-lipped, severe, and pious, but it was simultaneously frank, strongly sexed, and somewhat romantic. Except for the extreme forms of Calvinism, it was as much an offshoot of the Renaissance as a reaction against it. The frigidity and neuroses associated with Puritanism belong to a much later date: hellfire-and-brimstone sermons reached their zenith in the middle of the eighteenth century, and the suffocating prudishness of the Victorians came in the middle of the nineteenth.

Modern men and women often speak of struggling to free themselves from their "Puritanical" background, but they misunderstand the tradition they have inherited; it is really the nineteenth-century emphasis on respectability and gentility they are speaking of. Actually, the early Puritan was rather close to modern man in many of his attitudes toward adultery, sexual enjoyment, love, and marriage. Milton hailed wedded love in a spirit much like our own; like many another prophet, however, he was too far ahead of his time, and died in a world that seemed increasingly to scorn the ideals he believed in.

Chapter VIII
THE CONTACT OF TWO EPIDERMISES

Love Becomes Ridiculous

✿   ✿

✿

ove, Jonathan Swift earnestly assured a young lady who was
about to be married, is a "ridiculous passion which hath no
being but in play-books and romances." It was the year 1723, and
most people of wit and good breeding throughout Europe were of
a similar opinion; it was the Age of Reason, and love had fallen into
disrepute among the upper classes and the intellectuals—the very
people who had made so much of it ever since William, Duke of
Aquitaine, wrote his first troubadour songs six centuries earlier.

There was good reason for the change. By the middle of the
seventeenth century, the religious and philosophical wars between
Catholicism and the Reformation had exhausted Europe and ended
in the only possible solution: hostile toleration. Intellectual Euro-
peans were disillusioned and disenchanted with the several traditions of the Middle Ages, the Renaissance, and the Reformation, and
sought instead a new, calm, humane philosophy that would be more
stable and productive of well-being. They turned away from emotion, authority, and the past, seeking to base a way of life on reason,
the individual, and the present. Theology and metaphysics yielded
to mathematics and physics, and it was in all seriousness rather than
in a spirit of satire that Alexander Pope wrote:

> Nature and Nature's laws lay hid in night:
> God said, Let Newton be! and all was light.

Along with so much else, the romantic, suffering, idealizing way
of love seemed to them merely another superstitious folly of the in-
fancy of mankind. The loutish sons and pious daughters of tradesmen and the lower classes might still indulge in this and other
"enthusiasms," but the educated aristocracy and upper-middle-class

men and women scorned to be enslaved by emotion. They chose to consider love a matter of natural sexual desire, a normal hunger that should be gratified whenever convenient—with suitable style, perhaps, but certainly without any barbarous exaltations or nonsense about ethical values.

Rationalists not only put these principles into practice, but were dismayingly lucid and outspoken about them, and perhaps it was for this sin above all others that succeeding generations condemned them. Giuseppe Parini, an Italian poet, defined love in terms free of all romantic nonsense simply as "the satisfaction of desire in noble liberty"; the Comte de Buffon, a naturalist, said acerbly: "There is nothing good in love but the physical part"; and the sarcastic wit, Sebastien Chamfort, uttering perhaps the ultimate rationalist word on the subject, said that love was nothing but "the contact of two epidermises." Little wonder that later generations disapproved: one can forgive a mute sinner, but not an articulate one.

Yet the Age of Reason, despite its contempt for emotion and its insistence that man's intellect should govern his actions, was obsessed with love, or rather with that special variant of it called "gallantry"—a socially required, intricate, ritualistic routine of flirtation, seduction, and adultery. The history of love has many an enigma, but none more intriguing than this, that the very men and women who spoke most nobly of subordinating their passions to their reason were helplessly addicted to squandering their time and money in amorous intrigues and ruining their health in excesses of lechery.

The light of reason, in short, did not illuminate all of the human soul; love in the Enlightenment was not as simple as it seemed. The amiable, cynical view of sex and love may look charming when seen from a great distance and sound delightful when set to Mozart's music, but for those who lived with it, it must often have been otherwise. Listen, for instance, to Madame d'Esparbès, speaking to her distraught young lover, the Comte de Lauzun, who is in an agony at learning that she has tired of their affair:

> Believe me, little cousin, being romantic does not succeed, but makes one ridiculous and nothing more. I have had a fancy for you, my child; it is not my fault that you have taken it to be a grand passion and convinced yourself that it would never end. It should matter little to you that this fancy has passed, and I have taken another lover. You have many qualities to please women with; make use of them to do so; be convinced that the loss of one

love can always be repaired by another, and that this is the means
of being happy and agreeable.[1]

It is the pure authentic voice of enlightened love. The gracious,
well-mannered words, though chilly, sound harmless; yet there is a
tendency implicit in them which has not even a good name yet, but
will gain one a century later from a practitioner of the ultimate
development of this viewpoint, the Marquis Donatien de Sade.

2

Gallantry and the "Aching Void"

❀　　　❀

❀

Gallantry had a long pedigree, particularly in France, but during
the Age of Reason it underwent notable changes. From the
time of Marguerite of Navarre on, it had meant Petrarchan affections, allegedly painful emotions, intricate "services" and
proofs of devotion, loquacious and didactic courting, and, perhaps
at last, assignations and love-making. But the mysticism and affected
emotionalism of all this was intolerable to the men of the Age of
Reason. They still wanted to cluster about women who combined
sex and intellect—but they sought a new kind of woman who could
be detached and perfectly cool about love. Here is how one of the
women they most admired wrote to her young lover, in about
1670, in terms perfectly expressing the new spirit:

Shall I tell you what makes love dangerous? It is the sublime
idea we are apt to form of it. But to speak the exact truth, love,
considered as a passion, is nothing but a blind instinct that one

[1] *Mémoires de M. le duc de Lauzun,*
quoted in Edmond and Jules de Goncourt: *La Femme au Dix-Huitième Siècle*, p. 172.

must know how to appreciate properly—as an appetite which
directs us toward one object rather than another without our being able to account for our taste. Considered as a relationship of
friendship, when reason presides over it, it is no longer a passion,
and indeed it is no longer even love.

That was Ninon de l'Enclos speaking—the greatest beauty, courtesan, and salonière of the latter half of the seventeenth century. In
her home, men of intellect and breeding met regularly to exchange
pensées, and to become her lover, if she beckoned. Ninon herself
would placidly choose one of her admirers and inform him when he
might begin to reign as her lover. His office would last a few weeks
or months, and then he would be informed that the affair was over
—but so charmingly and courteously that he remained a friend
and a member of the salon. Ninon would then select the next favorite and notify him of his selection. None of her lovers was permitted to show signs of affection in public, either before being
chosen or during the period of grace; each, however, was allowed
to contribute to her upkeep.

Yet to none of them did this relationship seem like a form of
prostitution. The distinguished men who were her friends were of
the opinion that they had been in love with her and she with them;
her lifelong friend, Saint-Évremond, congratulating her in her later
years on a life well and richly lived, summarized the best side of
gallantry in two sentences: "I consider you, in full life as you are,
the happiest creature that ever was. You have been loved often
enough to leave nothing untasted in pleasures, and wisely enough to
avoid the disgusts of a languishing passion." Less than two centuries
had passed since Castiglione wrote *The Courtier*, but it might as
well have been twenty.

The most influential exemplar of rationalist gallantry was the
young man who, at the very time of Ninon's zenith, took over the
control of France and became its greatest king. He was, of course,
Louis XIV, *le roi soleil*, the sun-king whose effulgence was so great
that Father Hébert, a priest at Versailles who knew him intimately,
wrote: "He is a very tall man, and very well proportioned; he is six
feet tall as near as makes no matter," whereas in fact Louis, standing
erect, was only five feet five. Father Hébert, however, and all of
Europe, saw him with bedazzled and admiring eyes. In all things,
Louis was the beau ideal of the aristocracy, and what he did in the

matter of gallantry, each lesser man would try to do as best he could.

Louis had started out ungallantly by falling romantically in love, when still only a foolish lad of eighteen, with Marie Mancini, a niece of his prime minister, Mazarin. Like any country bumpkin, the boy-king thought that love was reason enough to marry her, but Mazarin and the Queen-Mother were horrified. They were fishing for larger game—the Infanta of Spain—and packed Marie off without further ado, lecturing the distraught Louis on his royal duty and the folly of romantic passion. Sullen and embittered, the young king married the Infanta and turned to gallantry.

Louis did not record his inner feelings, but one can judge much from the fact that thereafter he bedded impartially with chambermaids, peasant girls, and ladies of noble blood; it was only necessary that each make a suitable pretense of loving him, and he, being the greatest of gentlemen, did likewise. But if the pretense of love was important to Louis, equally important was the avoidance of all real feeling. He established a remarkable set of rules of etiquette at Versailles not only to enhance his stature, but to suppress all evidence of emotion in his court. Even to *tutoyer* (use the verb forms with "thou") in the King's presence was the height of bad manners. To stay away from court because of mourning was considered illbred or disrespectful, and to fail to conceal one's grief with gaiety and cheerfulness was highly improper. When a prominent court lady died suddenly, Madame de Maintenon described Louis's reaction to a friend: "The death of Madame d'Espinois," she wrote, "was a surprise and nothing more. The King rids himself of unhappy ideas as soon as possible."

Though he was the very embodiment of politeness and good breeding, Louis could treat his women with remarkable callousness. His homely Spanish wife genuinely loved him, but he required her to live on intimate terms with his mistresses and to keep a cheerful face about it. When he transferred his affections from Louise de la Vallière to Madame de Montespan and wished to conceal it from the world, he made La Vallière the confidante, and had her sit guard in the outside chamber while he sported in the bedroom with the new favorite. His *Mémoires* give little indication how he felt about either of them, but it contains advice to his son which is a good clue. "Our first thoughts," he wrote, "should always be toward the preservation of our glory and power. . . . A mistress is the most dangerous of favorites." He once told a group of his courtiers: "I command each of you that if you notice a woman, any woman in the world, gaining control over me, you will tell me at once. It will not take me twenty-four hours to rid myself of her."

Madame de Montespan, however, lasted for years, but in the end Louis tired of her tantrums, her jealousies, and her stormy scenes, and chose as his next mistress the lovely, dignified Madame de Scarron, whom he made Madame de Maintenon. She was three years older than he, calm, placid, and given to unremitting self-control; in three decades she never let him see the least boredom or annoyance on her face, but sought to please and cheer him. It little mattered that she was nearing middle age, and no longer a ravishing beauty. This liaison was the right one for him; when the Queen died in 1683, he even married Madame de Maintenon secretly, gave up outside gallant affairs, and became almost domestic. What was this woman like whom King Louis, still only forty-six, found so satisfactory—so much so that he quit all others for her, performed almost all his state business in her drawing room, and increasingly followed her sober and religious bent? She was handsome, charming, and polished; but a remarkably frank letter by the Abbé Gobelin, one of her spiritual advisors, yields this astonishing information: "She had a marked disgust for the state of marriage. . . . Despite the affection she bore for Louis XIV, she retained these revulsions; she submitted to the conjugal duties only with regret and . . . her spiritual director had to exhort her to conquer herself on these painful occasions." Aside from the act of physical union, how the King and Madame de Maintenon felt about each other is far from clear, for she carefully burned all letters addressed to herself, and left only her own, composed with great care and edited to a fare-thee-well. "I wish to remain an enigma to posterity," she once remarked, but not too enigmatically she retired from the King's side during his final illness and shut herself up at her girls' school at St. Cyr, apparently unconcerned and oblivious of his condition. This was the woman whom the handsomest and greatest king of Europe, after all his experience with gallantry, chose to marry when he was still in his prime, and whom he kept beside him for thirty-two years to give him what he evidently thought of as love.

Like Louis XIV, upper-class men and women of the late seventeenth and eighteenth centuries concealed their feelings by the aid of cold reason and carefully rehearsed manners; after a while, they almost forgot they had any feelings. Philibert, Count de Gramont, a gallant and extravagant playboy, came to England in 1662 after being exiled by King Louis. Gramont became quite friendly with two young aristocrats, Anthony and George Hamilton, and at the same time fell in love with their sister, Elizabeth, a court beauty who unfortunately had no great purse. The courtship progressed under the stimulus of her blond good looks and his smooth talk of marriage; finally it arrived at a critical, indeed irretrievable, stage. In December 1663, when Gramont was recalled by King Louis, and hurried off without her, the Hamilton brothers felt obliged to chase after him and only succeeded in overtaking him at Dover. With deep bows and ceremonious phrases, they assured him of their enduring respect and humble service, and inquired if perhaps he had not forgotten something. "Ah, true," said Gramont with admirable aplomb, undoubtedly taking a pinch of snuff, "I have forgotten to marry your sister."

Back they went together in the most amiable fashion possible, and seven months later Gramont became the father of a handsome legitimate son. Neither he nor the Hamilton brothers ever harbored any ill will about the incident, and, in fact, many years later Anthony Hamilton wrote a glowing eulogy entitled *The Memoirs of the Comte de Gramont*, retailing the Count's military and gallant adventures; with great good taste, however, Hamilton said nothing of the incident at Dover.

Gramont had been perfectly comfortable at Whitehall, for Charles II of England, having spent his years of exile at the French court, had brought its manners and morals back to England upon his restoration in 1660; there they were eagerly adopted as part of the reaction against the asceticism of the recent Puritan regime. He and his courtiers wore immense, curling, chest-length French periwigs, and when they bowed deeply, they tossed their curls back into place with a swooping movement known as "the French wallow." They spoke French fluently, danced gracefully, and observed a new and more formal etiquette, somewhat similar to that of Versailles. Yet at the very same time, being newly freed from Puritan regulation, they were wild and ruffianly to a previously unknown degree. The marks of a gentleman were arrogance, the

bullying of lower-class people, and a reputation for drinking,
wenching, and cheating at cards. Sir Charles Sedley, a typical Restoration rake, peeled off his clothes and, stark naked, harangued a
crowd from the upper floor of a building in such obscene terms that
they threw stones at the windows; the Earl of Oxford seduced an
actress by rigging up a false marriage ceremony, and it took the
King himself to fine him for it; and men of distinction like Sir John
Coventry and John Dryden were beaten and wounded by hired
thugs for having insulted or offended nobles too grand to demean
themselves by fighting.

The several well-known vices, especially adultery, were practically a political necessity in the court of Charles II. The Puritans
had opposed them all; debauchery, therefore, was the easiest proof
of loyalty to the King. But social prestige was at stake, too; without
adequate scandal and proof of sexual attractiveness, neither lord nor
lady could reach the pinnacle of success. A nobleman named Henry
Jermyn was the favored stallion of the 1662 season and Mrs. Theo-
dosia Hyde, a court lady, was said by no less an authority on gallantry than the Count de Gramont to feel about him as follows:

> Mrs. Hyde had just married a man whom she loved. . . . How-
> ever she was of the opinion that so long as she was not talked of on
> account of Jermyn, all her other advantages would avail nothing
> for her glory: it was therefore to receive this finishing stroke that
> she resolved to throw herself into his arms.

One must not gather from this that such couplings were accomplished quickly or crudely; with ladies of quality, the gentleman
had to observe an elaborate ritual of courtship. Sir John Evelyn,
himself something of a Puritan, described the process with evident
distaste, but with reportorial care:

> You must often treat her at the play, the park, and the music;
> present her at the raffle; follow her to Tunbridge at the season of
> the drinking of waters, though you have no need of them your-
> self. You must improve all occasions of celebrating her shape, and
> how well the mode becomes her, though it be ne'er so fantastical
> and ridiculous; that she sings like an angel, dances like a goddess,
> and that you are charmed with her wit and beauty. . . . If the
> whole morning be spent between the glass and the comb, that
> your perruque fit well, and cravat strings be adjusted, as things
> of importance, with these and the like accomplishments, you'll
> emerge a consummate *beau*, or, in English, a coxcomb. . . .
> Thus you see, young sparks, how the style and method of woo-

ing is quite changed, as well as the language, since the days of our forefathers.[2]

Charles himself was the standard-bearer of English gallantry, as Louis XIV was of French gallantry. With his position and income as King, Charles could make a score to set other men's teeth on edge. He publicly acknowledged fourteen bastards, and history has the names of thirteen of his mistresses; there were many others whose names are lost. Being amiable and lazy, he generally chose his mistresses from among the females brought to him by his intimate advisors; but not being *too* lazy, he also indulged in a number of gutter escapades, including a famous visit to a brothel when his money was stolen and he very nearly got a beating for nonpayment before being recognized. The court rakes adored him for these follies, but the ordinary people of England were not so enchanted: the Duchess of Cleveland cost them £15,000 a year, the Duchess of Portsmouth £8,600, and Nell Gwyn, just as loving but made of common clay, £4,000. Nell was the most honest of them all, concerning royal love; she often called herself the King's whore, and once, being coolly treated by the Duchess of Cleveland, amiably clapped her on the shoulder and said: "I presume persons of one trade love not one another." Despite the handsome fees he paid, there is little evidence that Charles felt anything like tenderness or strong affection for any of them, and Bishop Gilbert Burnet, who knew the King well, said that despite his genial manner and outward bonhomie, Charles "did not think there was either sincerity or chastity in the world out of principle," and had a very ill opinion of mankind in general.

That same combination of elegance and animality, of stylized desire and cynical coldness, appears again and again in the annals of gallantry. A friend once chided the Count de Gramont, as follows: "Is it not a fact that as soon as a woman pleases you, your first care is to find out whether she has any other lover, and your second how to plague her; for the gaining of her affection is the last thing in your thoughts. You seldom engage in intrigues but to disturb the happiness of others; a mistress who has no lovers would have no charms for you." And a gentleman named Francis Osborn, advising his son against marrying a beautiful but poor woman, revealed the meaning love had for him in a crude anatomical witticism: "I have heard a well-built woman compared in her motion to

[2] Preface to *Mundus Muliebris* (a rhymed satire on women).

a ship under sail," he wrote, "yet I would advise no wise man to be
her owner if her freight be nothing but what she carries between
wind and water." But having delivered himself of twenty pages of
sentiments comparable to this, Osborn added a postlude for any
ladies who might have read the piece: his heart, he protested, "is no
less ready to be your footstool in age than it was to be one of your
triumphant chariots during youth." And that, in a word, is the
spirit of gallantry.

Clearly, it was not just zestful, charming, and delightfully
naughty. Even Madame de Maintenon once wrote to a young
friend that her beauty, her pleasures, her royal favors and great
years at court, had all left "an aching void." And for every Ninon
de l'Enclos, whose life has busied generations of biographers, there
were many women whose stories, being less agreeable and less
titillating, have remained unknown except to scholars. One such
was Mrs. Grace Worthley, a young beauty of good family who
lost her husband in the Dutch War in 1665 and became the mistress
of Henry Sidney, Earl of Romney. Sidney kept her in London
where she was both comfort and ornament to him, until the passage of time and the advent of bigger game made her seem undesirable. Here are a few words from a letter she wrote to a cousin after
she had been Sidney's mistress for nearly seventeen years and was in
her fading forties:

> He treats me with a great deal of cruelty, which I think is very
> severe, first to have spent my precious youth as I have done, and
> now, for a reward of all my sufferings, to be abused and despised,
> and my son rejected as if he were none of his, and all this to please
> his great Mistress.[3]

About this time, Sidney cut her allowance nearly in half, had her
forcibly turned away from his door by a constable, and tried to
make her leave London so as to be out of his way. Finally she appealed to King Charles, who ordered Sidney to do his duty by his
mistress. After Charles died, she was back in the same fix, and had to
beg, threaten, and cajole Sidney year after year in this fashion:

> How happy should I now esteem myself if I could do or say
> something that would make you reassume your former good-na-
> ture! But do not misconstrue me, my Lord; I mean only that part
> of your good nature that would oblige you to do what is reason-
> able, and not to return to your embraces. . . . All that at present

[3] Probably the Countess of Sunderland, with whom Sidney was having an affair.

I desire your Lordship to do is let me have half a year's money next Monday. How poor and how ignoble a revenge is this of yours to me, a poor deluded woman. . . .[4]

And so it goes, year after year, until 1694. Then the letters ceased, though Sidney was still alive; one can only assume that Grace Worthley had quietly died, and so found the only lasting solution to the economic difficulties of gallantry.

3

A One-man Sample of Restoration Love

❀   ❀

❀

If the early part of the Age of Reason was dominated by gallants and rakes, it also had its subdued Puritans, its stolid country gentry who were traditionally conservative in morals, and its men of decent and philosophic temperament such as exist in almost every age. Somewhere in the middle of all these types there was a median, an average kind of upper-class man; and by extraordinary good luck, during the first ten years of the Restoration, one of them wrote the world's most intimate, honest, and unbeautified diary. He was Samuel Pepys, fairly well born, fairly well-to-do (after a while), and both a fairly good husband and a fairly successful rake. Scattered throughout the six fat volumes of Pepys's coded memoirs is an unsparing portrait of one man's love life in Restoration England—an ill-blended amalgam of license and shame, exuberant sen-

[4] Both letters (and many more like them) were found in the Sidney correspondence, and printed in the introduction to Sidney's published letters, which appear under the title: *Diary of the Times of Charles the Second* (1843).

suality and feeble efforts at restraint, cheerful adultery and sincere
marital affection.

Pepys came of minor gentry of Huntingdonshire and was reasonably well educated, but he lacked the arrogance and polished
manner that only rank and wealth could give, and did not even learn
to dance until he was twenty-eight. He even somewhat favored the
Puritans for a while during the Civil War, but by 1660, when he
was twenty-seven, he went along with the fleet that escorted
Charles II from France back to England in glory. Through good
connections, Pepys became Clerk of the Acts in the Navy and
proved to be so devoted and accomplished an administrator that he
eventually rose to the post of Secretary of the Admiralty. Though
he was not very handsome (having a rather long bulbous nose and
an over-heavy lower lip), and affected none of the extreme fop-
peries of the time (it took him days to muster up enough courage to
wear his first ordinary periwig out on the street), he won the respect of his betters, mingled with them freely every day, and admired their looks, their habits, and their pleasures. As much as he
could, he tried to act like one of them.

Before he began to model himself upon them, Pepys had done a
very irrational and unaristocratic thing: he married for love. Having been enraptured by a fifteen-year-old French beauty, he wedded her without considering the fact that she had no property. For
a while, he was mightily enamored of her; commenting years
later on a new piece of music he had just heard, he wrote: "The
wind-music . . . is so sweet that it ravished me, and indeed, in a
word, did wrap up my soul so that it made me really sick, just as
I have formerly been when in love with my wife." But he learned
that, in the world of the wealthy and the rational, men and women
asked other questions first and looked for love later. As a result, he
so meddled in his younger brother's affairs, haggling and arguing
for adequate dowry, that the latter died a bachelor. Samuel Pepys
could even reflect, in one of his less charming moments, how ironic
it was that "all my troubles should arise from my disorders in my
family and the indiscretion of a wife that brings me nothing almost
(besides a comely person) but trouble and discontent."

But she *was* pretty, and Pepys once remarked of himself in some
astonishment: "A strange slavery that I stand in to beauty that I
value nothing near to it." What he meant by this "slavery to beauty"
was nothing metaphysical or pseudo-Platonic, but a simple, urgent

response to almost any attractive female, from a court beauty to a streetwalker; he tried to make love to all of them, and often succeeded, being equally ready to use a bed in his own home, a carriage, or an unlit alleyway. Whether he caught hold of the maid while his wife was out shopping, or flirted with ladies at a court reception, he recorded everything unsparingly and without pretensions, and his utter candor has a charm about it, even in the tawdrier moments. In a public alehouse he had the bad taste to thoroughly paw Doll Lane, a trollop, yet the disapproving reader can only chuckle with him when Pepys ruefully comments: "She has a very white thigh and leg, but monstrous fat." The sight of a homely woman, whom he had been told was a great beauty, once put him in bad humor for a whole day; the sight of an attractive woman would make him gay, and if the occasion permitted, start him on an immediate flirtation. Even when the occasion was not appropriate, Pepys was often galvanized into action by the irresistible force of his slavery to beauty; on August 18, 1667, for instance, he went to St. Dunstan's Church,

> where I heard an able sermon of the minister of the place; and stood by a pretty, modest maid, whom I did labor to take by the hand and the body; but she would not, but got further and further from me; and at last I could perceive her to take pins out of her pocket to prick me if I should touch her again—which seeing I did forbear and was glad I did spy her design. And then I fell to to gaze upon another pretty maid in a pew close to me, and she on me; and I did go about to take her by the hand, which she suffered a little and then withdrew. So the sermon ended, and the church broke up, and my amours ended also.

No wonder it is easy to like him: he is always willing to laugh at himself.

Yet much about Pepys was far from being modeled along rakish lines. "God forgive me," he wrote one time after fondling a lady, "I had a mind to something more." He did not enjoy gambling; winning upset him almost as much as losing, and he prayed God not to tempt him. Though he loved the theater, he frequently swore never to go back when he had seen some particularly licentious comedy, but he always did return. He carried off his infidelities with suitable coolness, but once, when his wife sweetly and with deliberate malice asked him to read aloud a letter by Sir Philip Sidney that dealt with such matters, he was more troubled than he allowed her see: "My conscience told me it was most proper for me, and therefore was touched at it, but took no notice of it, but read it out most frankly, but it stuck in my stomach." His peccadilloes even bothered him privately, and although his diary was written in cipher, he fooled his conscience by turning some of the more lurid episodes into an idiotic jumble of schoolboy's foreign phrases, to wit: "Doll Lane, and con elle I went to the Bell Tavern, and ibi je did do what I would con elle as well as I could. She sedendo sobre thus far and making some little resistance. But all with much content and je tenai much pleasure com ista."

Like any bourgeois, Pepys was stodgily conservative about his wife's appearance in public; when she first donned a blond wig, he refused to let her wear it, and only with great reluctance did he let her begin to use black beauty-patches in the courtly fashion. Yet he was pleased when she showed up to advantage: "My wife, by my troth," he once wrote, "appeared I think as pretty as any of them; I never thought so much before." And also like a bourgeois, he took a great interest in household management, considering himself the immediate master of all affairs; the result was an interminable series of criticisms, scoldings, quarrels, and tears. He and his wife quarreled about many other things, too, and as often as he remembered, Pepys would act the real man of the seventeenth century, reducing her to abject submission merely by maintaining stony silence. Sometimes, however, he would call her names and swear at her, and occasionally might even frighten her into silence by making a fist at her ("She, poor wretch, was surprised with it and made me no answer all the way home.") Once in a while he went still further: "Find my wife in a dogged humor for my not dining at home, and I did give her a pull by the nose and some ill words." Yet there is also much in his diary that seems warm and affectionate:

> December 27th, 1663: . . . So home to dinner with my wife very pleasant, and pleased with one another's company, and in our general enjoyment one of another, better we think than most couples do. . . .
> February 25th, 1667: . . . Talking with pleasure with my poor wife, how she used to make coal fires, and wash my foul clothes with her own hand for me, poor wretch! in our little room at my Lord Sandwich's; for which I ought forever to love and admire her, and do.

Yet Pepys was too much a man of his time to take her problems seriously. Mrs. Pepys was childless and bored, and all Pepys could think of was that she lacked work to keep her busy. He made a few brief and ineffectual efforts to divert her with music, dancing, and geography, but once when she handed him a written statement about the boredom of her seclusion, he fell into a rage, tore it up, and for good measure tore up some of his old love letters to her. Towards the end of the diary (which Pepys abandoned, because of weakening eyesight, when he was thirty-six), there occurred a monumental struggle between husband and wife over the matter of Pepys's affair with Deb, his wife's personal maid. It went on and on for over a week, and culminated in a tear-streaked quarrel in the moonlit bedroom, lasting half the night. Deb was discharged, but Pepys hunted her out and indulged in more intimacies; his wife found out, and there ensued another terrible fight. And this time Mrs. Pepys won; Pepys signed an affidavit not to see or speak with Deb, and even declared, in the privacy of his diary, that he was

> most absolutely resolved, if ever I can master this bout, never to give her occasion while I live of more trouble of this or any other kind. . . . Did this night begin to pray to God upon my knees alone in my chamber, which God knows I cannot yet do heartily.

The London rake and moralistic Christian in one soul—a complicated combination, and sometimes an awkward one, but very likely the pattern of the typical upper-class male in the year 1668. If other men of that period appear in history to have been more urbane, cynical, and egocentric, it may be only that we have not had the chance to eavesdrop and hear them on their knees, wrestling with what they liked to call their "natural desires."

4

Love and Polish
in the Eighteenth Century

❀   ❀

❀

By the early part of the eighteenth century the Enlightenment
had come of age. The educated and aristocratic classes had
very generally subscribed to a new scientific and rational outlook
on the world, replacing the mystical and intuitive ones of the past.
The views of such men as Descartes, Galileo, and Newton about
the physical world supplanted those of the Old Testament. A humane, amused, and tolerant view of man as a feeble but admirable
animal took the place of sin-laden theologies which saw him as the
guilty center of the universe. The ideal of human conduct was
thought to be behavior in which cool, dispassionate reason guided
every act, rather than emotion, revelation, or ancient custom.

On every side the rationalists found evidence of the logical and
orderly nature of the physical world and of human character. The
advances in astronomy, the growth of commerce, the emergence of
stable monarchies, and the increase in material comforts all lent
credence to the view that the universe was an excellent mechanism
made by a Master Mechanic who wound it up, set it ticking in accordance with scientific and mathematical laws, and thereafter did
not presume to interfere in its operation. Just as by detached reason
He therefore was responsible for the conduct of both atom and star,
so by reason ought man, His little likeness, govern himself and
society—humanely, sensibly, and without prejudice.

The Enlightenment appealed to several groups in European society. Liberals and scientists rejoiced in it because of its rejection of
ancient religious authority. The mercantilists found it good be-

cause it lent the sanction of philosophy to the present social order and justified the status quo. As Alexander Pope said, assuring everyone that the world was just as God meant it to be and needed no man-made improvements:

> *And, spite of pride, in erring reason's spite,*
> *One truth is clear, Whatever is, is right.*

But above all, the Enlightenment had the sympathy of the aristocracy, for it not only sounded their note of complacency, but expressed and justified their attitudes toward emotions, sex, and especially manners.

Never had there been such emphasis on manners, for an artificial code of formal behavior, applied consciously and deliberately, was the ideal technique for masking one's emotions and governing the irrational part of one's personality. Skill in the use of elegant courtesy, perfection in the maintaining of icy self-control, and the display of highly civilized politeness even in the tensest situations were the marks both of good breeding and of reason. Sometimes, to be sure, the overly civilized observance of politeness threatened to halt all normal human activities: the Duc de Coislin once saw a departing guest as far as his carriage, which was required; the guest, as also required, saw the Duc back to his own suite; but Coislin, the politest man of his time, then insisted with utmost assurances of his respect and devotion upon seeing his guest back to the carriage again, and the guest, seeing no other way to end the process, finally rushed out ahead of the Duc and managed to lock him in. Coislin, not to be outdone, leaped out the window and met him at the carriage. Having sprained his thumb in the leap, he then got it set by a surgeon, contested with the surgeon for the honor of opening the door for him, and sprained it again.

In England, manners continued to undergo refinements moderating the excesses and crudities of the Restoration period. Prior to 1703, at the fashionable resort of Bath, for instance, gentlemen wore their swords in public buildings, came to dances roaring drunk, talked vulgarly before ladies, and brawled and wenched without restraint. But by 1703 or 1705 Richard Nash ("Beau Nash") became the recognized Master of Ceremonies at Bath, and instituted new rules of deportment: gentlemen might not wear their swords, drunkenness was impermissible, and brawling, swearing, and undignified forms of flirtation were ruled out. Young dandies learned to bow and "make a leg" with all the Gallic grace in the world, offered each other snuff with matchless flourish, kissed each other on the cheek, and swore such pretty little oaths as "Why, blister me! Enfeeble me! Impair my vigor!" At other resorts, and in London, society rapidly changed in the same direction, and copied the manners of Bath and Paris.[5]

The emotional life of human beings almost disappeared behind the repressions of reason and the façade of stylized manners. Lord Chesterfield once cautioned his son never to say anything so crude to a bereaved friend as: "I am sorry for your loss," when good manners would call for: "I hope, Sir, you will do me the justice to be persuaded that I am not insensible of your unhappiness, that I take part in your distress, and shall ever be affected when you are so." Polished wit replaced overt anger: Richard Brinsley Sheridan, replying to an opponent in Parliament, said with flawless urbanity: "The Right Honorable gentleman is indebted to his memory for his jests, and his imagination for his facts," and when Chesterfield received the famous terrible letter of rebuke from Samuel Johnson, scorning his tardy patronage, he smilingly displayed it to friends and carefully pointed out in it certain excellent turns of phrase.

The customs of love likewise developed some bizarre aspects. A lady could receive visits from gentlemen while in bed or even in a covered bath; it was perfectly in order for a gallant to pretend to conceal tender feelings under such circumstances. Fond words and straightforward endearments were considered the *gaucheries* of inferior classes. In place of direct emotional expression, ladies learned from their French dancing-masters the code of the fan: it could be dropped, fluttered, closed with a clap, spread across a bosom, spread only partway across the bosom, or used as a weapon. Masks and masquerade balls were never more popular; anything was permissible if only emotion were concealed, and rules of etiquette observed. Casanova reported in his *Memoirs* that when he visited England, a strange lady once offered him a lift in her carriage, and though she refused to tell her name, allowed him to proceed from a squeeze of the hand to an inevitable conclusion before the ride was over; some time later, when he met her in someone's home and asked if she had

---

[5] The lower classes were meanwhile being improved by sterner methods. Dissenters (as Puritans were now called) and Anglicans joined hands in the formation of several Societies for the Reformation of Manners, one of which, between 1696 and 1730, brought about 99,380 prosecutions, almost all of lower-class people, for drunkenness, swearing, lewdness, and similar vices.

forgotten him, she frostily replied: "I remember you perfectly, but a frolic does not constitute an introduction."

The language used by eighteenth-century lovers is particularly intriguing. Words do not follow mere vagaries of fashion; the choice of language is governed by deep-seated forces of the human personality. It was not merely neo-classical style, but basic character structure, which made for the invariable use of such tepid abstractions as "witty nymph," "obliging modest fair," "endearing charms," "lively transports," and "pleasing flames"—expressions so conventional, polite, and formalized as to allow one to hint at emotion while nearly eliminating its power. Alexander Pope wrote some love letters to Lady Mary Wortley Montagu, and when she pretended he was merely being airily gallant, he protested in the rationalist equivalent of a throbbing confession:

> It would be the most vexatious of all tyranny if you should pretend to take for raillery what is the mere disguise of a discontented heart that is unwilling to make you as melancholy as itself; and for wit, what is really only the natural overflowing and warmth of the same heart as it is improved and awakened by an esteem for you.

Even in private amorous conversation, educated men and women used much the same sort of language and the same stilted, remote words and phrases. When young James Boswell was in London in 1762, he met and began visiting Mrs. Louisa Lewis, a pretty young actress, and hoped to have an affair with her. After some visits, he pleaded his passion and begged her to be "kind," a request she promised to think about. A week later he called on her to learn her answer, and since he copied down his own conversation as faithfully as he later did Samuel Johnson's, we have a chance to eavesdrop upon him and hear the very words an eighteenth-century gallant and a lady spoke, just as they spoke them, during that crucial scene. The dialogue went as follows:

> *Boswell:* The week is now elapsed, and I hope you will not be so cruel as to keep me in misery. (*He begins to take some liberties.*)
> *Mrs. Lewis:* Nay, Sir—now—but do consider—
> *Boswell:* Ah, Madam!
> *Mrs. Lewis:* Nay, but you are an encroaching creature! (*He deftly lifts up her petticoat.*) Good heaven, Sir!
> *Boswell:* Madam, I cannot help it. I adore you. Do you like me?
> *Mrs. Lewis* (*kissing him*): O Mr. Boswell!

Boswell (*still struggling against her resistance*): But my dear Madam! Permit me, I beseech you.

At this juncture, Mrs. Lewis pointed out that her landlady might come in at any moment, but she agreed to make Boswell "happy" on Sunday at 3:00 p.m., when all would be safe; and this quaint specimen of erotic semantics concludes thus:

Mrs. Lewis: Whenever you cease to regard me, pray don't use me ill, nor treat me coldly. . . .
Boswell: Pray, Madam, don't talk of such a thing. Indeed, we cannot answer for our affections. But you may depend on my behaving with civility and politeness.[6]

Boswell was duly made happy, but a week afterwards had a rather different conversation with Mrs. Lewis equally remarkable for the manners in which it clothes its subject matter:

Boswell: Do you know that I have been very unhappy since I saw you?
Mrs. Lewis: How so, Sir?
Boswell: Why, I am afraid that you don't love me so well, nor have not such a regard for me, as I thought you had. . . . I have but too strong, too plain reason to doubt of your regard. I have for some days observed the symptoms of disease, but was unwilling to believe you so very ungenerous. But now, Madam, I am thoroughly convinced.
Mrs. Lewis: Sir, you have terrified me. I protest I know nothing of the matter.

After some further talk, however, she admitted to having been infected three years earlier, but protested she had been entirely well for the past fifteen months. She swore solemnly that she had been ignorant of being still infected, and assured Boswell she was in misery at losing his esteem and being in jeopardy of getting a bad reputation. Boswell rose to the occasion superbly.

Boswell: I give you my word of honor that you shall not be discovered.
Mrs. Lewis: Sir, this is being more generous than I could expect.
Boswell: I hope, Madam, you will own that since I have been with you, I have always behaved like a man of honor.
Mrs. Lewis: You have indeed, Sir.
Boswell (*rising*): Madam, your most obedient servant.

Aside from such misadventures, the average rationalist, having nothing but scorn for the glooms and fears of earlier forms of

[6] *Boswell's London Journal, 1762–1763*, pp. 115–16.

Christianity, no longer thought of woman as a painted evil and the gateway to hell; on the other hand, he disdained the mystical fantasies of Neoplatonism. But his view of woman, if realistic and sane, was far from including an acceptance of her as his equal, or as a whole human being. She was still, in the eyes of the upper-class male, an ornament and a toy, a legal incompetent, and a congenital nitwit; having no religious grounds for disliking woman, he justified her continued subservience in the Age of Reason by claiming she was inherently unreasonable.

"Your sex," wrote Jonathan Swift to that same young lady who was about to be married, "employs more thought, memory, and application to be fools than would serve to make them wise and useful. When I reflect on this I cannot conceive you to be human creatures, but a sort of species hardly a degree above a monkey." Even those amiable reporters of English life Addison and Steele repeatedly portrayed the frivolous, useless life of woman, ostensibly with the object of reforming it. Steele complained that the typical young girl was delivered straight from her nurse to the dancing-master and was "taught a fantastical gravity of behavior, and forced to a particular way of holding her head, heaving her breast, and moving with her whole body, and all this under pain of never having an husband, if she steps, looks, or moves awry." He was hardly exaggerating; a typical advertisement of a girls' boarding school in the time of Queen Anne listed the following as the subjects taught: "The needle, dancing, and the French tongue, a little music on the harpsichord, or spinet, to read, write, and cast accounts in a small way."

The best-mannered Englishman of the century provides us with an ideal example of how the rationalist gentleman regarded love and women. He was Philip Dormer Stanhope, fourth Earl of Chesterfield, whom we heard a few pages back enunciating a formula for condolences. Chesterfield, who lived from 1694 to 1773, was the very embodiment of the gentlemanly ideal. A distinguished diplomat and statesman, a man of letters, and a generous patron of writers (with the notable exception of Johnson), he valued, above all, good manners, a sense of taste, and the cultivation of personal polish. He once commented that the very essence of gentility lay in the easy and graceful use of the arms and hands. He never laughed aloud, deeming it uncouth to do more than smile. Even his enemy, Johnson, conceded that Chesterfield's manner was "exquisitely

elegant," and most people, on meeting him, got the impression that
he was distinguished in appearance; in actual fact, he was rather
short, thickset, and had a broad, rough-featured face. He was, all
in all, a triumph of art over matter.

Chesterfield disdained the simple lechery of the rake; any foot-
man or porter, he felt could do as much. Instead he practiced gallantry in the grand style, and in addition, during his time as ambassador to the Hague, he openly took a Frenchwoman, Mlle Elizabeth
du Bouchet, as his mistress, and by her begot an illegitimate son,
Philip Stanhope. At thirty-nine Chesterfield finally married, having
been skillful enough to win the hand of Melusina von Schulemberg,
an illegitimate daughter of the late George I, who was nearly
forty and devoid of charm, but possessed a portion amounting to
£50,000 plus an annual income of £3,000. The newly-weds lived
separately in adjoining houses from the very first and Chesterfield
celebrated his marriage by taking a great beauty, Lady Frances
Shirley, as his new mistress. His wife seems not to have minded,
since as might be expected of him, he treated her with perfect
courtesy.

The private principles that guided his actions were all explained
by Chesterfield in certain of the famous confidential letters he
wrote to Philip Stanhope over a period of twenty years in an effort
to make something of the boy, and which were published against his
wishes. In one of them, written when his son was sixteen, Chesterfield confided to him the gentleman's real view of women:

> Women are only children of a larger growth; they have an
> entertaining tattle, and sometimes wit; but for solid, reasoning
> good sense, I never in my life knew one that had it. . . . A man
> of sense only trifles with them, plays with them, humors them,
> and flatters them, as he does with a sprightly, forward child; but
> he neither consults them about, nor trusts them with, serious mat-
> ters, though he often makes them believe that he does both.

Nevertheless, he added, they have so great an influence on other
men that they can make or break a man's reputation, and "it is
therefore absolutely necessary to manage, please, and flatter them,
and never to discover [7] the least marks of contempt, which is what
they never forgive."

As his son grew older, Chesterfield began coaching him in the
rudiments of gallantry. Women, he said, have only two passions—

[7] i.e., reveal or display.

vanity and love—and flattery is therefore the certain method of managing them. "He who flatters them most, pleases them best; and they are most in love with him who they think is most in love with them." He added a list of specific types of flattery, but despite his instructions, Chesterfield evidently felt that the boy was not making progress, and when young Stanhope was eighteen years old, Chesterfield began to urge him to attach himself to some older woman, long experienced in gallantry but now fading, who would be grateful for a young man's interest and would perfect his manners and gallant attentions. ("Nothing would do you more good than such a passion," he later added, making it sound almost medicinal.) But as the boy matured and failed to report any successful affairs of a high order, his father tried to to guide his aim for him:

> I am assured that Madame de Blot, although she has no great regularity of features, is, notwithstanding, excessively pretty; and that, for all that, she has as yet been scrupulously constant to her husband, though she has now been married above a year. Surely she does not reflect that woman wants polishing. I would have you polish reciprocally.

Sensing that Philip lacked daring and confidence, his father assured him repeatedly that, given good manners, a man could seduce almost any woman with perfectly standard gallant techniques:

> Force, assiduities, attentions, tender looks, and passionate declarations on your side will produce some irresolute wishes at least, on hers; and when even the slightest wishes arise, the rest will surely follow. . . . If you are not listened to the first time, try a second, a third, and a fourth. If the place is not already taken, depend upon it, it may be conquered.

The end of the story is beautifully ironic. Despite the brilliance of the coaching he received, Philip remained only an affable sort of fellow, neither distinguished, gallant, nor especially graceful. He died in 1668 at the age of thirty-six, leaving his aging father to learn with dismay that he had for some time been secretly married to an unattractive woman of humble origin, with whom he had apparently been perfectly content and perhaps even happy.

5

The Trouble with Don Juan

❀   ❀

❀

In bewildering contrast to the philosophic talk of self-control and the discipline of politeness, there was another face to the eighteenth century—a face of barbarity, cynicism, and unpitying cruelty. In the early part of the century, the French government was still propelling its galleys by means of chained, whipped, human beings—not only criminals, deserters, and Turkish captives, but French Huguenots. The southern British colonies in America were building an economy based upon a system of slavery far more severe than that practiced by the imperial Romans. Throughout Europe, gambling was a general obsession, estates and fortunes being freely flung onto the gaming tables, and dueling was at a peak of popularity, gentlemen thinking it entirely proper and ethical to kill one another for trifling insults. Londoners of good breeding liked nothing better than going to Hockley-in-the-Hole to watch a cockfight or to see a bear or bull torn to bits by maddened dogs. Heavy drinking had never been so common; in London alone there were 17,000 gin shops at mid-century, and Hogarth's squalid scenes of mass alcoholism were not exaggerations. Men spoke about self-control through the use of reason, but the law specified 160 capital offenses in eighteenth-century England. Executions were held publicly, and nobles, merchants and riff-raff alike turned out in holiday mood to eat fruit and gingerbread, swill gin, and watch the lads swing.

Rationalist love, too, though often portrayed as lustily lecherous and amusingly naughty, had about it a distinct malevolence. In the seventeenth and eighteenth centuries, poets and dramatists in every major European country were inescapably attracted by the story of

[278]

Don Juan Tenorio, a semi-legendary libertine of fourteenth-century Seville whose adventures and philosophy they magnified and added to until his fictional figure loomed menacing and satanic, more real than reality. There had always been stories of seducers, but it took the Age of Reason to exalt the archetype, at once detesting and admiring him, fearing and emulating him. In their denial of medieval and Christian values, the descendants of the same aristocracy who had once idolized the mythical Tristan—adoring, courteous, true, and long-suffering—now idolized the mythical Don Juan—lustful, haughty, false, and sadistic. Like all myths, it was drawn larger than life, but there were men something like Don Juan in Europe, less vindictive and monomaniacal, but dedicated to the art of cold-blooded seduction; the Duc de Lauzun, the Duc de Richelieu, Bezenval, Sedley, and Bolingbroke are only a few examples of the type.

Edmond and Jules de Goncourt, who made a highly perceptive study of eighteenth-century woman from the perspective of the mid-nineteenth,[8] said that not only had love in the Age of Reason been reduced to mere sensuality, but that its strongest motive was a desire to seduce and desert, for malicious sport. "This warfare and this game of love," they wrote, "perhaps disclose the most profound characteristics of the century." The dedicated seducer concocted plans, feigned emotions, and played his part with the skill of an actor and the dedication of a soldier; but the crown of his victory was to do all this without the slightest emotional involvement, so that when the woman, conquered and submissive, begged at last: "At least, tell me that you love me!" he could affect a disdainful smile and refuse. This, according to the Goncourts, was the grand style of seduction—seducing by pure caprice, so as to abandon without compunction. No wonder the eighteenth century found so superlatively clever that maxim of La Rochefoucauld's: "If love is judged by most of its effects, it resembles hate more than friendship."

To some degree, the deep antagonisms between man and woman may have stemmed from the economics of aristocratic marriage, which built every union upon a foundation of financial bickering, bargaining, and mistrust. Eligible young men of good family openly hunted heiresses, offered themselves to the richest, and even advertised in the papers, naming the minimum amount required to make

[8] Edmond and Jules de Goncourt: *La Femme au dix-huitième siècle*.

a girl suitable. Squire Guise, a country gentleman in search of a wife, left this plain indication of the prevailing callousness:

> Being on the bench at quarter-session, a Justice of the Peace took me aside and asked me whether I would marry a woman worth twenty thousand pounds. This lady I had seen but never spoke to, and upon the whole readily accepted his offer.

Few offers were so speedily accepted, however; in the average courtship, representatives of both sides cold-bloodedly and doggedly haggled about every detail of jointure (the inheritance guaranteed to a widow from her husband's estate), portion (her dowry), pin money (her guaranteed personal allowance), and the inheritance by the grandchildren of money or land; love or mutual attraction of the prospective bride and groom was rarely an issue. Considering the possibilities for later dissatisfaction with one's bargain, it is little wonder that the system produced as much sexual antagonism as it did.

Not every society which based marriage on property-trading has produced Don Juanism. In the eighteenth century, however, the matter was aggravated by the idea that man should—and can—subdue and repress all his emotions, a notion Ortega y Gasset has called the greatest error of Western man from the Renaissance on. Only much later would man scientifically relearn what many men had always intuitively known: that the stifling of biologically inevitable emotions results in human sickness and in destructive conduct.

A common explanation of Don Juanism, derived from modern psychoanalytic practice, is that it arises from a deep-lying fear of impotence, which is in turn frequently traced to a heavily repressed mother-attachment. But this rationale, if meaningful for modern Don Juans, is much less so for those of the Age of Reason, particularly since the emotional ties between aristocratic parents of that period and their children were extremely thin. Indeed, the principal cause which underlay Don Juanism may have been the faulty family relationships of the aristocracy, who entrusted their children to servants and saw them for a few minutes of polite conversation each day, if that much. According to contemporary psychology, it is only when the parent-child relationship is intimate, warm, and generous that the child learns a pattern of love involving empathy, altruism, and kindness, and develops a conscience consonant with those traits. If, however, the parent-child relationship is cold, barren, and distant, the child will remain psychologically a self-centered, angry infant, his concept of love being that of a struggle to grasp, seize, and hurt the unloving beloved, and his conscience, stunted in its growth, will fail to inhibit him from taking revenge for his frustrations.[9] In such persons, love can mean at best a sensual delight with a modicum of friendliness; at worst, the sodomy, tortures, and obscene self-gratifications of the Marquis de Sade; and between these extremes, the half-genial, half-hostile lecheries of the actual Don Juans.

The best-known of the latter, and the only one who wrote out a complete record of his amorous experiences, was the Chevalier de Seingalt, better known as Giovanni Jacopo Casanova. Born in Venice in 1725, he was the son of an actor and actress of Spanish descent. Possibly the most important event of his life occurred when he was one year old; at that age, he was abandoned by his parents, who handed him over to be raised by a disinterested grandmother. His character early showed its bent: at fifteen he was expelled from the University of Padua for excessive gambling debts, and at sixteen from a Venetian seminary for immoral and scandalous conduct. The rest of his life was a series of variations on these themes.

Having a brilliant mind and a talent for impersonation, Casanova became not only a man of many talents, but a consummate adventurer who played perfectly the role of a gentleman of quality. He translated the *Iliad* into Italian rhyme, wrote two dozen books on mathematics, history, astronomy, philosophy, and belleslettres, and conversed easily with men like Voltaire and d'Alembert. George III of England, Frederick the Great, Louis XV, and Catherine the Great were only a few of the monarchs who personally received him and welcomed him. He was variously secretary to an ambassador and a galley captain; director of state lotteries in Paris; diplomatic agent for Portugal; spy for the Venetian Inquisition; and above all, swindler and gambler. Time and again his adventures would follow the same inevitable pattern. Tall, sinewy, white of tooth, eloquent and elegant, he would arrive somewhere, make a dazzling social success, and win his way into an excellent position or post of confidence; after a while he would be found

[9] Several recent works deal with this phenomenon and offer abundant clinical and laboratory evidence; among them are psychoanalyst Abram Kardiner's *Sex and Morality*, anthropologist Ashley Montagu's *The Direction of Human Development*, and anthropologist Weston La Barre's *The Human Animal*.

out to be a rogue, or would get into some scrape; muffled and disguised, he would decamp and begin again elsewhere.

Three quarters of his *Memoirs,* however, are concerned with his love affairs, but like his business affairs these are marked throughout by rascality, showmanship, and a need—often forced by circumstances—for rapid movement and constant change. His first completed sexual experience consisted of coitus with two young sisters in one bed, all three of them enjoying the performance both as participant and spectator (Casanova was his own principal spectator then and ever after). He was always fond of this particular procedure, and in old age could reflect on it with benign wickedness:

> I achieved my best results, however, by attacking novices—whose moral principles and prejudices hindered the carrying-out of my intentions—in the company of another woman. I learned already in my early youth that young girls are difficult to seduce because they lack the courage, whereas in the company of a friend they easily surrender: the weakness of one excuses the fall of the other.

The fat volumes of his *Memoirs* are full of love affairs at this level. Casanova mentioned 116 mistresses by name and claimed that he had possessed hundreds of women. They ranged from noblewomen to chambermaids, and he made love to them standing, sitting, and lying down, in beds, alleys, on staircases, in coaches, and in boats. Typically, he would feel himself to be "passionately in love" a few moments after meeting a new woman; he would then launch himself upon any one of a hundred routines, using compliments, adoring words, gifts and money if necessary, stratagems of ambush if helpful or possible, and offers of marriage when all else failed. Finally he would bed the woman—and in the morning, or sometimes after a few days or weeks, he would be off on his way to the next one, for the prey, once taken, soon palled. It was the pursuit, the intrigue, the conquest that he found delightful, and a capitulation under duress was sometimes the sweetest of all. Casanova was once riding in a carriage with a pretty woman who had refused all his advances. Suddenly a severe thunderstorm broke over their heads; she clung to him in terror in the swaying coach, and then and there, wrote Casanova smugly, "my victory was most complete."

Some people find that the bulky *Memoirs* are a vast delicious meal, others that it rapidly produces surfeit and even nausea. The women in it form a surrealistic procession of lips, breasts, and thighs, but are scarcely individualized as human beings. Casanova himself must have felt ennui, for he required ever spicier dishes to stimulate him. "Madly in love" with a beautiful nun who had a semi-impotent lover, he put on one of his most prodigious displays of versatility and endurance after she told him the impotent man wished to watch through a peephole. He once met a young girl at the opera and was so smitten that he proposed marriage almost at once; before anything happened, he met her mother, who turned out to be an old mistress of his and who informed him that the girl was his own daughter. Only momentarily daunted, he hastened to bed with the mother, while the daughter shared their bed and watched them. Several years later he met the daughter again; this time she was married to an impotent marquis who wanted a child, and Casanova thereupon obligingly made love to his daughter three times and got her pregnant.[1]

In his forties he started collecting pornographic pictures, was "inflamed" by caressing a nine-year-old girl, and in the course of a swindle had sexual connection with a seventy-year-old marquise as part of an allegedly magical ritual. By the time he was forty-nine he had had at least eleven cases of venereal disease, and his powers had greatly waned or even vanished. In his aging years, when he was gouty, afflicted with prostatitis, and bored by his placid existence as librarian to Count Waldstein in Bohemia, he decided to live the good years all over again, and poured forth an unparalleled mass of recollections, without having changed his opinion or feeling about any of it. His final judgment of his entire life was contained in three words: "I regret nothing."

On a few rare occasions, however, Casanova seems to have felt a momentary awareness of the emotional impoverishment of his life, but the mood is fleeting. He wrote, for instance, how one night, in poor health and bad fortune, he stopped at an inn where thirteen years earlier he had been forced to part, with tears and suffering,

---

[1] The repetition of such themes as satisfying a woman whose lover or husband is impotent, making love to a woman while another watches, and indulging in the delights of incest has about it the suspicious sound of fantasy; one wonders if an aged man did not daydream about the acts he had never dared to do in actuality. European scholars, however, have verified a number of details in the *Memoirs*, identified some of the people involved, and found letters addressed to Casanova by a number of women. If some of his stories are fantasy, the larger number are evidently genuine.

from his young French mistress, Henriette, whom he loved with all
the intensity of his Latin soul. Yet on this second visit to the inn he
had completely forgotten the affair, the parting, and even the inn
itself, until suddenly he saw on a window the prophetic words she
had scratched there with a ring: "You will forget Henriette, too."
Casanova's reflections at this point are immensely interesting:

> Overcome, I dropped into a chair. . . . Comparing the self I
> was now with the self I had been then, I had to recognize that I
> was less worthy to possess her. I still knew how to love, but I real-
> ized I had no longer the delicacy that I had had in those earlier
> days, nor the feelings which really justify the transports of the
> senses, nor the same tender ways . . . *but what frightened me was
> to have to acknowledge that I no longer possessed the same vigor.*

As much as anything else, this final comment is Casanova's own
best evaluation of the meaning of love.

6

The Bourgeois Gentleman

❀   ❀

❀

The aristocratic and rationalist ideals penetrated eighteenth-
century society deeply enough to make Casanova, a mere
actor's son, into an excellent pseudo-aristocrat; even more remarkably, they infiltrated that stout bulwark of sentimentality, piety,
and family life, the middle class, and produced in it a number of
piebald specimens of mixed cultural values.

Intellectual salons, for example, had traditionally been held by
ladies of noble rank or by the courtesans of noblemen, but in the

latter half of the eighteenth century a number of salonières became prominent who were of neither category, and who even had certain distinctively bourgeois qualities. Madame Geoffrin, daughter of a dauphin's valet, was a virtuous, prim-looking woman who dressed simply, usually wore a modest lace cap on her head, and was thoroughly maternal in appearance; Madame d'Épinay, the wife of a tax collector, was not so virtuous nor so prim, yet she felt impelled to raise her child herself, a strikingly bourgeois action for a wealthy Parisienne of that time.

In England, a number of intellectual ladies known to history as the "Bluestockings" imitated the French salons beginning in 1750, and some of the most notable of them—Fanny Burney, Mrs. Hester Thrale, and Mrs. Hester Chapone, for instance—were serious intellectuals and perfectly moral wives of well-to-do middle-class citizens. They wore ordinary clothing to their meetings (hence the name "Bluestockings"), and ruled out cards, gambling, and other foolish pastimes. A tradition rooted in aristocratic flirtation had finally come fully around to the point where flirtation was no longer a part of it. Fittingly, the greatest luminary of their world was the ponderous pundit Dr. Samuel Johnson, a neoclassicist and rationalist, but a conservative, old-fashioned moralist all the same. Detester of "enthusiasm" and romanticism though he was, he summed up what was really a bourgeois reaction to the genteel ideal in his famous estimate of Lord Chesterfield's *Letters:* "They teach the morals of a whore, and the manners of a dancing master."

Voltaire, the friend of monarchs and chief prophet of the Enlightenment, was actually of sound bourgeois stock, his father having been a notary (a fact Voltaire preferred to say little about). All his life, this greatest propagandist of rationalism regarded passions as a prime source of human folly, and he once typically advised a wedding couple that the surest way to love forever was not to love each other too much. His well-known affair with the Marquise du Châtelet ("the divine Emilie") lasted sixteen years until her death and was carried on in the most enlightened fashion possible—with the tolerant consent of her husband, who for some years lived with them in a *ménage à trois.* Yet there was a distinctly bourgeois flavor about the way Voltaire and Emilie kept house together so long and so completely, and they were so thoroughly identified by the world as lovers that when they no longer made love and Emilie wished to break off so as to devote herself to a new affair, Voltaire would not let her for reasons of propriety. "He owed it to his public, he said, not to make a scandal which would cover him with ridicule and contempt," writes Nancy Mitford in her recent study, *Voltaire in Love*. "He thought it right to follow a straight line and to respect what he called, with his usual inaccuracy, a liaison of twenty years (really about fifteen)."

The prevailing ideas on love and women even had some influence in America, wherever the standard of living made it possible to emulate the British aristocracy. From New York to the South, the well-to-do gentry copied such English customs as fox-hunting, gaming, dances, and duels. Even in staid New England, an English traveler in 1740 remarked that aside from the theater and similar entertainments, the Boston gentry disported themselves in tempered emulation of the English:

> Both the ladies and the gentlemen dress and appear as gay in common as courtiers in England on a coronation day or birthday. And the ladies here visit, drink tea, and indulge in every little piece of gentility to the height of the mode, and neglect the affairs of the family with as good a grace as the finest ladies in London.

But that was only at the most elegant level of colonial society. More generally, the middle-class influence and the frontier philosophy caused great changes in the imported European ideas. Colonial libraries had a good sprinkling of rationalist writing on love and women, but typically the most popular books on these subjects were the conservative, moralistic ones, critical of the gallant life and full of sound, homemaking advice. Despite a considerable amount of intellectual scorn for romantic love, and the imitation and importation of English and French manners, marriage itself was generally praised in American books and magazines; even in the cities the frontier and pioneer feeling of a woman's immense usefulness and importance was still dominant.

One can see the hodge-podge of attitudes clearly in Benjamin Franklin. America's outstanding rationalist thinker came under the influence of the Enlightenment in his boyhood and adolescent years. Despite his New England background, he took a rationalist's guiltless view of sex, but had neither the money, skill, nor leisure for fancy gallantry; as a result, he took an obvious course, though he disapproved of it on purely practical grounds. "That hard-to-be-governed passion of youth," he later commented, "had hurried me frequently into intrigues with low women that fell in my way, which were attended with some expense and great inconvenience, besides a continued risk to my health by a distemper."

Too thrifty to waste his hard-earned money on a mistress, he turned his thoughts to marriage and approached it in the same cool, thoughtful spirit. Having started his own printing business in Philadelphia in 1728, he began to court a young lady with her parents' encouragement; after a suitable time, he candidly let them know "that I expected as much money with their daughter as would pay off my remaining debt on the printing-house, which I believe was not then above a hundred pounds." Bluffing, the parents said they did not have that much to give, and even denied Franklin the right to call on the girl. He rightly interpreted this as a ruse to get him to elope with the girl and forfeit all dowry, and was so annoyed by it that he would have nothing further to do with her even when the parents tried to draw him back.

He switched his interest instead to Deborah Read, a young woman he had courted years earlier. Unfortunately, in the meantime she had married a worthless fellow named Rogers who had deserted her and who was thought to have died. The situation was awkward: if Rogers had not died, another marriage would be bigamous, and if he had died, his wife's next husband might be liable for any debts he had left. The prudent Franklin therefore made only a common-law marriage with her, avoiding any ceremony or record. In his autobiography he summarized their relationship as follows:

> She proved a good and faithful helpmate, assisted me much by attending the shop, we throve together, and have ever mutually endeavored to make each other happy. . . . It was lucky for me that I had one as much disposed to industry and frugality as myself.

It was a workable, businesslike partnership, evidently devoid of inspiration or intensity. Deborah Franklin, though handsome, spirited, and devoted to Franklin's welfare, was not interested in his philosophic and scientific speculations, and was no intellectual company for him. He may have been fond of her, but was not strongly tied to her, for he spent what were the last ten years of her life in Europe without her.

From his middle years on, by which time he had become wealthy, famous, and sophisticated, Franklin adopted some of the airs of gallantry, but only at the verbal level. He corresponded warmly with Catherine Ray for many years, but kept what he called "a prudent but tender distance" between them. In London he acquired several young female admirers and treated them with affection and with gallant phrases, but his relationships with all of them remained chaste. An old tradition holds that during his years in France, he became a septuagenarian lecher; actually, he kissed the ladies he met, allowed the audacious young Madame Brillon to sit on his lap, and very pleasantly used to ask her for the ultimate favor which she always very pleasantly refused. Far from being lecherous, Franklin was merely being a good diplomat, and an amiable human being. The rationalist gallant in him was evenly matched by the New England Puritan.[2]

Franklin's writings on love, sex, and marriage, widely read and quite influential in America, are a jumble of enlightened cynicism, bourgeois earnestness, and vaguely Christian morality. The maxims in *Poor Richard's Almanack* range from "You cannot pluck roses without fear of thorns, / Nor enjoy a fair wife without danger of horns" to "A house without a woman and firelight is like a body without soul or sprite." Franklin's typical attitude toward sex was thoroughly rationalistic, yet not in the least licentious: "Rarely use venery but for health or offspring," he wrote, "never to dullness, weakness, or the injury of your own or another's peace or reputation." He was equally against marriage-by-infatuation and marriage purely for a good property settlement. The best-known of his writings on love is the mildly scandalous *Letter to a Young Man on the Choice of a Mistress*—a bit of Chesterfield in homespun— which tells the young fellow to choose an older mistress because she will be prudent, wise, infertile, and grateful. But it is really mostly spoofing; first and last, Franklin urges the young man to get married instead, since marriage "is the most natural state of man, and therefore the state in which you are most likely to find solid happiness."

So it went with the middle-class intellectuals: they borrowed ideas and gestures from the Enlightenment and the aristocracy, but lived for the most part very much like the bourgeoisie they really were. In 1751, an impecunious young Englishman named Richard Griffith, an amateur scribbler and rationalist, succeeded in seducing

---

[2] The case for the chastity of Franklin's gallantries has been convincingly made by Carl Van Doren, after a thorough sifting of the evidence, in his *Benjamin Franklin*, pp. 234–42, 411–12, 653, and 639–41.

his philosophic friend, Miss Elizabeth Griffith (no relation), a young girl without dowry. Where Casanova conquered in a matter of days or even hours, the middle-class Griffith had required five years of talk, letters, pleas, schemes, and promises. As luck would have it, she became pregnant, appealed to him in anguish, and he did what the genuine libertine would never have done: he married her. They achieved a warmly sentimental marriage, and even built literary careers on their own sentimental love letters, which they shortly published. Nevertheless, when Griffith drew up a will in 1753, he still had some lingering pride in his by-gone dreams of libertinage and rationalism, for on the wrapper of the will he wrote:

> I was not over-reached into this match by art, nor hurried into it by passion, but from long experience of her sense and worth I reasoned myself into it. . . . I found I had so engaged her affections that no other man could make her happy, and so dallied with her character that only myself could repair it.[3]

It was the last defiant nose-thumbing of a wicked little boy, who has been trapped into becoming a respectable husband.

7

A Most Unlikely Love Story

And so we have before us a portrait of rationalist love drawn from life. Yet is there not something lacking? Some final stroke, some bit of shading, that will vitalize the expression and add the final illusion of reality? Perhaps we will find it in one more story of

[3] Quoted in J. M. S. Tompkins: *The Polite Marriage*, p. 1.

love—a brief one, a pathetic one, a wildly improbable one that could have happened only during the Enlightenment.

It begins in the fall of 1765, when, at the salon of the Marquise du Deffand in Paris, two human beings met who were the least likely of all protagonists of a love drama. The man was Horace Walpole, English gentleman: a fragile, refined bachelor of forty-eight, a Member of Parliament, a literary amateur, a devotee of refined manners, a collector of curiosa and relics of whom a friend once remarked that his house was a museum and himself the best-preserved mummy in it. His behavior was marked by extreme polish and artificiality; he would never even think of striding manfully into a roomful of people, but would enter in a fashionably delicate manner almost on tiptoe, his knees slightly bent, as if afraid of a wet floor. "Walking is not one of my excellences," Walpole himself confessed. "In my best days . . . I tripped like a peewit." Thin-lipped, high of forehead, and frail of build, he was plagued by gout and subject to fatigue; not surprisingly, he took great comfort in rationalist philosophy, and summed up his opinion of emotion in a famous sentence: "The world is a comedy to those who think, a tragedy to those who feel." Accordingly, he thought about everything, and found everything material for his wit, for despite his prissy and affected manner, with friends or fellow intellectuals he was a marvelous conversationalist (though some thought he prepared his remarks in advance), and one of the most prolific and entertaining letter-writers of all time. In a word, he was one end-product of the era—all manners, all intellect, all gentility, sterile, inbred, and on the way to extinction.

The woman of the story was the hostess herself, the famous salonière, Marie Anne de Vichy-Chamrond, Marquise du Deffand, whom Walpole was meeting for the first time—a birdlike wisp of a woman, seventy years old. No, it is no tasteless jest, no stupid error by the historian; these are indeed the two protagonists. When he first met her, she was already tiny and withered, her clear blue eyes totally blind these twenty-odd years, her chiseled profile still exquisite but her once-translucent skin now dry and pale, her frothy imperious wit surviving on a rich daily diet of intellectual conversation. In her youth she had married and shortly been separated from the Marquis du Deffand, but her beauty and extraordinary mind soon won her the honored position of mistress of the Duc d'Orléans, Regent of France; later she had long-term liaisons with a few other men of importance and high rank, was for some years the principal ornament and intellectual lady of the court of the Duchesse du Maine, and had for many years maintained one of the principal salons of the century at her quarters in Paris. Among her habitués were many leading aristocrats, intellectuals, and encyclopedists (Voltaire, Montesquieu, Madame de Staal-Delaunay and d'Alembert, for instance), and some of the major creative writers of the era. Still alive to every new idea, still restless, energetic, and endlessly eager to talk about everything, she reigned as queen in her salon, her barbed wit as keen as ever, her gestures as graceful and elegant as always even though her hands were now as frail as two dead leaves.

It was a day in October 1765, when Walpole first came to her salon to look and listen. He was mildly displeased to find such vivacity and such pleasure in cleverness on the part of so venerable a lady, and in a letter to his cousin Henry Conway, he referred to her as "an old, blind debauchee of wit." Yet he was fascinated by the vitality and the charm of the spirit imprisoned in that faded body; he came again and again, and shortly was describing her to a friend as "the old, blind, charming Madame du Deffand." He talked to her for hours, visited her continually, and by late January wrote to his friend, Thomas Gray, that she

> . . . retains all her vivacity, wit, memory, judgment, passions, and agreeableness. She goes to operas, plays, suppers, and Versailles; gives suppers twice a week; has everything new read to her; makes new songs and epigrams, ay, admirably. . . . Her judgment on every subject is as just as possible; on every point of conduct as wrong as possible; for she is all love and hatred, passionate for her friends to enthusiasm, still anxious to be loved, I don't mean by lovers, and a vehement enemy, but openly.

For her part, Madame du Deffand found something rare, shy, and beautiful in the mind and soul of the crotchety, middle-aged bachelor; she responded to him with an outpouring of talk, effusions of flattery, and rapturous expressions of her feeling of *amitié* (friendship) for him that startled and frightened him. Yet it was Paris, and the salon habitués seemed to find nothing laughable or incongruous about the situation. Walpole was hypnotized into staying five months, and toward the end of that time he called on her daily, sat by her side during the salon gatherings, and in private even gingerly spoke of his own warm regard for her.

Then he had to go home, and the very touch of English soil produced a remarkable metamorphosis. Suddenly he was afraid of his involvement with her, shocked at his own actions, and genuinely alarmed lest English friends suppose he had been an old woman's lover and ridicule him for it. Meanwhile he was hotly pursued by letters in which she poured forth adulation, despair, and flattery in cascades of fluent rhetoric. What had seemed utterly charming in Paris seemed hideously inappropriate in England, and he wrote her, sternly scolding her for her indiscretions and romantic extravagances. She replied with warmth, but not the heat of anger: "Where, pray tell, did you get the idea that I am given to indiscretions and romantic transports? . . . I, the declared enemy of all that has the least resemblance to romance!" But two weeks later, completely forgetting this ringing declaration, she wrote in another vein, blurting out an incredible confession like an infatuated schoolgirl, even while pretending to find unobjectionable names and reasons for her feelings:

> I forget that I have lived; I am only thirteen. If you do not change and you come to find me again, my life will have been a happy one. You will wipe out all the past and I will date only from the moment when I met you. . . . Don't tell me that I have romance in my head—I am a million miles away from it, I detest it; everything which resembles love is odious to me, and I am almost glad to be old and hideous—not to mistake any profession of feeling for me, and happy to be blind, to be very sure that I am incapable of anything but the purest and most sacred friendship.

And only a few days after this palpitating message, she sent him one that was, in a way, still worse, since it plainly asked for pity and succor:

> All I can see is our separation, which it seems to me must be eternal. . . . I shall never see you again; it was not worth your coming here to revive me and help me, if it only meant making me die twice. You see how sad I am; it is really a kind of despair.

All of this produced in Walpole something akin to panic, and on May 20, 1766, he wrote her a shocking reply:

> On my return from Strawberry Hill[4] I find your letter, which gives me the utmost possible annoyance. Ought not your lamenta-

---

[4] Walpole's miniature mock-Gothic castle near Twickenham; he had just come back from there to his town lodgings when he wrote this letter.

tions ever cease, Madame? You make me repent my frankness.
. . . Really, if friendship is to have all the sorrows of love without its pleasures, I see no reason for trying it. . . . If you wish
our relation to continue, conduct it on a less tragic note.

So began what is surely the most incredible correspondence in
the annals of love—840 letters from her and nearly as many from
him over a fifteen-year period—filled with repeated outpourings,
confessions, quarrels, and apologies; on her part an endless stream
of emotional outbursts, on his a series of formal, cranky, and sometimes frozen replies ("*Je suis refroidi*," he actually wrote—"I am
refrozen"), unsuccessfully trying to make her hide or at least
moderate the intensity he found so upsetting and embarrassing.
(Walpole realized how these letters would sound to the world and
later asked for them back and burned them; only eighteen survive,
plus phrases or sentences from eighty-two others; Madame du Deffand's remain complete, not a word missing.)

To Walpole's most unconscionable attacks, Madame du Deffand
replied neither with icy scorn nor vitriolic rage, but a variety of
softer moods. Sometimes it was gentle sarcasm: "The English are
conceited and insolent. Declarations of friendship, of boredom, of
sadness . . . —they take all that for unrestrained passion." Sometimes it was with petulant tearfulness: "I think I have a friend, I
console myself by telling him my troubles, I take pleasure in
speaking to him of my friendship . . . and he is scandalized, ridicules me, and abuses me in every possible way!" Sometimes she
promised to reform: "You will find on your return (if you do return) that I am much improved. . . . I have a kind of fear and
respect for you that has very good effects." And sometimes she
resorted to exquisite flattery: "You make my setting far more
beautiful and happy than my noontime or my rising. I am only
frightened of not living long enough to see you again and tell you
all that I know not how to write you." And when, occasionally,
he would unbend a trifle, it would send her off into an ecstasy; once,
for instance, he wrote in a kindly vein to ask about her health and
got back this delirious burst of thankfulness:

> Your insults, your roughness, even your cruelties, have never
> blinded me to the goodness and the tenderness of your heart.
> . . . Your letter has upset me so that I feel as if I were drunk.

If Walpole could not tame her, neither could he make himself
break it off. Indeed, he finally succumbed to the lure and visited her

for six weeks in 1767. In her own salon in Paris the transformation
in him again took place; once more he was the urbane charming
conversationalist, witty, gentle, and solicitous, offering his arm to
the frail little Marquise and acting as her prince consort. But when
he returned to England, he was *refroidi* again. It happened a third, a
fourth, and a fifth time, yet she never despaired or gave him up.
During his last visit to her, when she was seventy-nine, she could
still act like an impulsive girl: when he arrived, seasick, dirty, and in
need of a complete change, she rushed to his room at once, insisted
that her blindness made it permissible for her to stay, and chattered
gaily while he washed and dressed. They talked until 2:00 a.m.;
then she let him retire, but she was still full of things to say; when
he awoke in the morning, he found a long effusive letter awaiting
him which she had dictated while he was sleeping.

The entire affair was as baffling to her as it was to him; she
twisted her words and tortured her explanations, fearing always to
seem ridiculous. A letter she wrote about a year after they met is
typical of many others that indulged in the same confusions:

> It is a misfortune and a very great one, this friendship I have
> conceived for you. Ah! *mon Dieu*, how far it is from romance and
> how little you have known me to have suspected me of it! I love
> you only because of the esteem I have for you, and because I be-
> lieve I have found in you the qualities I vainly sought for fifty
> years in so many others.

But the letter is not unclear, after all. Whatever she may call it,
whatever she might deny it was, this was the one emotion Madame
du Deffand had never known in all her long, glamorous, gallant
life, and for which her unknowing heart had always been starved.
It was the bitterest of ironies that she was seventy when she first felt
it, and that Horace Walpole was the last man in Europe who could
return it. There may never have been a more hopeless love affair
in the world.

This, then, is the last stroke in the portrait; this is the final touch
that gives meaning. Love in the climate of rationalism could produce a frigid Madame de Maintenon, a rakehell Gramont, a cal-
culating Chesterfield, a libertine Casanova, and a sexless Walpole;
then, for good measure, it could give everything that was best
about the gallant life to a dazzling Madame du Deffand, only to let
her discover, hopelessly late, that all her life she had completely
lacked the thing she wanted most.

Chapter IX

THE ANGEL IN THE HOUSE

I

The Unmeaning of Romanticism

❦   ❦

❦

In his later years Lord Chesterfield, that paragon of good breeding and exponent of rational gallantry, grew deaf and lived in seclusion, largely out of touch with society. Perhaps it was just as well; before his death in 1773, the world of the absolute monarchs in which the Enlightenment had flourished was mortally ill. But even in advance of the wars and revolutions that destroyed it, the finely polished pattern of upper-class European life was being tarnished by influences a fastidious gentleman like Chesterfield could view only with revulsion. Factories were starting to befoul the good air, and businessmen with porky faces and soiled linen were growing wealthier than many an aristocrat. Some of these *nouveau riche* tried to copy the ways of the upper class, but the more distressing spectacle was the upward infiltration of the tastes and customs of the lower and middle class. The Methodism of John Wesley—a reformer of morals who was so strict that he disapproved even of tea-drinking or lying abed of a morning—gained such ground in the latter half of the eighteenth century that the Established Church itself was following suit with a reforming movement known as Evangelicalism. The taste of chambermaids and merchants' daughters for the sentimental novels of Richardson and his imitators was spreading to people of the better sort. Throughout educated society, the urbane control of one's emotions was losing its popularity and being supplanted by a benighted, bourgeois attitude summed up in the word "sensibility"—a hyperemotional frame of mind, deeply affected by every event or thought. It became the style to exhibit languor, pallor, and a physical "decline" as proof of one's great sensitivity of soul, and some-

[297]

times an even more extreme result was attributed to it, as witness
this inscription on the Oxfordshire gravestone of a young lady:

> Her artless beauty, innocence of mind, and gentle manners
> once obtained her the love and esteem of all who knew her. But
> when nerves were too delicately spun to bear the rude shocks
> and jostlings which we all meet with in this transitory world, Na-
> ture gave way; she sank and died, a martyr to excessive sensibility.

Rationalist gentlemen like Chesterfield had wooed and philan-
dered with aplomb, considering love an excellent pastime, and they
had held a skilled style of seduction to be a necessary social grace.
Sensibility changed all that; men of the newer generation considered
love as a mighty force and a noble goal in life, but the higher they
prized it, the more they seemed to grow shy with women, inhibited, and fearful of rebuff. Men spoke of love in rhapsodic terms,
but shied away from sexuality; they began to prize not the dazzling
flirtatious woman, but the shy, virginal one, and themselves acted
just as shy, and nearly as virginal. In the very era when love poetry
again came into its own, a number of literary journeymen were re-
vising and purifying the love poetry of earlier eras; not only bawdy,
lusty, or passionate expressions were trimmed out, but even those
that might make the unwary reader think of sexual love, and, accordingly, one James Plumptre even emended Shakespeare's lyric
from "Under the greenwood tree/Who loves to lie with me," to
read "Under the greenwood tree/Who loves to work with me."

These were but a few of the signs of a major change in European
social ideals—a broad counter-trend to reason and neo-classicism
usually given the general title "romanticism." The label may itself
be the most confusing in the history of ideas, having been freely
pinned on unrelated areas of literature, politics, and psychology, on
events of brief duration and on movements lasting centuries, and
on such disparate phenomena as Rousseauism and horror novels,
free love and idealized chastity, Methodism and the Catholic revival,
and the French Revolution and the reaction that followed it. In
recent years, indeed, some scholars have at last thrown up their
hands in disgust and decided that the terms "romantic" and "romanticism" are an academic scandal and have become quite useless.

Fortunately for us, in the area of love these words are still meaningful and valuable. We have already seen romantic love in earlier
manifestations and observed its characteristics; in the late eighteenth
century it is this tradition that re-emerges from partial obscurity

and guides a larger fraction of society than ever before. And yet if it is still recognizable, it is not what it once was. The term "romantic love" refers really not to one thing, but to a loose aggregation of ideas and customs. As it passed down the centuries, some were continually sluffed off and others added; it is somewhat like the philosopher's much-darned socks, the fabric of which was eventually altogether changed, but which never lost their identity as a specific pair of socks.

One rarely thinks of the businessmen of the Industrial Revolution, for instance, as being the inheritors of a love tradition that was originated by the feudal knighthood, adapted to the needs of chivalry, and designed to provide extramarital adventures; and when one looks at the nineteenth-century family photograph of the round-bellied patriarch, stiff and unbending, surrounded by his well-scrubbed progeny and demure wife, it seems unlikely that he had been personally influenced by the eloquent preciosities of sixteenth-century Neoplatonism. Yet such was the case; the tradition of romantic love was clearly identifiable, but had become so modified that it suited the needs of a business-oriented society. To see how that society was able to blend feudal, Renaissance, and Puritan traditions, and why romantic patriarchalism seemed so important to it, we will concentrate our attention on an extreme and clear-cut example—Victorian love, or romantic love in nineteenth-century England, an archetypal pattern for much of Northern Europe and America.

If it may surprise one to find that the Victorians were the latter-day romantics, it may seem equally surprising that the romantics of Byron's own era were—with a few such notable exceptions as Byron himself—nearly as prissy and puritanical as the Victorians who would follow them. And though one usually thinks of the nineteenth century as being marked by high moral standards, a close-knit family life, and a tender, worshipful view of woman, it was also an age in which prostitution and deviation were endemic, the ancient structure of marriage was crumbling, and women themselves were making a determined revolt against their glorified status. Why all this was so we will understand better after doing our utmost to invade that sacrosanct shrine of shrines and mystery of mysteries, the Victorian bedroom.

2

An Apostle of Romanticism
and His Gospel

❀   ❀

❀

But the Victorian bedroom is neither easily seen into nor invaded; it was well shuttered and firmly locked. We need to go back, and borrow both passkey and lamp from a pre-romantic whose life illuminates nineteenth-century love although he died in 1778, whose ideas were immensely influential in conservative England though he had been a somewhat radical Genevan who lived in France, and whose ideals were vastly admired although his personal life had been more or less shocking.

This was Jean-Jacques Rousseau, composer of operas and plays, novelist, political theorist, educational reformer, and social philosopher. Every college student learns that he was one of the most influential forces in fostering romanticism, political liberalism, and sentimentality. Everyone knows of his nature worship, his concept of the "natural man" spoiled and debauched by civilization, his pro-republican theory of the "social contract," and his quarrels with the rationalist *philosophes*. Generally by-passed in college, however, are the unusually frank *Confessions* Rousseau wrote in later life, recounting in detail not just his career, but his endless ailments, depressions, and complaints of plots against him (David Hume described him unforgettably as a man not only naked in the world, but without a skin), and in particular retailing his amorous history. Extraordinarily, in the age when Don Juan was the fictional ideal, Rousseau was pleased to recount about himself a series of sexual and erotic tales involving incompetence, misadventure, and frustration. Sentimental tears, timidity, unsatisfied passion, and renunciation seemed to him at once pathetic and noble; he wept for his shortcomings, and was thoroughly proud of them.

Rousseau was born in Geneva in 1712, the son of a watchmaker of French Protestant origin; his first piece of bad luck was the death of his mother nine days later. When he was a small boy, his father would sentimentally tell him about his dead mother's beauty, virtue, and goodness. "Jean-Jacques," he would say, "let us speak of your mother," and the small boy would knowingly reply: "Very well, father, then we are going to cry." Though Isaac Rousseau was fond of his son, he never let him forget that it was his birth that had killed his mother. "Ah, give her back to me!" he would cry out to Jean-Jacques, and the child would weep helplessly.

When the boy was ten, his father had to flee from Geneva. Jean-Jacques was farmed out in the succeeding years to an uncle and a tutor, and later apprenticed to an engraver. Some of his neurotic amorous proclivities began to appear quite early.[1] At the age of twelve, for instance, when he was boarding with a pastor named Lambercier, the pastor's sister threatened to whip him for misbehavior. He misbehaved anyhow, got whipped, and found to his astonishment that while it was painful, it was also peculiarly delicious. He loved her the more for the beating, and the very next time Mlle Lambercier beat him, she saw an evident symptom of his erotic feelings and thereafter refused to paddle him. It is tolerably obvious that this propensity stemmed from Isaac Rousseau's mishandling; the boy desperately sought to find a loving mother-substitute, yet expected punishment for having killed his real mother. For the rest of his life, Rousseau hungered for cruelty and beatings at the hands of women; fearing to ask for them outright, he transmuted his desire into an acceptable form by employing the older traditions of romantic love:

> To fall on my knees before a masterful mistress, to obey her commands, to have to beg for her forgiveness, have been to me the most delicate of pleasures. . . . This way of making love does not lead to rapid progress . . . [and] consequently I have possessed few women, but I have not failed to get a great deal of satisfaction in my own way, that is to say imaginatively. So it is that

[1] In some cases the dating of the episodes to follow does not coincide with that in the *Confessions*, but Rousseau's memory was inaccurate, and his paranoia far advanced, by the time he wrote it; scholars have managed, with considerable effort, to correct some of the discrepancies.

my sensibility, combined with my timidity and my romantic nature, have preserved the purity of my feelings and my morals, by
the aid of those same tastes which might, with a little more bold-
ness, have plunged me into the most brutal sensuality.

At sixteen, Rousseau ran away from the engraver, and a few miles
from Geneva met a kindly curé who sent him to the home of a
recent Catholic convert, the widow Louise Eleanore de Warens.
Rousseau expected to find a pious, cranky old woman; instead, he
came upon an angelic ash-blonde lady of about twenty-eight, whose
sweet face and gentle manner captivated him instantly. For a while
she housed and supported the short, nervous, black-eyed youth;
then under her influence he went to Turin, studied Catholicism and
became a convert, and after several years of vagabondage returned
to her home at Annecy, the only place he felt happy and secure.
Madame de Warens, whom he always called "Mamma," saw to it
that her "Little One" got a decent education and a knowledge of
music, and she secured him several government positions, each of
which he muffed; but she always understood and forgave, and continued to take good care of him.

At twenty-one Rousseau, too shy to make advances to women,
was still a virgin. At last the mother of one of his music students
began to make some approaches toward him, and brought about
one of the truly significant episodes of his life. Mamma, having
learned of the impending situation, took him into the garden one
beautiful day and told him, in the sweetest and kindest fashion
possible, that promiscuity was dangerous; to save him from it, she
proposed to grant him her own favors, but wanted him first to
think it over for eight days. Rousseau could hardly answer her, so
wild and vivid were his fancies. He had always considered Mamma
extremely pretty, and the thought of the promised fulfilment threw
him into a very fever of anticipation, but as the days passed he was
all but sick with anxiety, fear, and even revulsion, a condition he
found infinitely perplexing. "I loved her too much to desire her,"
he wrote half a life later, still perplexed. "That is the clearest idea
I have on the subject."

The eighth day arrived; Rousseau went, all atremble, into her
bedroom and learned his lesson. To appreciate the extraordinary
emotions he felt, one has only to imagine the palpitating youth, in
the moment of highest passion, murmuring "Mamma! Mamma!"
His own comments on the episode are wonderfully revealing:

> [I] found myself for the first time in the arms of a woman I
> adored. Was I happy? No; I tasted the pleasure, but I knew not
> what invincible sadness poisoned its charm. I felt as if I had com-
> mitted incest and, two or three times, as I clasped her rapturously
> in my arms I wet her bosom with my tears. As for her, she was
> neither sad nor excited; she was tranquil and caressing. . . . She
> neither received sexual pleasure nor knew the remorse that fol-
> lows.

It was the blueprint for romantic love—the burning but remorseful
man, the frigid but charitable woman, the love-making compounded of yearning and tears, desire and guilt.

Tears and guilt notwithstanding, Rousseau remained Mamma's
lover for some six or seven years, though one gathers that the actual
sexual episodes were relatively infrequent and always colored by
sinful overtones. Although Mamma remained perfectly kind and
sweet despite Rousseau's instability and petulance, she finally took
a better lover in 1738 or thereabouts, gently assuring Rousseau that
she did not propose to deny him her favors and that he had only to
share them with the new lover. Bursting into tears at her feet, he
said that although he would always adore her, he would not so degrade her. "It is to our heart's union that I sacrifice my pleasures,"
he cried, but he chose this alternative so readily that perhaps it
represented a relief; he stayed on in her house without discomfort
another year before finally leaving to make his own way in the
world.

In Paris, Rousseau began in his early thirties to achieve some success as an opera composer. Meanwhile, lacking the pleasures Mamma
had provided, he took a fancy to Thérèse le Vasseur, a young, very
shy, and simple girl who was a servant at the inn where he lived,
and rather easily seduced her; what was more important, he found
in her a companion who became attached to him by a doglike devotion. Telling her he would neither marry her (on some vague
principle of rebellion against social custom) nor desert her, Rousseau began a permanent association with Thérèse, finally setting up
housekeeping with her in a plain fourth-floor apartment and openly
acknowledging her to his friends and the world.

What sort of woman was it that this greatest of the pre-romantics
chose for his common-law wife? Neither a very pretty nor a
charming one, and certainly not a clever one. Thérèse learned to
write under Rousseau's prodding, but never to read properly; she
never was able to tell time, count money, or name the months of

the year in proper order; and her malapropisms were so outrageous
that Rousseau compiled a little anthology of them for the amusement of one of his patrons. Five children were born of their union,
but since Rousseau felt that he could neither support them properly
nor write with children around the house, he turned all five over
to a foundling home. Although he and Thérèse wrangled somewhat in later years (particularly after Rousseau ceased being her
lover), he never left her; in fact, after twenty-five years of this
union, he married her in 1768, his middle-class origins and his boyhood Calvinism asserting themselves after all his years of intran-
sigence. As to what the relationship meant to him, he left this mys-
tifying summary:

> From the first moment I saw her until this day [circa 1770] I
> have never felt the least glimmering of love for her [and] no more
> desired to possess her than I had desired Madame de Warens. . . .
> The sensual needs I satisfied with her were for me purely sexual
> and had nothing to do with her as an individual. . . . Love did
> not enter into the feelings that attached me to the woman who has
> been dearest to me.

Famous at last as a writer and thinker, in his forties Rousseau
began to brood that he would die without ever having truly loved.
Day after day he would leave the country cottage in which they
were then living and go alone into the woods to spin daydreams of
love and tragedy; these he began to set down in the form of a
novel filled with painful and exquisite sentiments. In the middle of
this, a neighbor of his, Sophie, the Countess d'Houdetot, dropped
in at the cottage one day when her carriage got stuck in the mud
near by. She was an attractive vivacious woman of about twenty-
seven, with gentle features, a bubbling wit, and waving black hair
that she could let down to her knees. It was inevitable that Rousseau
should see in her the heroine of his novel, and in himself the hero;
moreover, since she had a lover named Saint-Lambert to whom
she was fervently devoted, and since Rousseau was suffering from
a chronic bladder ailment that made him all but impotent, his
chances of success in love were nil, and thus the entire situation was
perfectly suited to his inclinations. He fell in love with her wildly,
his emotion being so great as to produce trembling, palpitation, and
convulsive movements of the limbs; later he said that this was the
only real love of his life.

One perfect night, in the moonlit garden of her house, his tongue was fully unloosed and he poured forth with consummate eloquence all his emotions, weeping "intoxicating tears" at her knees, and making her weep likewise. But though she called him the most charming of lovers, she said she could not love two at one time and must remain faithful to Saint-Lambert. "I sighed and was silent," wrote Rousseau. "I kissed her. What a kiss! But that was all." And he supplied a rationalization which superbly covered the situation —an explanation that might have been written by Bernard de Ventadour, the Provençal troubadour who had sung the praises of pure ladies six centuries earlier:

> The light of every virtue adorned in my eyes the idol of my heart; to have soiled that divine image would have been to destroy it. . . . I told her a hundred times that, if it had been in my power to gratify myself, if she had put herself at my mercy of her own free will, except in a few short moments of madness I should have refused to purchase my own happiness at such a price. I loved her too well to wish to possess her.

This bizarre emotional life was in considerable part the product of neurosis, but Rousseau adapted it to a cherished ancient tradition, thereby idealizing and dignifying his disease. Moreover, it happened to reflect the growing sentiment and inclinations of his time, and his ideas therefore had immense success and influence among the liberals and intellectuals of late eighteenth-century Europe; so does fortune immortalize a man for his sickness in one age, and merely hospitalize him for it in another. Two works in particular carried Rousseau's ideas on love to the public. The first was *La Nouvelle Héloïse*, the novel he began before his unhappy love for Sophie, and completed after it, in 1761; the second was *Émile*, a novelized tract on education, published in 1762. The former told of the love of a man of low position and a girl of rank, her marriage (at her father's request) to a man of her own station, the sufferings of her lover, her purity as a wife and mother, and the partial easing of her lover's misery through the exercise of noble sentiments. *Émile* had little plot, but dealt with a young man's choice of an ideal wife and discussed the importance of domestic virtues and the proper upbringing of children.

Both novels, in short, put forth surprisingly conservative doctrines, considering Rousseau's cantankerous nature and untidy manner of life. Actually, all his thoughts about women and love were essentially old-fashioned and bourgeois, rather than radical and

avant-garde. Julie and Saint-Preux, for instance, the protagonists of
La Nouvelle Héloïse, were platonic lovers for a long while before
finally becoming physical lovers. Julie, after her marriage, became
an ideal wife and mother and was unswervingly faithful to her husband, even when Saint-Preux returned, his old love for her burning as brightly as ever. Much of Saint-Preux's sorrow at having lost
her stemmed from the fact that true love is unique, and not to be
found twice in life, each person having but one ideal soul mate.
This was a romantic concept of considerable age, and in Rousseau's
own time it already seemed hopelessly antiquated and barbaric to
rationalists; Dr. Johnson snorted that there were fifty thousand
women in the world a man might be as happy with as any one particular woman. *Émile* offered still more conservative doctrines. Its
major theses on woman are that her intellect is much inferior to
man's, and that she therefore requires a different kind of education;
that she should be weak and timid, and strive to make herself agreeable and obedient to her husband all the time; and that her proper
business in life consists of domestic affection, child-rearing, and the
cultivation of tender sentiments.

If there seems to be a striking inconsistency between his adoration of woman and his view of her as an acquiescent homebody, one
need not be surprised; in his private love life Rousseau had been
chronically inconsistent, and it had never bothered him. He wrote
ecstatically of the love he felt for Madame de Warens, but claimed
that the only true love he ever felt was for Sophie; he was sick for
Sophie's embraces, but believed that his love was too great to let
him possess her; he lived comfortably with a woman vastly inferior
to him, used her as concubine and housekeeper, and married her
only after marriage had lost its value for her; and having given
away his own children, he wrote sentimentally about home life and
child-rearing.

The truth was that Mamma, Thérèse, and Sophie represented
three aspects of woman that he strove to amalgamate; in his own
life he never succeeded, and even in fiction he scarcely managed it,
but he assured the world that it could and should be done. For well
over a century after the publication of his books, the middle class
and even some upper-class young men and women in Europe were
deeply under his influence; many of their problems in love and in
marriage were surely due to the fact that the amalgam was not much
easier for anyone else to make than for Jean-Jacques Rousseau.

3

The Practices of Romantic Love

❀　　　❀

❀

Within a few years after Rousseau's death, many of the phenomena collectively called romanticism were flourishing
in Europe; in particular, the practices of romantic love which he
idealized were fast becoming the ruling fashion. Despite his ec-
centricities, he had not been speaking only for himself, but had
cogently expressed much of the domestic morality and sentimental
piety of the growing middle class. The sooty factory towns and
grubby counting-houses of the Industrial Revolution hardly look
like a fertile soil for the growth of that tender plant, romantic love.
In folklore and fiction, it is generally associated not with tradesmen, but with poets, musicians, rebels, and nonconformists; yet the
principal elements of romantic love had entered middle-class life by
the seventeenth century, and in that shelter survived the cold win-
ter of rationalism. When industrialization caused the middle class to
grow rapidly in size and power, its ideals of love and marriage began first to color and then to dominate Western thinking. Nonconformists like Rousseau were not really the typical romantics,
but only the extremists who put into words what the mercantile,
the professional, and the business people had long felt.

There were other reasons beside tradition for the sympathy the
middle class felt for the ideas Rousseau had espoused. His thoroughgoing individualism matched and expressed the general philosophy
of the bourgeoisie, especially that of Protestant England. Just as
laissez-faire economics and Puritan conscience were forms of individualism, so too was sensibility: it was individualism in the realm
of emotional life—a reliance on one's own inner feelings rather
than some external or rational standard. It is not so surprising after
all that the plant should have thrived in the soil of industrialism.

Rousseau's ideas, furthermore, appealed to the new middle class by their very earnestness and seriousness. His *Confessions*, though they tell of sexual transgressions, are soul-searching, serious, and almost entirely humorless. These were qualities the upward-striving middle class approved and prided itself on. Even before Rousseau's death, the *Sentimental Magazine* in England observed with approval that laughter and wit were going out of style, and by 1815 the *Edinburgh Review* was pleased to note that the change had gone still further:

> Our very advances in politeness have an undeniable tendency to repress all the extravagances of mirth or indulgence in humor . . . and to restore our original English taste for honest, manly good sense. . . . Artificial spirits and mere frivolous glitter, we believe, were never in so little request among us.

This latter-day Puritanism was not limited to the lower-class Methodists, but spread to the Church of England; it was an Evangelical reformer who persuaded George III in 1787 to close gaming houses, prosecute the drunk and the lewd, and suppress licentious publications. But no official edict was the cause of the closing of Ranelagh Gardens, one of London's famous pleasure parks, in 1803; it was, rather, the gradual conquest of England by a revived Puritanism that made Ranelagh's business wither away after sixty successful years.

Rousseau's paeans to the pure and the motherlike in woman also accentuated a growing middle-class emphasis on female delicacy and modesty. The earlier Puritans had called things by plain names, but the new Puritans and the Rousseauists became linguistic prudes. As early as the 1790's, no decent woman used good old expressions like "with child" or "brought to bed," but substituted "pregnant" and "accouchement," words which would spare tender sensibilities. By 1805 various expurgated classics were being put on the market, and the most famous of them appeared in 1818—Thomas Bowdler's *Family Shakespeare*, a version which excluded "whatever is unfit to be read by a gentleman in the presence of ladies." Although ladies' fashions continued to feature décolletage in upper-class circles, the romantic-bourgeois preference was for greater modesty; by 1798, in fact, a lady named Priscilla Wakefield, surveying the status of woman in a book, was all aflutter over the gross indelicacy of mortuary practice. "How shocking," she wrote, "is the idea of our persons being exposed, even after death, to the observation of a parcel of undertaker's men."

The typical romantic prided himself on the ability to fall tumultuously and passionately in love; at the same time, there runs throughout romanticism a persistent theme of sexual inhibition or limitation similar to Rousseau's, though seldom so severe. Goethe and Beethoven were both frequently very deeply in love, but succeeded in possessing few of the women they loved, and Keats, despite his sensuous poetry and his throbbing love letters, probably died a virgin. In 1798 it seemed perfectly reasonable to Reverend Thomas Malthus, fretting about the problem of overpopulation, to suggest that young people, though they fall in love, spend a number of years as abstinent lovers, marry late, and thus produce fewer children. Even to anti-Malthusians this seemed easy enough for women, for the emerging female ideal of the time was a sweet, tender, girl-mother (Madame de Warens again) in whom sexual desire seemed inappropriate, if not downright wicked. In a rape trial in 1804, Miss Rachael Lee, who had been abducted and ravished by two men, admitted that when resistance seemed pointless, she had flung away a magic charm supposed to preserve her chastity, and cried: "Now welcome, Pleasure!" In view of this shocking conduct, the judge dismissed the two alleged rapists forthwith, to loud huzzahs by the spectators.[2]

In place of sexuality, the romantics delighted in being demonstratively sentimental, melancholic, tempestuous, or tearful, according to the occasion. Tom Moore, the Irish poet, singing some pathetic ballads to an audience, so moved them that one by one they slipped off, reduced to helpless sobbing; Moore himself, equally moved by his own songs, at last bolted in a fit of tears. Brides were known to swoon at the altar, and ministers sometimes wept at the Table. Keats was moved by an urn and Shelley by the wind, but Coleridge was deeply stirred by a mere jackass and Wordsworth by things even more prosaic:

> To every natural form, rock, fruit, or flower,
> Even the loose stones that cover the highway,
> I gave a moral life: I saw them feel,
> Or linked them to some feeling.
> Prelude, III, 127–30

[2] M. J. Quinlan: *Victorian Prelude*, pp. 66–7, 154, 245–8; C. W. Cunnington: *Feminine Attitudes in the Nineteenth Century*, pp. 28–9.

When love was the cause, it produced cascades of rhetoric and frenzied actions. A young French medical student, distraught at not seeing the woman he loved for three weeks, wrote her as follows: "In the forest I shouted like a demon, rolled on the ground, crunched branches between my teeth. . . . In a rage I took my hand between my teeth and bit convulsively; blood spurted forth and I spat out at heaven a piece of living flesh. . . . I would have liked to spit out my heart at it." [3] It may be that emotional compensation is as simple as a law of physics: where the rationalists had repressed their emotions and acted out their sexuality, the romantics restrained their sexuality and poured forth their emotions.

One other compensatory device deserves mention—the development of the clinging-vine personality in women of the romantic period. Along with modesty, virtue, sweetness, and similar qualities, she was supposed to be weak, fearful, and anxious to lean on, and be dominated by, a strong kind man. Having no tradition of land inheritance, middle-class women had no marriage settlements and were wholly dependent on their husbands, any dowry being completely controlled by the husband, and divorce being all but impossible. Cleverness and education, never prized by the middle-class husband, went out of vogue, and "Bluestocking" became a term of reproach. Industrialism itself directly fostered the clinging-vine concept; the making of clothing, food, and medicine, and the teaching of children, were moving outside the home, depriving the middle-class wife of many of her functions, though leaving her cloistered—a situation paralleling that which we saw earlier with the women of Periclean Athens. An Edinburgh physician, Dr. John Gregory, advised his own daughters in 1774:

> The intention of your being taught needlework, knitting, and such like is not on account of the intrinsic value of all you can do with your hands, which is trifling, but . . . to enable you to fill up in a tolerably agreeable way some of the many solitary hours you must necessarily pass at home.

The reasonably well-off romantic did not need a woman-of-all-work as did his forefathers; he could therefore concentrate more on her value as a love ideal. Since, however, she was supposed to be uneducated, demure, frail, and modest, she was fading out as a person and becoming something of a wraith. The medieval troubadour

[3] G. M. Young: *Early Victorian England*, Vol. II, p. 424; L. Maigron: *Le Romantisme et les moeurs*, p. 153.

had met a similar situation by simply attributing the same divinity and perfection to any lady he loved. An analogous phenomenon took place in the romantic era: men sought an ideal woman rather than a real one, and pinned their ideal image on some girl of whom, because she had been so quiet and retiring, they knew very little.

William Hazlitt, the literary critic, is a case in point. In 1820, when he was forty-two and separated from his wife, he fell in love with his landlord's twenty-year-old daughter, a pretty, uncommunicative, uneducated girl. Each morning when she brought up his breakfast, Hazlitt would speak extravagantly and at length of his love for her, uttering innumerable statements like this: "Ah! enchanting little trembler! You are an angel, and I will spend my life, if you will let me, in paying you the homage that my heart feels towards you." He attributed to her every virtue, every beauty, every uplifting influence, and assured her that she could, if she would, remake his life for him. After each of his interminable speeches, the girl would reply in a monosyllable, or sometimes, extending herself, would make as long a statement as: "Indeed, you greatly overrate my power." Hazlitt supplied her with all the qualities he wanted her to have, and even was charmed by her lack of speech. "Her words are few and simple," he told a friend, "but you can have no idea of the exquisite, unstudied, irresistible graces with which she accompanies them, unless you can suppose a Greek statue to smile, move, and speak." His friends were not so ecstatic; Bryan Procter, a poet, met her through Hazlitt and saw her more plainly:

> Her face was round and small, and her eyes were motionless, glassy, and without any speculation (apparently) in them. Her movements in walking were very remarkable. . . . She went onwards in a sort of wavy, sinuous manner, like the movement of a snake. She was silent, or uttered monosyllables only, and was very demure.

Benjamin Haydon, another intimate of Hazlitt's, considered her nothing but a "lodging-house hussy" who would be the death of Hazlitt, and he wrote to a mutual friend: "He is really downright in love with an ideal perfection which has no existence but in his own head." [4]

[4] Hazlitt published the details of the affair anonymously under the title *Liber Amoris;* his statements quoted above appear on pp. 16 and 129; Procter's quote is from his *An Autobiographical Fragment,* pp. 181–2; Haydon's letter is quoted in P. P. Howe: *The Life of William Hazlitt,* p. 349.

For a year and a half Hazlitt loved her to distraction and believed her coolness to him was only the result of extreme maidenly modesty; he begged her to admit her feelings, but although she would sometimes sit on his lap and permit him a few chaste kisses, she would never admit anything and refused to promise to marry him. Nonetheless Hazlitt went to Scotland for half a year to obtain a divorce, but when he returned, he found her chillier and more disinterested in him than ever. He went berserk with rage and smashed things in his lodging-house room; then he went walking to calm down, saw her with another man, and discovered that she had had a lover all along. Suddenly she looked different to him; he saw her as a "lodging-house decoy" and a "callous jilt" who was small, indifferent-looking, and affected in manner. But disillusion did not mean the end of pain. For nearly two years he was despondent, disorganized, and almost unable to work properly. Mrs. Shelley, having run into him some time later, wrote to a friend: "I was never so shocked in my life; he has become so thin, his hair so scattered, his cheekbones projecting; but for his voice and smile I would not have known him." Hazlitt married a well-to-do widow shortly afterwards, but the marriage lasted only a short while; he lived the remaining five years without seeking or finding love again. Having judged so wrongly, he had had quite enough of it.[5]

As far as woman was concerned, her new role—that of the passive, quiescent, clinging vine—was a necessary adaptation to her changing problem of winning man. She was becoming less useful to him; it made sense, therefore, to attract him by flattering his ego through the claim of frailty and dependency. Hannah More, once a Bluestocking and a friend of Samuel Johnson, became later on a pious Evangelical and an exponent of the clinging-vine view. "To be unstable and capricious," she wrote to a friend in 1793, "I really think is but too characteristic of our sex; and there is no animal so

---

[5] The ability to imagine all the hoped-for perfections in a non-entity or someone relatively unknown was likewise the basis of the love-philosophy of Stendhal, who, incidentally, knew and admired Hazlitt. Stendhal called the process "crystallization"; just as a common twig (he said), if immersed for a time in salt water, becomes covered with glittering crystals, so does the ideal of a woman, residing in a man's mind, become the focus for a crystallizing of perfections and ideal attributes. Stendhal knew it to be a willful folly, but lived by it all the same. Being a Frenchman, he had more physical achievement in love than Hazlitt, but of the eleven women he adored in his life, the six with whom he had success all suffered from decrystallization after he won them; the perfect loves in his life were the ones who never yielded. See his De l'amour, pp. 6-7, 11, and 324f, and Howard Clewes: Stendhal, p. 32f.

much indebted to subordination for its good behavior as woman." Within a few years she was actively campaigning against all forms of female education that might give women interests outside the home. Even in America, where the frontier influence and the slower development of industrialization had retarded this view, the percentage of women who worked outside the home decreased markedly in the decades following the Revolution. In every country with a strong middle-class influence, men showed a new patriarchalism that went hand in hand with the feminine retreat. Napoleon stated flatly that "a husband ought to have an empire absolute over the actions of his wife," and saw to it that his Code embodied laws to that effect; Thomas Jefferson argued that the vote should never belong to women, since "the tender breasts of ladies were not formed for political convulsion"; and Keats, ecstatic about the new woman, burbled: "God! she is like a milk-white lamb that bleats/For man's protection."

The new-style patriarchs, unlike those of old, saw home life with their tender lambs as the be-all and end-all of existence. The footloose master, coming home when he wished and then only to attend to his own comforts, was an outmoded male ideal; the new one was that of a devoted stay-at-home husband. In 1829 William Cobbett, the newspaper publisher and parliamentary reformer, described the good marriage in terms that clearly anticipated, and even outdid, the much-touted "togetherness" of suburban home life in the late 1950's. In Cobbett's picture of nineteenth-century marriage (given in his book, *Advice to Young Men*), the wife stays at home to care for the house and tend the children; only the shameless woman trips around town paying idle visits and seeking diversion. The good wife's husband shares every available hour with her; he spends no time away from home except on business, always comes home punctually, plays with his children, helps his wife with the chores, and tells her of the affairs of his day. But there is no togetherness in the making of decisions; though the menu, furniture, and servants are her affair, he alone decides on their home location, their scale of living, their politics, the children's education, and other major questions. Still, his absorption in her and hers in him is complete and exclusive; Cobbett even disapproved of the custom of separating wives from their own husbands at dinner parties, and for that matter saw little point in dinner parties altogether or in entertaining in general. "What company," he asked, "can a young man and woman want more than their two selves, and their children, if they have any? If here be not company enough, it is but a sad affair."

It all begins to sound familiar. It is still romantic love, in a tradition eight centuries old—but newly domesticated, puritanized, and tailored to the measure of middle-class Anglo-Saxon culture; romantic love chastened, tamed, and grown cautious in its manners. In a word, it is nascent Victorianism.

4

Household Romanticism

The crown was set upon Victoria's head in 1837, but many of the attributes of Victorianism were already evident in England and elsewhere. In retrospect the nineteenth-century bourgeoisie look insufferably smug, complacent, and secure, but this is partly the effect of distance and nostalgia. The newly arrived middle class was, in fact, quite insecure in many ways. Its own industrialism was spawning a self-aware proletariat, and already agitators were loudly touting socialist ideas; farmers were counterattacking the growing power of the cities via uprisings and new political movements; and the rapid advance of the sciences was posing myriad questions that established religion could not answer. Most important of all, the free-for-all of economic liberalism was greatly accelerating that dissolution of ancient social ties, loyalties, and customs that had been going on ever since the Renaissance. "The Old has passed away," Carlyle wrote in 1831, "but, alas, the New appears not in its stead; the Time is still in pangs of travail with the New." And the travail only grew more intense. By the 1870's Matthew Arnold was lamenting the "break-up of traditional and conventional notions respecting our life, its conduct, and its sanctions, which is undeniably befalling our age." The era was far from being that fairyland of certainty and security we often imagine it to have been.[6]

The desire to find or achieve stability in a rapidly changing world led the Victorians to take many social actions of a constructive nature—political reforms, Sunday schools, hospitals, religious revivals, poor relief, and the like—but in private life it found its chief expression in the exaggerated worship of home life and in the domestication of romantic love. "This is the true nature of home," said John Ruskin, "—it is the place of Peace; the shelter, not only from all injury, but from all terror, doubt, and division." But home was more than shelter; in a commercial world where ancient loyalties and affections had dissolved, it was the only place where a man could prove to himself that he still possessed warm emotions and decent human feelings. As James Froude, a Victorian historian, wrote:

> When we come home, we lay aside our mask and drop our tools, and are no longer lawyers, sailors, soldiers, statesmen, clergymen, but only men. We fall again into our most human relations. . . . We cease the struggle in the race of the world, and give our hearts leave and leisure to love.

Anything threatening that shelter and refuge of warm emotion met violent hostility, be it talk of female suffrage, agitation for divorce reforms, free love experiments, or bloomers. And in May 1842, when the Commission on Child Labor prepared a report to Parliament on the terrible working conditions in the coal mines, Lord Londonderry was outraged because copies of the *Report*, containing what he called "disgusting pictorial woodcuts" of women and children hauling carts in the shafts, had reached the boudoirs of decent ladies and disturbed their domestic tranquility. It might also be added that Lord Londonderry himself owned a number of mines.

With the home being the only locus of emotional behavior and human kindness, woman's love was once again thought to be the source of ethical value. Typically, a popular manual for wives written by Mrs. Sara Ellis in 1843 stated that it was a wife's func-

[6] This is definitively documented by Walter Houghton in his recent study, *The Victorian Frame of Mind.* See especially chapters one, two, and three.

tion to "raise the tone" of her husband's mind and lead his thoughts to dwell on a "higher state of existence" than his daily concerns. Not for centuries had there been so general a belief that woman's love uplifted and spiritualized man. Unlike the medieval troubadours and the Renaissance Neoplatonists, Victorian men thought this improvement through love was exclusively a product of wedded domesticity, yet other than that their words sounded like conscious echoes of the past. Robert Browning's plea to Elizabeth Barrett—"Give me your counsel at all times, beloved: I am wholly open to your desires, and teaching, and direction. Try what you can make of me."—might almost have come straight from Andreas Capellanus.

The same belief, in slightly different form, could even sometimes appear on the American frontier, where ordinarily one would expect the valuation of woman to be more candidly procreative and economic. In 1864 and 1866, for instance, Asa Mercer, a young college graduate who had moved out to the Oregon Territory, went back East and arranged for the transport of several dozen unmarried females to the Puget Sound area, a project which later won him election to the Oregon legislative assembly. His motives, however, had not been political, but thoroughly romantic: "I had been taught to believe, and did believe," he later explained, "that practically all the goodness in the world came from the influence of pure-minded women. At that time there was not a single woman of marriageable age on Puget Sound . . . [and] the bachelor element was almost wholly beyond the reach of female influence and its wholesome results."

The female, in such a view, had to be spotless and unimpeachable, and every word or action that might conceivably have an immodest implication was therefore transmuted into a "respectable" form. Even the word "pregnant" was now too blunt, and instead ladies were said to be "in an interesting condition" or "visiting in the country." Grown women would mincingly say of a newborn baby that he "had been discovered under the gooseberry bush." The anxieties of the ambitious middle class about its own social status and respectability led to the invention of numerous new taboos. A gentleman could no longer offer a lady the leg of a chicken, but only its breast—and he called even that the "bosom"; the books of male and female authors were separately shelved in some Victorian libraries; advertisements of ladies' underclothing always showed them folded so one would be unaware of the crotch; and some women, when describing a pain to the doctor, would point out on a doll where the hurt was so as to be at one remove from making an indelicate gesture. The fictional Mrs. Grundy, a figure of satire in a play of 1798, had become the uncrowned ruler of English social mores half a century later, but Grundyism was by no means limited to England; there was a similar prudishness in France—a thing hard for the Anglo-Saxon to believe—and likewise in the United States. From the latter, in fact, comes the most delightful (though apocryphal) of all examples of prudery: according to Captain Frederick Marryat, a visiting Englishman, certain American ladies in an excess of modesty fitted up the legs of their pianos with crinoline pantalettes.

Ladies had been celebrated for purity before, but the extremes of the Victorian taboos were something new. So, too, was a notable new extension of modesty to bathroom functions, which had formerly been treated frankly; the result was that since modesty covered both excretion and sexuality, the two were more or less confused and identified with each other. Fear of nudity, of dirt, and of sexuality were all mingled in the minds of those who sought to be acceptable and respectable. They laid great stress on personal cleanliness, strenuously forced primitives and natives of tropical lands to put on English-style clothing, and generally felt that the sex act in marriage, though certainly not sinful, was an animal activity stemming from man's "lower nature," and was therefore "disgusting" or "indecent." A typical late Victorian, privately telling a doctor about his married sex life, candidly stated that he considered coitus with his wife a form of evacuation.

The emotional power behind prudery came from the romantic identification of the female with the pure mother ideal, and from the resulting inhibition of sexual desire. Conversely, the girl of the time, being a pure mother ideal, was forbidden to be sexually seductive in any way; she dared not even show any mild flirtatious interest in a man. "It is the privilege of the male, as superior and protector, to make a choice," the *Encyclopaedia Britannica* authoritatively stated in 1842. "The female preferred has no privilege but barely to consent or refuse." The young woman's permissible methods of attracting interest, or indicating her own interest, had shrunk almost to nothing. She might shriek delicately at the sight of a grasshopper, weep discreetly at a play or concert, or even, if the occasion merited it, faint (some manuals of deportment even taught the proper ways of fainting). But for the most part, her only way of showing any response to a young man's interested appraisal was, according to an etiquette book of the period, to summon up a "timid blush" or "the faintest of smiles lurking within the half-dropped eye."

Assuming that these feeble signals got across, and that the young man then obtained her father's permission to call on her, she might spend some time with him, talking, playing the piano, singing, or, on rare occasions, dancing—but always with a chaperone present; and even under these inhibiting conditions, his visits were limited in frequency, since they might otherwise produce "that undesirable familiarity which oftener lessens than increases esteem."

Somehow, despite these impediments, Victorian lovers eventually managed to convey to each other the knowledge that love existed in their hearts. The actual proposal might be made in writing to the father, but sometimes circumstances and a co-operative chaperone made a direct proposal possible. What such a proposal sounded like, or at least was supposed to sound like, may be judged from this sample declaration offered in an English manual of practical advice:

> If I can merit you by a love so chaste and illimitable as ever made the breast of man its tenement, you are mine already, my dear Miss Somersdown. . . . Heaven knows the purity of my intent and the affection which dictates it. . . . Your life of love with me shall be as near an approach to the utmost height of enjoyment as my pecuniary competence, my untiring zeal and infinite affection can make it. . . .[7]

What became of these purified and chaste sentiments on the bridal night and thereafter is not easy to discover; we are forced to imagine the quality of Victorian conjugal love on the basis of tangential hints. One woman, for example, who was married in the middle of the Victorian era and had borne several children, told Havelock Ellis when she was seventy that she had never seen a naked man in her life, and even those superlative lovers, the Brownings, are said never to have seen each other entirely nude. The typical attitude toward sensuous physical love can be inferred from the words of Tennyson's King Arthur (who hardly speaks in the

[7] *Courtship As It Is and As It Ought   History of Courting*, pp. 158–9.
To Be (1877), quoted in E. S. Turner:

tones of a fifth-century warrior): he knew of no greater power "to keep down the base in man" than "the maiden passion for a maid."

But if the base in man needed to be kept down by purifying love, woman supposedly had no such problem, for only prostitutes felt sexual desire or enjoyed sexual intercourse. This extraordinary idea was believed not only by poets, idealists, and prudes, but by a large number of physicians in various countries. Dr. William Acton, in a standard text on the reproductive system, said that the belief that woman had a sexual appetite was "a vile aspersion"; William Hammond, a surgeon-general of the United States, wrote that nine tenths of the time decent women felt not the slightest pleasure in intercourse; and at the University of Basel an eminent gynecologist named Fehling labeled sexual desire in young women "pathological." Even if a Victorian woman did feel those vile stirrings, she could only consider it shameful and degrading to yield to them; they were contrary to her nature. It was her business to lie still and be calm about the whole thing; in fact, in 1839 a highly successful English marriage manual written by a physician named Michael Ryan warned that female sterility was due, among other causes to "an excessive ardor of desire" or "passion strongly excited. . . . It is well known that complaisance, tranquility, silence, and secrecy are necessary for a prolific coition." [8]

From such scattered materials one can more or less visualize the Victorian act of love-making—hasty, ashamed, and uncommunicative, the husband "taking his pleasure" while the wife either was, or tried to seem, inert and passive. It is only natural that the Victorian bedroom was so heavily muffled, shrouded, and dark, for such surroundings must have somewhat reduced the embarrassment of performing so gross a function. This is not to say that Victorian marriages were loveless or unhappy, but that the quality of the love in them was partly, and in a special way, desexualized. The Victorians bred large families not because they were libidinous, but because of decreasing childhood mortality. Libido could not flourish where the woman's role was either that of a timid, virginal maiden or a sweet, pure mother, but never a sexual lover. Behind the sentiment that would later be expressed in the song, "I Want a Girl Just

---

[8] Acton, Hammond, and Fehling quoted in Havelock Ellis: *The Sexual Impulse in Women* (Studies, Vol. III), pp. 193–5; Michael Ryan: *The Philosophy of Marriage*, p. 260.

Like the Girl That Married Dear Old Dad," there operated both
an incest wish and an incest fear different in their trappings from
those which had affected the knight and the Renaissance courtier,
but comparable to them in power. Adolescent boys were endlessly
told to regard all women as mothers or sisters, more divine than
human; long engagements became ever more popular, possibly because a man who could worship a mother-sister divinity grew
shaky at the thought of copulating with her. In his mature years,
the Reverend Frederick Robertson recalled that, as a boy, when it
one day occurred to him that a pure young girl would someday
become his wife, he felt not rapture but pain at the thought of her
degradation.

But glorified and idealized as her role might seem, it was only a
new pretext for continued subjugation. And a new pretext was
needed. Formerly, one of the potent reasons for keeping woman
subordinate was that she had considerable productive importance
in the home. Industrialism robbed her of much of that, and to take
its place, there arose the fiction of female helplessness.[9] It was a
face-saving and ego-protecting device for woman; for man it was
the means by which he tried to make continued sense out of marriage in an era when its values were changing and its forms coming under attack.

Women carried out the scheme by making themselves literally
helpless through fashion. By the 1820's, Englishwomen had begun
to imprison themselves in laces, stays, and huge buckram-lined
sleeves. In the 1830's the English actress, Fanny Kemble, wrote
from Pennsylvania that American women too were lacing and pad-
ding themselves into virtual immobility. From the 1840's to the
1860's the crinoline and the huge skirt made nineteenth-century
woman not a two-legged human being but a seraphic image that
glided gingerly along to the sound of gentle rustling. So encum-
bered, she passed her time in the only pursuits convenient to this
condition. She gave the servants orders and instructed the children;
then she played the piano, read interminable novels, made anti-
macassars, painted on velvet, and shaped wax flowers. And then,
with time still heavy on her hands, she did things one finds hard to
believe: *Godey's Lady's Book and Magazine* for February 1864, for

[9] The loss of her productive importance was hardly true among the poor
or the frontier people in the United
States, but the helplessness of the female
was a social ideal, and even women of
the poorer or lower-middle classes
made a pretense of it whenever they
could.

instance, contains detailed instructions for making a netted ear-cover for a horse, decorated with eight charming tassels.

The role in which Victorian man had cast woman had its inevitable effect on man himself. Patriarchal he might be, stern to his children, frock-coated, mightily bewhiskered and not to be trifled with, but he played this part at the expense of his own sexual expressiveness and his own peace of mind. If he were a libidinous man, he was driven to resort secretly to brothels. If he were weakly sexed, the emphasis on the purity of woman might actually unman him. If he were an average man with an average drive, he might live his entire sexual life galled by the need for self-denial and self-restraint.

Doctors warned him against too early or too intense an enjoyment of his powers; intellectuals like Ruskin told him to conquer his lust through love; and even evolutionists found grounds to urge self-restraint, Tennyson telling him to

> *Arise and fly*
> *The reeling Faun, the sensual feast;*
> *Move upward, working out the beast,*
> *And let the ape and tiger die.*
> In Memoriam, cxviii

One of the wise men of the age—W. E. H. Lecky, the historian of moral development—said what must have been the regretful conclusion of many a thoughtful Victorian male:

> It must be owned that the progress of knowledge, which is usually extremely opposed to the ascetic theory of life, concurs with the theological view, in showing the natural force of this appetite to be far greater than the well-being of man requires.

Private Lives of Some Victorians

❀   ❀

❀

D espite all that we have seen, the private lives of the Victorians
remain elusive and obscure, for we hardly ever learn how
they actually behaved or felt behind closed doors. Novels of the
period dealt with the love life of the Victorians, but only in a purified or sentimentalized fashion; biographies, on the other hand,
either blandly pretended that there was no love life to record, or
stated flatly that it was nobody's business. The novelist Anthony
Trollope wrote an autobiography that filled two volumes, but on
the subject of love he had only this to say: "If the rustle of a
woman's petticoat has ever stirred my blood, of what matter is
that to any reader?"

In the heat of emotion, the Victorians occasionally forgot to be
so circumspect, and put their thoughts on paper, but almost invari-
ably they or their families later expunged these revelations; only
faint tantalizing traces remain, such as a note in Hallam Tennyson's
biography of his father: "These extracts [on Tennyson's courtship]
. . . are made from a series of letters from my father to my
mother extending over three years. I have not felt able to include
the many passages which would show the intensity of feeling expressed in these letters, but have burnt the correspondence according to my father's directions."

Yet in spite of the censor's fire, not all is hidden; there sometimes
remain ashes or a scrap of bone from which one can sketchily re-
create something. Hallam Tennyson does provide one or two clues
by which we can estimate that "intensity of feeling" he speaks of.
One evening in 1850, when Alfred Tennyson and his new bride

were honeymooning in the Lake Country, Mrs. Tennyson went to bed early while the poet stayed up with two friends who had come to visit. The conversation came around to love, women, and Tennyson's bride in particular. The poet puffed his pipe thoughtfully, then slowly removed it and in his deep rich voice uttered a statement no bridegroom but an ultra-Victorian one could possibly have made: "I have known many women," quoth he, "who were excellent, one in one way, another in another way, but this woman is the noblest woman I have ever known."

Sometimes, too, the diligent scholar can, by heroic and patient reconstruction, recover evidence the Victorians thought they destroyed—only to be astonished at what they thought it necessary to conceal. Nathaniel Hawthorne wrote 164 letters to Sophia Peabody before and during their marriage; she preserved them for posterity, but spent a great deal of time carefully inking out a number of phrases and sentences, even making false blots above and below the line to mislead any prying scholar. Scholars pry all the same; a couple of decades ago several of them used a microscope, filtered light, and infinite patience, and after several years of recovering one character at a time, were able to read almost all of what gentle, maidenly, intellectual Sophia deleted.[1] And what was it like? Here is a typical deletion: "Shall there be no holy kisses in the sky? Shall I not still hold you in my arms, when we are angels together?" Why did she blot it? Apparently because she and Hawthorne were unmarried at a time when he indicated he had held her in his arms.

Later, but still before their marriage, he wrote to her from the Transcendentalists's co-operative at Brook Farm, saying: "There is a brook, so near the house that we shall be able to hear its ripple, in the summer evenings." This she allowed to stand, but canceled the rest of the sentence: "—and whenever we lie awake in the summer nights." She was equally cautious with letters written long after their marriage. "There is no thinking how much I love and desire thee," wrote Hawthorne while away on a trip; she struck out "and desire." There is perhaps only one truly surprising statement she canceled; as retrieved by the scholars, it shows Hawthorne writing from New York and saying, because he did not have the cash: "Thou shouldst not ask me to come to Boston for the purpose of sleeping a night in thy dearest arms." Sophia, of course, deleted the

[1] Randall Stewart: "Letters to Sophia," *Huntington Library Quarterly*, Aug. 1944.

words following "Boston" and purified herself, but the scholars with their microscope found her out; she was a woman, after all.

From such bits and scraps we gain an occasional flash of insight into Victorian love. One man, however, gives us much more than a flash: he not only experienced an ideal Victorian marriage, but made it his goal in life to write the definitive portrait of such a relationship. Coventry Patmore was his name; he is all but forgotten today although the Victorians liked his portrait of love and marriage well enough to buy a quarter of a million copies of it in his own lifetime.

Patmore, the son of a writer, was born in 1823 and early decided on a career in poetry. He took a position as an assistant librarian in the British Museum, and began diligently writing poetry in his spare time, but he had little success until after meeting and marrying Emily Andrews, for domestic love was to be his forte and his grand theme. Patmore, when he married her in 1847, was a tall, shy, somewhat stern young man of twenty-four with a sensuous mouth, powerful nose, long waving hair, and (when he thought about it) a Byronic expression. Emily was pretty, but her elongated face was always carefully composed into a grave, madonnalike expression, accentuated by hair which was parted in the middle and drawn down tightly on either side; Mrs. Carlyle, in some irritation, once grumbled that Emily Patmore tried to look like a medallion. Obviously they were typecast as the ideal Victorian couple.

Emily played to perfection the unassuming but omnipresent role of Victorian wife; when Patmore's friends—who included Tennyson, Ruskin, Carlyle, and Browning—came to call, she was always the hospitable charming housewife, listening appreciatively to male talk but unassumingly doing a bit of needlework the while. She herself had an urge to write, but appropriately produced only a book of child's verse, which she entitled *Nursery Rhymes by Mrs. Motherly*. She reared her own children with skill and care, lavished admiration upon her creative husband, accepted without complaint his varied moods of brusqueness, imperiousness, sensitivity, and dejection, and was his principal inspiration in life. It is therefore intriguing to see his personal estimate of her. In a private diary, he jotted down that she was unshakably mild, that she had a "milkmaid-like absence of pretensions" but a certain degree of "severity of feature," that her heart saw the right moral answer to every question, and that she could keep a house in a state of "gem-like neatness." His life with her, he wrote, was ideal and flawless; but with great honesty he confessed that it was easily forgettable, for after her death in 1862 he wrote himself the following note of reminder:

> Remember, above all, the 5,410 days she was my wife, and on each one of which, though nothing happened to be remembered, she did her duty to me, her children, her neighbors, and to God, with a lovely, unnoticeable evenness and completeness.[2]

This "unnoticeable evenness" was not the result of love alone, but of a complete and unquestioning acceptance on Emily's part of the role of the obedient woman; she once even wrote to Patmore in some amusement that a visitor, seeing "my appearance of instant submission to your slightest wish," had supposed it came from fear. It did not; Emily accepted his right to rule, and thus had no reason to fear him.

Early during this marriage, while recuperating from an illness, Patmore was struck by an idea he felt to be of major importance. In a state of great excitement, he told his friend and fellow poet Aubrey de Vere what he had suddenly realized—that poets through the ages, however much they had written of love, had overlooked or slighted the greatest theme of all—married love. He was dumbfounded to realize how universally they had failed to see this, and proposed to make good the lack himself; as he later put it:

> *The richest realm of all the earth*
> *Is counted still a heathen land:*
> *Lo, I, like Joshua, now go forth*
> *To give it into Israel's hand.*

The first product of this revelation was a long poem he wrote at blinding speed in a mere six weeks, and which was published as a separate book in 1854 entitled *The Betrothal*; it told of the conversations, moods, and ordinary incidents in the routine courting of a dean's daughter, first by one suitor and then by another. Two years later there appeared a second installment carrying the girl, Honoria, into marriage with her suitor, Felix; two more installments appeared in the next six years, painting in detail the unruffled tenor of marriage, the tragedy of her death, and the survival of love in the faithful husband. Patmore gave the over-all epic a brilliant title

---

[2] These private documents are quoted in Basil Champneys: *Memoirs and Correspondence of Coventry Patmore,* Vol. I, pp. 142–6.

—*The Angel in the House*—thus epitomizing in five words the
Victorian conception of woman and marriage. For the rest, the
monumental poem is anything but brilliant. Here and there occur
lyrics of reasonable merit, but for the most part Patmore had undertaken to celebrate in banal verse the minutiae of daily life, under
the impression that these were the essence of love. When the young
hero of the story writes to Honoria, for instance, his letter, suitably
rhymed, begins like this:

> *Dear Saint, I'm still at High-Hurst Park.*
> *The house is filled with folks of mark.*

Later one finds versified by the yard such material as a homely
wedding sermon, the honeymoon travel arrangements, and the
purchase of a pair of new shoes; lines such as these—

> *Our witnesses the cook and groom,*
> *We signed the lease for seven years more,*

—are all too frequent. Constructed of such realistic materials, the
sprawling work undertook to exemplify the familiar Victorian beliefs that love arises immediately when a man and maiden, pre-
destined for each other, finally meet; that love, whether successful
or not, "leaves the heart more generous, dignified and pure"; that
the supreme function of woman is to reign as the angel of the household, though despite her divinity she meekly and sweetly acquiesces
to her husband's wishes—and thus rules him by her very weakness;
and that conjugal sex relations are better than any others because
"life is sweetest when it's clean."

The *Angel in the House* became the most popular poem of the
era and a kind of national epithalamium. But after 1860 the Victorian frame of mind began to crack and disintegrate, and, before
he died, Patmore heard critics referring to him as a "laureate of the
tea-table" who wrote "humdrum stories," and even "goody-goody
dribble." The purely literary merit of his work to one side, though,
Patmore did succeed in portraying a typical Victorian marriage,
and although he denied that the Honoria of the poem was identical
with his own Emily, any comparison of the two makes it clear that
except for superficial characteristics they are the same and that
Patmore's own married life was the inspiration and source of material for the poem.

That being the case, the most interesting thing about Patmore is
the direction his life took after the completion of *The Angel in the*

House. It was finished in 1862, the same year Emily died; Patmore never again wrote in the same vein or style. Although he had portrayed Felix as being faithful to his love for his wife after her death, Patmore himself two years later, at the age of forty-three, married Marianne Byles, a forty-four-year-old spinster, serious, pious, and unbending, but wealthy enough to enable him to retire and give himself over to poetry. Although he rapidly managed to see in her all the same virtues he had seen in Emily, something in him was groping for a different solution to life; he became a Catholic like his wife, but simultaneously abandoned tea-table stories for poems dealing with the theme of sensual love versus spiritual love, and using irregular, free-moving verse forms. The result, published in 1877, was *The Unknown Eros,* a long work which came to Catholic conclusions only after extended passages of sensuous description. In his mid-fifties, this psalmist of placid marriage, this acolyte before the icon of the angelic wife, was consulting erotic reference books and producing lines such as these in which Psyche addresses her lover, Eros:

> *Kiss, tread me under foot, cherish or beat,*
> *Sheathe in my heart sharp pain up to the hilt,*
> *Invent what else were most perversely sweet;*
> *Nay, let the Fiend drag me through dens of guilt;*
> *Let Earth, Heav'n, Hell*
> *'Gainst my content combine;*
> *What could make nought the touch that made thee mine!*
> Bk. II, No. 12

Patmore's second wife died in 1880 after fifteen years of marriage; a year later, at fifty-eight, the tall, somber, greatly mustached poet fell in love and married once more. This time his wife was Harriet Robson, a woman a generation younger than he and a former schoolmate of one of his daughters. In this marriage, too, he seems to have been deeply affectionate and worshipful, but after some years he began to manifest a new and more significant symptom of unrest: without wishing to leave his wife, he conceived a grand passion for a married woman—Alice Meynell, the poet—and tried to win her. After all his thinking and pontificating about love, the seventy-year-old Patmore seemed to feel he had missed something all along. What he thought it was is not quite clear, but it must not have been pure Neoplatonic affection, for he made unsuccessful overtures to Mrs. Meynell and confessed to a friend that his feelings for her were "too much for the balance, peace, and purity of my religion." After she gently refused him, the aging Patmore, who should have been uplifted and enriched by his love (according to his own earlier doctrines), was instead desolate and wretched. Bundled in warm clothing on a sweltering July night, he complained to his son, Francis, that he was cold. His son said that that was impossible on so hot a night, but Patmore replied in the best romantic tradition: "Ah, it is a spiritual cold I feel." Love had been a pillar of fire, leading him a long way from *The Angel in the House,* but the Promised Land had never materialized. Now it was too late and he was lost, and would never know where he had been trying to go.

6

Emancipation and Confusion

"hastity," said a wealthy English textile-manufacturer, "is sexual intercourse with affection." "I doubt not," wrote a French novelist, "that [marriage] will be abolished if the human race makes any progress towards justice and reason." "Yes, I am a free lover!" shouted an American lady lecturer to a heckler in the audience at Steinway Hall. "I have an inalienable, constitutional, and natural right to love whom I may, to love as long or as short a period as I can, to change that love every day if I please!" [3]

Paradox of paradoxes, only in the era of bourgeois dominion,

[3] The manufacturer, the novelist, and the lecturer were, respectively, Robert Owen, George Sand, and Victoria Claflin Woodhull.

when the wife was worshipped as the angel in the house, did free love become both a doctrine and an organized form of social protest. Nor was it a rare or isolated phenomenon, but part of a broad fight for greater rights for women and for emancipation from the purdah-like seclusion of the Victorian home. Throughout the century, an evergrowing army of people, including liberals, radicals, and some crackpots, fought for women's rights of one sort of another, and though most of the women of the period complaisantly accepted the role Victorian society assigned to them, many of them secretly hankered for some of the demanded freedoms and gladly accepted them when they were won. If helplessness was one female adaptation to a shrinking utility, militancy was the other alternative; woman could either barricade herself in the home with the myth of frailty, or struggle to get outside it and find some new definition of femininity.

Many a woman tried a little of each, but from the very first the aims of even the moderate feminists were confused and entangled with radical and seemingly dangerous notions. In 1792, Mary Wollstonecraft made the first comprehensive attack on bourgeois marriage and the subjugation of women in the form of a widely discussed book, *A Vindication of the Rights of Woman*. She was not against marriage as such, but against its existing inequities; she argued for increased social and economic rights and education so that in marriage women would be not submissive, pleasing housewives, but equals, capable of friendship with their husbands—a type of relationship she felt was surer and sounder than romantic adoration-and-domination of the female. These ideas might in themselves have seemed merely objectionable to the middle class, but coming from Mary Wollstonecraft they acquired the coloring of dangerous radicalism, for all the literate world knew that she had lived in Paris during the early years of the French Revolution, and been the unmarried wife of Gilbert Imlay, an American businessman, to whom she bore a child. Seemingly pleased with this arrangement, she had even written the daring statement: "I am acquiring the matrimonial phraseology without having clogged my soul by promising obedience." Worse yet, she had thrown herself off a bridge in England when she learned that Imlay was unfaithful; still worse, after being saved by a boat and recovering, she next fell in love with the anarchist writer William Godwin. With him she again lived in unwedded bliss until Godwin, in an uncharacteristic fit of conformity, married her during her pregnancy.

From this point on, the woman's rights movement continued to incorporate radical elements. Shelley absorbed extremist political and social ideas from Godwin, wrote revolutionary pamphlets (some of which he sent to sea in bottles) and included in his *Queen Mab* a passionate defense of free love. Robert Owen, having practiced benevolent capitalism in his textile mill at New Lanark, became Utopian in his thinking and, beginning in 1825, poured most of his fortune into a short-lived social experiment at New Harmony, Indiana, where he tried to mingle communism, religious free thought, and equalitarian marriage. New Harmony failed, but from the 1820's to the 1840's there were, in the eastern United States, nine other Owenite and several dozen Fourierist communities, all of which mingled economic radicalism with experiments in modified love and marital relationships.

Although the woman's rights movement had been spawned by the industrial revolution, it was from the beginning allied with forces the bourgeois class could only fear and fight. The middle class had been all for increasing freedom while it had few rights of its own, but was ready to call a halt when the vote and the distribution of rights threatened to spread to the unpropertied class and to women. It was thus inevitable that these two dispossessed groups should either ally themselves, or seem allied in the minds of the rulers of society, who had all the proof they needed when Fourierists spoke of replacing marriage by some "new system of license" and Saint-Simonians justified the practice of "men and women giving themselves to several without ceasing to be united as a couple." [4]

The most alarming radicals, however, may have been those who offered their ideas in a mild, palatable form. Owen's son, Robert Dale Owen, leaving free love to one side, got himself married properly, but challenged the nineteenth-century marriage laws by making a written agreement with his wife and publishing it for all the world to see. In part, it read:

New York, Tuesday, April 12, 1832
This afternoon I enter into a matrimonial engagement with Mary Jane Robinson, a young person whose opinions on all important subjects, whose mode of thinking and feeling, coincide

---

[4] Later, the Marxists spoke of liberating both workers and women at the same time, but the tie-up of the two radicalisms was not their invention.

more intimately with my own than do those of any other individual with whom I am acquainted. . . . This ceremony involves
not the necessity . . . of repeating forms which we deem offensive, insomuch as they outrage the principles of human liberty and
equality. . . . Of the unjust rights which in virtue of this ceremony an iniquitous law tacitly gives me over the person and property of another, I can not legally, but I can morally divest myself.

Robert Dale Owen

Other parts of his statement repudiated a number of romantic
concepts—the permanence of love, the clinging-vine nature of
woman, and so on—but it was the challenge to man's rights over
woman's own property and her body that was most fundamental
and most dangerous. As late as the eighteenth century, women were
actually not far advanced toward freedom from the female serfdom
introduced a millennium and a half earlier by Teutonic tribesmen,
compounded with Christianity, and later codified by feudalism.
They still had few property rights or legal rights, no political
rights, and very little status in intellectual, artistic, or business life.
The Victorian male had no desire to change this situation, but
only to intensify it. On economic grounds, too, he found it ideal;
a subjugated wife, even if cranky, was simpler and cheaper to deal
with than an equal at law who could decamp with her own property if displeased, or could sue for redress if mistreated.

Moreover, from the business viewpoint it made good sense: during much of the nineteenth century, subjugated womankind in
English, French, and American industry were paid only one quarter
to one half as much as male workers. It was only natural that any
plea for female education or reform of marriage should seem to be
linked with atheism, socialism, abolition, teetotaling, sexual immorality, and other despicable forces. But the counterattacks, even
when couched in terms of ultra-romantic woman worship, began
to sound ever more clearly like the slave-owner's paternalism; in
fact, one of the typical condemnations of the woman's rights movement came from a Southerner, and was transparently analogous to
the apology for slavery:

> So long as she is nervous, fickle, capricious, delicate, diffident
> and dependent, man will worship and adore her. Her weakness is
> her strength, and her true art is to cultivate and improve that
> weakness. . . . In truth, a woman has but one right, and that is
> the right to protection. The right to protection involves the obli-
> gation to obey. . . . If she be obedient, she is in little danger of

maltreatment: if she stands upon her rights, is coarse and masculine, man loathes and despises her, and ends by abusing her.[5]

Despite all resistance to it, the woman's rights movement inexorably gained ground all through the century; the very industrialization that had robbed woman of many of her essential functions left
her time to yearn and fight for others. In 1833 Oberlin was the
first man's college in the United States to admit women, and four
years later Mount Holyoke, the first woman's college, was opened;
in England the same process began in 1849 when Bedford College
was established. In America the first Woman's Rights Convention
met in Seneca Falls, New York, in 1848, and by the 1850's such
respected intellectuals as the New England Transcendentalists were
allying themselves to the movement; in England the Unitarians and
other liberal elements were doing so likewise, and in 1869 John
Stuart Mill's thoughtful work *The Subjection of Women* gave the
stamp of absolute respectability to English feminism.

Meanwhile, women who had nothing to do with feminism and
never dreamed of attending conventions or marching in protest
parades were eagerly accepting by-products of the woman's rights
movement. By the 1860's they began to discard their crinolines and
gradually slimmed down their skirts until only the bustle was left.
Once again they could and did begin to take exercise and play simple games of sport such as croquet and lawn tennis; and unchaperoned they could once again walk arm in arm with men, a thing
impossible all during the crinoline period. A new "fast" girl, de-
plored by conservatives, appeared on the scene; she was flippant,
gay, unsentimental, and even used such shocking words as "jolly."

All during the second half of the century, furthermore, a series
of legal reforms were giving the lie to the myth of the angel's
happiness in her house. In England, for instance, where divorce law
had been so conservative and the procedure so expensive that only
184 divorces were granted between 1715 and 1852, a great divorce
debate raged in mid-century and a new divorce law was enacted
over violent opposition in 1857. It took the business of granting
divorces out of the public hands of Parliament, gave it to a relatively private civil court, and eliminated the need for a preliminary
ecclesiastical separation. The grounds remained few, but the right
to obtain a divorce on those grounds was made unquestionable and
the cost of doing so was greatly decreased. In the United States,

[5] George Fitzhugh: *Sociology for the South* (1854), pp. 213–20.

similarly, the general trend during the nineteenth century was to remove divorce suits from the legislatures, where it was awkward, expensive, and subject to political motivations, and put it in the hands of special courts; in addition, there was a general increase and broadening of the grounds for which it might be granted. Even in Catholic France, where divorce had been eliminated by the Napoleonic Code, it was restored in conservative form in 1884.

Victorian society furthermore found itself, willy-nilly, granting to woman economic privileges such as she had not had since the time of the Roman Empire. An act of 1857 granted a deserted wife the right to own any property she acquired after being deserted; prior to that, unthinkable as it may seem, a deserter could reappear and calmly seize whatever his wife had earned or been given in his absence. In 1870 and 1882 Parliament carried this further, granting all wives, deserted or not, ownership of whatever they earned after marriage or had owned before it; more than that, they won the right to make contracts, bring suit, and generally act as "persons" at law. In the United States, most jurisdictions had taken similar actions by 1900, and the same trend was visible in various European countries.

Even more valuable and influential were the rights, granted to woman by changing custom rather than by law, to support herself by her work without loss of self-respect or face, and to begin forcing her way not only into business but the various professions. Toward the end of the century one finds, for the first time, tracts and essays which argue that to remain single and to support one's self is better than to become the wife of a dissipated man. The right of lowly and of genteel women alike to work provided the means of escape from unhappy or loveless marriage, and the new divorce laws were used by ever-increasing numbers of women. In the United States, where the woman's rights movement was especially well advanced, the divorce rate showed an astonishing increase: between 1870 and 1905, while the population of the United States slightly more than doubled in size, the annual divorce total multiplied six-fold. The greatest rate of growth, almost predictably, was in the South, where the Civil War had broken up the feudal-romantic pattern of life and permitted the entry of industrialism with all its concomitant effects. Life with father, at the turn of the century, was not really life in a rigid patriarchy; by then, that was already only a nostalgic memory of earlier days.

In view of all these changes taking place at the very height of
Victorianism, the entire philosophy and practice of Victorian love
seem curiously unreal. Victorian love was at best a desperate rear-
guard defense against the inevitable changes made by industrial
civilization; it could be nothing more than a delaying action. Still,
why was woman not content with the romantic exaltation offered
her? Was it not enough to be honored, sung, and deified? Evidently
not, if such worship also meant her exclusion from all the other
areas of social and personal achievement. In the Victorian scheme,
woman was denied every form of status and achievement except
one, but in an industrial urban world that one was no longer as
meaningful as it once had been. She yearned, instead, for the achieve-
ments reserved for men, and her feminist spokeswomen argued that
she was the natural equal of man and deserved the same opportunities as he. But the very nature of this argument created in her
mind a confusion as to what part she could, or should, play in life;
the choice seemed to be between that of the unwed, childless, career
woman, and the subjugated, dependent, housewife-mother. If
there were some other answer, some other personality she could assume, Victorian women had no idea what it might be.

7

Perfect Love and
Some of Its Imperfect Results

❀   ❀

❀

Victorian love, wrote William H. Mallock, a late nineteenth-century novelist, was undoubtedly "far the highest" man had ever known; even Shakespeare, he said, had never been able to conceive of love in terms as sublime as those of Elizabeth Barrett Browning. His attitude was typical; most Victorians were convinced, by the analogies drawn from Darwinian evolution, that love had progressed undeviatingly upwards from a universal bestiality among primitives to the ultimate goal of sentimental monogamy.

In recent years the world has so lacked the seeming stability and optimism of the Victorian era that some people have become nostalgic and respectful of the Victorian world and its ways. Not long ago, for instance, the historian Esmé Wingfield-Stratford flatly stated (without offering statistics) that "the married lives of Victorians were, in an extraordinary number of instances, crowned with a happiness that no dreams of romance could have surpassed," and recent biographies have tended to make the Victorians seem genuinely estimable, well balanced, and content.

To some extent, it was true. Certainly a great majority of Victorians pledged their allegiance to a wholesome form of love directly concerned with the preservation of the family and the stability of society. But even in its heyday there were certain aspects of Victorian love which were neither "high," wholesome, nor indicative of contentment. The history of feminism, which we have just glanced at, is major evidence of the discontent and instability

inherent in Victorian love. Many other symptoms indicated that
not all was gold that glistened. In the second half of the century,
for instance, bourgeois morality was defiantly violated by an outburst of sensuality in literature—the "fleshly" and "erotic" poets in
England, Balzac and Zola in France, Whitman in America, and
many others. And there was more than mere sensuality: often the
writers displayed decadence and perversion, dwelling on scenes of
sadistic coition, gamy details of masochism, and elaborate fantasies
of the *femme fatale* or insatiable devouring temptress; Swinburne,
Gautier, Flaubert, and Wilde are only a few of the cases in point.[6]
And even where perversion was not involved, the combination of
love and death—typically, a product of unresolved incest-wishes,
according to the late Dr. Ernest Jones—was immensely popular,
appearing on every level from tear-jerking short stories in *Godey's
Lady's Book* to the libretto Wagner wrote for his own *Tristan und
Isolde*.

Apart from legitimate literature, the great hunger for a fantasy
sex life that would make good the deficiencies of the real sex life
of the time manifested itself in a considerable increase in pornographic and indecent publications, prudish London being something
of a European center for such materials. In America, meanwhile,
when the conventional propriety was occasionally breached by
pornography in disguise, the reception was astonishing; Maria
Monk's *Awful Disclosures of the Hotel Dieu Nunnery of Mont-
real*, ostensibly an exposé, but actually a fraud designed for prurient prudes, sold 300,000 copies, a remarkable record for the pre-
Civil-War period.

The symptoms were not only literary. During the century, there
was a notable increase in prostitution; estimates of the numbers of
prostitutes in mid-century London varied widely according to the
source (ranging from 7,000 to 80,000), but a few years later Taine,
an impartial Frenchman, claimed there were 50,000. His figure is
believable, for 42,000 illegitimate children were born in England
in 1851, most of them to "fallen women." Even more noteworthy
was the existence, among the London brothels, of many which
specialized in providing flagellation to a large clientele of men who,
without it, were sexually inoperative; this taste was so character-

---

[6] This tendency was exhaustively illustrated and traced to its romantic origins by Mario Praz in *The Romantic*
Agony; see especially chapters four and
five.

istically Victorian as to receive the name, *le vice anglais.*[7] Against
these ills bourgeois society struggled fitfully, seeking symptomatic
relief, if not real cure, through police activities, the actions of anti-
vice societies, purity crusades, and spasmodic efforts at the suppression of erotica. These countermoves, though most in evidence
in countries with a Puritan tradition, appeared elsewhere too. As
the historian G. M. Young has pointed out: "Much nonsense about
'the Victorians' is dissipated by the reflection that it was the French
Government that prosecuted *Madame Bovary*"—and, he might
have added, convicted Baudelaire for corrupting public morals
with his sickly poems, *Les Fleurs du Mal.*

Beneath the placid exterior of bourgeois marriage, furthermore,
there was much well-hidden misery. Toward the close of the era,
Balzac, Breuer, Freud, and Havelock Ellis, among many others,
collected evidence that wedding-night rape, vaginismus (painful
vaginal spasm), frigidity, impotence, homosexuality, and other
aberrations of sexual love were far more common than the official
doctrine of nineteenth-century romantic love ever admitted. When
even a leading American gynecologist said, before a convention of
doctors in 1900: "I do not believe mutual pleasure in the sexual act
has any particular bearing on the happiness of life," what could
one expect of the average male? Doubtless not much, and it is
therefore not surprising to find turn-of-the-century reports from
different parts of northern Europe and America claiming inci-
dences of female frigidity ranging from ten per cent to seventy-
five per cent.[8]

We can actually see in clinical detail what one such woman's love
life was like, thanks to the fact that by the end of the century the
changing attitudes toward medical investigation had lifted some of
the veils of secrecy, at least as far as concerned the recording of
anonymous case reports. The case in point, reported by Havelock
Ellis, is that of "Mrs. B.," an Englishwoman in her early thirties
at the turn of the century, and characterized by Ellis as attractive,
healthy, the mother of several children, and leading an active life.
As a girl, she had been decently brought up; she was modest and
thoroughly "pure," but fond of dancing and of male attention, and
much given to romantic imaginings. Ignorant of sex until she fell

[7] Houghton: *Victorian Frame of Social History*, pp. 490–1; Praz: *Roman-
Mind*, p. 366; G. M. Trevelyan: *English tic Agony*, pp. 421–3.
[8] Havelock Ellis: *Sex in Relation to Society (Studies*, Vol. VI), pp. 512, 525–7.

in love and became engaged, she feared to drive away her fiancé
by excessive prudery and therefore let him fondle her breasts at
length, but such was her state of inhibition that she desired neither
this nor any other physical act except what she imagined love-
making to consist of—lying in each other's arms all night and kissing. Reality came as a surprise, and her romantic lover assumed, in
her eyes, a new look and personality:

> She was somewhat shocked and disgusted by the experience of
> the wedding night. It seemed to her that her husband approached
> her with the violence of an animal. . . . Coitus, though incom-
> plete, took place some seven times on that first night. . . . For
> two months subsequently there was great pain during intercourse,
> although she suppressed the indications of this. . . . She has sel-
> dom obtained complete gratification. For a long time she disliked
> seeing or touching the penis, and the feel, and especially the smell,
> of the semen produced nausea and even vomiting. . . . Feelings
> of friendship for her husband have been [occasionally] potent in
> arousing the sexual emotions . . . [but] she has been for many
> months at a time without sexual intercourse. . . . She eventually
> discovered that her husband's abstinence from marital intercourse
> was due to infidelity. This led to a definite separation. She still oc-
> casionally experiences sexual desire . . . but she herself believes
> that her sexual life is at an end.[9]

So ended in failure the attempt by one couple, and, it would seem,
a great many others, to make a reality out of the dream of Victorian love.

[9] Havelock Ellis: *Studies,* Vol. III, Appendix B, pp. 303–6.

Chapter X
THE AGE OF LOVE

1 By Love Obsessed

2 The Sexual Revolution

3 The New Romanticism: Dating and Sex

4 The New Romanticism:
Illusions and Realities

5 Love as Panacea

6 Who Is Woman? What Is She?

7 Grand Design, with Flaws

8 Conclusion

I

By Love Obsessed

❁   ❁

❁

Social critics have pinned so many special labels on our own era—
the Atomic Age, the Age of Conformity, the Age of Anxiety
—that we may as well add one more, equally cogent: the Age of
Love. Nor is this a mere literary artifice. At no time in history has
so large a proportion of humanity rated love so highly, thought
about it so much, or displayed such an insatiable appetite for word
about it. There are no contemporary Tristans, nor even any Jane
Eyres, but only the likes of Stanley Kowalski and John's Other
Wife; still, it is a safe guess that never before have so many of the
plays, novels, and stories of an era centered about, or at least included, themes of love and sex. And this is true not only of fiction.
The news media are crammed with reports of the romances, marriages, infidelities, and quarrels of the famous; in the love affairs of
the celebrities, millions of the obscure live out their own dreams.
When Princess Margaret obeyed the call of duty in 1955 and gave
up Group Captain Townsend, millions of persons in the Western
world were genuinely sad and sympathetic; when the Czechoslo-
vakian government recognized the supremacy of love in 1957 by
allowing its lady discus champion to marry an American hammer-
thrower, the citizens of Prague joyously turned the wedding day
into a spontaneous city-wide revel; and when in 1958 Crown Prince
Akihito of Japan succeeded in breaking an ancient tradition and
chose his fiancée on the basis of love, the youth of that nation all
but rioted with enthusiasm, and the rest of the world was, if not
exactly riotous, at least very favorably impressed.[1]

[1] Some informed observers, however,
believe that Akihito's action involved
practical considerations: it may have
been expressly designed to persuade the
world of Japan's new democracy, and
to introduce new blood among the "six
families."

The contemporary millions who are thus insatiably hungry for news and stories of love also try diligently to make it an actual part of their own lives. As lovers, modern men and women may not be nearly as graceful as the Renaissance courtiers, as lusty as the rationalists, nor as sweetly eloquent as the Victorians; yet more than any of these they consider love the *sine qua non* of the happy life. Americans, who make more of marrying for love than any other people, also break up more of their marriages (close to 400,000 annually), but the figure reflects not so much the failure of love as the determination of people not to live without it. Large numbers of the world's people, while regarding American divorce with evident disapproval, seem irresistibly drawn toward the same general conception of love and marriage. East Germany, after a decade of attacking romantic love as "bourgeois trash," recently gave up the unequal struggle and urged its writers to produce love stories to meet the needs of its people; feminists throughout the Moslem world are throwing away the veil and warring against polygamy; and the love patterns of most primitive societies are rapidly disintegrating and being replaced by Western models.

It is almost incredible that so many different peoples should be attracted by a pattern of love that is essentially Western, strongly Anglo-Saxon, and relatively new on earth. Western love, in a manner scarcely to be found in earlier history, attempts to combine sexual outlet, affectionate friendship, and the procreative familial functions, all in a single relationship. Romantic attraction is considered to be the adequate, and indeed the only, basis for choosing one's lifelong partner; the sexual desires deliberately aroused in courtship are supposed to be held in check until after marriage; the sexual drives of both partners are supposed to be completely and permanently satisfied within marriage even though there was no testing period beforehand; and tenderness, mystery, and excitement are expected to coexist with household cares, child-rearing problems, and the routine of fifteen thousand nights together. All in all, anthropologists consider it one of the most difficult human relationships ever attempted; just as certainly, it is also one of the most appealing.

Much of the appeal is based on the aesthetic and morally elevated atmosphere of this love ideal; yet with total inconsistency the very same societies which have so glorified the synthesis of love and sex have at the same time commercialized and mechanized sex. To judge by the major news media, for instance, the Western peoples are afflicted with endemic *voyeurism*, and have an untiring morbid need to gaze at, and compare, the breast development of young actresses. The cigarette, clothing, and cosmetic industries continually suggest that their products can assure sexual conquest, and the suggestion is frequently couched in terms clearly referring to illicit seduction, rather than marriage and companionship: typical recent perfume advertisements say, for instance: "Not for the timid," "A whispered invitation for a man to be masterful," and "Depend on it —for anything!" And in the name of science, sex has been stripped of all emotional meaning and viewed as a purely mechanical activity; never before did it occur to men to count and tabulate millions of orgasms like grains of wheat, giving exactly the same statistical value to a one-minute back-alley copulation as to the transcendent climax of a genuine love affair.

How can anyone make sense of this Age of Love? All over the world women want emancipation, which will enable them to love and be loved in the modern way; but over two thirds of America's emancipated women stay at home after they marry, fearful that in throwing off domesticity they might throw off femininity, and even make no cry of outrage when a contemporary college president tells them it is in their nature to be as satisfied by soufflés as by philosophy. It is an age in which failure to marry is taken as a sign of personal incompetence or even neurosis, yet one in which ten million Americans have been willing to end their marriages— some of them because (or so they swore in court) their mates played the television set too loudly, had noisy false teeth, or refused to let the cat share the nuptial bed.

It is an age when the experts themselves are all at sixes and sevens about the whole subject of love. Some sociologists see modern love in terms of greed, sensuality, and social ruin, while others see it as the basis of equalitarian marriage, in harmony with modern democracy; some anthropologists feel that lifelong fidelity is unrealistic and unworkable, but any number of psychiatrists diagnose infidelity as a symptom of a disease (emotional immaturity) and do their best to "cure" it.

Perhaps, however, these are not so much contradictory interpretations of the same phenomena, but of different and coexistent phenomena. Modern man is so ambivalent about love and so much in the midst of transition from old orders to new ones that he is liable

to pick and choose whatever facts he needs to bolster his own uncertain inclinations. In any case, this much is clear: he is even more
perplexed about love, in the very Age of Love, than he was at any
time in the past 2,500 years.

2

The Sexual Revolution

❀   ❀

❀

Before looking more closely at modern love, we need to go back
briefly and remind ourselves of the process by which it broke
away from the Victorian pattern. As we saw in the previous chapter, when the industrial middle class became dominant early in the
nineteenth century, it set up as the standard of European and American love a domesticated romanticism, prudish, patriarchal, and sentimental; but the same changes in the techniques of production that
brought the businessman power over society spawned at the same
time a powerful feminist movement which successfully challenged
his power over his wife and family.

Science, the humus of Victorianism, was also the seedbed of the
revolution in love. For it was the new work in medicine, sociology,
and anthropology that made sex once again a legitimate matter of
study, and caused sexual outlet, so long viewed with shame and disgust, to be re-evaluated as a necessary, health-giving, and even a
noble function. The revolution was anything but giddy and light-
hearted about sex; its leaders were earnest, high-minded, and me-
thodical, and in the process of liberating sexuality they sometimes

accomplished the almost impossible task of making pleasure seem like a medical necessity.

It was, for instance, in the interest of combating disease that men like Krafft-Ebing, Forel, Weininger, and Havelock Ellis produced their various studies of sexuality and sex pathology in the latter part of the nineteenth century, and that same tradition, rather than any bent towards licentious reveling, was responsible for the epochal discoveries of the Karl Marx of the sexual revolution, Sigmund Freud. Indeed, Freud had originally had no intention of studying sexuality as such; he began his medical career as a neuropathologist, attempting to treat nervous disorders at first by electrotherapy, and later by hypnosis. In the late 1880's, working in collaboration with Dr. Joseph Breuer, also of Vienna, he found that a number of patients with severe nervous disorders seemed temporarily improved when they discharged their pent-up emotions under hypnosis. The matter might have rested there, with a modest improvement in symptomatic relief, but Freud was struck by the fact that the emotions vented during the trance very often concerned sexual desires and fears which the patient, at all other times, was either unaware of or even vehemently denied. From this early beginning Freud was inevitably led along that road of investigation, discovery, and theoretical formulation which ended by profoundly affecting the Western conceptions of sex, love, morality, and human psychology. It was particularly ironic, that this rather puritanical, romantic, and inhibited young man should become in the eyes of conservatives the licentious and prurient instrument of Satan; the apostle of the sexual revolution was himself chaste before his marriage, devotedly monogamous after it, and far from being a satyr, was a man with a rather mild and early terminated sex drive.[2]

Freud and Breuer published their findings in the book *Studies on Hysteria* in 1895, a date which in effect marks the discovery of the dynamic processes of the unconscious, and the introduction of this concept into Western psychology. Soon Freud discovered that when he encouraged his patients, without hypnosis, to speak freely and without the usual inner restraints on thoughts, they produced a free-associative flow of talk that revealed far more of their problems and motivations than did the trance-produced material. This was the origin of psychoanalysis; with this powerful tool of in-

[2] This is the picture of Freud that emerges from the recent definitive biography of him by Dr. Ernest Jones. See especially Vol. II, p. 386.

vestigation and treatment, Freud made discoveries in rapid succession and developed many of his principal theories. None of his findings led him to advocate or sanction anything like sexual libertarianism, yet they were thoroughly alarming to conservatives in the medical profession and to many others. People at many sorts felt his insistence on the paramount importance of the sex drive to be vile and indecent; more importantly, they were shocked by his claim that everyone has an unconscious—a psychic closet stuffed with the skeletons of infantile, homosexual, incestuous, and perverse desires.

At first the medical profession tried to ignore him, but a decade after the book on hysteria appeared he was beginning to acquire a following and to receive international recognition, and the opposition became overt. Between 1906 and 1910 Freud and his major ideas were regularly denounced at medical meetings and in the press; various doctors castigated psychoanalysis as "mental masturbation," Freud himself as a "Viennese libertine," and his followers as ripe for lunatic asylums. It was in vain, of course; even before World War I psychiatry and psychology were rapidly coming under the influence of psychoanalytic theory, and after the war it penetrated literature, philosophy, and the social sciences. Since then it has been so thoroughly absorbed into popular thinking that psychoanalysts have become familiar, friendly figures in television dramas, and perhaps more significantly, millions of parents have read the ubiquitous baby-book of Dr. Spock and never winced at—or even noticed—the psychoanalytic concepts on almost every other page.

If Freud's ideas had arrived at the beginning of the nineteenth century, they might have had relatively little immediate effect; as it was, they came at a time of sexual reconstruction attendant upon the successes of feminism. During the nineteenth century the feminists had slowly won important financial and social rights; now the long campaign approached its final victories. Eleven of the Western states in the United States granted women the vote before World War I; Finland, Norway, and Denmark did so between 1906 and 1915; suffragettes marched down Fifth Avenue in 1912, got the Bull Moose Party to endorse female suffrage, and Congress passed the Nineteenth Amendment in 1919, with ratification coming in 1920.

During this same period the more radical feminists were demanding and actually putting into practice some of the increased sexual freedoms which only now became practicable. For at last women could support themselves, and hence remain free of the need to barter their love for lifelong maintenance. Olive Schreiner, the English feminist and writer, argued that only by total economic independence could sexual love be freed to become "the essentially Good and Beautiful of human existence." Logically, Ellen Key pleaded for woman's right to maternity, in or out of marriage. And putting these ideas into flamboyant practice, Isadora Duncan became the very symbol of flaming feminism: in America and Europe alike, she scandalized and fascinated the public by her rapt, interpretive dances, performed only in a transparent veil, and by her well-advertised love affairs and her defiant unwed motherhood.

She was, to be sure, an extreme type, but she did exemplify a basic position of feminism—that sexual love should be an ecstatic experience for woman. Indeed, Isadora was apt to ascribe to her own physical responses a cosmic importance. When, for instance, she was still a young virgin in Paris before the turn of the century, she introduced herself to Rodin one day, admired his work, and then privately danced for him at home in her diaphanous tunic. Not unreasonably, Rodin advanced upon her with glittering eye and bared tooth, whereupon she promptly took fright, threw on a dress, and sent him away thoroughly irritated. But for many years she reproached herself, feeling that she had cheated the entire world: "How often have I regretted this childish incomprehension," she wrote in *My Life*, "which lost me the divine chance of giving my virginity to the Great God Pan himself, to the mighty Rodin. Surely Art and all Life would have been richer thereby!" Belatedly she did her best by Art and Life with a series of other men, each love affair seeming to her like "the final resurrection" of her life, and each, by her own admission, ending badly. In her fading, thick-waisted middle age, she married a young Bolshevik poet, Sergei Essenin, drank too much, quarreled bitterly, saw her popularity vanish, and was fortunate enough to die in an automobile accident in 1927 before things got much worse.

Margaret Sanger, an American housewife and mother, was meanwhile waging a historic fight for woman's sexual freedom on a very different front—the control of pregnancy. As a visiting nurse, she had seen the squalid results of ungoverned fertility among the poor in the slums of New York City, and she felt that not only were health and happiness ruined by excessive childbearing, but that married love remained uncivilized and brutish as long as it could not be practiced without the fear of unwanted consequences. In France she collected birth-control information for a year; then in 1914, back in New York, she began publishing her data in a newspaper entitled *Woman Rebel*, which she sold mostly to labor and socialist groups. But her challenge was one all feminists could respond to: "A woman's body belongs to herself alone," she wrote, and insisted that unless woman had the absolute right "to dispose of herself, to withhold herself, to procreate or suppress the germ of life," all other feminist gains were empty.

Puritanical and Catholic elements alike were outraged. She was arraigned for violating the Comstock Law, published a still more detailed pamphlet called *Family Limitation*, fled to England for a year, and then returned to stand trial. By that time feminists were solidly aligned with her, and the government first delayed trial and then dropped the case. In 1916 she opened a birth-control clinic in Brooklyn, was arrested, and served a thirty-day sentence in the workhouse, but in 1918 the Court of Appeals put a new broader interpretation on the dissemination of birth control information; she reopened the Birth Control Clinical Research Bureau in 1923, and thereafter clinics multiplied rapidly, despite continual opposition from the Catholic Church. By the late 1930's there were over three hundred of them in the United States, and a survey made in 1940 showed that over nine tenths of upper-middle-class Protestant couples and nearly as many Catholic ones were making at least some efforts to regulate their own parenthood.[3]

Birth control, like divorce and feminism in general, was succeeding, in large part, because of a fundamental change in the nature of marriage and family life. The Industrial Revolution had been causing a gradual shift from the country to the city, which became more rapid by the close of the century: in 1880 only twenty-eight per cent of the American population lived in cities, but by 1910 forty-six per cent did, and today roughly two thirds live either in cities or city-suburb complexes. The rural families of earlier centuries had raised much of their own food, built their own shelters, made their own foods and medicines, and taught their own young; in the shift

[3] J. W. Riley and M. White: "The Use of Various Methods of Contraception," *Amer. Sociol. Rev.*, Vol. 5 (1940), pp. 890–903.

to the city, men began to work for wages, used the cash to purchase the goods and services they needed, and sent their children to public schools. Women were left with childbearing and housework, but little else that was irreplaceable or challenging. Men, if they chose, did not actually need women in order to survive in the city. As for children, they were no longer an economic asset with candle-making, cow-milking, and crop-harvesting value, but a costly luxury, valuable only for reasons of love and pride.[4] Margaret Sanger, after all, had been horrified not by fertile peasants, but by fertile slum-dwellers. The Industrial Revolution had spawned the Victorian family in one century, only to undo it in the next by giving the right to love priority over the act of begetting.

For the natural result of separating love-making from procreation was to bring the traditional bourgeois ideal of monogamous faithful marriage under attack. The most frequent argument was that since love did not always last for life, the promise to love and be faithful for life was meaningless; it was the right of every human being to seek new love when the old died. If children were involved, the marriage should continue, but with complete freedom by each partner to conduct outside love affairs. This general solution was given by a number of intellectuals—H. G. Wells, Bertrand Russell, and Havelock Ellis, among others—and restrictions on sex freedom were seen as an unreasonable, even outrageous, interference with human rights. Marriage, Havelock Ellis concluded, would conquer adultery in only one way—by absorbing and tolerating it. In the United States a somewhat similar attitude was displayed by Judge Ben Lindsey in his widely publicized writings on marriage, and in the mid-20's he suggested a scheme of legal but exploratory union, to be called "companionate marriage" and terminable at will by husband and wife as long as no children had been born. A more typically Jazz Age notion was put forth by Fannie Hurst, who advocated "visiting marriage," with separate households for husband and wife, and meetings by appointment—a proposal not likely to appeal to any but the well-to-do.

[4] Adam Smith reported in 1776 that an American child was worth £100 clear profit to his parents before he left home (in 1959 terms, at least $1,000 and possibly two to three times that); for 1910 city-dwellers, in contrast, each child reared to maturity cost thousands of dollars. (The actual per-child cost had risen to over $16,000 by 1944, and in 1959 is probably above $25,000. See Metropolitan Life Insurance Company *Statistical Bulletin*, Jan. 1944, p. 10.)

All these suggested modifications of marriage were widely discussed from the turn of the century on, but except for a handful of intelligentsia and radicals, not many tried them except in the old, furtive fashion. Some of the most articulate advocates of emancipated marriage—Wells, Russell, D. H. Lawrence—themselves had rather untidy and painful personal lives; it often appeared that modernized marriage would satisfy one mate nicely, while making the other wretched.

The marriage of that saintly, bearded scholar of sex, Havelock Ellis, was a case in point; it seems more like one of the case histories of aberration in his own *Studies in the Psychology of Sex* than anything else. Ellis and the novelist Edith Lees fell in love and were married in 1891, but Ellis required her to agree in advance that they would always maintain separate homes, live by their own incomes, and retain complete personal freedom in outside relationships. Throughout their twenty-five years of married life, they generally spent only half of each year together, and then moved apart for the other half of the year to their separate lodgings. When the marriage was only a few years old, they ceased being lovers physically because of waning interest, according to Ellis's account in *My Life* (although there is some reason to suppose that Ellis himself may have been partially impotent at times); despite this, he wrote that their love for each other grew ever more intense and "passionate." In accordance with his modern ideas, Ellis told her in the friendliest possible fashion about his various love affairs, Platonic and otherwise, and in *My Life* he repeated again and again that Edith surmounted her initial jealousies and found security and genuine love in their marriage. Yet one has only to open his lengthy book at random to find Edith suffering, agonized, jealous, despondent, and always in the midst of some tear-streaked resolve never again to make a fuss; and always the trouble was his feelings for, or relations with, other women—never money, never politics, never religion, only love. As early as 1895 she was writing like this:

> *My poor boy*, my heart is aching and aching for you. . . . Oh! dear, oh, dear! *why* have you and I to keep making one another miserable, when no other person could ever be really as much to the other as you and I are?

In 1898, chin up (but quivering) she was sure things were going to be all right:

> I only have realized lately how much more I love you than I ever did, or you could not make me suffer so hideously. And though I may not yet comprehend you, you also don't quite see why I feel things; but all is sure to come right, for love carries folk through everything in the end.

And so it went. Ellis seemed to feel constant improvement, enrichment, and spiritual exaltation in their love; the disinterested reader may see nothing but unvaried torment, and wonder why Mrs. Ellis continued to subject herself to it. Apparently she loved him far too much to break off with him, but despite her struggles to understand and to accept him, she could not help suffering for a reason the great scholar would not admit: namely, that love in the modern world is not painlessly divisible, that sex and affection, play and earnest, love affairs and marriage, cannot be easily or neatly maintained in separate compartments of the personality. When Margaret Sanger, during her flight from America, became Ellis's very dear friend, he wrote of her to Edith, whose reply said nothing of her own long years without his physical love, and yet showed unmistakably the nature of her agony at not being her husband's choice:

> I have no heart or strength to write long letters. . . . It is not that you have ceased to care—it is—well, just what it is, and perhaps only a woman knows what that is. . . . That you cannot see it is the comedy—that I do is the bathos and the pathos in one. . . . God keep you and bless you in this new thing and may she make up for all our failures. Your comrade who loves you.

Not long after, she swallowed morphine unsuccessfully, then jumped into a well and later out of a window, surviving both acts; finally she died of a chill in 1916, and so found the only state in which she could cease to care.

There is, however, a postscript to the story, and an important one. After his wife's death, Ellis took as his constant companion and friend a Madame Françoise Cyon. His dear friend, the poet Hugh de Selincourt, doing little more than living by Ellis's own recommendations, fell in love with her and had an affair with her. Ellis, deeply hurt, broke off with both of them. Mme Cyon, understandably dumbfounded, eventually gave up De Selincourt and begged her way bank into Ellis's grace; even the poet, two years later, was readmitted to the white-bearded Mosaic presence—but only on the clear, if unuttered, understanding that the emancipated theory of love be practiced with someone other than the philosopher of love's own consort.

While some of the sexual revolutionaries were philosophizing about the improvement of love through adultery, many others seemed fascinated by the purely mechanical aspects of the sex act; as a corollary of this, they recognized the existence of female desire and, like the suffragettes demanding the vote, loudly asserted woman's right to orgasm. In 1918 Mrs. Marie Stopes, an English-woman who had known the frustrations of an unconsummated marriage, published her startling book *Married Love*, which had immense influence in Europe and, later, in America. In terms that would have made any Victorian lady faint away instantly, she ardently proclaimed that the wife should be a full partner in sexual pleasure, and should obtain full gratification every time. It was doubtless a salutary reaction to what had long existed, but Mrs. Stopes, in her fascination with the moment of climax, showed that queer tendency of the sexual revolutionaries to view the orgasm as a kind of excellent thing-in-itself, detached from the partner, the meaning, and the emotion. She often dissected out the act from its human context, and came up with many a disembodied description of a woman's climax such as this: "The critical pinnacle of the orgasm broke like the towering crest of a sun-sparkling wave."

In 1926 the Dutch physician Theodoor H. van de Velde issued his classic work *Ideal Marriage*, the philosophy of which was of the same type and placed upon husbands a moral burden of no mean sort: "Every considerable erotic stimulation of their wives that does not terminate in orgasm, on the woman's part, represents an injury, and repeated injuries of this kind lead to permanent—or very obstinate—damage to both body and soul." That same year there appeared, in German, Wilhelm Reich's *Function of the Orgasm*, a work of maverick psychiatry whose author alleged that orgasm failure, of either man or woman, was the cause of major mental and physical diseases (later Reich even advocated masturbation as a way to combat cancer by promoting the flow of sexual energy). In the United States the psychiatrist Gilbert V. Hamilton made one of the first major statistical studies of married life and sexual conduct, paying particular attention to orgasm frequency in women; he reported that a considerable number of women did not experience it regularly, and he claimed that this lack was a principal cause of weariness, ill health, adultery, and divorce. One might, however, wonder how much of this was a sexual revolutionary's preconception, for he also admitted, with mild surprise, that the happily married women of his sample were only about seven per cent more climactic, on the average, than the unhappily married women.[5]

A similar attitude of detached biological concern was characteristic of the Lost Generation of the Twenties, though they assumed the pose of hard-boiled pleasure-seekers. By their time, all circumstances conspired to it: feminism had given woman the right to put her foot on the rail, even in a prohibition speakeasy; World War I had created an atmosphere of cynicism combined with a desperate hunger for wasted years; and the widespread dissolution of Victorian morality had left a vacuum, still unfilled by any new rules and standards. It was not only an American or Western phenomenon; in the Soviet, where nineteenth-century ideas had been even more abruptly repudiated, the state philosophically and legally encouraged sexual freedom and made divorce and abortion no harder to get than a newspaper or a new hat. The reigning Communist attitude was that one should seek sexual intercourse just as one did a glass of water—to satisfy a physical need—with no admixture of outmoded philosophy. Lenin himself was horrified at this "glass-of-water" theory and spoke out against it, but to no avail.

In the United States, meanwhile, middle-aged people were likewise horrified at the young generation, who defiantly made bold of their hip flasks and bootleg gin, wild rides and petting sessions, loose talk and roadhouse parties. Even in the small towns of the Midwest there was no escaping it, for the movies and the radio had come into their own; no matter where one lived, he was subjected to the impact of Clara Bow, the "It" girl, and such edifying tunes as "Diga Diga Doo," and "Makin' Whoopee." Even the aesthetic and intellectual *avant-garde* was committed to the tough, cynical, and physical view of love; the new woman, being still in part the same old woman, was therefore both witty and brokenhearted, gay and pathetic. No one said it better than Edna St. Vincent Millay:

> *I shall forget you presently, my dear,*
> *So make the most of this, your little day,*
> *Your little month, your little half a year,*
> *Ere I forget, or die, or move away,*
> *And we are done forever; by and by*
> *I shall forget you, as I said, but now,*

[5] The same concentration upon orgasm as *Ding-an-sich* has persisted to our own time among some researchers. The late Dr. Kinsey was its ultimate exemplar, firmly discarding from sex studies all questions of love and applying to sex a boilermaker's sense of values which reduced everything to a matter of tension and "outlet."

If you entreat me with your loveliest lie
I will protest you with my favourite vow.
I would indeed that love were longer-lived,
And oaths were not so brittle as they are,
But so it is, and nature has contrived
To struggle on without a break thus far,—
Whether or not we find what we are seeking
Is idle, biologically speaking.

3

The New Romanticism:
Dating and Sex

❀   ❀

❀

The era of "It," however, was short-lived and superficial; its bright, brassy, emancipated doctrines never really dominated modern love except among the *avant-garde*, and then only briefly. As for the bulk of Americans, they showed the influence of change in milder, more bourgeois ways. In the middle of the Twenties, the Lynds made their famous anthropological expedition into darkest Indiana and studied the restless natives of Middletown (Muncie); the Midwestern Americans, they found, had indeed lost their patriarchal and functional view of family life, but rather than replacing its moral code with that of free love or emancipated marriage, they had switched to what has become a typical American answer— divorce and remarriage, or as it is sometimes referred to, progressive polygamy. Their attitude toward adultery was unchanged, but they were getting six times as many divorces as they had in 1890.

They had genuinely accepted the modern conception of sexual enjoyment as a human right, but basically they believed in romantic personal love, not mere biology, and assigned it a major role in holding society together.

In part, this represented simply the spreading-out of middle-class values to the whole society, for by the present century Americans were almost all thinking of themselves as "middle class," despite wide variations in income, occupation, and habits; one study shows that seventy per cent of even the low-income groups claim to be of the middle class. But there was more to it than tradition which had become widespread; the isolation and anonymity of modern life made men and women desperately long for firm ties, personal loyalties, and a sense of individual importance. Even D. H. Lawrence, that tormented exponent of sexual freedom, declared in the very last year of his life that it was not really sex that man needed. "It is a great blow to our self-esteem that we simply *need* another human being," he wrote in a magazine article. "I do not mean a mistress, the sexual relationship in the French sense. . . . It is in relationship to one another that [people] have their true individuality and their distinct being. . . . It is a living contact, give and take."

It was just such a hunger for self-definition, for a reassurance of one's importance, that made a new form of romantic love more important than ever. The growing deluge of movies and of radio soap operas in the Twenties was characterized by themes of love, heartbreak, and eventual happiness, and however factitious and trashy their portrait of life was, the immense appetite for them indicated some considerable need on the part of the general population. The Depression only accentuated this trend, sweeping away the superficial follies and extremes of the previous decade, and making the comfort and reassurance of love more vital than ever; as in the latter part of the nineteenth century, when the Victorian certainties were disintegrating, there seemed only love to cling to, and Matthew Arnold's words, written in 1867, seemed to have a new relevance:

> *Ah, love, let us be true*
> *To one another! for the world, which seems*
> *To lie before us like a land of dreams,*
> *So various, so beautiful, so new,*
> *Hath really neither joy, nor love, nor light,*
> *Nor certitude, nor peace, nor help for pain. . . .*

The value placed on the emotional life was so high, in fact, that it became fashionable among social scientists to regard it as a kind of national disease. The anthropologist Ralph Linton made a scathing appraisal of it in 1936 which has become something of a classic in the field:

> All societies recognize that there are occasional violent attachments between persons of opposite sex, but our present American culture is practically the only one which has attempted to capitalize these and make them the basis for marriage. . . . Their rarity in most societies suggests that they are psychological abnormalities to which our own culture has attached an extraordinary value just as other cultures have attached extreme values to other abnormalities. The hero of the modern American movie is always a romantic lover just as the hero of the old Arab epic is always an epileptic.

Many of the sociologists who were turning their attention to American love and marriage in the Twenties and Thirties used the term "romantic love" derisively or scoldingly to refer to powerful, irrational emotions and expectations that mark the courtship period but not, presumably, marriage. Whether or not this is a fair use, the term had clearly undergone important changes in meaning in half a century. In the twentieth-century version of romantic love, for instance, the whole concept of woman's part in courtship had changed radically; no longer was she the timid maiden, blushing and looking at the ground, hoping to be observed at church by some young man who would then ask her father if he might come calling. That marketing mechanism had worked adequately in small, stable towns, but in the rapidly growing cities of the industrial era it left many a girl on the back shelf of spinsterhood, dependent on relatives or forced to seek the loveless compensation of feminism and factory work.

By the 1920's, however, when the ideal of shy, passive femininity had been discarded, a technical revolution in courtship became possible. It rested upon the spontaneous invention of dating—the most significant new mechanism of mate selection in many centuries. In place of the church meeting, the application to father, and the chaperoned evenings in the family parlor, modern youth met at parties, made dates on the telephone, and went off alone in cars to spend their evenings at movies, juke joints, and on back roads. But the mechanical devices, however essential to the new pattern, did not create it; they were absorbed by it because they were so sorely needed. Society worked out the new procedure because it had to; young people urgently required a new way of developing themselves into marriageable persons through social experience, and a new broader exposure to possible mates in order to make the process of falling in love less risky.

The crucial part of dating, therefore, was its freedom from commitment as compared to the Victorian entrapment known as "keeping company." Young people needed years in which to acquire their social skills and to experiment with relationships to the opposite sex; then they needed still more years in which gingerly to try out a series of tentative choices before settling upon one. The pattern that developed was strikingly different from the forms of sexual mingling and mate selection known elsewhere in the world. American children scarcely got beyond puberty when their mothers began to arrange a heterosexual social life for them via dancing classes and parties, but as soon as possible most of the control and initiation of the social life was handed over to the children themselves, who then made their own choices (subject to some parental pressures, of course), set up their own appointments, and sought to escape the parental eye as rapidly as possible. In back seats, senior proms, and bull sessions, boys and girls would try to piece together some knowledge of what it meant to be a male or a female. By their late teens, most of them had been through a "crush" or two, done a fair amount of necking, and, in an increasingly large number of cases, some "heavy petting." Finally these components would begin to coalesce into the more serious attachment known as "going steady"; at this point, too, it became necessary to exhibit one's tentative choice to one's parents. The typical parental attitude towards a "steady" was one of wary, grudging acceptance—an understandable attitude, since parents had not selected the mate, yet could seldom exercise a real veto power. But only a very small percentage of rebellious youths crossed religious, social, or color lines in any dramatic fashion; for the most part, young people fell in love with other young people very much of their own background and position, and hence were rarely in serious conflict with their parents. In due course overt engagement followed, and then marriage, both of them involving the participation of both families. Characteristically, however, this was only a superficial return to the bosom of the clan; the ideal was for the couple to rush off alone as soon as possible to experiment with their sexuality and their love unobserved, and to set up their own home even in a drab single room in order to have privacy. The freedom and isolation of the dating couple were, in other words, harmonious with the emerging image of married life, and it is not surprising that the entire process has undergone only very minor changes since its inception.

Some social scientists have bluntly charged that dating is only simulated courtship behavior, its real purpose having little to do with love. The late Willard Waller coined the term "rating and dating complex" in 1937 and described it as a competitive game in which the primary goal is prestige and a high rating; boy and girl alike attain this by making a high score in getting dates with desirable people, and by sexual success—the latter, for the boy, consisting of obtaining thrills, and for the girl, of distributing as few of them as possible while remaining as enticing as she can. Critics of American love such as Margaret Mead and Geoffrey Gorer have developed Waller's analysis still further. Dr. Mead says that dating is not courtship, but a loveless contest designed to give the adolescent a feeling of success and popularity, neither of which he has much other way to gain in our culture until later in life, and she believes that the entire system works to the distinct disadvantage of marriage. The girl who has long practiced coyness and has fended off approaches, for instance, has been badly trained for the role of equal and joyous wifely sexuality.

One might reply that the Victorian premarital conditioning of the girl was a good deal worse; furthermore, although the theory of the rating and dating complex points up certain undeniable aspects of dating, it quite ignores the others. To say that competition, status-seeking, and personal gratification exist in the dating pattern is not to prove that emotional attachments do not. The average American adult, thinking back to his or her own adolescence and youth, recalls most vividly and fondly the bittersweet memories and not the score racked up, the long talk on a moonlight night or the walk hand-in-hand in the soft new snow, rather than the back-seat fumbling and the nervous efforts to advance the hand an inch or two.

A fair number of sociologists, at any rate, disagree with the sour interpretations of the dating pattern, and view it not only as a generally cheerful and happy activity of youth, but as an educational process gradually leading from playful heterosexual behavior to companionship and love capable of initiating a marriage; so seen, it is an adaptation of older courting behavior to a present need. Several years ago Samuel Lowrie, a sociologist at Bowling Green State College, Ohio, asked 1,595 boys and girls in high schools and colleges why they dated. The responses, all anonymous, indicate the reasons the young people themselves consciously have for dating. Only six per cent of the boys and one half of one per cent of the girls specified necking. One out of four did, however, specify affection, a word which evidently had considerably more meaning and appeal to them. Very nearly as many specified "to gain poise or ease," but only about half as many specified "to get to social affairs." All in all, Professor Lowrie concluded, reasons of the competitive-prestige type made up only about one quarter of all responses, but one third had to do with education and self-improvement, and well over a third had to do with affection, courtship, and marriage.

One of the most valuable functions of dating is the chance it gives young people to learn something about each other's character, opinions, and plans for living—a need which hardly existed in the stable small-town life of earlier centuries, when every young man was known, or known about, by nearly every young girl he was likely to court. A few years ago a group of typical college girls in Ohio told a researcher that they had averaged four dates a week with their prospective fiancés in the period preceding engagement; their grandmothers told him *they* had averaged only one a week. The granddaughters put their extra time to good use: fully half of them had discussed with their future husbands every one of the six major problem areas the researcher asked about (money, children, where to live, religion, the wife's work, and the husband's occupation), but only 4.5 per cent of the grandmothers had done as well. (One out of four grandmothers, in fact, had discussed none of the problem areas, while less than two per cent of the granddaughters were similarly reticent.) Evidently, even if adolescent dating is competitive and status-seeking in its early phases, it becomes increasingly oriented toward the task of obtaining a good fit, and in its later phases even involves some relatively realistic testing of the conditions which might cause love to diminish or die in actual marriage. This, then, is the shape of the new romanticism: it is at once unromantic in the sense that it is practical, inquisitive, and cautious, and romantic in the sense that it seeks a "right one" with whom love can be powerful, legitimate, and enduring.

The criticisms of dating may, in part, have carried much conviction because of the fears of mature persons that through dating the younger generation was becoming wild and sexually ungoverned. And the impartial, unemotional statistics collected by Kinsey and his co-workers do show the evidence of a considerable change. To take a single example, of the females interviewed by Kinsey only fifteen per cent of those born before 1900 had ever petted to the point of climax by the time they were twenty-five, but of the women born in the first decade of the twentieth century, thirty per cent had done so, of those born in the second decade, thirty-four per cent had done so, and of those born between 1920 and 1929, forty-three per cent had done so. Of the women born before 1900, only one in four had had intercourse before marriage; of those born after 1900, half did. (The change was less marked for men, but one can assume that most of the worry about Flaming Youth concerns the girls.)

The figures are impressive. Yet other data from the same study clearly indicate that the change was not solely due, or even largely due, to wildness and thrill-seeking. Of all the females who had had premarital coitus, nearly half had done so only with their fiancés, and another seven per cent with only one man; the over-all amount of activity for girls under twenty was on the order of only once every five to ten weeks, which is something less than a riotous abandonment to sensuality. An earlier study by Terman reported that fully two thirds of the girls who are not virgins at marriage have had relations only with their fiancés. One might interpret such data cynically as a delivery of the goods only upon commitment to purchase, but it makes more sense to interpret them, in the context of the prevailing American romantic expectations of marriage, as an indication that American women are coming to consider sexual expression legitimate where love exists (although, unlike their sisters in some European countries, it is a love definitely implying or aimed at marriage).

It would even seem that young people living in the milieu of American romanticism are not drawn to each other primarily by sexual attraction, nor is it chronologically the first force they feel. Ernest Burgess and Paul Wallin made a notable survey of a thousand engaged couples, all college students in the Chicago area, during the years 1937–9, and followed their subjects through beyond marriage. The majority of all these people specifically replied, in answer to a question, that strong physical attraction had not been a conscious part of their initial interest in each other, but that it developed as time passed, and that in general it increased in intensity as the relationship itself became a closer one.[6] Over one third of the engaged couples eventually had intercourse before marriage, and nine tenths of them considered that it strengthened their over-all relationship to each other. There is no evidence in either the Burgess-Wallin study or any of the Kinsey studies to show that such premarital intercourse is hurtful to the ensuing marriage, and some evidence, at least, that it is correlated with good marital adjustment.

If dating were geared to thrills rather than to the romantic-marriage ideal, one would hardly expect to find American youth marriage-minded; what can be obtained for the price of a motel room need not be purchased at the cost of one's freedom. Yet in the very decades when family life has been losing its personal survival value and Victorian morals have been discarded, young Americans have become ever more bent upon marriage and ever readier to undertake it in the expectation of rich emotional rewards. The median age at first marriage in 1890 was twenty-six for men and twenty-two for women; by 1958 men were marrying three years younger and women two years younger. In 1890 only fifty-four per cent of all persons over fourteen years old were married; in 1958 seventy per cent of males and sixty-six per cent of females over fourteen were married.

We can appreciate the extraordinary significance of these bald statistics by recalling again the conditions in the Roman Empire during the reign of Augustus Caesar. At that time, Roman women had won an economic and legal emancipation of sorts, the economic functions of home life had all but vanished for the well-to-do city dwellers, children had become a luxury rather than an asset, and sexual enjoyment was deemed a right and a natural privilege of every human being. All this seems generally comparable to the conditions of our own time; yet we remember that Augustus was grieved and concerned by the resulting preference of his Romans for bachelorhood, and by the infertility of marriage, the high divorce rate, and the deterioration of family life and morality in general; we recall his heroic efforts to enforce his Julian Laws, and his tragic failure. In our own time there are no such laws, and none are needed; the same conditions have produced an almost opposite result.

[6] Burgess and Wallin: *Courtship, Engagement, and Marriage*, pp. 117, 164.

Evidently, courtship in the new romanticism follows a complex prescription: one part youthful amusement, one part social striving, one part sexual attraction, one part infatuation and glamour, one part practical searching for a mate, and a considerable number of parts of quasi-mystical expectation of love, joy, and personal fulfillment to come in marriage. How far the prescription is fillable, how far the great expectations in it are met in marriage and how far frustrated, are matters of endless debate among the experts. But not among Americans in general. When marriage fails, they precipitately drink of the magical elixir again, expecting that this time it will work; and if marriage does not fail, but only disappoints, they smile indulgently upon their romantic young as though the potion had never proven ineffective and never could.

4

The New Romanticism:
Illusions and Realities

❀   ❀

❀

Van Nuys, Cal., Nov. 18—UNIVAC goofed 20 times as an electronic matchmaker but finally came up with a winner. Bob and Shirley Kardell are UNIVAC's lone success. The machine introduced them on the TV show "People are Funny," and declared them to be compatible marital partners. And so they were married.   —*New York Post*, Nov. 18, 1958.

However strong the faith of Americans in romantic love may be, it is far from being pure and unalloyed. They are delighted to entrust to a machine, programmed with scientific marriage-prediction criteria, the task of selecting perfectly matched love candidates; yet it is plain that they are still more delighted that the machine fails ninety-five per cent of the time to yield true love. For Americans are firmly of two minds about it all—simultaneously hardheaded and idealistic, uncouth and tender, libidinous and puritanical; they believe implicitly in every tenet of romantic love, and yet know perfectly well that things don't really work that way.

Among the articles of faith in the American credo of romanticism, for instance, is what we might call the "one-person" theory, or the romantic conviction that for each individual there is a "right one" (also thought of as "the only one in the world") waiting to be found. It is the task, and indeed the moral duty, of every unmarried person to wait or to search until that one is located. "Somewhere I'll find you" and "somewhere in the world she is waiting for you" are only two of a hundred familiar expressions of the belief. The

[363]

romanticists of the late eighteenth century knew it as the doctrine of elective affinities, and in fact it had its ultimate source in Plato. This one-person theory is combined, for Americans, with the belief in free choice: it is up to man and woman alike to refuse all substitutes and to choose the right one on the basis of feeling "the real thing," unswayed by such unworthy considerations as geographical nearness, availability, or similarity of background.

Yet Americans, even young ones, are not utter fools, and they know perfectly well that if a youth lives in Maine, the only one in the world for him is not going to live in Calcutta, and not even in California. Romanticism sometimes admits reality and waxes sentimental about the boy next door—a very reasonable love choice. In major surveys made in Philadelphia and New Haven not many years ago, sociologists found that half of all people applying for marriage licenses lived within twenty blocks of each other. Somewhere in the world she is waiting for you, and it is a fifty-fifty chance that you can walk that far in less than an hour.

More importantly, scores of painstaking studies show the importance of "homogamy" in mate selection: to an overwhelming extent Americans fall in love not with ideal persons freely found and freely chosen, but with persons very narrowly limited to those of similar economic status, social class, religion, and educational level. The emotion may feel as strong even under these circumstances as if one had chosen from among all the world's people, and as if the test of rightness overrode all deterministic factors, but the realistic truth known to all American romantics is that love is largely a matter of opportunity and familiarity.[7]

A second article of faith in the credo concerns the meaning of "falling in love"; generally people are supposed to be unsuspecting and unprepared for the attack, which occurs suddenly and powerfully either at first sight or soon afterwards, the victim being helpless in the grip of a superior force. Some enchanted evening one sees a stranger across a crowded room, and it happens, unmistakably and irrevocably. This belief is almost a required convention in popular fiction, television, and the movies; oddly enough a large number of the teachers in marriage and family courses in colleges seem to believe it too, since they so consistently inveigh against it

[7] Another measure of the narrowness of selection was provided by a survey of Navy men; even the twenty-five-year-olds had dated, on the average, only seven different girls. See *Family Life*, Vol. 6, Oct., 1946.

and warn their students against the pitfalls of rushing hastily into marriage because of violent romantic feelings. They point with alarm to such evidence of its existence as news stories of lightning romances; the following one, for example, was cited in a sober sociological work from the San Francisco *Chronicle* of a few years ago:

> On Monday Cpl. Floyd H. Jackson, 23, and the then Mary Ella Skinner, 19, total strangers, boarded a train at San Francisco and sat down across the aisle from each other. Johnson didn't cross the aisle until Wednesday, but his bride said, "I'd already made up my mind to say yes if he asked me to marry him." "We did most of the talking with our eyes," Johnson explained. Thursday the couple got off the train in Omaha with plans to be married. Because they would need the consent of the bride's parents if they were married in Nebraska, they crossed the river to Council Bluffs, Iowa, where they were married Friday.

But most people, including the alarmists, are aware in some other part of their minds, that it really does not happen that way except in rare cases. Even the adolescent "crush" is not so precipitate or overpowering at its inception as is said; the young boy and girl do not so much fall in love as push themselves down a slide of love— after first looking things over. Realistically, most people know what careful sociologists have reported: American boys and girls play cautiously at light love, or mock love, the boy "handing a line" and the girl playing whichever role best suits her (coquette, charmer, aloof one) until each is fairly sure the other is more or less equally interested and ready to fall. Then, and then only, do they wilfully submit to the inexorable force; then do they fall, but by design. Helpless passion, one-way love, and unrequited suffering, belong largely to fiction and to the medieval knight's long service of his lady. In our own time, they exist chiefly in the form of the bobby-soxer's hopeless adoration of the remote idol, but among maturing young people they are more illusion than reality, believed in but not practiced.

As for the culmination of lightning romance in hasty weddings, that too is more myth than fact, according to the statistics one can glean from various surveys of American marriage. For it is a fact that at least two thirds of American husbands and wives have known each other two or more years before marrying; and it is also a fact that only one out of every six or seven love affairs becomes a marriage.[8] The myth that people fall in love and promptly rush into marriage fades out of sight in the harsh glare of the data.

Supplementing these dry figures, sociologists have also provided something new in the annals of love confessions—the clinical, undramatic, and artless interview, protected by anonymity and published not in the name of literature, but that of scientific research. Here is what falling in love is like in our time, according to one college student whose story was selected by Burgess and Wallin as most nearly typical of the pattern they observed in their study of a thousand engaged couples:

> I had my first date with her about three months after we both started to work in the firm. One day we worked together on an assignment and we made a date for that Saturday night to go to a movie. At that time it was nothing but another date. I liked her general appearance and personality. . . . I would say that I was definitely interested our first night out. I know that on my first date I wanted more dates. . . . I would say that within the first two months we were going together I felt I was in love with her, and that I'd like to marry her. Our understanding was brought on very gradually, however. It was never actually stated, but I gave her my frat ring about nine months after we started dating and that was it. I don't know which of us fell in love first. I think it came on both of us in the same way. I think it just started out as plain dating, and gradually developed into love from there on.

Not exactly exciting, not very communicative, but it undoubtedly has the sound of truth and the feeling of authenticity.

Still a third article of the romantic credo holds that love is blind, and that the lover neither observes his beloved's imperfections of character or beauty nor will admit them when they are pointed out. And certainly everyone does know that young adolescents have mad crushes for quite inappropriate people, and fall in love on the basis of wavy hair, a "heavy" look, a giddy manner, or a cream-colored convertible, rather than on the basis of more fundamental aspects of the human being. Yet once again, if we turn to the many competent field studies rather than impressionistic diatribes against American love, we find impressive evidence, heaped up in windrows of statistics and morains of case histories, to show that during the years of dating and growing up, young Americans generally begin

[8] The ratio of love affairs to marriages is from G. V. Hamilton: *A Research in Marriage*, Ch. 10. Hamilton included the love affairs of childhood, but even if one excludes those, and the affairs broken up by *force majeure*, the average man or woman experiences two to three love affairs before marrying.

to discard, or push into the background, their image of the ideal mate or dream mate; they find themselves, often to their own surprise, being attracted to people whose "type" they never cared for, but with whom they find a workable degree of companionship and a comfortable sense of fitness, and with whom the sensations of love derive from, rather than precede, the recognition of these attributes.

Such maturing people describe their emotions as "true" or "real" love rather than "puppy love" and "infatuation." That being the case, real love may be myopic, but it is not blind, for among Burgess and Wallin's two thousand engaged people, two thirds of the men and three quarters of the women were willing to name defects or things they wished were different in their partners. Some of the admitted defects concerned lofty matters such as too serious an attitude toward religion, too sharp a temper, or too great a tendency to stubbornness, but many were in the area of physical shortcomings which simply had to be accepted without hope of change, such as shortness, crooked teeth, and ears that stuck out a bit too much. Even nail-biting and dandruff were honestly named, and were evidently no impediments to love.

A fourth article of belief holds that love conquers all. When Virgil wrote *Omnia vincit Amor* long ago, he was merely being poetic, but Americans, intractably democratic and unreasonably optimistic, take it in earnest that the mighty force of love can overcome all obstacles, all reasonings, all ties that bind; love can easily best parents and professors, is superior to laws and in-laws, is greater than logic or logistics. The daughter of a coal-miner who emigrated from Lithuania wins a beauty contest and is seen by Winthrop Rockefeller; what could be more inevitable than that they fall in love and marry? Americans are delighted; this is proof indeed that love surmounts all barriers and leaps easily across all chasms. But when Bobo and Winthrop separate a year later, Americans (having a remarkable ability to feel two ways about love) look sourly wise and ask what did we expect? And when five years later she gets a divorce plus $5,500,000, they snicker and avow that all along they knew what she must be up to.

The scientists of marriage are generally aligned with them in this realistic (or cynical) side of their thinking. The sociologist has computed to the last decimal point the effects of differences in cultural background, social class, personal tastes, and the like, and finds them all bad; every difference increases the likelihood of unhappiness, maladjustment, and divorce. *Omnia vincit Amor* . . . but it seems, really, that everything conquers love. The marriage counselor, too, finds that the unusual love choice—the person of another color, another country, another religion—is very often only a means of rebellion against one's parents. And at least some psychoanalysts consider "being in love" an obsessional state in which old forgotten angers, sadistic and masochistic tendencies, sibling rivalries and the like all make the fond fool suppose himself in love while he is merely in the grip of his own unconscious motives.

In view of these several discrepancies between theory and actuality, a number of the sociologists who have studied love and marriage in the past several decades have soundly belabored romantic love, and praised in unbounded terms its supposed opposite—conjugal or companionship love. They attribute to the former a number of follies, especially that of "romanticization" or "idealization," that is, the imagining or attributing of ideal beauty and ideal personality to some perfectly ordinary youth or girl. And indeed this is, historically, one of the classic characteristics of romantic love; we remember Ulrich von Lichtenstein's idiotic devotion to the cruel princess, Hazlitt's infatuation with the lodging-house girl, and Stendhal's theory of "crystallization." To the sociologists, this is the core of romanticism, and a distinctly malign and hurtful tendency.

"No marriage can be classified as wholly romantic or as based entirely on companionship," writes Professor Burgess, ". . . [but] all our data bearing on the question point to the conclusion that, on the average, marriages resulting from comradely affection turn out happier than those chiefly inspired by romantic attitudes." "It is an ironic paradox," writes Professor Ray Baber, "that this cult of romance, with its sincere desire to refine and beautify the marriage relationship, should do it more harm than good." And the late Willard Waller (who took so dim a view of dating) even advocated a certain amount of quarreling in the early years of marriage in order to "liquidate the effects of the romantic complex" and thereby establish a firmer basis for the marriage.

But despite the collection of data to prove this general thesis, the natural history of love does not justify the sweeping attack on romantic love. To begin with, it has changed its character very considerably over a period of nine centuries, but its earnest opponents are often still slaying medieval dragons. The uneasy and imperfect blend of illusion and reality, idealism and hardheadedness, which we have described under the name of "the new romanticism," cannot properly be considered identical in spirit with abject troubadour woman-worship, Rousseauistic idealization-plus-impotence, or Stendhalian crystallization.[9]

Some of the historical components of romantic love, such as the linking of love and death or the impossibility of love existing within marriage, have vanished altogether. Others, such as extreme idealization, remain in modern romantic love, but typify early puppy love and adolescent infatuation. The adolescent wants to be in love and is surcharged with love before he has anyone in mind; it therefore takes a mere face, of which he hardly knows the name, to precipitate a very thunderstorm of adoration. As we have seen, during the process of dating and courtship some of these excesses disappear, and a degree of realistic testing and learning enter; nevertheless, the principal sources of attraction remain heavily romantic, including refined or beautified sexual desire, a sense of enrichment and fulfillment at feeling love and being loved, and a sense of completion at finding a soul mate.

In marriage, finally, the inhibition, mystery, and masking of defects that is typical of courtship come to an end. The sociologists who decry romantic love would have us understand that this shedding of romanticization is a painful transition, that true married love is based not on romantic love but comradeship, and that therefore romantic love should be eliminated from the culture as much as possible; but in historical perspective it would seem that modern marriage does, in fact, incorporate certain other residual values of romantic love, and that these are in part responsible for its success in the present age.

Before the advent of medieval courtly love, for example, the Catholic-Teutonic tradition made the husband godlike in his dominion over his wife. Courtly love reversed the roles and gave the woman sovereign, if make-believe, power over her suitor. The end result, after centuries, was to strike a rough balance, each partner

[9] But the modern sociologist really does equate them; see, for instance, Winch's *The Modern Family*. He and others also cite the scholar Denis de Rougemont, who considers passion and marriage irreconcilable and traces the former back to the Albigensian heresy of the eleventh century which linked love to a desire for sorrow and death. See above, pp. 148-9 and 170.

in love trying to please and serve the other; and this, it can hardly be denied, is considered the ideal of modern marriage.

Courtly love likewise greatly refined sexual expression (often to the point of partial impotence), and linked it to devotion, deep feeling, gentleness, long service, and similar traits of behavior. This combination of characteristics originally existed only in illicit connections, but was gradually absorbed into Christian monogamy beginning in the Renaissance. The major absorption took place later, however, among the Protestant bourgeoisie who badly needed romantic love as a cement for marriage, to replace the sacramental bonds they had broken. The dominant love ideal of modern adolescents derives from this source, but so does that of modern adults. Everyone knows that adolescents are romantic, but even for the long-married couple, love involves not only comradeship and mutual interests, but tenderness, moments of intensity, waves of compassion, joyous sexual play, and spells of candlelight and soft music. That the middle-aged do all this is the best-kept secret of our era; neither movie-makers, fiction-writers, nor advertising men can bring themselves to admit that any but the young can feel and act so.

Again, one of the most original contributions of courtly love was its attribution of character improvement and ethical value to the condition of loving. The theme appears strongly in every incarnation of romantic love: the Neoplatonists made love the stairway to spiritual excellence, Puritans such as Milton considered wedded love the fulfilment of life, and the Victorians saw love as the redeeming experience that saved men from brutalization by business.

Seen in this perspective, the contemporary ideal of marriage is distinctly romantic, since it definitely allies love to ethical goals; modern men and women are overwhelmingly convinced that without married love, life is barren, selfish, ungenerous, and pointless. The very critics of romantic love agree on this ethical value of married love. Psychiatrists view the ability to love givingly and generously as a sign of maturity, and maturity is agreed to be good. Anthropologists grant to love a life-preserving value (the scientist's equivalent of ethical good), since it meets two creatures' emotional needs and in the process continues the species and the society. Even some of the younger sociologists begin to suspect that modern companionship marriage—supposedly opposed to romantic follies

—in large part owes its existence and continuation to the cohesive power of romantic love.[1]

The antithesis made in so much of the sociological literature between romantic love and conjugal love thus appears to be artificial, unhistoric, semantically unsound, and misleading. Romantic love seems to be a continuum in the life of modern men and women—an ever-changing but ever-present entity, altering slowly and smoothly from the wild, foolish, and self-centered love of young adolescents to the tempered, realistic, and mutual love of mature adults. Contradictory views of love exist in each of us because it is the nature of man to be ambivalent about many things, and because even the most mature of us have never altogether conquered our juvenile desires; the more foolish illusions we claim to believe in are not a hurtful alien philosophy we cannot live by, but the unerased record of our youth and growth.

Romantic love may not be the ultimate or best way to choose a mate or build a marriage, but it is the only functioning one modern man has. The subtle and fine adjustments required of a maturing marriage relationship cannot be made without some stability, some force insuring a continuation of the efforts, some motivation for doing so. But modern man and woman are not linked by patrimonies, indissoluble law, clanship ties, or social pressures; it is romantic love that first draws a boy and girl into marriage, and then is the principal bond holding them together until they have forged the other ties of habit, shared experiences, adaptation to each other's needs, and children.

Yet even after that, it continues to give to modern marriage its distinctive character; for despite the follies and disillusionments, the divorces and infidelities, all alleged to come from romantic love, without it modern man and woman could not find in each other that unique, difficult, and fragile blend of protector and protégé, child and parent, comforter and tempter, friend and lover, that is nowadays implied in the word husband and the word wife.

---

[1] For several sociological contributions granting that romantic love has ethical value in this sense, see W. L. Kolb in *Social Forces*, May 1948; H. G. Beigel in *Amer. Sociol. Rev.*, June 1951; and J. F. Cuber in *Marriage and Family Living*, Vol. XI, p. 95.

5

Love as Panacea

❊   ❊

❊

Whatever ethical values and practical purposes love may happen to encompass in modern life, however, men and women do not hunger for it primarily on their account; love itself is the goal, the thing beyond price, the good in itself. Other rationalistic and materialistic eras have treated it lightly and considered it nothing more than the agreeable sensations and the sporting pleasure accompanying the sexual drive; our own era makes of it a high, noble, and essential human relationship. One might reasonably suspect, therefore, that there is in it today a value and purpose above all values and purposes—the fulfilment of a major human need that happens to be greater in certain eras of history than in others.

To some extent, the need is one created by civilization itself. The primitive man lived in the most intimate continual contact with all the members of his village; he was linked to scores of his clan-relatives by a web of powerful loyalties and affections; he was rarely restricted to a single sexual partner or severely penalized for sexual adventures. He could not know the feelings and the hungers that made Athenian men endlessly discuss the importance of friendship and love, or caused medieval courtiers and ladies to spend days at a time in conferences concerning the meaning and the rules of love.

But with the coming of industrialization and the growth of the modern city, love achieved in the Victorian period an unprecedented significance. And since these changes were further accentuated in the present century, the sexual revolution had to fail in its attempt to deromanticize love. The impersonality of urban life and the shrinking size of the family produced that central paradox of modern life to which David Riesman several years ago gave a

memorable label—the lonely crowd. And to the lonely, love seemed
the cure for pain, the harbor for wandering souls. No Greek youth,
pleasantly loitering all day with the ever-present gathering of men
in the Athenian agora, no knight, constantly surrounded by friends
and retainers or lingering for years in the intimate society of his
liege-lord's castle, could have known anything like the feelings of
the modern bachelor (or career girl) returning at evening to a
rented room or tiny apartment, an anonymous cell in a vast prison
where one can weep and be unheard, can die and remain undis-
covered for days.

The physical isolation and rootlessness of modern life, however,
is only half of the reason love has assumed such great significance.
The other half lies in the fact that our society, more so than most
others, conditions us from earliest childhood to measure and rate
ourselves by the amount of love we receive. According to Freudian
theory and the observations of a number of students of child development, the typical middle-class technique of controlling and
training the child is to give him love when he is good or does something well, and to deny him love when he is bad or does something
poorly. This ever-present threat, though highly useful in socializing
the child, makes him chronically insecure about love and obsessed
by the task of keeping it. It is the key to his personal worth, and he
interprets every gain as a reward for goodness, and every loss of
love—including the death of a parent—as due to his own badness.[2]

In the context of a competitive society, the child thus rapidly
comes to identify success in general with personal worth, and to
gauge his own success and worth by the degree to which he is liked
and loved by others. He has as yet no access to a career or to social
prestige, and all the more, therefore, he measures his own merit by
popularity (a thin-spread form of love) or, as an alternative, by the
intensity and overpowering quality of his youthful love feelings.
Everyone knows how the thirst-stricken man in the desert interprets every shadow as an oasis, and clinical psychologists have
found that when poor children are shown coins, they later recall
the coins as being much larger than they really are; rich children do
not make the same error. Similarly, the teen-ager, unsure of his
own merit and his eventual status in our fluid society, needs love

[2] Freud: *Group Psychology*, pp. 74–5;
J. C. Flugel: *Man, Morals, and Society*,
pp. 55–7; Talcott Parsons: *Essays in So-* *ciological Theory*, p. 257; and many
others.

more than he ever did as a child, and so is able to see rare beauty and infinite charm in a giggling dumpling of a bobby-soxer. The jaunty step, new-minted optimism, and smug contentment of the adolescent in love mean that he has found two things to be of great value—his beloved, and himself.

By the time he starts to earn a living or attains the social status of a college man with its attendant career expectations, he is achieving at least some small degree of real success; his image of himself therefore somewhat improves and the intensity of his need to bolster his ego through an idealized love object somewhat decreases. It is not only experience that introduces some realism into love during courtship, but actually a decreased need to have love be a form of magic, solving all one's problems. But it still has enough of them to solve, for at the very time the youth has these first successes, he has also left home and begun to sense in full the isolation so typical of contemporary life.

Meanwhile, what of the girl? She, too, has finished school or is in college, yet her career expectations are nothing like the boy's. She is already aware that she will probably never have a career, make her mark, or seem important to any but a very few people; the result is—and there are a number of serious studies to prove what everyone intuitively recognizes—that girls are more romantic than men, both at the courtship level and after marriage. The young female's addiction to movies and the married woman's equal addiction to soap opera clearly indicate that her romantic needs are greater than those of men in our culture; or as Groucho Marx once put it, a wife is a person who doesn't think she goes dancing enough.

But this difference in need between young men and young women is actually minor; after all, it is these self-same young men who marry the young women. For our own time is one in which a variety of well-known social forces, plus the rapidity of social change itself, conspire to create psychic insecurity in the adolescent and the adult alike. And so love has come to have somewhat the character of a panacea, a medicine curative of career discontent, anemia of the ego, loneliness, over-all anxiety, and lack of purpose. These and other by-products of industrialization are rapidly appearing in many new areas of the world, and it therefore makes sense that in the very same areas, modern love is now beginning to exercise its immense appeal.

In America itself, meanwhile, the use of love as panacea seems to be on the increase. Parents thrust their children into dancing-classes and parties even before puberty, and the young begin to date at twelve and thirteen, when masculinity and feminity are still only uncomfortable and unjustifiable poses. All too soon, they become anxious to "go steady," and tend to do so earlier and more fixedly than used to be the case. Going steady evidently is reassuring in that it signifies they have been accepted by someone; unfortunately it reduces the utility of the dating pattern itself, since it limits the chances for the wider testing of personalities and possible meanings of love.

But having been in the love competition since the age of twelve, the young people are ready ever earlier to marry and attain still greater security. And this represents not just a breakdown of the Victorian pattern of long engagement and late marriage, for the shift is continuing; since 1930, for instance, the average age at first marriage has dropped a year and a half for men and a year for women. *The Reader's Digest* of August 1957 expressed the popular viewpoint on all this, seeing it through a roseate haze of optimism:

> The girl of 19 and the boy of 21 who walk down the aisle to-day, however, often are far different from the wild, eloping kids of a generation ago. Usually they have tested their affection and loyalty for each other during three or four years . . . [and] acquired an intimate knowledge and a deep tolerance of each other's habits, reactions and attitudes. Thus, marriage poses no overwhelming problems of adjustment.

To test, however, means little unless one has some comparisons by which to measure the results; in any case, to be really valid, much of the testing would have to be done in the period of more mature, secure personal development. Despite the benign cheerfulness of the *Digest* and the wedding-loving American public, the census data show that a girl who marries under twenty is three times as likely to be divorced as one who marries between twenty-two and twenty-four. The hunger for love and marriage, like the hunger for food, is necessary and healthful—and can likewise become exaggerated to a pathological degree.

Similarly, under the pressure of insecurity the healthful interaction of personalities in love can become an actual disease. There is good evidence to show that, normally, people tend to fall in love with other people whose emotional needs complement their own (in this sense, at least, the adage is correct that says opposites attract). The achievement-oriented man or woman tends to pick a partner who is relatively quiescent and passive, the parent-like and care-taking person tends to love and marry someone who is dependent and clinging, and so on. These choices, needless to say, are often unconscious; people frequently think they want someone like themselves, and yet choose otherwise.[3] This is thought to be a normal basis for love, yet a mere exaggeration of it produces what psychoanalysts and marriage counselors call "neurotic marriage," which often involves pain and symptom formation of a kind sufficient to ruin health and destroy careers. But the people involved in such a marriage, though suffering, may be completely unable to do without each other or to cut themselves off from what they think of as love. A typical case from the files of Family Service of Highland Park (Illinois) involves an exhausted, ailing man over whose face flickered a nervous desperate smile, and who told his story to the marriage counselor as follows:

> I had a premonition before I married Lucille that this is the way my marriage would turn out. I guess I was flattered that she chose me instead of some of the other guys. It was pretty tough competition. . . . I was just a nobody—and still am. In fact, if you listen to Lucille, I'm not only a nobody but a complete flop—as husband and as a man. . . . If I don't ask for a raise at work, she ridicules me. If I should happen to get a raise, she says it isn't enough and it proves I'm a sucker. . . . I've lost my last five jobs because she called me so often at work, talking endlessly and telling me off. She has thrown everything at me that she can lift. . . . We haven't lived as man and wife for twelve years.

His wife, a vigorous, voluble woman, frequently tearful but nevertheless in blooming health, came in separately and told her side of it:

> Joe is a poor excuse of a man. He won't stand up to his boss and demand a raise. He won't argue with a clerk who overcharges him. . . . At times when I look at him, I get so mad I just can't control myself. Generally I just don't try. I just let him have it. . . . I wanted a strong, successful man I could lean on, depend on. What did I do instead? When I get after Joe, he gets a smile on his face that looks like the smile of Christ. . . . It's that damned smile that causes me just to throw whatever I can lay my hands on.

[3] Robert F. Winch: *Mate-Selection,* especially Ch. 6.

But when the counselor asked each one individually whether it might not be better to break up, their answers were remarkably similar. Joe, clearly horrified at the suggestion, replied with an air of explaining the obvious:

> Oh, I *couldn't* leave Lucille. I love her very much. I decided one night to leave and I did. But I couldn't sleep for thinking about her, wondering what she was doing and if she was all right. I was scared to come home because I knew she would be furious that I had left—and she was, but *I had to come home.*

Lucille, too, was aghast at the idea:

> What would I *do* if I left him? I would be absolutely *lost.* I have thought of it often enough, but when I try to imagine what it would be like without him, I know I just couldn't go on without him. I would miss him, strange as it may seem. I just couldn't get along without him.[4]

In rather more eloquent terms the same pattern was brilliantly portrayed by Eugene O'Neill in *A Touch of the Poet.* The "poet" of the title is only a low-born Irishman who held a commission and fought under Wellington in the Napoleonic wars, but was cashiered for amatory indiscretion. He has moved to the United States and spent his years pretending to be an English gentleman. While he drinks, dresses like a lord, and rides a fine horse, his withered little wife runs the failing inn that is their sole support, but she adores his swaggering gallantry, accepts his roaring abuse without a whimper, and ardently defends the ruinous relationship to her daughter in several throbbing speeches about the glory of love. The sad truth, known to playwright and marriage counselor alike, is that a human being may cherish his disease, cling to the source of his pain and self-destruction, and call the whole thing love; more than that, it may *feel* like love to him or her, and which of us can prove to him that it does not?

The panacea, in other words, may itself produce an addiction that is no better than the ills it is supposed to cure. Infidelity is the prime case in point. As we have seen, it was acceptable, normal, and even required in many other times and places; in our own, however, where faithful monogamy is the professed ideal and the general practice, infidelity is often a symptom of some pressure or need over

[4] Case reported by Martha Winch, executive director, Family Service of Highland Park, in Winch, ibid., pp. 314-16.

and above the ordinary.[5] This may be one meaning of Kinsey's revelation that men of the upper educational levels tend to increase their
extramarital activities in their late thirties. Many professional and
business men either reach a career plateau at that time, or see clearly
that their potential success in life has fairly distinct boundaries.
Roughly thirty per cent of them try infidelity, as against half that
many, in their early twenties; like whiskey, it alleviates the feelings
of one's limitations and induces an illusion of general well-being, but
it similarly involves multiple dangers and after-effects.

Even without reference to the Kinsey data or career-satisfaction
studies, most psychiatrists and marriage counselors have long considered neurotic drives the most important ones behind both male
and female infidelity. Behind this lies the Freudian theory of the
development of love from the selfish infantile level to the mature
and giving level, but there is also statistical evidence to support it; in
one careful study of a sizable group of female psychiatric patients
and a comparable group of normal women, six times as many of the
abnormal women had had extramarital affairs. And if one may judge
from the case histories reported by marriage counselors, many of
the men and women who believe they have found real love outside
their marriages have actually chosen highly inappropriate persons
with whom they are unlikely to be better off than they have been.
In the more successfully treated cases, therapy typically results in a
revival of love and sexual enjoyment with the marriage partner, and
a simultaneous fading of the glamour and intensity of the outside
love affair.[6]

And thus once again, as so often in the past, love is a thing of paradoxes. In a society which is not only mechanized and impersonal,
but in which religious and philosophic goals have lost much of their
power, love meets the emotional needs of the individual, gives him
a sense of security, and provides him with much of the impetus and
inspiration to effort. But at the same time modern love has assumed

[5] Fidelity still is the general practice,
though many have supposed that the
Kinsey data prove the contrary. Kinsey
concluded that half of all American husbands are unfaithful at some time or
other, but his figures show that many of
these have had only one or a few scattered episodes, a very different phenomenon, psychologically speaking, from
repeated, habitual, or practiced infidelity.

[6] For the typical psychoanalytic view
of infidelity as neurosis or immaturity,
see Abraham N. Franzblau: *The Road
to Sexual Maturity;* for the comparative
study of normal and abnormal women,
see Carney Landis *et al.: Sex in Development,* especially p. 97; and for case
histories treated successfully, see Emily
Mudd *et al.,* editors: *Marriage Counseling, A Casebook,* Ch. 6.

in the lives of many people the role of a cure-all, or at least an ano-
dyne. The immature, the discontented, the lonely, and the neurotic
all dose themselves with love; like most panaceas, it seems for a
while to lessen their ills, but rarely cures them, and if its analgesic
powers later fail, the ailments may be beyond healing.

6

Who Is Woman? What Is She?

Most of the foregoing treats of love in America as it applies
equally to men and women. Indeed, it was the intention of
the feminists to make all things, love included, apply equally to both
sexes; they expected that when they gained legal and educational
equality, women would desire the same goals in life, work at the
same jobs and careers, live and love as they saw fit, and marry and
rear children without being relegated to the home and required to
depend on man. They were sure that when the goal was reached,
the abilities and personality of woman would be almost indistin-
guishable from those of man, and in the crop-haired, flat-chested
Twenties even the differences in appearance seemed to be diminish-
ing.

But the feminists won their rights two or three decades ago, and
still modern woman is by no means the equal of man. The principal
reason is love itself: she is afraid to be his equal—afraid that it will
cost her the chance for love, and leave her a juiceless old maid. Furthermore, she does not *have* to do the things he does, for in the
name of love he will still pay her way and permit her to be depend-

ent on him. And so she buys love at the price of remaining unequal and inferior, and being discontented with her bargain all her life.

Her inequality, of course, is no longer a matter of law. After the many centuries of woman's subjugation, she is now completely a person at law, with the same rights as man to hold and control money, make contracts, use the courts, and vote for representatives. To be sure, a number of laws remain on the books which restrict her right to work, but they are minor and all ostensibly for her own good: seventeen states, for instance, prohibit her from working in mines, eight will not let her mix or serve liquor in public bars, and almost all the states set limits on the number of hours she may work per day and per week. But by and large these remaining inequities are trifling. The only important one is in her favor, and is more a matter of practice than actual legislation: in defiance of all the facts, it is still assumed by divorce courts throughout the land that as soon as a woman goes to bed with her husband, she becomes permanently helpless and is entitled to life-long support. And herein lies the crux of woman's problem: she is painfully torn between the desire to use her hard-won rights and become as fully developed a being as man, and the desire to be man's temptress, darling, and dependent.

In the course of Western history, women have never been educated equally with men; imperial Rome came the closest, but even then there was no genuine coeducation. Today girls go to the same public schools as boys, and average half a year more education than the boys do, and in college they now get over one third of all degrees granted. All this equips women to want and to perform most of the kinds of work men do. And indeed, in the past sixty years the percentage of all females of working age who have full-time jobs has more than doubled (it is now thirty-seven per cent), while that of wives who work has nearly quintupled (it is now thirty per cent). But what is far more remarkable is the fact that, decades after the major victories of feminism, seventy per cent of American wives still do *not* work, and neither do fully one quarter of all single adult women.

To a man, in our culture, work means not only money but what he *does* and what he *is*. Woman has won equal education and one third of all the jobs in this country, but work remains to her only something she does to earn money. The Department of Labor surveyed 9,000 working women in 1952 and found that only about three per cent worked because of job satisfaction; the rest all did so purely for the money. One sees the career woman in evidence in large Eastern cities and a few other places, and career women are always in the news, but they are still a rarity. Women make up only three per cent of America's dentists, six per cent of its doctors, and one per cent of its U.S. Senators, but sixty-nine per cent of its clerical workers. A generation ago girls who went to college talked earnestly of becoming botanists, psychologists, or scholars; nowadays, although more girls go to college than ever, half of them have no intention of working after they marry, another thirty per cent vaguely hope to combine marriage and motherhood with part-time work, and only twenty per cent are really bent on careers.[7] In the classroom the college girl briefly flares up into a bright flame of talent, intellectual curiosity, and determination; then she graduates and fitfully subsides into an ember on someone's hearth.

Yet it is not easy for her to do so. Although there is no device for measuring the total quantity of satisfaction or dissatisfaction in any society, the overwhelming consensus of such close observers as psychiatrists, sociologists, and marriage counselors is that many American wives suffer from a chronic low-grade dissatisfaction with themselves and with life; they are bored, fearful of "going to seed," fatigued by their duties despite all the mechanization of housekeeping, and jealous of the lives their husbands lead.

The central problem of modern women, causing these dissatisfactions, is known as "role conflict" or "role confusion." The modern woman does not really know what she wants to be; even if she knows, she also has reason for wanting to be something very different. For she still lives in a man's society. Ours is no longer a thoroughgoing patriarchy, but it is still a world in which men give the family and its children their last name, run most businesses and all governments, and are able to philander, gamble, or get drunk at the cost of being criticized but not ruined. And it is a world in which nearly all the gratifications of prestige and importance accrue to men. Of the people listed in *Who's Who*—the criterion of which is to be well known in some form of "useful and reputable achievement"—only six per cent are women. Even if this does not prove homemaking to be useless or disreputable, it unquestionably shows that it does not make one well known.

---

[7] The figures on college girls have been extracted by Dr. Mirra Komarovsky from a number of studies and surveys. See her *Women in the Modern World*, pp. 92–9.

Some sociologists have likened women to Jews, Negroes, and immigrants—persons caught between two worlds, who live amid the upper world but are not part of it, who long to escape from their own group and are ashamed of their desire, who yearn to enter the upper world but resent its members, and who are both defensive and harshly critical of their own kind. Nobody can lampoon a Jew like a Jewish comedian; nobody can paint the female character in as detestable colors as a caustic woman. And very much like the southern Negro who grins, cackles, and shuffles in order to make the white man feel safe, modern woman often adopts the role of the "sweet thing" and the nitwit so as not to frighten men away. On two different campuses, roughly four out of every ten undergraduate women admitted to surveyors that they "played dumb" with interesting men, deliberately misspelled occasional words, and on dates consciously adopted the "I-don't-care-anything-you-want-to-do" stance.

The potential fear they are trying to allay is no mere illusion. In our society, success, generally equated with love, is for men specifically equated with masculinity. Many a male feels genuinely alarmed by a woman who can match wits with him, beat him in a debate, more quickly solve a problem in calculus, or write a better piece of advertising copy. He uneasily tells himself she is "cold" and "unfeminine," but at the unconscious level he feels a threat to his traditional male superiority and hence to his very potency. No wonder he shuns her; no wonder the career woman so often remains single.

But the noncareer woman is also caught between two worlds, and her jealousy of the male and suppressed desire to compete with him frequently reappear after marriage in the form of attempts to dominate him by nagging, or hostile criticism of his shortcomings and lack of success, and the like. The man often reacts as though it were literally his maleness which she criticized; according to Dr. Karl Menninger, for every woman who complains of her husband's excessive virility, a dozen complain of their husband's sexual apathy or impotence.

If woman were really certain of her nature and character, she might not suffer from these uncertainties and conflicts. Suppose, for instance, that all those things were true that scornful and domineering men have been saying about her for 2,500 years. Suppose she were really less intelligent than he, weak, vain, and wanton, designed

by God to live under man's dominion, and intended by nature to devote herself to making man happy. If all this were true and she believed it, she could accept her exclusion from the affairs of the world
without serious misgivings and accept the nurturing and homemaking role as the best that fate had given her.

But her equal education has made her want the things of the masculine world and shown her she can do its worthwhile work as well
as he; moreover, modern psychology has made it plain to her that
her intelligence is the equal of his and that most of the differences
between feminine and masculine abilities are acquired rather than
innate. Sir Thomas More once found one of his daughters in tears
over a difficult Latin text she was working on; gently he took it
away from her and told her that such difficult mental effort was not
for women. But to a century which has seen women like Marie
Curie, Eleanor Roosevelt, Marianne Moore, Madame Pandit, Margaret Mead, and Suzanne Langer, Sir Thomas looks more like a
medieval gentleman than a Renaissance one. (And medievalism of
that sort was still a part even of the nineteenth century; it was Kings-
ley who wrote that incredible line, "Be good, sweet maid, and let
who can be clever.") It is not really her *abilities* modern woman is
unsure of, but her *nature;* even if she has talents, she feels herself
trapped in a recalcitrant body, a gentle prison in which it seems
abnormal and unnatural to use those talents. The threat she most
fears is that if she does try to use them, she will become unlovable.

In a seeming resurgence of traditional ideas, a chorus of voices
has been raised in the past fifteen years, assuring woman that to win
love she must accept the dictates of nature and content herself with
being a fond, emotional, subservient homebody. It is particularly
impressive when the voice is that of an extremely wealthy and successful career woman. Marlene Dietrich, for instance, advised modern woman in a recent issue of the *Ladies' Home Journal* to accept
her husband's superiority without so much as the tiniest doubt, complaint, or wish of one's own. "Love him," she urged, "uncondition-
ally and with devotion. You chose him. He must be wonderful." In
practical terms, Miss Dietrich explained, this meant adapting one's
self completely to his needs and whims, worshipping him and treat-
ing him as the unquestioned lord and master of the house, pampering
and comforting him, and devoting full time to making him happy
without thought of one's self. Even Alfred Tennyson—no, even
Tertullian—was not more patriarchal.

In recent years there has been a good deal of such writing (though not all so extreme) by social critics, educators, and others, but the psychoanalysts have been the major intellectual power behind modern antifeminism. Oddly enough, Freud himself is responsible; although he seemed an ally of the feminists two generations ago, he actually had a thoroughly Victorian outlook on woman's proper role. In 1883, long before he had theoretical grounds for his beliefs, he wrote to his fiancée, Martha Bernays, as follows:

> It is really a stillborn thought to send women into the struggle for existence exactly as men. If, for instance, I imagined my gentle sweet girl as a competitor it would only end in my telling her, as I did seventeen months ago, that I am fond of her and that I implore her to withdraw from the strife into the calm uncompetitive activity of my home. It is possible that changes in upbringing may suppress all a woman's tender attributes, needful of protection and yet so victorious. . . . Nature has determined woman's destiny through beauty, charm, and sweetness. . . .

This is plainly only run-of-the-mill nineteenth-century patriarchalism. But years later, when Freud was struggling to theorize about the character of woman, he decided that the determining factor in her psychological development was the realization that nature had failed to provide her with the admirable equipment boys possess. The result was that she felt painfully inferior, and by way of adjustment assumed a passive, submissive, and dependent role in life. The "normal" woman turned to dependency and domesticity; the woman who sought a career could only be suffering from neurosis or a "masculinity complex." Freud thus provided himself with a theoretical justification for those Victorian prejudices with which he was already equipped, and took for natural laws the ephemeral opinions of his own time. Yet he seems to have sensed the fact of his own rationalization, for years afterwards he said to a dear friend: "The great question that has never been answered and which I have not yet been able to answer, despite my thirty years of research into the feminine soul, is: *What does woman want?*" [8]

[8] This theory of female personality can be found in "Psychology of Women" in his *New Introductory Lectures on Psycho-Analysis*. Although many psychoanalysts have followed Freud in this, some, at least, have held that he mistook effect for cause, and that penis envy is not so much an inevitable cause of woman's inferiority as one more proof that, in a man's world, she would like to be a man. Dr. Abram Kardiner has criticized the Freudian theory from this standpoint in *Sex and Morality*, pp. 46–8. So have Karen Horney and Clara Thompson; see the discussion citing them and others in Viola Klein: *The Feminine Character*, pp. 72–85.

Many contemporary psychoanalysts accept his theory about women but not his doubts. Typically, a well-known two-volume *Psychology of Women* by Dr. Helene Deutsch develops its whole scheme of the female personality on the assumption of a "genital trauma" which occurs when the girl realizes her own shortage of external plumbing. The inclination of psychoanalysts of this persuasion has been to urge women—as Freud did—to stay at home and *be women*. Perhaps the most familiar exposition of this view was the one made in 1941 by that well-known analysand Moss Hart in the form of his delightful but clearly didactic show *Lady in the Dark;* the lady, a successful but unhappy editor, found love and a sense of identity as a woman only when she relinquished her top job to her male assistant, married him, and presumably settled down in a healthful atmosphere of chintz, roast beef, diapers, and rosebushes.

An even more thoroughgoing advocate of traditionalism is the psychoanalyst Dr. Marynia Farnham, who calls modern woman "the lost sex," and claims that her neuroses and dissatisfactions are due solely to her failure in love—a failure which comes from her inability to be a real woman. The trouble is the lack of prestige accorded to real womanhood; Dr. Farnham and her collaborator Ferdinand Lundberg therefore suggest that our government re-establish the dignity of womanhood by such means as giving honorary degrees and cash grants to good mothers, and energetically teaching and repeating the doctrine that careers are "not generally desirable for women . . . [and are] the disordered fantasies of the masculine-complex woman." The individual woman can find ample means of self-expression and achievement in returning to the handicraft stage of housekeeping, and making her own bread, canning her own food, sewing her own curtains, and the like. "Very possibly," wrote Dr. Farnham and Mr. Lundberg, "good food is no more susceptible of commercial exploitation than mother love. . . . The decline of woman's interest in food preparation parallels the decline in many of them of the capacity for affection."

But it is a vain hope. Ruskin, Gandhi, and other reformers have tried at various times to restore a changing morality by calling for a return to older ways; but when it means giving up increased productivity and returning to a more difficult struggle for existence, mankind ignores the advice. Dr. Farnham and analysts of a like viewpoint may convince a few hundred patients to take their expensive advice, but the Industrial Revolution is not likely to be easily undone. Females of the poorer and even middle classes cannot afford the luxury of playing frontierswomen; more than that, society itself could not survive the abandonment of the productive power that has helped fill the globe with people. In any case, it is far from certain that baking bread and canning peaches would produce true love; modern man's motives in seeking a woman are not, as we have seen, those of a householder in search of a housekeeper, but those of a human being in need of emotional satisfaction.

The fact is that to a woman who has been trained during twelve years of school and four of college to be interested in many things, the routines of housework are as dull and at least as time-consuming as the most tedious assembly-line job. Even in the age of mechanization, a woman with three children and no servant has thirty-five beds to make per week, 170 pounds of food to prepare, and 750 items of glass and 400 of silver to wash (which involves a lot of handling even with an automatic dishwasher). Next week it all starts again. Important as her children and husband may be, the chores themselves occupy most of her time; she may be pardoned for not finding in them an adequate meaning to life or definition of womanhood. The following letter from the twenty-five-year-old wife of a college instructor in a large city, offered by Professor Mirra Komarovsky as typical of many she has received, exhibits nearly all the problems of modern woman in microcosm:

> Believe me there is not enough stimulation in the incessant dishwashing, picking up, ironing, folding diapers, dressing and undressing the kids, making beds day in and day out. My social life with the other mothers on the park benches is depressing. I cannot get them away from the same old talk. . . . My husband is very sympathetic and tries to help me on weekends, but he has his own work to do and must be allowed to do it if he is to advance in his job. I must confess I envy him. Here we were two college students, he a few years ahead, each interested in his own field. I majored in art and as you know even had some ambitions of my own. Now he still has a very interesting life. He meets in the course of the day some of the most interesting people in his field. Even his daily lunch at the Faculty Club is more exciting than anything that happens to me.

But the significant thing is that this young woman voluntarily accepted her self-denying role (for mothers *can* work these days, if they really want to), in order to solve her dilemma of role conflict —and only ended up pitying herself and envying her husband. In such an atmosphere, love is lucky to thrive; lucky, even to survive.

But for all the discomforts and frustrations of her choice, there has been an unmistakable trend since the war for women to accept their traditional place in the home, though without their ancient submissiveness. Not only are they marrying younger, but they are having children earlier and in larger numbers. The rise in fertility is by no means a phenomenon only of the upper-middle-class suburbs; taking all women throughout the nation, those between twenty and twenty-four years old had thirty-two per cent more children in 1957 than did women of the same age range only seven years earlier, while the average for all women of childbearing age went up twenty-two per cent. The average family size, to be sure, has increased only slightly so far: there is no evidence of a movement toward the large old-fashioned family of early America, but childless or one-child families are becoming less frequent, while two-child and three-child families are increasing. As usual, the poor and the rich are having more children than the middle economic groups, but the national tendency at the moment seems to be in the direction of the three-child family.

The young American woman is thus muddling through her major dilemma by several kinds of compromises, all only moderately satisfactory; meanwhile, for the most part she ignores another one that is clearly in store for her. For by choosing early marriage and early motherhood, and abandoning any serious lifelong planning for career and work, she inevitably condemns herself to nearly half a life of the so-called empty nest. Her three children will all be in school when she is in her early thirties, and the youngest will be a self-sufficient teen-ager when she is still under forty. With over thirty years of life ahead of her, at least twenty of which represent the very pinnacle of her powers as a personality, she has nothing worthwhile to do—neither continuing reproduction nor career to give her a genuine purpose in life. Bored, useless, and disconnected, her emotional needs may again become very great—greater than her familiar, preoccupied husband can meet. The Kinsey figures seem to bear this out: the percentage of female infidelity is at its maximum for women in their mid-thirties and early forties. Whether or not they find what they are seeking, the data do not say; but that they are seeking something more than mere "outlet" seems beyond reasonable doubt.

Some students of modern woman have suggested a less unsatisfactory compromise. Professor Komarovsky, Alva Myrdal, and others reject the thesis that womanliness lies in homemaking and childbearing. They agree that the well-being of society depends on adequate mothering of young children, and, furthermore, that the biology of woman predisposes her to find genuine fulfillment in childbearing and mothering. But these are not identical with house-work, and chores are not a substitute for a purpose in life. They suggest that the young woman pursue a career or a job seriously until she is certain that she can re-enter it even after an extended furlough; then she can take her leave and pursue her other role in life, working only part time or not at all, but making generous use of the child-care facilities of co-operative sitting pools, nurseries, and camps, to gain leisure for herself so as to engage in stimulating activities. Finally, when her youngest child enters school, she can begin to re-enter her working life part time, and then full time. If she devotes twenty-five years to it, from the age of forty on, she will have had almost as much time at her career as did men a cen-tury ago.

But all this is not yet actuality; it is only the recommendation and hope of certain moderate contemporary feminists. Whether it has any likelihood of being realized it is impossible to say. For the time being, most American women seem to be solving their role conflicts by accepting the conservative answer. In their uncertainty as to what they are, they make a choice, but many of them are not wholly happy with it afterwards; they bargain away their other selves for love, and are seldom completely convinced that they paid the right price for it.

7

Grand Design, with Flaws

❀   ❀

❀

Despite the faults of latter-day romanticism, the weaknesses of love as a cure-all, and the discontents of modern woman, history shows an erratic but seemingly purposeful movement toward the present-day pattern of love. Although the Dark Ages and the Enlightenment were major reversals of direction, the long-term movement towards the joining of romantic passion, sensuous enjoyment, friendship, and marriage has about it such seeming inevitability that Lionel Trilling has even spoken of "the dialectic of the history of love." Like the Victorians, we often believe that our present way of love is the ideal and ultimate one at which history has been aiming all along.

Advertising art assures us of this with its endless images of handsome young smiling Dad, pretty young smiling Mom, jolly freckled smiling children, all in an environment of house, car, freezer, and perky almost-smiling dog. Newspapers, television, and magazines reinforce the image of the family as an amiable democratic team in which, from time to time (as one may intimate from the misty mood of the ad in which Dad is slipping a bracelet on Mom's wrist), romance exists and finds its expression when the children are sleeping.

A quite different interpretation of modern marriage is available in the strictures of such social critics as Philip Wylie, in the endless flow of studies and articles on divorce, and in the acidulous accounts by fiction-writers of suburban boredom, ambitious wives, harried and disenchanted husbands, and grubby experiments in adultery. From all of this, it is fairly evident that the modern form of love is something less than perfect, and every critic is ready and willing to

[389]

lay the blame someplace. The laying of blame is not our business in this book, but since we have observed the positive values of modern marriage, it behooves us to notice also its conflicts and imperfections.

One of them, of course, is the dilemma of modern woman which we have just seen to be deeply rooted in the culture and unlikely to be solved soon. Even more basic is a conflict felt by men and women alike, present in nearly every society but greatly exaggerated in our own. It is an artificially created discontinuity, contradicting biology for society's sake, that requires every child to be thoroughly sexless during his formative years, but suddenly become sexual as an adult. Moreover, it particularly prohibits the sexual impulses he feels toward his parents even while teaching him to love his father and mother and to be affectionate toward them. Herein lies the primary disconnection between love and sex, peculiar to man among all animals, and the source of all those tangled, tortured arguments throughout the ages about the relationship between them.

The Greeks, according to Demosthenes, tried a solution-by-specialization: they had concubines, hetaerae, and wives, for sex, love, and housekeeping respectively. But with the advent of ascetic Christianity, the primal disconnection became so severe that men almost supposed love and sex to be antithetical; even the amorous medieval knights had to keep love partly desexualized in order to be comfortable with it, and the Victorians, similarly, when they moved love into marriage and at the same time made mothers of their wives, had to repair to brothels for their lustier moods. Our present society has kept something of the Christian condemnation of sex and blended it (but poorly) with the rational and scientific ideas emerging from the sex revolution. Each person's life is an inconsistent mixture of the two. In the first decade of life the boy and girl learn that love is good and sex is evil; in the second decade that love is still better, while sex has been slightly upgraded to the status of a forbidden fruit; and in the third decade that love is better than ever, while sex has suddenly become normal and healthful and is, in fact, a major means of expressing one's higher sentiments.[9]

[9] Sexual love within marriage has become generally accepted as not primarily a means of procreation, but an affectionate, pleasure-giving end in itself. In a major survey in 1947, it was shown that among the relatively fertile four fifths of a large sample of married couples in Indianapolis, ninety-eight per cent tried to control the number and spacing of births by various contraceptive measures; see P. K. Whelpton and C. V. Kiser in *Milbank Memorial Fund Quarterly*, Jan. 1947, pp. 63–111. The official position of the Catholic church

But the disconnections in each person's life are not easily repaired after twenty-odd years of conditioning. The files of doctors and marriage counselors are filled with the case histories of young people who have joyfully entered marriage only to find that disgust, frigidity, impotence, vaginismus, and similar surprises awaited them to blight their love, and although the evidence indicates that these afflictions are less common than in Victorian times, they are still all too frequent. Even with large samples of supposedly normal people it has been found that by and large the sexual relationship is the slowest of all major areas of marital adjustment to become genuinely satisfactory—and this in a country that is absorbed and fascinated by sex, greatly values sex appeal, and prides itself on its frankness and modernness in sex matters.

Contemporary marriage upholds the ideal of sexual equality between husband and wife, yet here too remains a built-in contradiction. Despite all the changes brought by the sexual revolution, girls are still supposed to be chary of their favors before marriage (while the boy takes all he can get), and to be at once sexually attractive and yet reserved and inexperienced. Many a modern girl, for all her freedoms, is astonishingly ignorant of the usual or average feelings of other women concerning sex; situations like the following—recently reported by a psychologist doing marriage counseling—are far more common than one would suppose:

> *Mrs. N. (an attractive young woman from New England)*: Do you think my husband is normal or is he oversexual? He wants it two or three times a week.
> *Counselor:* Two or three times a week sounds very normal for a man his age. And I am sure that a great many wives would feel disappointed if their husbands didn't want it that frequently.
> *Mrs. N. (incredulous)*: You mean there are *women* who really want it that often?

Although actual physiological reasons for female frigidity are extremely rare, the extensive records of the Margaret Sanger Research Bureau and the findings of various investigators indicate that about one out of four women is sexually unresponsive, having feelings about the sex act ranging from disinterest to violent disgust;

---

remains basically unchanged, but the Archdiocese of New York, in reaffirming procreation as the God-appointed purpose of marriage during a 1958 controversy, added: "This does not deny secondary purposes for the exercise of the generative faculties of men, as the expression of love between husband and wife."

among men, however, the proportion of total unresponsiveness is
only about one per cent in youth, and does not match the female
ratio until age seventy.

Not all the contradictions in modern marriage involve sex, however. One of the more serious ones, for instance, exists between the
vastly increased importance of marriage and its greatly diminished
structural strength. Gone are the bonds of law and religion that
once made divorce all but impossible; gone from the family are its
valuable food-raising, medicine-making, and other productive functions; gone, for the most part, are its responsibilities for education,
defense, and security against age and disease. In place of all these
values, modern marriage offers primarily sex, affection, and companionship; even the decision to have children is made largely on the
basis of expected pleasure. Unlike food, marriage does not fill a vital
need, and no one dies without it; it is a way to seek that highly valued, but nonessential, commodity, happiness. But having no vital
functions it alone can perform, a marriage stands or falls precisely
according to whether it does or does not yield happiness—a fragile
and slippery basis of existence. In past centuries an unhappy husband
or wife sought ways to get along with minimum discomfort, but
did not live in constant fear of seeing his or her world shattered; today an unhappy husband or wife lies rigidly awake in the night,
turning over and over the sickening prospect of dissolving the partnership and starting the long dismal process of trying to build another one. In past centuries the functional family was a large, close
association of loyal relatives who knew each other's troubles and
were ready to help each other in any crisis; today the marriage of
love requires privacy and isolation, and when troubles or crises
come, husband and wife must wrestle with them at home alone and
assume the inevitable look of optimism as they step out the front
door.

The weaknesses and the hedonistic basis of modern marriage have
led to many gloomy predictions about it. Two decades ago, for example, the sociologist Pitirim Sorokin made this glum pronuncia-
mento:

> Divorces and separations will increase until any profound dif-
> ference between socially sanctioned marriages and illicit sex-rela-
> tionship disappears. . . . The main sociocultural functions of the
> family will further decrease until the family becomes a mere inci-

dental cohabitation of male and female, while the home will become a mere overnight parking place mainly for sex-relationship.

But the forecast was thoroughly and embarrassingly wrong. The divorce rate has been fairly steady for nearly a decade at a level far below its 1946 peak; as for the rest, the valuation of marriage has, as we have seen, tended to prize it more as a vehicle of love and emotional security than as a convenient means of copulation.

As opposed to the view of marriage as a casual meeting for coitus, many contemporary observers agree that the most distinctive characteristic of modern marriage is the extent to which it yields a merger or identification of the husband and wife with each other in every aspect of their lives. Their personalities so completely interact in all roles and at all levels that they seem to be genuinely intermingled and fused, each individual coming to have desires, to think, and to act in terms of the composite ego rather than of his own alone.

This, too, though greatly prized by modern lovers, is achieved at the cost of a contradiction. For where the merging and adjustment become total over a period of years, a dependency may be established so great that the death of one partner becomes an almost irreparable blow to the other; even the absence of one of them on a trip may produce in both waves of irrational paniclike anxiety. In primitive society or the societies of earlier centuries in Europe, the death of one spouse was the death of only a small fraction of one's self; today the fraction is a half, and the sundered remainder has all it can do to survive.

Apart from death or separation anxiety, the total merger of the selves over the years also may produce the irony of a relationship in which there is no longer anything to give each other, no unexpected riches to offer, no private chambers of the mind from which to step forth refreshed and desirable into the beloved one's sight. Margaret Mead says that such husbands and wives "have become so much like a single person that, like most individuals in America, they feel the need of others to complete themselves, to reassure them that they are good, to rid them of the self-searching that comes from being left alone." The young lovers are all in all to each other, utterly comforted in their isolation; the middle-aged couple may, in the same circumstances, feel desperately alone and in need of someone else to talk to, play cards with, just *be* with. Modern love is a nourishing, but it can also be a devouring; two can consume each other and have nothing left when hunger returns.

The merger of personalities, even when it avoids the danger of mutual devouring, runs into still another conflict with the basic mammalian sexual pattern. By and large, faithful monogamy does not seem to be a natural pattern, but a socially fabricated one; even so, it is rare to the point of seeming almost abnormal. Of one hundred and eighty-five societies analyzed in the Human Relations Area Files at Yale University, only about five per cent were monogamies in which all outside sexual activity for men was disallowed or disapproved. Fidelity thus seems to some scholars difficult, unnatural, and greatly overpriced, and the insistence on it the cause of hypocrisy, guilt, unhappiness, and broken marriage. All this is the product of the identification of the selves, for infidelity is a sharing of a very intense experience with someone other than one's principal love partner, and therefore it breaches the merger. Even if the infidelity is perfectly concealed, it sets up in one person hostile barriers and dark places into which the other cannot penetrate. Dr. Abraham Stone has reported that in nearly three decades of marriage counseling he has found infidelity almost never innocuous, but practically always a cause of concealment, guilt, and impairment of personality interaction and total love.

Nevertheless, the discomforts of fidelity may be the price at which one buys considerable happiness and stability in marriage. Men in the lower economic and educational groups, according to the Kinsey studies, are both less apt to link sex to tender and affectionate relationships, and far more likely to indulge in extramarital coitus, than men of higher education and economic status. But in the context of our society, this simplicity and freedom does not make for stability or satisfaction in marriage as it has in some other societies and as people like Havelock Ellis and Bertrand Russell had hoped. For although the divorce rate is often thought to be highest among the neurotic, success-driven middle class, actually it is highest among the lower economic classes: national census data show that men earning less than $3,000 a year are two to four times as likely to be divorced as men earning over $4,000 a year.[2]

How shall one finally judge the vitality and health of modern love? Biologically and socially it is clearly successful, for it is pro-

[2] William J. Goode: *After Divorce*, pp. 53–4.

viding a more than adequate supply of children, making marriage more popular than ever, and providing what seems to be a reasonable stability in family life, as judged by the present plateau of the divorce rate. But in view of all its internal conflicts and tensions, is it proving successful in terms of its own major promise—the promise of happiness?

Many professional studies have been made on this very point, but the results vary widely, with as few as forty-two per cent and as many as eighty-eight per cent of the husbands and wives interviewed claiming to be happy in their marriages. The width of this range is due to many causes, but the principal one is the inability of the researchers to make the word happiness precise or to measure it in accurate units. Yet despite this grave shortcoming, most of the results point significantly in one direction: a guesswork summary of them is that some seventy-five per cent of the married people in the United States are happy in their marriages.[3] There is no way to prove statistically that this figure exceeds the average happiness of Athenian men and women, or medieval knights and ladies, or the good proper people of Victorian times, but the evidence we have seen certainly would make us suspect, on a subjective basis, that it does.

The most impressive fact is that in a time when divorce is generally easy to get and relatively acceptable to society, the great majority of Americans prefer to accept what happiness marriage has brought them rather than seek further for it. They may not have realized their daydreams, but they have found something they are willing to accept as a realistic substitute; few people have ever loved superbly, and few really expect to, but many are moderately well pleased with the love they have. This is, after all, Earth, not Heaven.

---

[3] The summary is that of Clifford Kirkpatrick in *The Family*, p. 448. The major surveys have been by Davis, Terman, Burgess and Cottrell, Lang, and Hamilton.

8

Conclusion

❀ ❀

❀

Looking through the history of Western love, we can see how love changed both in importance and in quality as primitive clans grew into city-states and then into nations, as agricultural and feudal societies turned into industrial ones, and as theocracy yielded slowly to democracy. We can perceive the shaping influence on love of family structure and of woman's position; we can discern the molding of love by philosophy and by the growth of leisure; we can watch the flourishing and proliferation of love in the climate of urban loneliness and insecurity. But all these factors only modify love and determine the limits of its importance; they do not offer an explanation as to what prime mover sets it in motion and provides its momentum. Though they have directed, deflected, or enlarged the affectional needs in a variety of ways, we may still wonder why there are such needs at all and from what source they draw their strength.

A number of answers have been offered in modern times. Freud believed that the ultimate secret of love's power was biological, and derived from the imperious libido. The sex drive, he held, is first directed by every child toward his parents, but being severely prohibited in that direction, it is transmuted into acceptable forms of affection; love, in other words, is "aim-inhibited sexuality." Other students of man also suggest that biology is the source of love's power, but in quite a different fashion. Ashley Montagu points out that the young of many animals, including man, react favorably and healthfully (in terms of better digestion and circulation, for instance) to gentle touching, stroking, and comforting; sensuous stimulation is structurally linked to total creature health, and the emotion of love therefore draws its power from the instinct of self-preservation, the most basic of them all. In complete contrast, the Jesuit student Father M. C. d'Arcy will have none of this; like many another theologian, he learnedly argues that human love is a mighty force only because it succeeds in palely imitating divine love: even the poor copy has about it something of the greatness of the original.

Curiously enough, psychoanalyst Erich Fromm holds a somewhat comparable view; he argues that the strength of mature love derives from its allowing one to become parentlike (or godlike), giving without thought of return. But Edmund Bergler, another psychoanalyst, speculates in rather gloomier vein that all love originates in self-love: it is, so to speak, a reflecting-back from someone else of one's own self-worship—a kind of emotional moonlight mistaken for the light of the sun. Worse yet, some sociologists think that much of love's power is mere "cultural expectation," or learned behavior without ultimate biological or emotional roots; if they are right, they are only restating more ponderously the caustic observation of La Rochefoucauld that "people would never fall in love if they had not heard love talked about."

But it has not been our business here to decide which, if any, of these explanations of love's power is the correct one. We set out to collect and describe, rather than to create a philosophy or elaborate a metaphysic. We have therefore limited ourselves to observing love's power as it makes itself manifest, rather than seeking for its quiddity, its essence: we have seen how love sometimes harms and sometimes benefits men and women, how it is sometimes nothing more than a game but sometimes almost a religion, how it is sometimes only a cruel sport and yet again is sometimes a partial remedy for life's ills. Above all, we have seen love's ways passing down the centuries and found modern love to be a composite and patchwork of much that has gone before, a *pasticcio* of ancient and modern, mystical and rational, sacred and profane. If not in any final metaphysical sense, each of us has seen enough to say, like Virgil's shepherd in his moment of illumination: *Nunc scio quid sit Amor*— Now do I know what love is.

Notes on Sources

❀   ❀

❀

"A man will turn over half a library to make one book," said
Dr. Johnson. Even if this is a trifle exaggerated, space does
not permit me to give a complete bibliography of the sources consulted, much less of those I might have looked at but decided to
pass by. But for the benefit of any who may wish to extend their
reading on the subject of this book, I have listed here chapter by
chapter almost every source mentioned in the text or footnotes,
giving bibliographical information for those not easy to find, and
for modern works; in addition I have included the other principal
sources I drew on, even when not specifically named or alluded to
in the text or footnotes.

CHAPTER I: *Introduction*

FOR GENERAL DISCUSSIONS of the nature of love from several very
dissimilar contemporary points of view, see the works listed below by Huxley, Ortega y Gasset, and Fromm, and the little anthology by Montagu, *The Meaning of Love*. Montagu's *The Direction of Human Development* and La Barre's *The Human
Animal* are both excellent interdisciplinary studies of human nature and culture, and both discuss love from the biological, sociological, and psychological viewpoints. Of the general histories of
love, the one by Lewinsohn (published too late to be cited or used
in this book) is excellent, though its emphasis is more on sexual
mores than the emotional meaning of love itself. Taylor sketches
sexual history in the West in psychoanalytic and sociological
terms, and much sexual and marital history is scattered throughout the old but indispensable work of Ellis. The monumental
work by Westermarck, and the briefer one by Müller-Lyer are

dated, but give a still-useful panorama of marital patterns among primitives and civilized peoples. Love among the primitives, as reported by more modern anthropologists, can be found in the works by Danielsson, Firth, Kaberry, Mead, Richards, and Schapera; the somewhat older books by Briffault and Malinowski take opposite points of view and are both still useful, and the still older one by Sumner continues to be an indispensable mine of data. The questions of the relation between fiction and reality, and the unreliability of fiction as primary evidence of human behavior, are discussed by Jones, Lesser, and Lucas.

Bölsche, Wilhelm: *Love-Life in Nature*. London: Jonathan Cape; 1931. First published in German in 1900.

Briffault, Robert: *The Mothers*. New York: The Macmillan Company; 1927. A massive three-volume anthropological study of sex and love.

—— and Bronislaw Malinowski: *Marriage: Past and Present*. Boston: Porter Edward Sargent; 1956. A reprint of a series of radio debates in 1930 on primitive love.

Danielsson, Bengt: *Love in the South Seas*. New York: Reynal & Co.; 1956.

Descartes, René: "The Passions of the Soul," in *Selections*, edited by R. M. Eaton. New York: Charles Scribner's Sons; 1927.

Ellis, Havelock: *Studies in the Psychology of Sex*. Philadelphia: F. A. Davis; 1901–28. Of the seven volumes, Vols. I, III, IV, and VI are particularly useful for the historian of love.

Firth, Raymond: *We, the Tikopia*. London: George Allen & Unwin; 1936.

Freud, Sigmund: *Civilization and Its Discontents*. London: The Hogarth Press and The Institute of Psycho-Analysis; 1939.

Fromm, Erich: *The Art of Loving*. New York: Harper & Bros.; 1956.

Huxley, Julian: *New Bottles for New Wine*. New York: Harper & Bros.; 1957. Has an excellent chapter on love.

Jones, Ernest: *Essays in Applied Psycho-Analysis*. London: The International Psycho-Analytical Press; 1923.

Kaberry, Phyllis M.: *Aboriginal Woman, Sacred and Profane*. London: George Routledge & Sons; 1939.

La Barre, Weston: *The Human Animal*. Chicago: University of Chicago Press; 1954.

Ladies Dictionary, The (anon.). London: J. Dunton; 1694.

Lesser, Simon O.: *Fiction and the Unconscious*. Boston: Beacon Press; 1957.

Lewinsohn, Richard: *A History of Sexual Customs*. New York: Harper & Bros.; 1959.

Lodge, Henry Cabot: *Studies in History*. Boston: Houghton Mifflin Co.; 1884.

Lucas, F. L.: *Literature and Psychiatry*. Ann Arbor: University of Michigan Press; 1957.

Malinowski, Bronislaw: *The Sexual Life of Savages in North-Western Melanesia*. New York: Halcyon House; 1929.

Mantegazza, Paolo: *The Physiology of Love*. New York: Cleveland Publishing Co.; 1894.

Mead, Margaret: *Coming of Age in Samoa*. New York: New American Library; 1949.

Montagu, M. F. Ashley: *The Direction of Human Development*. New York: Harper & Bros.; 1955.

——, ed.: *The Meaning of Love*. New York: The Julian Press; 1953.

Müller-Lyer, F. C.: *The Evolution of Modern Marriage*. London: Allen & Unwin; 1930. First published in 1913.

Ortega y Gasset, José: *On Love*. New York: Greenwich Editions; 1957.

Plato: *Symposium*.

Plutarch: *Conjugal Precepts*.

Putnam, Emily: *The Lady*. New York: Sturgis & Walton; 1910.

Richards, Audrey J.: *Bemba Marriage and Present Economic Conditions*. Livingstone, Northern Rhodesia: The Rhodes-Livingstone Institute; 1940.

Schapera, I.: *Married Life in an African Tribe*. London: Faber & Faber; 1940.

Sewall, Samuel: *Diary of Samuel Sewall: Collections of the Massasetts Historical Society*, 5th series, Vols. V–VII (1878–82).

Sumner, William Graham, and A. G. Keller: *The Science of Society*. New Haven: Yale University Press; 1927. Written, in large part, prior to 1906.

Taylor, G. Rattray: *Sex in History*. New York: Vanguard Press; 1954.

Westermarck, Edward: *The History of Human Marriage*. New York: The Allerton Book Co.; 1922. First published in 1889.

CHAPTER II: *Dilemma in Greece*

AMONG THE GENERAL SECONDARY SOURCES which include useful introductions to Greek love are the books listed here by Durant, Robinson, and Wright; the older works by Blümner, Gulick, Mahaffy, and Tucker sometimes sound a trifle Victorian, but are still excellent standard references. The primary sources have already received special singling out in the text. On the subject of Greek character structure and the distinctions between shame cultures and guilt cultures, see the works by Benedict, Dodds, and Piers.

Aristotle: *De Generationa Animalium*, II, i, iii. *Ethica Nichomachea*, VII, iv, and VIII, iii. *Politica*, II, iv.

Athenaeus: *The Deipnosophists*, Book XIII.

Benedict, Ruth: *The Chrysanthemum and the Sword*. Boston: Houghton Mifflin Company; 1946.

Benson, E. F.: *The Life of Alcibiades*. London: Ernest Benn; 1928.

Blümner, H.: *The Home Life of the Ancient Greeks*. New York: Cassell & Co.; 1893.

Butler, Samuel: *The Authoress of the Odyssey*. London: Longmans & Co.; 1897.

Demosthenes: "Against Neaera," and "Erotic Oration."

Diogenes Laertius: "Socrates," in his *Lives*.

Dodds, E. R.: *The Greeks and the Irrational*. Berkeley: University of California Press; 1951.

Döllinger, J. J. I.: *The Gentile and the Jew in the Courts of the Temple of Christ*. London: Gibbings & Co.; 1906. Originally published in 1857.

Durant, Will: *The Life of Greece*. New York: Simon and Schuster; 1939.

Finley, Moses I.: *The World of Odysseus*. New York: Viking Press; 1954.

Greek Anthology (*Anthologia Graeca*). With a translation by W. R. Paton. New York: G. P. Putnam's Sons; 1916–18.

Gulick, C. B.: *The Life of the Ancient Greeks*. New York: D. Appleton & Co.; 1902.

Herodotus: *Historiae*, III, 118 (on Intaphernes).

Homer: *Iliad. Odyssey.*

Jones, W. H. S.: *Greek Morality.* London: Blackie & Sons; 1906.

Keller, A. G.: *Homeric Society.* New York: Longmans, Green & Co.; 1902.

La Barre, Weston: *The Human Animal.* Chicago: University of Chicago Press; 1954.

LaCroix, Paul: *History of Prostitution.* Chicago: P. Covici; 1926.

Lyra Graeca, edited and translated by J. M. Edmonds. New York: G. P. Putnam's Sons; 1928. Contains all of extant Sapphic fragments, and all the classical biographical evidence about her.

Machon. Quoted extensively in Athenaeus, q.v.

Mahaffy, J. P.: *Social Life in Greece.* London: Macmillan & Co.; 1925. First published in 1874.

Piers, Gerhart, and M. B. Singer: *Shame and Guilt.* Springfield, Ill.:

C. C. Thomas; 1953.

Plato: *Charmides. Laws. Lysis. Menexenus. Phaedrus. Republic. Symposium.*

Plutarch: "Alcibiades," "Demetrius," and "Pericles," in *Lives. Conjugal Precepts. Of Love.*

Robinson, C. E.: *Everyday Life in Ancient Greece.* Oxford: Oxford University Press; 1933.

Sappho. See *Lyra Graeca*, Vol. I, for biography and extant poems.

Theocritus: *Idylls.*

Tucker, T. G.: *Life in Ancient Athens.* Chautauqua: Chautauqua Press; 1917.

Weigall, Arthur: *Sappho of Lesbos.* New York: F. A. Stokes Co.; 1932.

Westermarck, Edward: *The Origin and Development of the Moral Ideas.* London: Macmillan & Co.; 1917.

Wright, F. A.: *Greek Social Life.* London: J. M. Dent; 1925.

Xenophon: *Oeconomicus. Memorabilia. Symposium.*

CHAPTER III: *Bread and Circuses, Love and Games*

A GOOD MODERN SURVEY of Roman sexual customs and love can be found in the book by Carcopino; the old work by Friedländer is still marvelous and gives some special attention to sex and love. For biography, topical studies, and general background, the standard sources include Pauly, Daremberg, and the *Cambridge Ancient History*. Lecky's history of morals is Victorian in tone, but remarkable for scholarship. Goodsell's history, covering much of the same ground, is briefer and modern in tone.

Boak, E. R.: *Manpower Shortage and the Fall of the Roman Empire in the West.* Ann Arbor: University of Michigan Press; 1955.

Buchan, John: *Augustus.* Boston: Houghton Mifflin Company; 1937.

Cambridge Ancient History, Vol. X (especially for Antony and Cleopatra).

Carcopino, Jerome: *Daily Life in Ancient Rome.* New Haven: Yale University Press; 1940.

Catullus: *The Poems of Catullus*, edited and with comments by William A. Aiken, in translations by various hands. New York: E. P. Dutton & Co.; 1950.

Cicero: "Philippics" and "Pro Caelio" in *Orations. De Legibus*, iii. *Letters to Quintus* in *Letters to Friends.*

Daremberg, C. V., and E. Saglio, eds.: *Dictionnaire des Antiquités*

Grecques et Romaines. Paris: Hachette; 1877–1919.

Dio Cassius: *Dio's Roman History* (Loeb Classical Library), lv (on Julia).

Durant, Will: *Caesar and Christ.* New York: Simon and Schuster; 1944.

Ferrero, G.: *The Greatness and Decline of Rome.* New York: G. P. Putnam's Sons; 1907.

Fowler, W. W.: *Social Life of Rome in the Age of Cicero.* New York: The Macmillan Company; 1909.

Frank, Tenney: *Aspects of Social Behavior in Ancient Rome.* Cambridge: Harvard University Press; 1932.

Friedländer, Ludwig: *Roman Life and Manners Under the Early Empire.* Seventh edition. New York: E. P. Dutton & Co.; n.d.

Goodsell, Willystine: *A History of the Family as a Social and Educational Institution.* Revised edition. New York: The Macmillan Company; 1934.

Haywood, Richard: *The Myth of Rome's Fall.* New York: The Thomas Y. Crowell Company; 1958.

Highet, Gilbert: *Poets in a Landscape.* New York: Alfred A. Knopf; 1957.

Horace: *Epodes. Satires.*

Juvenal: *Satires,* esp. No. 6.

"Laudatio Turiae": in M. Durry: *Laudatio Turiae: Éloge Funèbre d'Une Matrone Romaine.* Paris: Belles Lettres; 1950.

Lecky, W. E. H.: *History of European Morals.* New York: D. Appleton & Co.; 1869.

Livy: *Roman History,* Bk. XXXIV.

Lucretius: *De Rerum Natura,* Bk. IV.

Macrobius: *Saturnalia,* Bk. II (on Julia).

Ovid: *Amores. Ars Amatoria. Tristia* (contains letters written from exile).

Pauly, A. F. von, and G. Wissowa: *Real-Encyclopädie der Classischen Altertumswissenschaft.* Stuttgart: J. B. Metzler; 1894–1919.

Pliny the Younger: *Letters.*

Plutarch: "Antony," "Cato the Younger," "Caesar," and "Cicero," in *Lives.*

Polybius: *Histories,* XXXIV, ii–iii.

Putnam, Emily: *The Lady.* New York: Sturgis & Walton; 1910.

Sellar, W. Y.: *Roman Poets of the Republic.* London: Oxford University Press; 1905.

Seneca: *De Beneficiis,* iii. *De Clementia,* i. *Ad Helviam,* x.

Seneca the Elder (L. Marcus Seneca): *Controversiae,* iii.

Suetonius: *Augustus* and *Julius Caesar* in *Lives of the Caesars.*

Tacitus: *Annals,* iii, 24–5. *Dialogue Concerning Oratory.*

Tucker, T. G.: *Life in the Roman World of Nero and St. Paul.* New York: The Macmillan Company; 1910.

Wright, F. A.: *Catullus; the Complete Poems.* London: George Routledge & Sons; 1926.

CHAPTER IV: *It Is Better to Marry Than to Burn*

AMONG VARIOUS GENERAL HISTORIES which give some attention to the Christian influence on love, the *Cambridge Medieval History* and Bury are worth looking at, though neither is recent; Lecky and Westermarck are indispensable classics. Lot and Boak pay special attention to the declining Roman society and the mood it engendered. The two *Dictionaries* are very generally useful for topics and biographies, as is also the *Encyclopaedia of Religion and Ethics.* Baring-Gould offers a massive compilation of saints' lives, referring back to original sources, but is frequently inaccurate and unscholarly. Westermarck and Cadoux both survey Hebrew and early Christian attitudes toward sex, woman, and love, and the details of clerical unchastity and papal corruption are exhaustively documented by such varied sources as the *Cambridge Medieval History*, Lea, Lecky, McCabe, Milman, and Westermarck.

Ammianus Marcellinus: *Ammianus Marcellinus*, translated by John C. Rolfe. Cambridge: Harvard University Press; 1937. Vol. II, Book XXII, discusses Emperor Julian (the Apostate).

The Ante-Nicene Fathers, edited by A. Roberts and J. Donaldson. New York: Charles Scribner's Sons; 1899–1900.

The Apostolical Constitutions: in *Ante-Nicene Fathers*, Vol. VII.

Athanasius: *Stories of the Holy Fathers . . . Compiled by Athanasius, Archbishop of Alexandria, Palladius*, etc., translated by E. A. W. Budge. Oxford: Oxford University Press; 1934.

Augustine: *Confessions. City of God. Treatises on Marriage.* (In *Fathers of the Church* series.) New York: Fathers of the Church; 1947.

Baring-Gould, Rev. S.: *The Lives of the Saints.* London: John C. Nimmo; 1897.

Battenhouse, R. W., ed.: *A Companion to the Study of St. Augustine.* New York: Oxford University Press; 1955.

The Bible.

Boak, A. E. R.: *Manpower Shortage and the Fall of the Roman Empire in the West.* Ann Arbor: University of Michigan Press; 1955.

Brittain, Rev. Alfred, and Mitchell Carroll: *Women of Early Christianity.* Philadelphia: Rittenhouse Press; 1907.

Bury, J. B.: *History of the Later Roman Empire.* London: Macmillan & Co.; 1923.

Cadoux, Cecil J.: *The Early Church and the World.* Edinburgh: T. & T. Clark; 1925.

Cambridge Medieval History, Vol. III.

Chrysostom, St. John: "Letters to Theodore," in *Nicene Fathers*, Vol. IX.

Clement of Alexandria: *Stromata*, in *Ante-Nicene Fathers*, Vol. II. Includes his discussion of heretics. *Paedagogus*, in *Fathers of the Church* series: New York: Fathers of the Church; 1947.

Cyprian: *Epistle* lxi in *Ante-Nicene Fathers*, Vol. VIII.

Dictionary of Christian Antiquities, edited by W. Smith and S. Cheetham. "Agapeti," "Betrothal," etc. Boston: Little, Brown & Co.; 1875.

Dictionary of Christian Biography, edited by H. Wall and W. C. Piercy. Boston: Little, Brown & Co.; 1911.

Eginhard (pseud. of G. Buschman): *Life of Charlemagne.* New York: American Book Co.; n.d. (but copyright 1880 by Harper & Bros.).

Ellis, Havelock: *Sex in Relation to Society*, Vol. VI of *Studies in the Psychology of Sex*. Philadelphia: F. A. Davis; 1901–28.

Encyclopaedia of Religion and Ethics, edited by J. Hastings. "Agapetae," "Chastity," "Marriage," etc. New York: Charles Scribner's Sons; 1908–26.

Ephraem, St.: "Life of Saint Mary the Harlot," in *Vitae Patrum*, q.v.

Gregory (the Great), Pope: *Epistles*, in *Nicene Fathers*, Vol. XIII.

The Dialogues of St. Gregory. London: Philip Lee Warner; 1911.

Gregory of Nyssa: "De hominis opificio," in *Nicene Fathers,* Vol. V.

Gregory of Tours: *History of the Franks.* Oxford: Clarendon Press; 1927.

Jerome, St.: *Against Jovinianus; Epistles* xxii, xxxviii, xlviii, cvii, cxxii; Preface to *Ezekiel,* all in *Nicene Fathers,* Second Series, Vol. VI.

Julian (the Apostate): *The Works of Emperor Julian* (see especially *Misopogon*). New York: The Macmillan Company; 1913.

Kligerman, Charles: "A psychoanalytic study of the *Confessions* of St. Augustine," *Jour. Amer. Psychoanal. Assn.,* Vol. III, July 1957.

Lea, H. C.: *Historical Sketch of Sacerdotal Celibacy.* Boston: Houghton Mifflin Company, 1884.

Lecky, W. E. H.: *History of European Morals.* New York: D. Appleton & Co.; 1869.

Lot, Ferdinand: *The End of the Ancient World.* New York: Alfred A. Knopf; 1931.

McCabe, J.: *Crises in the History of the Papacy.* New York: G. P. Putnam's Sons; 1916.

Menninger, Karl: *Man Against Himself.* New York: Harcourt, Brace, & Co.; 1938. Includes a psychoanalytic discussion of martyrs and ascetics.

Milman, H. H.: *History of Latin Christianity.* London: John Murray; 1872.

Nicene Fathers. A Select Library of the Nicene and Post-Nicene Fathers edited by P. Schaff. New York: Christian Literature Co.; 1887–1900.

Palladius: *Historia Lausiaca,* in *Vitae Patrum,* q.v.

Russell, C. E.: *Charlemagne, First of the Moderns.* Boston: Houghton Mifflin Company; 1930.

Socrates ("Socrates Scholasticus"): *Ecclesiastical History,* in *Nicene Fathers,* Second Series, Vol. II.

Tacitus: *Germania,* 18.

Tertullian: "On the apparel of women" ("De Cultu Faeminarum") and "To his wife" ("Ad Uxorem"), both in *Ante-Nicene Fathers,* Vol. IV.

Theodore of Canterbury: *Penitential,* in A. W. Hadden and Wm. Stubbs: *Councils and Ecclesiastical Documents,* Vol. III. Oxford: The Clarendon Press; 1871.

Todd, James H.: *St. Patrick, Apostle of Ireland.* Dublin: Hodges, Smith & Co.; 1864. Contains the story on Scuthin and Brendan.

Verba Seniorum (by various compilers), in *Vitae Patrum.*

Vitae Patrum, edited by J. P. Migne. Paris, 1849–50. (Appears as Vols. LXXIII–LXXIV of Migne's *Patrologiae Cursus Completus,* Ser. Lat.). An excellent and easily located English translation of selections from the *Vitae Patrum* is by Helen Waddell, and entitled *The Desert Fathers.* Ann Arbor Books: University of Michigan Press; 1957.

Westermarck, Edward: *Christianity and Morals.* London: Paul, Trench, Trubner & Co.; 1939.

——: *The Origin and Development of the Moral Ideas.* London: Macon; 1917.

CHAPTER V: *The Creation of the Romantic Ideal*

AMONG THE MANY SOCIAL HISTORIES portraying the general background against which courtly love appeared, Painter is one of the best and most recent, and the works by Coulton, Durant, May, and Vossler are all stuffed with helpful details. Of books paying special attention to troubadours and courtly love (either in a chapter or throughout), those by Kelly, Lewis, De Rougemont, Schultz, and Taylor are especially noteworthy, and display a variety of viewpoints. Andreas and Chrétien provide the two best medieval discussions of the subject; many others, in Provençal, are included in Raynouard, and Smythe gives a sampling of troubadour verses translated into modern English.

Andreas (Andreas Capellanus, or Andrew the Chaplain): *The Art of Courtly Love*, translated by John J. Parry (from *Tractatus Amoris et de Amoris Remedio*). New York: Columbia University Press; 1941. Parry's introduction is excellent.

Aquinas, St. Thomas: *Summa Theologica*, Supplement of: LXXXI, 3. *Summa Theologica*, II, ii, Quaest. CLIV, Art. 4.

Bernard, St.: Sermon XI, in *Life and Works*, translated by S. J. Eales. London: John Hodges; 1896.

Briffault, Robert: *The Mothers*. New York: The Macmillan Company; 1927.

Butler, P.: *Women of Mediaeval France*. Vol. V of *Woman, in All Ages and in All Countries* (by various authors). Philadelphia: The Rittenhouse Press; 1907–8.

Cambridge Medieval History, Vol. III.

Chaytor, H. J., Rev.: *The Troubadours*. Cambridge: The University Press; 1912.

Chrétien de Troyes: *Le Chevalier de la Charrette*, in English as *Lancelot* in *Arthurian Romances*, translated by W. W. Comfort. London: J. M. Dent & Sons; 1913.

Coulton, G. G.: *Life in the Middle Ages*. Cambridge: The University Press; 1930.

——: *Medieval Panorama*. New York: Meridian Books; 1955.

Dante: *La Vita Nuova. La Divina Commedia.*

De la Tour Landry: see Landry.

Denomy, Father Alexander J.: "Fin' Amors: The Pure Love of the Troubadours," *Mediaeval Studies*, Vol. VII (1945), p. 139f.

——: *The Heresy of Courtly Love*. New York: The Declan X. Mc-Mullen Company; 1947.

Durant, Will: *The Age of Faith*. New York: Simon and Schuster; 1950.

Gesta Karoli Magni ad Carcassonam et Narbonam, edited by F. E. Schneegans. Halle: Max Niemeyer; 1898.

Huizinga, J.: *The Waning of the Middle Ages*. New York: Doubleday Anchor Books; 1956.

John of Salisbury: *The Statesman's Book (Polycraticus)*, translated by John Dickenson. New York: Alfred A. Knopf; 1927.

Kelly, Amy: *Eleanor of Aquitaine and The Four Kings*. Cambridge: Harvard University Press; 1950.

Kroeger, A. E.: *The Minnesinger of Germany*. New York: Hurd & Houghton; 1873.

Landry: *Le Livre du Chevalier de La Tour Landry*, edited by A. de Montaiglon. Paris: Bibliothèque Elzévirienne; 1854.

Lee, Vernon (pseud. of Violet Paget): *Euphorion*. Boston: Roberts; 1884.

Lewis, C. S.: *The Allegory of Love*. Oxford: The Clarendon Press; 1936.

Lucka, Emil: *Eros; the Development of the Sex Relation through the Ages*. New York: G. P. Putnam's Sons; 1915.

May, Geoffrey J.: *Social Control of*

Sex Expression. London: George Allen & Unwin; 1930.

Neumann, Freidrich: "Ulrich von Lichtenstein's Frauendienst," in *Zeitschrift für Deutschkunde*, 1926, p. 373f.

Owst, Gerald R.: *Literature and Pulpit in Medieval England*. Cambridge: The University Press; 1933.

Paget, Violet: see Lee, Vernon.

Painter, Sidney: *French Chivalry*. Baltimore: Johns Hopkins Press; 1940.

Raynouard, F. J. M.: *Choix des Poésies Originales des Troubadours*. Paris: F. Didot; 1816-21.

De Rougemont, Denis: *Love in the Western World*. New York: Pantheon Books; 1956.

Schultz, Alwin: *Das Höfische Leben zur Zeit der Minnesinger*. Leipzig: S. Hirzel; 1889.

Smythe, Barbara, translator: *Trobador Poets*. New York: Duffield; 1911.

Taylor, G. Rattray: *Sex in History*. New York: Vanguard Press; 1954.

La Tour Landry: see Landry.

Ulrich von Lichtenstein: *Ulrich's von Liechtenstein Frauendienst*, edited by R. Bechstein. Leipzig: F. A. Brockhaus; 1888. For a modern German translation, see *Der Frauendienst des Minnesängers Ulrich von Liechtenstein*, translated by Michelangelo Baron Bois. Stuttgart: Robert Lutz; n.d.

Vossler, K.: *Mediaeval Culture*. New York: Harcourt, Brace & Co.; 1929.

CHAPTER VI: *The Lady and the Witch*

In the Renaissance (and thereafter) the available materials are so plentiful that it is not possible to list more than a fraction of the sources used. In particular, biographies are so numerous that I will limit myself, for the most part, to naming only works containing accounts of several lives in one volume, since individual biographies are easy enough to find.

A general introduction to the social history of the period can be found in Durant, Einstein, and the *Cambridge Modern History*, among many others. More specifically, Maulde's old work and Kelso's two recent ones give much space to Platonic love in theory and practice, while the theory and practice of the inquisitors concerning women is given in detail with rich documentation from the original sources by Jones, Lea, and Zilboorg. Castiglione and Sprenger, both readily available in English, are the two most valuable Renaissance documents giving the opposing points of view, and a vast number of lesser works dealing with the many questions of woman, sex, love, and married life are cited and quoted in Camden, Powell, and Stenton.

Aubrey, John: *Brief Lives*, edited by A. Powell. London: The Cresset Press; 1949.

Bligh, E. W.: *Sir Kenelm Digby and His Venetia*. London: Sampson Low, Marston & Co.; 1932.

Boulting, William: *Woman in Italy*. New York: Brentano's; 1910.

Bromberg, Walter, M.D.: *The Mind of Man*. New York: Harper & Bros.; 1937.

Burckhardt, Jacob: *The Civilization*

of the Renaissance in Italy. New York: Harper & Bros.; 1929. Reprint of a classic, still valuable.

Cambridge Modern History, Vol. 1 (1957 edition).

Camden, Carroll: *The Elizabethan Woman*. New York: Elsevier Press; 1952.

Castiglione, Count Baldesar: *The Book of the Courtier*, translated by L. E. Opdycke. New York: Charles Scribner's Sons; 1903.

Chambers, E. K.: *The Mediaeval Stage*. Oxford: Oxford University Press; 1903.

Cupid's School: Wherein Young Men and Maids May Learn Divers Sorts of New, Witty, and Amorous Compliments. By W. S. London: 1632.

Digby, Sir Kenelm: *Private Memoirs of Sir Kenelm Digby*, edited by Sir Nicholas Nicolar. London: Saunders and Otley; 1827.

Durant, Will: *The Renaissance*. New York: Simon and Schuster; 1953. Deals with Italy only.

——: *The Reformation*. New York: Simon and Schuster; 1957.

Einstein, Lewis: *The Italian Renaissance in England*. New York: Columbia University Press; 1902.

——: *Tudor Ideals*. New York: Harcourt, Brace & Co.; 1921.

Garcon, Maurice, and Jean Vinchon: *The Devil*. London: Victor Gollancz; 1929.

Hansen, Joseph: *Zauberwahn, Inquisition und Hexenprozess im Mittelalter*. München: Oldenbourg; 1900.

Henry VIII: *The Love-Letters of Henry VIII*, edited by Henry Savage. London: Allan Wingate; 1949.

Historia Regis Henrici Septimi, edited by James Gairdner (Great Britain Public Record Office: *Chronicles and Memorials of Great Britain and Ireland during the Middle Ages*). London: Long-

man, Brown, Green, Longmans and Roberts; 1858.

Innocent VIII, Pope: Papal Bull, *Summis Desiderantes Affectibus*, available in English in the Introduction to Sprenger, q.v.

Jones, Ernest, M.D.: *On the Nightmare: The International Psycho-Analytical Library, No. 20*. London: Hogarth Press; 1949.

Kelso, Ruth: *The Doctrine of the English Gentleman in the Sixteenth Century*. Urbana: University of Illinois Press; 1929.

——: *Doctrine for the Lady of the Renaissance*. Urbana: University of Illinois Press; 1956.

Lea, H. C.: *History of the Inquisition of the Middle Ages*. New York: S. A. Russell; 1956. Reprint of a classic.

Marguerite, Queen of Navarre: *The Heptameron*. New York: Alfred A. Knopf; 1924.

De Maulde la Clavière, R.: *The Women of the Renaissance*. New York: G. P. Putnam's Sons; 1900.

Paston Letters, The, edited by James Gairdner. Westminster: A. Constable & Co.; 1895.

Pastor, Ludwig: *The History of the Popes*. London: Kegan Paul, Trench, Trubner and Co.; 1910.

Pollard, A. F.: *Henry VIII*. London: Longmans, Green & Co.; 1951.

Powell, Chilton L.: *English Domestic Relations, 1487–1653*. New York: Columbia University Press; 1917.

Raleigh, Sir Walter: "Instructions to His Son," in *Remains of Sir Walter Raleigh*. London: 1675.

Saltini, G. E.: *Tragedie Medice e Domestiche (1557–87), Narrate sui Documenti*. Firenze: Barbera; 1898.

Sprenger, Jacob, and Henry Kramer: *Malleus Maleficarum*, translated by Rev. Montague Summers. [London]: John Rodker; 1928.

Stenton, Doris Mary: *The English*

Woman in History. London: Allen & Unwin; 1957.

Taylor, G. Rattray: *Sex in History.* New York: Vanguard Press; 1954.

Thorndike, Lynn: *History of Magic and Experimental Science.* New York: The Macmillan Company; 1923–41.

Zilboorg, Gregory, M.D.: *The Medical Man and the Witch During the Renaissance.* Baltimore: Johns Hopkins Press; 1935.

CHAPTER VII: *The Impuritans*

FOR A GENERAL INTRODUCTION to the Reformation, both Durant and Smith are readable and thorough; more specifically the social history of Puritanism in New England is covered in Wish. The over-all modifying and reshaping influence of the Reformation upon the laws and customs of marriage, divorce, fornication, and adultery is sketched rapidly by Goodsell, and in minute detail by Howard. Harkness gives much special detail on the experiment in Geneva. The surprising liveliness of Puritans in New England is dealt with by Lawrence, Morgan, and Oberholzer, through the convincing method of liberal citation and extracting of court cases, private correspondence, diaries, and the like.

Bainton, Roland: *Here I Stand.* (On Luther.) New York: Abingdon-Cokesbury Press; 1950.

Bradford, Governor William: *Of Plymouth Plantation,* edited by Samuel Eliot Morison. New York: Alfred A. Knopf; 1952.

Calvin, John: *Institutes of the Christian Religion,* translated by H. Beveridge. Edinburgh: T. & T. Clark; 1869.

Durant, Will: *The Reformation.* New York: Simon and Schuster; 1957.

Essex County Archives: *Salem Witchcraft, 1692.*

Funck-Brentano, Frantz: *Luther.* London: Jonathan Cape; 1936.

Gataker, Thomas: *A Good Wife God's Gift—A Marriage Sermon.* London: 1620.

Goodsell, Willystine: *A History of the Family as a Social and Educational Institution.* New York: The Macmillan Company; 1934.

Haller, William: "Hail Wedded Love," ELH (English Literary History), Vol. XIII, June 1946.

—— and Malleville Haller: "The Puritan Art of Love," *The Huntington Library Quarterly,* Vol. V, Jan. 1942.

Hanford, J. H.: *John Milton, Englishman.* New York: Crown Publishers; 1949.

Harkness, Georgia: *John Calvin.* New York: Henry Holt; 1931.

Howard, G. E.: *A History of Matrimonial Institutions.* Chicago: University of Chicago Press; 1904.

Hutchinson, Lucy: *Memoirs of the Life of Colonel Hutchinson.* London: J. M. Dent; n.d. This Everyman edition includes Mrs. Hutchinson's *Life of Mrs. Lucy Hutchinson,* which, though only a fragment, is useful.

Lawrence, Henry W.: *The Not-Quite Puritans.* Boston: Little, Brown & Co.; 1928.

Luther, Martin: *Tischreden.* Weimar: Hermann Böhlaus Nachfolger; 1912–21. (These six volumes are part of *Dr. Martin Luthers Werke: Kritische Gesamtausgabe,* same publisher.) See esp. *Tischreden* Nos. 3, 49, 55, 975, 1161, 1472, 1563, 1965, 2047, 2733a, 3523,

6567, 6925 and 6928. Also, the essay on married life in Weimar *Werke*, X–2, 276.

——: *Dr. Martin Luther's Sämmtliche Werke*, edited by G. Plochman and J. Irmischer. Frankfurt and Erlangen: C. Heyder, und Hender & Zimmer; 1826–57. Especially Vol. LX, 110 (*Tischreden* No. 1588).

——: *The Table-Talk of Martin Luther*, translated by Wm. Hazlitt. London: G. Bell & Sons; 1902. See Nos. 737, 752.

Masson, David: *The Life of John Milton*. New York: Peter Smith; 1946. Reprint of a classic.

Mather, Cotton: *Diary of Cotton Mather (1681–1708): Mass. Historical Soc. Collections*, 7th Series, Vols. VII–VIII. Boston: Published by the Society; 1911.

May, Geoffrey J.: *Social Control of Sex Expression*. London: Allen & Unwin; 1930.

Miller, Perry: *The New England Mind*. New York: The Macmillan Company; 1939.

Milton, John: *The Doctrine and Discipline of Divorce*, and *Tetrachordon*, both in *The Works of John Milton*, Vol. III. New York: Columbia University Press; 1931.

——*Apology*, in *Complete Prose Works of John Milton*, Vol. I. New Haven: Yale University Press; 1953.

Morgan, Edmund S.: *The Puritan Family*. Boston: The Public Library; 1944.

——: "The Puritans and Sex," in *The New England Quarterly*, Vol. XV, Dec. 1942.

Muir, Edwin: *John Knox*. New York: The Viking Press; 1929.

Oberholzer, Emil: *Delinquent Saints*. New York: Columbia University Press; 1956.

Powell, Chilton L.: *English Domestic Relations, 1487–1653*. New York: Columbia University Press; 1917.

Rogers, Daniel: *Matrimonial Honor*. London: 1642.

Schaff, Philip: *The Swiss Reformation*. New York: Charles Scribner's Sons; 1892.

Sewall, Samuel: *Diary of Samuel Sewall: Collections of the Massachusetts Historical Society*, 5th Series, Vols. V–VII. Boston: Published by the Society; 1878–82.

Smith, Preserved: *The Age of the Reformation*. New York: Henry Holt & Company; 1923 and 1936.

Whately, William: *The Bride-Bush*. London: 1617.

Winthrop, Governor John: *The History of New England from 1630 to 1649*. Boston; Little, Brown & Co.; 1853.

Wish, Harvey: *Society and Thought in Early America*. New York: Longmans, Green & Co.; 1950.

CHAPTER VIII: *The Contact of Two Epidermises*

SMITH AND THE *Cambridge Modern History* are two of the many general works on the era here portrayed. For greater detail on French social history, see the works by Lewis and Russell, and on English social history see Ashton, Traill and Mann, and Trevelyan; all these books quote copiously from original sources. On the subject of rationalist love in particular, the pre-Freudian work by the Goncourts remains wonderfully perceptive. As indicated in the chapter itself, my own interpretation draws upon modern ideas of the psychodynamics of family life and personality growth as found in Kardiner, La Barre, Montagu, and elsewhere.

Ashton, John: *Social Life in the Reign of Queen Anne*. London: Chatto & Windus; 1925.

Bertrand, Louis: *Louis XIV*. New York: Longmans, Green & Co.; 1928.

Boswell, James: *Boswell's London Journal, 1762–1763*. New York: McGraw-Hill Book Co.; 1950.

Cambridge Modern History, Vol. V.

Casanova, Jacques (or Giacomo, or Giovanni Jacopo): *The Memoirs of Jacques Casanova de Seingalt*, translated by Arthur Machen. New York: A. & C. Boni; 1932.

Chesterfield, Philip Dormer Stanhope, Earl of: *Letters to His Son*, edited by O. H. Leigh. New York: Tudor Publishing Co.; n.d.

Dobson, Austin: *Horace Walpole*. London: Oxford University Press; 1927.

Du Deffand, Madame: see Walpole.

Earle, Alice Morse: *Colonial Dames and Goodwives*. Boston: Houghton Mifflin Company; 1895.

Evelyn, John: *Mundus Muliebris*, in *Miscellaneous Writings of John Evelyn*. London: Henry Colburn; 1825.

Franklin, Benjamin: *Autobiography of Benjamin Franklin*, a restoration of a fair copy by Max Farrand. Berkeley and Los Angeles: University of California (in cooperation with the Huntington Library); 1949.

——: *Poor Richards Almanack*, published as "*The Sayings of Poor Richard*," edited by P. L. Ford. New York: G. P. Putnam's Sons; 1890.

Goncourt, Edmond et Jules de: *La Femme au Dix-Huitième Siècle*. Paris: G. Charpentier; 1882.

Gramont: see Hamilton.

Halsband, Robert: *The Life of Lady Mary Wortley Montagu*. Oxford: The Clarendon Press; 1956.

Hamilton, Count Anthony: *Memoirs of Count Grammont* [sic]. Edinburgh: John Grant; 1908.

Kardiner, Abram: *Sex and Morality*. New York: The Bobbs-Merrill Company; 1954.

Kesten, Hermann: *Casanova*. New York: Harper & Bros.; 1955.

La Barre, Weston: *The Human Animal*. Chicago: University of Chicago Press; 1954.

De Lenclos, Ninon: *Lettres de Ninon de Lenclos*. Paris: Librairie Garnier Frères; n.d.

Lewis, W. H.: *The Splendid Century*. New York: William Sloane Associates; 1954.

Magne, Emile: *Ninon de Lanclos*. London: S. W. Arrowsmith; 1926.

Maintenon, Madame de: *Correspondence Générale de Mme. de Maintenon*, edited by T. Lavallée. Paris; 1865–6.

Mitford, Nancy: *Voltaire in Love*. New York: Harper & Bros.; 1957.

Montagu, M. F. Ashley: *The Direction of Human Development*. New York: Harper & Bros.; 1955.

Osborn, Francis: "Advice to a Son," in *The Works of Francis Osborn*. Ninth edition. London: 1689.

Pepys, Samuel: *The Diary of Samuel Pepys*, edited from Mynors Bright with an introduction by J. Warrington. London: J. M. Dent; 1953.

Russell, Phillips: *The Glittering Century*. New York: Charles Scribner's Sons; 1936.

Shellabarger, Samuel: *Lord Chesterfield and His World*. Boston: Little, Brown & Company; 1951. First published in England in 1935.

Sidney, Henry (Earl of Romney): *Diary of the Times of Charles the Second*, edited by R. W. Blencoe. London: Henry Colburn; 1843.

Smith, Preserved: *A History of Modern Culture*, Vol. II. New

York: Henry Holt & Company; 1934.

Spectator, The: Nos. 2, 66, and 154; and The Tatler, No. 40.

Swift, Jonathan: "A Letter to a Young Lady, on Her Marriage," in Vol. IX of Prose Works of Jonathan Swift, edited by Herbert Davis. Oxford: Basil Blackwell; 1948.

Tompkins, J. M. S.: The Polite Marriage. Cambridge: The University Press; 1938.

Traill, H. D., and J. S. Mann, eds.: Social England, Vols. IV and V. New York: G. P. Putnam's Sons; 1909.

Trevelyan, G. M.: English Social History. New York: Longmans, Green & Co.; 1942.

Van Doren, Carl: Benjamin Franklin. New York: Viking Press; 1945.

Walpole, Horace: The Yale Edition of Horace Walpole's Correspondence; edited by W. S. Lewis. New Haven: Yale University Press; 1937–55. Includes Mme du Deffand's letters to Walpole.

Wilson, John H.: Nell Gwyn: Royal Mistress. New York: Pellegrini and Cudahy; 1952.

CHAPTER IX: *The Angel in the House*

OF THE VERY MANY HISTORIES of England in the Romantic and Victorian periods, the relevant sections of Wingfield-Stratford's *The History of British Civilization* are perhaps the most readable; many others, easily available, are more scholarly in format, but need not be listed here. On the characteristics of pre-Victorian society, Quinlan is a good recent study, rich in detail. On Victorian society itself, Wingfield-Stratford's *Those Earnest Victorians* and the book by Young are both useful, but Houghton is far and away the most thorough, detailed, and richly documented study available and includes the best modern discussion of Victorian love. (The best nineteenth-century discussions of it are by Ruskin and, of course, Patmore.) The woman's rights movement is treated in Calhoun (old, but indispensable), Ditzion (literary more than historical), Goodsell, and Stenton. Ellis frequently deals with the sexual and emotional ailments of the era, and Pearl lovingly gathers up all the evidences of its vices (and somewhat exaggerates them for effect).

Bagley, C. B.: "The Mercer Immigration," Quarterly of the Oregon Hist. Soc., Vol. V (1904).

Benson, Mary S.: Women in Eighteenth-Century America. New York: Columbia University Press; 1935.

Calhoun, Arthur W.: A Social History of the American Family. Cleveland: Arthur H. Clark Co.; 1918.

Champneys, Basil: Memoirs and Correspondence of Coventry Patmore. London: George Bell & Sons; 1900.

Clewes, Howard: Stendhal. London: Arthur Barker; 1950.

Cobbett, William: Advice to Young Men. London: 1829.

Cunnington, C. W.: Feminine Attitudes in the Nineteenth Century. London: Wm. Heinemann; 1935.

Dexter, Elisabeth A.: *Career Women of America, 1776–1840*. Francestown, N.H.: Marshall Jones Co.; 1950.

Ditzion, Sidney: *Marriage, Morals, and Sex in America*. New York: Bookman Associates; 1953.

Ellis, Havelock: *The Evolution of Modesty; The Sexual Impulse in Women;* and *Sex in Relation to Society*, in Vols. I, III, and VI of *Studies in the Psychology of Sex*. Philadelphia: F. A. Davis; 1901–28.

Encyclopaedia Britannica, 1842 edition: "Love."

Fitzhugh, George: *Sociology for the South*. Richmond: Morris; 1854.

Froude, J. A.: *The Nemesis of Faith*. London: J. Chapman; 1849.

Goodsell, Willystine: *A History of the Family as a Social and Educational Institution*. New York: The Macmillan Company; 1934.

Green, F. C.: *Jean-Jacques Rousseau*. Cambridge: The University Press; 1955.

Gregory, John, Dr.: *A Father's Legacy to His Daughters*. London: A. Millar; 1788. First published in 1774.

Hazlitt, William: *Liber Amoris, or The New Pygmalion*. London: Mathews & Lane; 1893. First published in 1823.

Houghton, Walter E.: *The Victorian Frame of Mind, 1830–1870*. New Haven: Yale University Press; 1957.

Howe, P. P.: *The Life of William Hazlitt*. London: Martin Secker; 1922.

Klein, Viola: *The Feminine Character*. London: Kegan Paul, Trench, Trubner & Co.; 1946.

Maclean, C. M.: *Born Under Saturn*. (Biog. of Wm. Hazlitt.) London: Collins; 1943.

Maigron, Louis: *Le Romantisme et les Moeurs*. Paris: H. Champion; 1910.

Malthus, Thomas: *An Essay on the Principle of Population*. London: Reeves & Turner; 1872. First published in 1798.

Owen, Robert Dale: Marriage letter printed in Calhoun, q.v.

Patmore, Coventry: *Angel in the House* and *The Unknown Eros*, both in *Poems*, edited by F. Page. London: Oxford University Press; 1949.

Pearl, Cyril: *The Girl with the Swansdown Seat*. New York: New American Library; 1958.

Praz, Mario: *The Romantic Agony*. New York: Meridian Books; 1956.

Procter, Bryan W. ("Barry Cornwall"): *An Autobiographical Fragment*. Boston: Roberts Brothers; 1877.

Quinlan, M. J.: *Victorian Prelude*. New York: Columbia University Press; 1941.

Reid, J. C.: *The Mind and Art of Coventry Patmore*. London: Routledge & Kegan Paul; 1957.

Rousseau, Jean-Jacques: *The Confessions of Jean-Jacques Rousseau*. London: Penguin Books; 1953.

Ruskin, John: "Of Queens' Gardens," in *Sesame and Lilies*. London: Cassell & Co.; 1907.

Ryan, Michael, M.D.: *The Philosophy of Marriage*. Philadelphia: Lindsay & Blakiston; 1867. First published in 1839.

Stendhal: *On Love*. Garden City, N.Y.: Doubleday Anchor Books; 1957.

Stenton, Doris Mary: *The English Woman in History*. London: Allen & Unwin; 1957.

Stewart, Randall: "Letters to Sophia," in *Huntington Library Quarterly*, Vol. VII (Aug. 1944). Nathaniel Hawthorne's censored letters.

Tennyson, Hallam: *Alfred Lord Tennyson*. London: Macmillan & Co.; 1897.

Trevelyan, G. M.: *English Social*

History. New York: Longmans, Green & Co.; 1942.

Turner, E. S.: *A History of Courting*. New York: E. P. Dutton & Co.; 1955.

Wingfield-Stratford, Esmé: *The History of British Civilization*.

London: George Routledge & Sons; 1928.

——: *Those Earnest Victorians*. New York: Wm. Morrow & Co.; 1930.

Young, G. M., ed.: *Early Victorian England, 1830–1865*. London: Oxford University Press; 1934.

CHAPTER X: *The Age of Love*

THE ORIGINAL SURVEYS and studies to which this chapter refers or on which it draws are so numerous that, with a few exceptions, I shall list only secondary sociological textbooks in which the bulk of the original statistics are collected, cited, and named. Among works of this type are Baber, Burgess and Locke, Folsom, Kirkpatrick, Nimkoff, and Winch's *The Modern Family*. Winch's *Mate-Selection* contains an excellent summary and listing of works on homogamy and heterogamy in the pairing of lovers. Mead's book includes an incisive, provocative, but non-statistical portrait of love in America today. Of the many available books on love in the 1920's, the anthology by Calverton and Schmalhausen is perhaps the most generous sampler. Statistics on marriage, divorce, fertility, and women workers come from the U.S. Census Bureau and the U.S. Department of Labor Women's Bureau.

Baber, Ray E.: *Marriage and the Family*. New York: McGraw-Hill Book Co.; 1953.

Beigel, Hugo G.: "Romantic Love," in *Am. Sociol. Rev.* Vol. XVI (1951).

Burgess, Ernest W., and Leonard S. Cottrell: *Predicting Success or Failure in Marriage*. New York: Prentice-Hall; 1939.

—— and Harvey J. Locke: *The Family*. New York: American Book Co.; 1953.

—— and Paul Wallin: *Engagement and Marriage*. Philadelphia: J. B. Lippincott Company; 1953.

Calverton, V. F., and S. D. Schmalhausen, eds.: *Sex in Civilization*. New York: The Macaulay Co.; 1929.

Cuber, J. F.: "Can We Evaluate Marriage Education?" in *Marriage and Family Living*, Vol. XI (1949).

Cyon, Françoise: see Delisle.

Davis, K. B.: *Factors in the Sex Life of Twenty-Two Hundred Women*. New York: Harper & Bros.; 1929.

Delisle, Françoise: *Friendship's Odyssey*. London: Wm. Heinemann; 1946.

Deutsch, Helene: *The Psychology of Women*. New York: Grune & Stratton; 1945.

Dietrich, Marlene: "How to Be Loved," *Ladies' Home Journal*, Jan. 1954.

Duncan, Isadora: *My Life*. New York: Liveright Publishing Corporation; 1933.

Ellis, Havelock: *The History of Marriage*, in *Studies in the Psychology of Sex*, Vol. VII. Philadelphia: F. A. Davis; 1928.

——: *My Life*. Boston: Houghton Mifflin Company 1939.

Farnham, Marynia: see Lundberg.

Flugel, J. C.: *Man, Morals, and So-*

ciety. New York: International Universities Press; 1945.

Folsom, J. K.: *The Family and Democratic Society.* New York: John Wiley & Sons; 1943.

Franzblau, Abraham N.: *The Road to Sexual Maturity.* New York: Simon and Schuster; 1954.

Freud, Sigmund: *Group Psychology and the Analysis of the Ego.* London: The Hogarth Press; 1922.

——: "Psychology of Women," in *New Introductory Lectures on Psycho-Analysis.* London: The Hogarth Press; 1933.

——: Letter to Martha Bernays, in Jones, q.v.

Goode, William: *After Divorce.* Glencoe, Ill.: The Free Press; 1956.

Hamilton, G. V.: *A Research in Marriage.* New York: A. & C. Boni; 1929.

Jones, Ernest, M.D.: *The Life and Work of Sigmund Freud.* New York: Basic Books; 1953–7.

Kinsey, Alfred C., et al.: *Sexual Behavior in the Human Male.* Philadelphia: W. B. Saunders Co.; 1948.

—— et al.: *Sexual Behavior in the Human Female.* Philadelphia: W. B. Saunders Co.; 1953.

Kirkpatrick, Clifford: *The Family as Process and Institution.* New York: The Ronald Press; 1955.

Klein, Viola: *The Feminine Character.* London: Kegan Paul, Trench, Trubner & Co.; 1946.

Kolb, William L.: "Sociologically Established Family Norms and Democratic Values," in *Social Forces,* Vol. XXVI (1948).

Komarovsky, Mirra: *Women in the Modern World.* Boston: Little, Brown & Co.; 1953.

Lader, Lawrence: *The Margaret Sanger Story.* Garden City, N.Y.: Doubleday & Co.; 1955.

Landis, Judson T.: "Length of Time Required to Achieve Adjustment in Marriage," *Am. Sociol. Rev.,* Vol. XI (1946).

Lang, R. O.: Unpublished study on happiness in marriage, quoted in Burgess and Cottrell.

Lawrence, D. H.: *We Need One Another.* New York: Equinox; 1933. A reprinting of two magazine articles.

Linton, Ralph: *The Study of Man.* New York: Appleton-Century; 1936.

Lowrie, S. H.: "Dating Theories and Student Responses," *Am. Sociol. Rev.,* Vol. XVI (1951).

Lundberg, Ferdinand, and Marynia F. Farnham, M.D.: *Modern Woman: The Lost Sex.* New York: Harper & Bros.; 1947.

Lynd, Robert S. and Helen M.: *Middletown.* New York: Harcourt, Brace & Co.; 1929.

Mead, Margaret: *Male and Female.* New York: New American Library; 1955.

Mudd, Emily, et al.: *Marriage Counseling: A Casebook.* New York: Association Press; 1958.

Myrdal, Alva, and Viola Klein: *Women's Two Roles: Home and Work.* London: Routledge & Kegan Paul; 1956.

Nimkoff, Meyer F.: *Marriage and the Family.* New York: Houghton Mifflin Company; 1947.

Parsons, Talcott: *Essays in Sociological Theory, Pure and Applied.* Glencoe, Ill.: The Free Press; 1949.

Reich, Wilhelm: *The Function of the Orgasm.* Vol. I of *The Discovery of the Orgone.* New York: Orgone Institute Press; 1942–8.

Riley, J. W., and M. White: "The Use of Various Methods of Contraception," *Am. Sociol. Rev.,* Vol. V (1940).

Sorokin, Pitirim: *Social and Cultural Dynamics.* New York: American Book Co.; 1941.

Stopes, Marie: *Married Love.* London: A. C. Fifield; 1918.

Sullivan, Mark; *Our Times.* New

York: Charles Scribner's Sons; 1926–35.

Terman, Lewis M., et al.: *Psychological Factors in Marital Happiness*. New York: McGraw-Hill Book Co.; 1938.

U.S. Bureau of the Census: *Characteristics of the Population*, in *Census of 1890, 1940, 1950. Current Population Reports:* Population Characteristics series, and Labor Force series, 1951–8.

U.S. Department of Labor: Woman's Bureau *Bulletins*, Nos. 157, 209, 239.

Van de Velde, Theodoor: *Ideal Marriage: Its Physiology and Technique*. New York: Covici Friede; 1930.

Waller, Willard: "The Rating and Dating Complex," *Am. Sociol. Rev.*, Vol. II (1937).

——: *The Family: A Dynamic Interpretation*. New York: The Cordon Co.; 1938.

Whelpton, P. K., and C. V. Kiser: *Social and Psychological Factors Affecting Fertility*. New York: Milbank Memorial Fund; 1950. Includes data given in a series of articles by same authors in various issues of *Milbank Memorial Fund Quarterly*, 1943–9.

Winch, Robert F.: *Mate-Selection*. New York: Harper & Bros.; 1958.

——: *The Modern Family*. New York: Henry Holt & Company; 1952.

Index